OXFORD REFE

C000293085

A Dictiona

Fly-Fishing

Dr C. B. McCully has been a lecturer in English Language and Literature at Manchester University since
1985. His publications include work on rhythm and
phonology, Anglo-Saxon literature, the history of the
English Language, literary criticism and poetry. He
has been fishing since losing his first trout on Conis-
ton Water, aged seven; his particular interest is now in
fly-fishing for wild brown trout, and for sea trout and
grayling.

A Dictionary of
Fly-Fishing

C. B. McCully

Oxford   New York

OXFORD UNIVERSITY PRESS

1993

Oxford University Press, Walton Street, Oxford OX2 6DP

Oxford New York Toronto
Delhi Bombay Calcutta Madras Karachi
Kuala Lumpur Singapore Hong Kong Tokyo
Nairobi Dar es Salaam Cape Town
Melbourne Auckland Madrid
and associated companies in
Berlin Ibadan

Oxford is a trade mark of Oxford University Press

© C. B. McCully 1992

The moral right of C. B. McCully to be identified as
the author of this work has been asserted

First published 1992 by Carcanet Press Limited,
Manchester, as Fly-Fishing: A Book of Words
First issued as an Oxford University Press paperback 1993

All rights reserved. No part of this publication may be reproduced,
stored in a retrieval system, or transmitted, in any form or by any means,
without the prior permission in writing of Oxford University Press.
Within the UK, exceptions are allowed in respect of any fair dealing for the
purpose of research or private study, or criticism or review, as permitted
under the Copyright, Designs and Patents Act, 1988, or in the case of
reprographic reproduction in accordance with the terms of the licences
issued by the Copyright Licensing Agency. Enquiries concerning
reproduction outside these terms and in other countries should be
sent to the Rights Department, Oxford University Press,
at the address above

This book is sold subject to the condition that it shall not, by way
of trade or otherwise, be lent, re-sold, hired out or otherwise circulated
without the publisher's prior consent in any form of binding or cover
other than that in which it is published and without a similar condition
including this condition being imposed on the subsequent purchaser

British Library Cataloguing in Publication Data
Data available

Library of Congress Cataloging in Publication Data
Data available

ISBN 0–19–283126–7

1 3 5 7 9 10 8 6 4 2

Printed in Great Britain by
Biddles Ltd.,
Guildford and King's Lynn

To my friend of the seasons

Bill Long

Dictionaries are like watches: the worst is better than none, and the best cannot be expected to go quite true.
– Samuel Johnson

Acknowledgements

I am grateful to the John Rylands Library, Manchester University, and to the Library of Trinity College, Dublin, both of whom have made their facilities available to me.

I would also like to thank the following publishers, fishing bodies and literary representatives for their permission to use copyright material:

Extracts from *The Complete Fly-fisher*, edited by C.F. Walker (1969), reprinted by permission of Barrie and Jenkins Ltd.

Extracts from

The Pursuit of Stillwater Trout by Brian Clarke (1975)

Trout Fly Recognition (1976 edn.) by John Goddard

Trout Flies of Stillwater (1979 edn.) by John Goddard

Lake, Loch and Reservoir Trout Fishing (1987) by Malcolm Greenhalgh

Trout and Grayling (1980) by Norman Maclean

50 Favourite Wet Flies (1986) by Donald Overfield

Nymphs and the Trout (1958) by Frank Sawyer

Minor Tactics of the Chalkstream (1924 edn.) by G.E.M. Skues

The Way of a Trout with a Fly (1949 edn.) by G.E.M. Skues, and

A Dictionary of Trout Flies (1986 edn., with additional section on modern trout flies by T. Donald Overfield) by A. Courtney Williams –

all these excerpts reprinted by kind permission of A. & C. Black (Publishers) Ltd.

Extracts from Lord Edward Grey's *Fly Fishing* (1899; rpr. 1984), John Waller Hills' *A Summer on the Test* (1930; rpr. 1983), Harry Plunket-Greene's *Where the Bright Waters Meet* (1936; rpr. 1983), and C.F. Walker's *Lake Flies and their Imitation* (1960; rpr. 1983) – all published in the 'Modern Fishing Classics' series (ed. Antony Atha) – reprinted by kind permission of André Deutsch Ltd.

Extract from 'The Monster of the Pool', a poem in *Game-bag and Creel* by W.G.M. Dobie (Edinburgh, 1927), reprinted by generous permission of Mr J.T.J. Dobie.

Extract from the May 1984 *Grayling Society Newsletter* ('Of graylings, large and small' by William Caine, from *An Angler at Large*, 1911), reprinted by kind permission of The Grayling Society.

Extract from *An Incompleat Angler* by Lord Hardinge of Penshurst (1976), reprinted by permission of Michael Joseph Ltd.

Extract from *The Haig Guide to Salmon Fishing in Scotland* (1981; ed. David Barr) published by Macdonald.

Extract from *To Cast a Trout Fly*, published by House of Hardy Ltd.

Extracts from *Fly-fishing for Irish Trout* by Niall Fallon (1983), published by Roberts' Books, Kilkenny, Republic of Ireland.

Several substantial extracts from *A Man May Fish* by T.C. Kingsmill Moore (1979), reprinted by kind permission of Colin Smythe Ltd, Publishers.

Extracts from articles in *Trout and Salmon* (EMAP Pursuit Publications) reprinted by permission of the editor, Sandy Leventon.

Extracts from the *New Illustrated Dictionary of Trout Flies* by John Roberts (1986), published by Unwin Hyman Ltd.

Extracts from *Sea Trout Fishing* by Hugh Falkus (revised second edition, 1981), Sidney Spencer's *Newly from the Sea* (1969) and *Game Fishing Tactics* (1974) reprinted by kind permission of H.F. and G. Witherby Ltd.

Every effort has been made to contact copyright holders. In the event of any inadvertent omission or error, please contact the publisher.

I offer my warmest thanks to the many who have taken an interest in this work from its beginnings: to my friends and colleagues in Newcastle and Manchester; to Owen Jacob, best of fishermen and friends, whose extensive fishing library and brain I tapped over the telephone lines to Dublin; to Mark Brown, scourge of trout wherever they rise; to John Roberts, who pointed me in the direction of John McDonald's historical work in *Quill Gordon*; to Helen Maclean, whose knowledge of English dialects saved me from severe embarrassment more than once; to Gerald Hammond, who commented so lucidly on my draft material that even I felt encouraged; and to Bill Long, a fellow spirit to whom this book is dedicated. Others have provided me with illustrative quotations: Douglas Dunn pointed out the splendid poem on the Greenwell's Glory by Ruthven Todd; Shelagh Aston quoted Ogden Nash's excellent 'ant and emmet' poem; Alan Dobie drew my attention to his grandfather's writing in *Game-bag and Creel* (1927); and others, such as David Palmer, have suggested lines of enquiry which otherwise would have gone unexamined. I would also like to record my thanks to my publisher, Michael Schmidt, whose comments, criticisms and practical advice have been constantly helpful. My final, and surely my biggest, debt is to my wife Janet McCully, who allows me to pursue two anti-social activities, fishing and writing, and who hardly ever complains.

Introduction

In a haunting and exactly-phrased paragraph, the fifteenth-century *Treatise of Fishing with an Angle* advised fishermen as follows: '... ye shall not vse this forsayd crafty dysporte for no couetysenes to thencreasynge and sparynge of your money oonly, but pryncypally for your solace and to cause the helthe of your body and specyally of your soule.' Because fishing is 'principally for your solace' it has spawned a great reflective literature. Poets from Cotton to Ted Hughes have contemplated fishing's intrinsic mystery. Writers from Walton onwards – Kingsley, Grey, Buchan, Farson, Hemingway, Ransome – have tried to explain and celebrate the connection between man and fish, hunter and hunted. Philosophers and Doctors of Divinity have analysed fishing's ethics. It is reasonable to claim that fishing has one of the most extensive, and certainly one of the best, literatures of any 'disport'.

Beyond fascination, one of the reasons angling literature is so extensive lies in the obvious fact that fishing has a longer recorded history than most other popular sports and pastimes. Even in English, where written records of rod-and-line fishing begin relatively late, we have five centuries of fishing writing to consider. Embedded in this literature are changing perceptions of fishing along with, and perhaps as a consequence of, changing styles and technical developments. This evolution is captured in the way people have spoken and thought about the pastime. Fishing, therefore, and fly-fishing in particular, has a large, rich, and rewarding vocabulary. The aim of this book is to examine that vocabulary in detail. It is primarily a book about language and history.

Fish and fishing have always been important to the inhabitants of the British Isles. Long before the records of rod-and-line fishing begin, Bede, in his *Ecclesiastical History* (*c.*700) explicitly mentioned that our waters teem with salmon, eels and pike. Ælfric, writing in *c.*1000, noted that a fisherman – presumably a man with a net, or a set line – might catch eels, pike, minnows, trout and lampreys, 'and as many other kinds as swim in the river'. That fisherman would then sell his freshwater fish to the 'ceasterware', the citizens; there was evidently a great demand, because the fisherman was 'unable to catch as many as I can sell'.

Place-names, too, attest the historical importance of fish and fishing. The original Germanic term for the salmon was *leax* (as in Modern German *lachs*). In Ireland, you may still watch salmon, or even catch them, at Leixlip, the salmon leap. In the far north-west of Scotland you may still ford the river at Laxford. In York-shire, you may still catch trout in Troutsdale. To name a place after a fish suggests not only the importance of the fish, but also that we have been captivated by it. We are, many of us, fascinated by fish and by water. The bridge-leaning habits we acquire in childhood, and which are endemic in Ireland, persist throughout our lives. The massed cars and stopped traffic one sometimes finds in summer, as hundreds gather near a salmon-leap to watch the genetic intensity of the salmon's spawning run, are a tribute to our absorption.

Given the long history of fishing, it is not surprising to find that the vocabulary of fly-fishing organises into a series of historical layers. The earliest terms concerning fish and fishing are native, deriving mainly from Old English (OE) but with one or two Celtic or Gaelic terms. The word *angle* itself comes from OE *angul*, 'fish-hook'; *beetle, creeper, drag, fish, gnat, hook, midge, wade* and many other terms derive more or less directly from OE. *Charr* is Gaelic (from *ceara*, 'red or blood-coloured'), as are *finnock* (from *fionnag*), *gillaroo* (from Irish *giolla ruadh*, 'red lad'), *loch* (or *lough*), *machair*, and, possibly, *parr*. These form the substratum, the lexical bed-rock, of fishing vocabulary. It is worth noting, though, that these are all words to do with fish, insects or water – words which would have occurred in the natural descriptive way; at this early date, before the Norman Conquest, they have apparently nothing to do with rod-and-line fishing.

As England is conquered, settled and reconquered, first by the Vikings in the ninth and tenth centuries, then by the Norman French in the eleventh, new words drawn from those languages infiltrate English, and another two layers are added to the fishing vocabulary. From Old Norse (ON) come *blae* and *bloa, grilse, mort*, and *voe*. From Old French – and here is more familiar lexical ground – we ultimately derive the words *blank, brace, cane, fry, mend, salmon, spawn, troll, trout*, and many others.

As the centuries pass, fly-fishing, like the English language itself, borrows terms voraciously from several different sources, and more lexical layers are added to those already present. From the four-teenth and fifteenth centuries onwards, the new, borrowed words have much more to do with the actual techniques of fishing, with natural and artificial flies or with fly-dressing. There are terms borrowed directly from the Classical languages, principally Latin, or borrowed from Latin via French: *action, antenna, barb, caudal* (fin), *chironomid*, *diptera*, *dorsal*, and *eclosion* are representative here, and several other examples will be found. From Welsh come the words *gwyniad* and *sewin*, from Irish, *croneen*, *dollaghan* and *sonaghan*.

This relative distribution of terms, and the dates at which they are first attested in an English fishing context, is a significant pointer towards the historical development of the pastime. The native OE vocabulary has to do simply with fish and food; the later, post-Conquest vocabulary has to do with fish, angling, and sport. In OE, our familiar trout was called a *scēote*, a 'shoat', a shooter and darter of currents. Like the salmon, it was primarily seen as a source of food (and income, if Ælfric's fisherman is to be believed). By the fifteenth century, though, English has borrowed the new word *trout* from French, and the trout has become, as the *Treatise* puts it, 'a right choice fish and also a fervent biter'. Such a lexical change, from *scēote* to *trout*, seems to reflect a wider change in the way the fish was regarded. Essentially, it is a change from utilitarian hunger to refined sportsmanship. It is at least plausible to think that this quiet revolution took place because fly-fishing was brought to England by the Norman aristocracy, those who had the leisure to fish, to hawk, and to hunt game in their far-flung estates.

There is a final point to be made, concerning the relationship between the fairly specialised vocabulary of fly-fishing, and the vocabulary of the English language itself. While some of our fishing words are in general use (*gnat*, *fly*, *line*, *trout* . . .), other terms, once specialised, have leaked back into the vernacular with an enhanced sense. To *rise to the bait*, to *land a sale*, to be *played out*, to swallow something *hook, line and sinker*, or to be *let off the hook* are all phrases which have acquired an extra resonance from being used in a fishing context. English is constantly being enhanced in this way, not only, of course, from fishing, but also from other popular pursuits: from cricket, *caught out*, *sticky wicket*, *straight bat*; from horse-racing, *cocktail*, *first past the post*, *finishing straight*, *hands down*. These language-internal borrowings and reborrowings indicate just how important are the vocabularies of our chosen means of solace. The words we use to a great extent condition the way we see the world around us.

For those interested in words, then, as much as for those who like to catch fish, the study of fly-fishing's language, from *alevin* to *whitling*, from *dapping* to *stockie-bashing*, offers many curiosities and many rewards.

Principally for your solace

Abbreviations

OE: Old English (*c*.600-1100)
ME: Middle English (*c*.1100-1450)
eModE: early 'Modern' English (*c*.1450-1700)
ModE: 'Modern' English (*c*.1700-present day).

AN: Anglo-Norman (*c*.1150-1300)
Da: Danish
Du: Dutch
Fr: French (ModF: Modern French)
G: German (ModG: Modern German)
Gk: Greek
Ir: Irish Gaelic
L: Latin
LG: Low German
MF: Middle French
MLG: Middle Low German
OF: Old French
OHG: Old High German
ON: Old Norse
Sw: Swedish

OED: Oxford English Dictionary, Second Edition (1989)

Material in braces:
    in [ ] = phonetic representation, e.g. [pʰa], 'parr'
    in / / = underlying phonemic representation, e.g. /pa:/
    in < > = written form of word, e.g. <parr>

References to important and often-cited sources such as Hills, Kingsmill Moore, Roberts, Trench, Walton, and Courtney Williams are given in shortened form. Full details may be found in the bibliography. Where a work does not appear in the bibliography, details have been taken from the OED's citation.

My chief debt, as it is for anyone who undertakes serious lexicographical work, is to the OED.

Abdomen   The body of a nymph or pupa, dun, or adult fly. The abdomen is joined to the *thorax*. 'Anglers usually refer to the "thorax" of a fly as the "shoulders" and to the "abdomen" as the "body"' (Harris, 16). In both immature and adult insects, the abdomen is distinctly segmented. This segmentation may be represented on the *artificial* by the use of e.g. marked *quill* as a body material, or by ribbing the body with hair, wire, *tinsel* or mylar. Anglers have attempted to imitate colour and segmentation of natural insects from the earliest times, e.g. the *Treatise* gives a dressing of the 'Shell Fly' (*?grannom*) with the 'body of grene wull and lappyd abowte wyth the herle of the pecocks tayle'. Ribbing fly bodies with hair or silk was usual by the 18th century (Hills, *History*, ch. IX).

The word *abdomen* is from L. *abdere*, 'to stow away, conceal, cover', although there may also be some connection with L. *adeps*, 'fat' (see *adipose*). It first occurs in English in the sense 'fat deposited around the belly', although by the early 17th century, our modern sense 'stomach' had developed. In a specifically zoological sense ('the posterior division of the body [of an insect]'), the word is first attested in 1788-89 (Howard, *New Royal Cycl.*: 'In insects of the third order...the head, thorax and abdomen are wholly different from those of the other orders').

acid and alkaline waters   *Acid* waters, especially lakes, typically lie on the uplands, on granite or peat, and are sometimes referred to as *oligotrophic*. These waters are characteristically poor in nutrients, phytoplankton, and plants, and consequently poor in food. If the lake is fed by a *spawning* stream, the result is a large number of small trout. Acid waters may also contain charr, and migratory fish such as salmon and sea-trout may be present during their summer runs.

Alkaline waters, also referred to as *eutrophic*, are usually lowland, typically lie on limestone, and contain mineral nutrients, plankton, extensive plant life, consequently are rich in food. These waters are able to support larger trout, although usually in smaller numbers. See Greenhalgh, ch. 2, and Frost & M.E. Brown.

acid rain   The cause of *acid rain* is disputed, but commonly thought to be an effect of sulphur dioxide emissions from power stations. Rainfall thereby contains excess acidity, and, by increasing the solubility of poisonous metals, causes ecological changes in the catchment, including the death of fish and other creatures. Areas of Scandinavia have been badly affected, also parts of the west coast of England and Scotland, particularly Galloway. Attempts have been made to counteract acid rain by placing lime in feeder streams in order to protect or restore the pH factor of the water.

action   From L. *actiōnem*, 'doing, performance'. The word first comes into English meaning 'exertion of energy or influence; working, agency, operation' (e.g. 1386 Chaucer: 'the acciouns or werkynges of Penitence'). The later sense, 'way in which an instrument acts', is attested from 1845 (*London Univ. Calend. Exam. Papers*: 'Explain the action (1) of the siphon, (2) of the air-pump').

In a fishing sense, the word *action* is a term applied to the *rod*'s curve when flexed under pressure. A *tip-actioned* rod, for example, also referred to as *fast-actioned*, has a relatively stiff *butt¹* and a more flexible tip; the action causes a tight loop in casting, great line-speed, and consequent distance. A middle-to-tip action, also referred to as *through-* or *progressive-action*, means that power is transferred through the rod evenly (not just through the tip), causing a wider loop. Most practical fly-fishers, particularly where distance-casting is not a priority, choose a rod with this kind of action (e.g. 'There should be a feeling of power in the flexions of the [salmon fly] rod, especially about the middle; the action should be appreciable right down to the hand . . .' (Taverner & Scott, 42).

On a good trout (or salmon) fly-rod, the action, the curve, should be even; there should be no flat spots around the *ferrules*. For this reason, spigot ferrules, which are built in to the rod, are preferable to sleeve-type joints. See also *cast²*.

adipose (fin)   From L. *adeps*, 'fat'. Much can be attributed to this tiny, fleshy lobe. To it is owed the distinction between coarse- and game-fish. The presence of the *adipose fin* is diagnostic for game-fish in the sense that they can be distinguished by this small, rayless adipose fin found between the dorsal fin and the tail.

The adipose fin seems to serve no purpose to the fish, but is useful to the angler as a distinguishing mark during a *scale-count*, i.e. a scale-count may be taken between the adipose fin and the *lateral line*, counting down and backwards. A salmon has 11-15 scales between adipose fin and lateral line, while the sea-trout has 14-19. (And see here H. Falkus, ch. 1.) See also *abdomen*.

advanced wings   These are single or divided *wings* on *dry fly* patterns, tied in with a pronounced forward list in advance of the *eye* of the *hook*. Courtney Williams (*Dictionary*, 418) states that this method of winging was first found on the Mole Fly; another pattern with an advanced wing is that excellent Yorkshire fly, the John Storey. Further information on the history of dressing the wings of artificial flies may be found under *wing*.

AFTM   abbr. American Federation of Tackle Manufacturers. The *AFTM* system is a way of rating line-weights, e.g. a line labelled AFTM (also symbolised '#') 4 is light, as #9, heavy. Lines should be chosen to suit the #-rating of the rod, i.e. a trout fly-*rod* rated #7-9 is designed for AFTM line weights 7-9, but will fish best with 10-15 yards of #8 line beyond the rod tip. The AFTM system superseded the 'H' system of line-rating when plastic-coated flylines were developed, and replaced silk lines, towards the end of the 1960s. See also *double taper; weight forward; fly line*.

alder   *Sialis lutaria* and *S. fuliginosa*. Only the first is found on stillwater (Goddard). A fly, with brown abdomen, darker thorax, and brownish wings with strong veining. At first glance, the adult is rather like a *sedge*. The life-cycle is partly terrestrial, partly aquatic. The larva is carnivorous.

The etymology of the word is noteworthy. The word occurs in OE as *al(e)r* (the tree, *Alnus glutinosa*), the /d/ being the result of a later phonetic development (by the late 14th century, for example, Chaucer could write of the 'birch, asp[en], aldir'). But our word *alder*, meaning the fly, apparently develops from dialectal *orl*, which is related to OE *alr* (again, the tree – possibly the fly gained its name from the fact that it is found in the vicinity of the trees?). In a fly-fishing context, then, the alder first occurs as *orl*, e.g. in Bowlker's *Art of Angling* (1747: 'The Orle Fly... is the best fly to Fish with after the May Flyes are gone'). But by the 19th century, *orl* (possibly via *olr*) has again developed a /d/, so that Davy, *Salmonia* (1828), could write of 'the alder fly [which] is generally in large quantities before the Mayfly' (evidently Davy had not read Bowlker).

The *alder* has been recorded (Harris) as common in lowland areas during May and the early part of June. Charles Kingsley, who called the fly 'hunch-back', developed a famous dressing (see below), but there are older patterns. Hills considered that the earliest known pattern is given in the *Treatise* (15th century) – 'The drake fly: the body of blacke wull and lappyd abowte wyth blacke sylke, wynges of the mayle of the blacke drake wyth a blacke head' – although unfortunately the dressing is difficult to construe, and moreover, the *Treatise* gives this as a fly for August, which is a little late. Kingsley's passage (from *Chalk Stream Studies*, 1859) on the alder runs as follows:

O thou beloved member of the brute creation – Songs have been written in praise of thee; statues would ere now have been erected to thee had thathunch-back and those flabby wings of thine been "susceptible of artistic treatment". But ugly thou art in the eyes of the uninitiated vulgar; a little stumpy old maid toddling about the world in a black bonnet and a brown cloak, laughed at by naughty boys but doing good wherever thou comest and leaving sweet memories behind thee; so sweet that the trout will rise at the ghost or sham of thee for pure love of thy kindness to them, months after thou hast departed from this sublunary sphere. What hours of bliss do I not owe to thee!...Would that I could give thee a soul...and make thee happy in all aeons to come! But as it is, such immortality as I can, I bestow on thee here, in small return for all the pleasant days thou hast bestowed on me.

Kingsley's pattern was in use, and familiar, fifty years after its inception. For further dressings, see Harris, 169; J. Goddard, *Trout Flies of Stillwater*, 151-2, and Courtney Williams, 75-81. See also *terrestrial*.

alevin   From French *alevin*, ultimately from OF *alever*, 'to rear' (cf. L. *adlevāre*, 'to raise'). Defined in the OED as a 'young fish, fry', the word is first attested in 1868 ('The havoc committed on the eggs, and alevins').

In our sense, the *alevin* is the stage between *egg* and *fry* in the life-cycle of a *salmonid*. Eggs of the brown trout take about sixty days to hatch into alevins, which live on the yolk-sac still attached to their bodies for approximately one month. When the yolk-sac has been used up, the fish is termed a fry, and begins to feed actively in the quiet water at the edges of the stream. See e.g. Sawyer, *Keeper of the Stream*: 'The alevins live on their yolk sacs for about five weeks...' (39). See also *redd*.

amadou   From F. *amadou*, literally 'lover' (perhaps because it is easy to ignite, see below), although there may be some connection with ON (e.g. ON *mata*, 'to feed'). A type of dried fungus, found on the Scottish birch. It is absorbent, and was used until recently to dry floating flies. *Amadou* is now difficult to obtain commercially, although at the time of writing (1990) some limited stocks are available from a supplier in Germany. It was also used to ignite fireworks, and to staunch blood (dentistry). It was replaced in fishing use by dry tissue, or by proprietary, water-absorbent crystals. Amadou was extensively used during the early years of this century, when the *dry-fly* cult was at its height. The term is not recorded before the 19th century (first attestation 1815: 'Some give to the amadow the name of pyrotechnical sponge').

The great G.E.M. Skues was an enthusiast for amadou, and *The Way of a Trout with a Fly* ends with an 'advertisement' for amadou:

Dentists use it for drying the hollows in teeth. Dry-fly men who know what is good for them use it for drying flies. Salmon-fly anglers are going to find it first-rate for drying and preserving their salmon flies. Wet and mangled May flies washed and then dried with it resume their pristine youth and beauty . . . (272)

On the fungoid origins of amadou see also David Beanland, 'Made in Scotland', *T&S*, May 1989.

anal fin   a single, rayed fin found on the underside of fish between the *ventral fins* and the *caudal* or tail fin. As with other fins (apart from the *adipose*), its function is to assist in the fish's balance and stability.

angle also **angling**   From OE *angul*, 'fish-hook'. The word is still older, and stems ultimately from an Aryan root *ank-* meaning 'to bend'. It occurs in a phrase of King Alfred's: *Swā swā mid angle fisc gefangen biþ*, 'just as fish are taken with a hook' (i.e. a hook on a set line). Later, the term comes to apply to the *rod*; the *Treatise* speaks both of the 'angle' ('fysshynge wyth an angle', meaning fishing with a rod rather than 'all other manere of fys-shyng', which 'is . . . laborious and grievous, often makynge folkes wete and colde'), of 'angling' ('the game of anglynge'), and of the 'angler'. *Angling* and *fishing* are already synonyms by the time of the *Treatise*, although clearly the former is less ambiguous: 'The beste [of all sports] to my symple dyscrecion . . . is fysshynge callyd anglynge wyth a roode and a lyne and an hoke'. The term *angle*, as a noun meaning 'rod', is virtually obsolete by the time of *The Compleat Angler* (first edition, 1653; first edition including Charles Cotton's work, 1676). Cotton, for example, spoke only of the rod ('These are to be angled with, with a short Line, not much more than half the length of your Rod' . . . 'The length of your line, to a Man that knows how to handle his Rod, and to cast it, is no manner of encumbrance' – *Angler*, 266). Fifty years before, William Davenant wrote of the 'angling rod' – perhaps to meet the demands of his metre: 'For angling rod he took a sturdy oak, / For line a cable that in storm ne'er broke . . .' (cited in Profumo & Swift, 80).

ant   *Ant* derives from OE *æmete*, which in ME becomes either *āmete* or *ēmete*; by suppression of the unstressed medial vowel, *āmete* ultimately becomes *amt* (or *ampte*); once this happens, the /m/ subsequently becomes an /n/ (because /n/ is phonetically closer to /t/ than is /m/). But there is also a dialectical word, *emmet*, which represents a survival of the original OE form. This intriguing relationship between *ant* and *emmet* is versed by Ogden Nash:

> . . . The modern ant, when trod upon,
> Exclaims 'I'll be a son-of-a-gun!'
> Not so its ancestor, the emmet,
> Which perished crying 'Zounds!' or 'Demmit!'

Ants are terrestrial insects, both black and red, which are sometimes blown onto the water, especially during hot days in high
summer. Theakston, writing in 1853, noted that in August the
'ants sometimes fall numerous on the waters this month and are
greedily taken by the fish.' Ronalds gave a very good illustration
of the red ant, citing Newman's *History of Insects*, which claimed
that ants are 'attracted by the brilliant surface of water, illumined
by an autumnal sun' (115). But the earliest artificial pattern is
perhaps that of Charles Cotton, who gave a dressing for the 'Ant-
flie, the dubbing of brown and red Camlet mixt, with a light grey
wing' (this he fished in June, see *Angler*, 207).

More recently, Arthur Ransome, *Rod and Line* (1929), extensively
reviewed artificial dressings, and gave one of his own, reproduced
in Courtney Williams, *Dictionary*, pp.82-6. See also *terrestrial*.

antennae   The etymology is intriguing. The word *antenna* derives
from L., where it means 'a sail-yard', this sense ultimately deriving from a Greek word meaning 'to stretch out or forth'. As the
OED notes, 'As the projecting "horns" or ends of sail-yards, in L.
cornua antennārum, were also called [Gk.] κεπαίαι, *antennae* was
aptly employed to render the same word when meaning the horns
of insects'. The second attestation of the word in English (1657)
nicely reflects this etymology: 'The horns are called by Aristotle,
Antennae, because they [insects] hold them forth before them'.

Antennae, then, are paired feelers found on the heads of certain
insects, notably the *sedges*. The antennae are represented on some
artificial patterns (e.g. the G & H Sedge) by *hackle* stalks.

I believe the first angler and fly-dresser to represent antennae
was the excellent Robert Venables (*The Experienced Angler*, 1662),
who wrote that 'some flies have forked tails, and some have horns,
both which you must imitate with a slender hair fastened to the
head or tail of your fly' (1969 facsimile, 15).

anterior wings   The large forewings of an adult insect, especially
the *upwinged* flies. See Harris, 91: 'All duns and spinners carry
a pair of anterior wings which arise from the mesothorax (second
segment of the thorax). Most species also possess a smaller pair
of hind or posterior wings...' Two insects which possess only
one pair of anterior wings (i.e. where the lack of hindwings helps
in recognition) are the Lake Olive and the Pond Olive. See also
dun; ephemeroptera; olive; wing.

artery forceps   A surgeon's tool made of stainless steel, having a
scissor-action and knurled, blunt points. These may be used to
extract hooks embedded in the gristle of a fish's mouth (see *maxillary; scissors*), and are superior to other unhooking devices or
disgorgers. As Alan Pearson writes, 'fingers will prove far less

efficient [for removing hooks] than artery forceps, which possess
the excellent facility of locking on to the shank of the hook for
manipulative purposes' (p.110).

artificial   This word, from F. *artificiel*, enters English as an adjective (with the sense 'made by or resulting from art or artifice')
during the early Middle Ages; in 1382, for example, Wycliffe
contrasted 'naturel ordre' with 'artificial ordre'. Later, the word
comes to be used as a substantive, in the sense 'artificial things;
products of art', as in Guillim's *Heraldry* of 1611: 'Such Artificials
as are in vse amongst men of Militarie Profession'.

The fishing terminology reflects the above distribution, since
anglers use the word both as an adjective and as a noun ('the
artificial'). Courtney Williams, for example, speaks in Part I of
his great dictionary of both 'the artificial fly' (or 'the artificial
pattern') and of 'artificials' ('many artificials which well represent
some natural insect as seen by the fish, may, in our eyes, bear
very little resemblance to it').

autopsy   From L. *autopsia*, 'seeing with one's own eyes'. The
word's first English attestation dates to 1651 ('Or by autopsie,
when by our observation, wee get a certaine knowledge of things'),
although our current sense, 'dissection of a dead body' is quick
to develop.

During the gutting of fish, especially brown and rainbow trout
(since neither salmon nor *sea trout* appear to feed in freshwater),
it is usual to inspect the stomach contents in order to determine
what the fish had been feeding on immediately before its capture.
The autopsy can confirm suspicions ('I thought this trout had
been taking green midge pupae'), or, on occasion, baffle them
entirely.

Skues called the autopsy a 'nauseating business', and preferred
the use of a *marrow-scoop* by the bankside as a quicker, more
convenient and more immediate way of ascertaining what his
trout had been eating prior to capture.

Hills (*History*, 27) pointed out that the autopsy ('usually
imagined to be the most modern of modern devices') has been
familiar to fishermen for over five hundred years, and is first
recorded in the *Treatise*, which gave the following good advice:
'For baytes for grete fyssh kepe specyally this rule: When ye have
take a grete fysshe, undo the mawe [stomach], and what ye find
therin make that your bayte, for it is beste.' Cotton also directed
Viator to '[fish] untill you have taken one, and then thrusting
your finger thorough his Guills, to pull out his Gorge, which
being opened with you knife, you will then discover what Flie is
taken, and may fit your self accordingly' (*Angler*, 284).

Backing   Thin, level line, usually of *nylon monofilament* or braided terylene, used to fill up the *reel* under the fly-line and to provide extra line capacity, e.g. as attested by the following: 'the [wide drum reels] will take the lines recommended [up to WF8] together with enough backing. I use 25lb . . . breaking strain monofilament . . .' (Greenhalgh, 107). Backing is joined to the fly-line by a *needle knot*, or a *splice*. Particularly large fish may, when hooked, run so far and fast that they take the fisherman 'onto the backing', which can be a delightfully worrying moment. Backing is also used with *shooting-heads*.

The word ultimately derives from OE *bæc*, which during the 18th century develops a verbal sense, *to back*, meaning 'to line the back of, make a back to'. *Backing*, in our sense 'anything used to form a back, or line a back' apparently develops from this verb (first attestation 1793: 'Not only flat backing, but Purbeck ashler in rough courses'). OED records no fishing sense.

backing-up   A technique for presenting the fly on rivers, used especially for *salmon* and *sea-trout*. The fly is fished down the pool in the normal way; when the pool tail is reached, the angler turns and begins to fish up the pool again, casting across, or up-and-across, allowing the line to belly in the current so that the fly fishes in a fast curve. The principal advantage of the method is that the fly works at a different depth and angle to that of a downstream presentation, and may therefore induce a recalcitrant fish to *take*[1]; as Falkus puts it, 'backing-up a pool is a very productive method of fishing – both for sea trout and salmon' (*Sea Trout Fishing*, 230).

OED records no fishing sense, but it is at least possible that *backing up* is related to *back up* in its sense 'to stand behind with intent to support or second . . .' (thus *backing up* in cricket and other sports). On the other hand, it seems more plausible to derive the phrase from a verb, *to back*, meaning 'to draw back, withdraw, to move back' (first attestation 1496, *Book of St Albans*, and the Treatise on Hawking: 'The terretys serue to kepe hir from wyndyng whan she backes'). This verb ultimately gives rise to the verbal phrase *to back out (of)*, e.g. 1818 Scott: 'Determined that Morris should not back out of the scrape so easily'. I believe our fishing practice of backing up derives from the ME verb.

baggot   From a verbal participle, *bagged*, meaning 'big with young, pregnant'. (*Sir Perceval*, 1400: 'The mere was bagged with fole'.) This is a term applied to *hen salmon* which have not spawned – McLaren & Currie refer aptly to such fish as 'thwarted matrons' (20). These fish are sometimes caught by anglers in the early spring, but, since they are still full of ova, baggots should be returned to the river. See also *kipper; rawner; shedder*.

barb From L. *barba*, 'beard'. The recurved process on the point of a *hook*. Strangely, OED records that this word is first found in English during the 14th century. This, of course, cannot mean that barbed hooks did not exist before that time, since there is ample evidence that barbed hooks were known since the time of the Ancient Greeks, who typically fished with hand-lines (although fly fishing itself also dates from this time, see *fly*). William Radcliffe, in *Fishing from the Earliest Times*, considers that the barbed hook was still older, having been developed from the bent, originally barbless hooks used in ancient Egypt (see p.313, where Radcliffe argues that the precursor of the 'Limerick hook with a single barb' dates from *c*.2000 BC).

The *Treatise* gives good illustrations of barbed hooks, along with instructions on how to make them from embroiderers' needles or shoemakers' awls. ('Thenne reyse the berde [barb] wyth your knyfe, and make the poynt sharpe' – see too Trench, 32). The *Treatise* calls hook-making 'the moost subtyll and hardyste crafte in makynge of your harnays [tackle]'.

In recent years, more trout anglers have been experimenting with the use of *barbless* (or de-barbed) *hooks* on the grounds of conservation; the use of barbless hooks makes it possible to return trout, especially *parr* and other undersized fish, without handling them. See Clarke & Goddard (*The Trout and the Fly*, 182-4), who write that the 'barbless hook...comes out with the merest twist of the fingers. There is little more damage to the trout, than would be caused by a pin-prick in a human'. (One popular and quick way of removing the barb from a hook is to flatten it with a pair of small pliers.) And see e.g. *Limerick; sneck*.

bass From OE *bast*. A bag made of plaited straw or similar material, used to carry the catch. *Bass* originally meant 'the inner bark of the lime or linden', and later, by extension, was a term applied to articles made of split rushes or straw (OED) such as mats or hassocks. The *bass* seems to come into use rather late; Walton spoke merely of the 'Fish-bag'. In the sense 'flat plaited bag or flexible basket', Howitt, *Rural Life* (1837), wrote of 'Carrying home a bass brimful of vegetables.' Many fly-fishers prefer to carry their catch in a bass since it is light and allows air to circulate, keeping the catch fresher than e.g. the unfortunately common plastic bag. See also *creel*.

beaching   A technique for landing fish, especially *salmon*, but also
sometimes used for *sea trout*. When the beaten fish turns onto its
side in the later stages of the *play*, the fisherman exerts rod-
pressure so as to bring the fish's head into the bank, which preferably shelves quietly into the stream. (It is difficult to beach a
fish on a steep, rocky, or wooded bank.) Thereafter the motions
of the fish's body are (usually) sufficient to bring the fish onto
the shore, when, in the case of salmon, it can be *tailed* and carried
away from the stream.

Bank fishermen on stillwaters also sometimes use this technique
with brown and rainbow trout, where the shoreline permits.

Given a good hook-hold, beaching is a relatively safe way of
landing fish, and particularly useful in situations where use of
the *gaff* or *landing net* is impossible, see e.g. Taverner & Scott,
238: 'If the river's edge shelves conveniently, you can safely beach
the fish you are forbidden to gaff or unable to tail by running it
gently up the shingle and cutting off its retreat by standing
between it and the river'.

beetle   From OE *bitula*, related to the OE verb *bītan*, 'to bite'.
Any of the various species of *Coleoptera*. The most important
beetles to the fly-fisherman are perhaps the *Coch-y-bonddu*, also
known as the June Bug and Bracken Clock, and the Soldier Beetle
(this last, especially on stillwaters in summer). Goddard (*Trout
Flies of Stillwater*, 153-6), gives a good discussion. Artificial flies
include the Coch-y-bonddu, Eric's Beetle, Black and Peacock
Spider, and many others (see Roberts, *Illust. Dictionary*, 13-14).
Representative artificial patterns do not appear to have come into
general use until the 19th century: Ronalds (1836), for example,
gave a dressing for the 'Coch-a-bonddu' (which he also referred
to as the 'Marlow Buzz'), saying that the insect 'is very abundant
in hot weather...from the beginning until the middle of June...
They are called Bracken-clocks in the North, and are well taken
by the Trout'.

black curse   See *black gnat; reed smut*.

black gnat   Any small black fly from the Bibionidae family,
although the term commonly refers to *Bibio johannis*, a *terrestrial*
insect which may be blown onto the water, especially in the early
summer (*johannis* from the fact that the natural insect is said to
be most prevalent around Midsummer Day, St John's Day). Both
Goddard and Harris point out that the term 'black gnat' is also
used to describe species of Simulium or *smuts* (and see *reed smut*).

Artificial dressings for the black gnat have been familiar since
Cotton, who wrote 'From the tenth of this Month [March]...is
taken a little black Gnat; the dubbing either of the fur of a black

water-Dog, or the down of a young black water-Coot; the wings
of the Male of a Mallard as white as may be, the body as little as
you can possibly make it, and the wings as short as his body'
(285). As Hills pointed out (*History*, 165), Cotton's is a most
accurate pattern, copying the three characteristic features of the
fly ('a small body, transparent wings, and, in the male, particularly short ones'). Cotton also gave two other dressings for gnat-
like flies, the first (possibly, owing to the month, another dressing
for the true *Bibio johannis*?) a black *palmer* for use in May ('The
next May-Flie is the black Flie, made with a black body of the
whirle of an Ostridg feather, rib'd with silver twist, and the black
hackle of a Cock over all'), the second, 'another little black Gnat'
for use in June. The last is probably an imitation of a smut ('the
dubbing of black mohair, and a white Grey wing'). For recent
dressings, see e.g. Goddard, Courtney Williams, Weaver, and
Fallon (p.27). Fallon also records the following anonymous verse:

There are trout in my river whose attitude,
Is one of the blackest ingratitude;
Though I offer them duns,
Most superior ones,
They maintain a persistent Black Gnatitude.

blae *Blae* is originally a Norse word (ON *blá*, Swe. *bla*, Da. *blaa*)
surviving into Northern English and Scots as *blae*, elsewhere as
blo or *bloo (bloa)*. OED suggests that *blae* means '[o]f a dark colour
between black and blue; blackish blue; of the colour of the blae-
berry . . . livid; also, of a lighter shade, bluish grey, lead-coloured';
it also records senses in 'bleak . . . dark . . . dingy-coloured, "grey"
as opposed to white'. The phrase 'beaten black and blue' was
originally ' . . . black and blae' (the colour of a livid bruise). In
fishing terminology, the word is applied to the Blae and Black,
an artificial pattern much used on stillwaters, particularly in Scotland, to represent e.g. the large black *midge* of spring, but which
was originally the 'old Scottish wet imitation for the iron blue'
(Roberts, *Illust. Dictionary*, 16). This is interesting because the
natural iron blue is so dark blue as to be almost a slaty-black, cf.
the definition above. Perhaps, too, the term blae also refers to
the grey colouration in the wing (starling or blackbird) of the
artificial. As hinted above, the Blae and Black is also effective
during hatches of black *chironomids*. See too Courtney Williams
(p.102), who refers to Blae and Silver, Blae and Blue and Blae
and Gold; and see *bloa*.

blank[1] The treated raw material of a *fibreglass* or *carbon fibre*
fishing *rod*, without cork handle, *rings*, or whippings. The material
is wrapped around a mandril, and then heated, sometimes being

strengthened by the addition of cross-weaved fibres such as kevlar.

No fishing sense is recorded in the OED. The earliest sense of *blank* seems to mean 'bare', but it is likely that our fishing-rod blanks derive from *blank* in its sense 'piece of metal, cut and shaped to the required size of the thing to be made, and ready for the finishing operations' (1596: 'Braid blancis hang above thair eis, With jewels of all histories'). In other words, the term transfers from metalwork (and coinage) into rod-building. See also *rod*.

blank²   Originally from F. *blanc*, 'white' (cf. OE *blīcan*, 'to shine'), which came to mean 'pale or colourless', later, in figurative use, 'void of result, unsuccessful, fruitless, nugatory; amounting to or producing nothing' (in this last sense from 16th century on).

Fishermen often have *blanks*, and also use the word as a verb ('How did you get on?' 'Oh, I blanked, I'm afraid.') – this usage is not recorded in OED. The phrase '(to have) a blank day' was first used, according to OED, in 1832 in Warburton's *Hunting Songs*: 'But I felt inclin'd in my inmost mind, To wish for a blank day'. No fisherman wishes for a blank day; if such a day looks imminent, anglers cast until the last knockings, hoping for a fish to 'save a blank'.

This usage is clearly related to the phrase *to draw a blank*. This was specifically a hunting term. *To draw* in hunting is 'to search (a wood, covert etc.) for game' (this sense of *draw* coming from 'drawing a net', searching the water for fish). So to 'draw (a covert etc.) blank' is to search (it) without success. The first attestation of this sense dates again from Warburton: 'The man...Whose heart heaves a sigh when his gorse is drawn blank'.

bloa   *Bloa* is the midland and southern form of *blae*, but used perhaps in a rather different sense. *Bloa* – as in the *artificials* Poult Bloa, Snipe Bloa, Waterhen Bloa – surely refers to the plumage on the dressing, especially to the colour of the *hackle*, which in each case, but particularly in the Waterhen, is a lead- or slate-grey. *Poult* (cf. *pullet*) is a young grouse; the hackle is slaty-blue. Courtney Williams wrote of the term as follows:

> Bloa is a curious term and purely of dalesman origin. In John Swarbrick's list of Wharfedale flies (1807), it is also spelt blo and bloo, but that may be because the gentleman of Austby was somewhat illiterate. Its meaning is by no means clear and north countrymen explain it in many divers ways, no two of which appear to agree. When I asked the late J.H.R: Bazley, he replied: "It refers, I think, to the cold cloudy bleak sort of weather feather, used frequently with a yellow or partially yellow body. This is my conception of it and I may be wrong,

but I don't think so. The word may possibly include a natural
fly which hatches in the conditions indicated, but I hardly
think this is so". (289)

It is difficult to agree that the term is 'purely of dalesman origin',
since *bloa* is clearly cognate with the more southerly forms *blo*
and *bloo*. What is more certain is that the *bloa* series of flies are
almost invariably associated with Yorkshire. Bazley was probably
right when he stated that the word did not refer to a natural fly.
The only possible candidate is the iron blue, which does hatch
in 'cloudy bleak sort of weather', but none of the dressings in the
bloa series are truly representative of this insect.

It may also be the case that the term *bloa* or *blo(o)* occurs in
the word *blow-fly*, the flesh-fly or bluebottle *(Musca vomitoria)*.
OED states that 'This sense is apparently connected with old
notions of natural history. It has nothing to do with the notion
of blowing or inflating meat.' Alternatively, it cannot be coinci-
dental that one of the senses of *blo(o)* means 'livid blue', and it
would be appropriate if the term was applied to the body coloration of the blow-fly.

blood knot   Taverner & Scott (63) describe the *blood knot* as 'by
far the best and safest knot for joining strands of gut or nylon to
make up a salmon cast. It was first described in print by Chaytor
(Letters to a Salmon Fisher's Sons, 1910).

Gut is now virtually obsolete (see *nylon monofilament*). As a
means of joining strands of nylon, the blood knot has to some extent
been replaced by the *Grinner Knot* and the *Water Knot*, which are
both reliable; the Water Knot is also easier to tie. See *knots*.

bloodworm(s)   The angler's term for the *larvae* of *midges* or
Chironomids, which larvae are typically bright red in colour owing
to the presence of haemoglobin, but which may also be green or
almost colourless (Goddard, *Trout Flies of Stillwater*, 89). Some
larvae are free-swimming, others live in tubes in mud or sand.
They are, as Goddard notes, a staple food item of many stillwater
trout and are commonly found in *autopsies*. Several artificial patterns are available, most using red wool or synthetic material tied
round the bend of the hook. Some writers report catching very
good bags of trout on stillwaters by inching a *bloodworm* pattern
along the bottom, e.g. Gordon Fraser (p.34): '[the fish] was still
full of bloodworms. They were half an inch long, and many were
still alive . . . I finished the day with 12 browns, the best 2lb. 10ozs.'

Bloodworms can survive in water with a very low oxygen content (owing to oxygen already stored in the haemoglobin) and are
found in considerable numbers in canals etc., where coarse fishermen sometimes use them as a hook bait.

The OED defines *bloodworm* in two ways, first, as '[a] small bright-red earth-worm used by anglers', and second, as the 'scarlet larva of a genus of crane-flies *(Chironomus)* found in rain-water cisterns and pools'. The first attestation of the word dates from 1741, and the earlier sense ('They will bite freely at the small Red-worm called the Blood-worm'), but by the nineteenth century our familiar sense (bloodworm = midge larva) had developed, e.g. J. Rennie's *Angling* of 1833: 'I mean here water blood-worms, and not the smaller bright red earth-worms sometimes so named in books on angling'.

See also *buzzer*.

blowline   An older term for the floss silk *dapping* line. There are references to the *blowline* from both Kingsley and Francis in the 19th century; Kingsley's is apparently the first attestation of the word in English (1857: 'Great anglers...who could do many things besides handling a blow-line'). More recently, there are references in e.g. Kingsmill Moore (p.64): 'As the natural is too delicate to be cast it has to be drifted out on the wind, which means using a long rod and a light line of undressed silk, known as a blow line', and in Taverner & Scott (p.171): 'Dapping for salmon with a blowline and a live Mayfly has become, more and more, a popular method in the south-western districts of Ireland ...Blowline fishing needs much experience...'. In recent years, the floss silk blowline has been replaced by a line made of synthetic material.

blue-winged olive   Often abbr. to *b.-w. o.*, this is an important river fly, hatching during the summer months, especially on warm evenings. See *dun; ephemeroptera; olive; quill*.

boat fishing   A means of approaching brown, rainbow and *sea trout* on stillwaters (also salmon). Boat fishing seems to have become increasingly popular, and there is currently great interest in 'over-the-front' fly-fishing methods using traditional (or traditionally-based) flies.

The basic technique of boat fishing is simple: the boat is rowed or motored upwind, to the head of a *drift* over promising water (not too deep – as a rough guide, ten feet or less), then is allowed to drift broadside downwind, each angler casting from respective ends of the boat. At the bottom of the drift, the process is repeated over a parallel strip of water. In this way, a large area of the lake may be explored.

There are alternative methods of boat fishing. One popular ploy, especially in a strong breeze, is to stream a *drogue* from the bow or stern of the boat, and allow the boat to drift downwind end-on, rather than broadside. Each angler fishes from respective sides of the boat, casting across-wind (rather than down-, or down-and-across wind, as in the traditional method). Another technique, although banned on some waters, is to employ a drift-controller or rudder, which enables a cross-wind drift, although it is often better to pay a *gillie* for this purpose, particularly on large or unknown lakes.

I have been unable to find references to boat fishing (in this specific sense) much before the nineteenth century, although Harris gives a plate of Irish trout flies tied in 1789 for use on Lough Mask, and in 1791 for use on Irish midland loughs (e.g. Sheelin and Ennell). The absence of a literature of boat fishing – indeed, stillwater trout fishing in general – before the nineteenth century is rather puzzling; as C.F. Walker notes, 'early angling writers seem to have dealt exclusively with river fishing' (*Lake Flies and their Imitation*, 17), although it is perhaps difficult to draw any firm conclusions from this. See also *Northampton style*.

bob fly   Another term for the *top dropper* (the fly nearest the rod) on a two- or three-fly *leader* (and see *cast¹*). The etymology is naturally connected with the term *dropper*, first attested in 1870 (although certainly in use earlier) from Blaine's *Encyclopaedia of Rural Sports*: 'When more than one fly is used ... the additional one is called a drop-fly, and by some a bob ...' The term *bob* derives from a much earlier verb, to bob, apparently onomato-poeic or mimetic, meaning 'short jerking or rebounding motion'. It is distantly related to the phrase 'bobbing for apples' – the general sense is 'to move up and down like a buoyant body in water'. Typically, and as used on stillwaters, the bob fly is a *palmered* or *bumble* pattern which, when retrieved and fished 'on the *dibble*', is semi-buoyant and causes an attractive wake.

References in fishing books up to the nineteenth century tend to speak just of the single fly, fished on a horsehair cast; it seems reasonable to suppose that the systematic use of droppered leaders cannot much antedate the development of silkworm gut, which only came into use in England during the later eighteenth century.

boron   A rod-building material which has partly superseded *carbon fibre* (or, properly speaking, may now be used in conjunction with it). The *blank* is light, strong, and of thin diameter. *Boron* fly rods seem to have been first introduced in the late 1970s or early 1980s, e.g. advertising material from 1980 explains that 'Boron is blended with carbon to produce very strong lightweight rods. Boron vibrates less than carbon so that the rods are very sensitive and the tubes do not go oval under stress so that power is retained. By introducing Boron to the rod blank where required the action can be carefully controlled ...' (*T&S*, July 1980, 5).

brace   From OF *brace*, 'two arms or their extent' (cf. ModF *bras*, 'arms'). A brace of trout, for example, are two trout, and, as Hills put it, '[w]hat a happy confidence it gives you to have caught a brace. A brace! It sounds so well. So much better than twice one. Even if you get no more . . . you can face the return home without a sinking heart' (*Summer on the Test*, 90-1).

Total catches are sometimes recorded in brace ('four brace', rather than eight), particularly by those schooled in earlier times. Our Edwardian grandparents – possibly through reticence, since they knew less of bag-limits in those days – spoke more often of 'so many brace . . .', and the word is perhaps less common today.

Fishing tickets on some waters detail the *limit* of fish in terms of brace (e.g. 'Limit: two brace of fish not less than 12"').

brook trout   The common term for *Salvelinus fontinalis*, the North American Brook Trout; also *brookie, brook charr*. Related to the *charr*, the fish is sometimes stocked into stillwaters, where it may subsequently attain weights up to 4lbs in certain cases. Like the *rainbow trout*, however, the brook trout spawns only rarely in this country, although there are records of self-perpetuating strains of these fish in remote parts of Scotland. The fish is distinguishable by the heavy marble-spotting on each flank, small scales (the skin is rather nastily smooth to the touch), and cream belly. There is little literature devoted exclusively to the species in England; Alan Pearson, pp.140-47, gives a useful discussion of fishing techniques.

brown trout   The common term for *Salmo trutta fario* (cf. *Salmo trutta trutta*, the *sea trout*); also *brown* or *brownie* (and see *trout*). The native trout of the British Isles, found from Caithness to Cornwall. Wild stocks are now often supplemented by the introduction of farm-reared fish. The fish thrives in clean, well-oxygenated water, both in rivers, and in lakes with a suitable spawning stream. In rich, alkaline environments (see *acid and alkaline waters*), the fish may reach weights in excess of 10lbs, although generally fish of 2lbs and upwards are considered heavy. In some lakes and lochs there are trout which are exclusively predatory, feeding on smaller trout; for long thought to be a separate species, and termed *ferox*, these trout may weigh anything up to 20lbs, and sometimes more. They are usually caught by *trolling* (and see *cannibal*).

It has always been known that the diet of the brown trout is extraordinarily eclectic (as the *Treatise* put it, the trout 'is a right deyntous [choice] fyssh and also a ryght feruente byter'). Walton, for example, spoke of trout eating frogs, water-rats and mice; at night, Walton wrote, 'he will sometimes rise at a dead Mouse, or a piece of cloth, or any thing, that seems to swim across the water, or to be in motion: this is a choice way [of fishing], but I have not oft used it...' (p.121). It is the brown trout's habit of feeding on natural flies, however, that makes it such an intriguing challenge for the fly-fisherman. In this respect it is worth noting that the earliest lists of artificial flies, from the *Treatise* to Venables, Cotton and beyond, suggest strongly that trout fishing in those centuries had begun as it was to continue, with more or less close representation of the natural insects on which the trout would feed at the appropriate season.

Very crudely speaking, the best of the brown trout fishing occurs in the early and late parts of the season – in May and early June (when large fish may be taken on the dapped or dry *mayfly*[2]), and again in September, when the fish feed heavily, especially on *fry*, in anticipation of *spawning*. This pattern is particularly apparent on stillwaters, although there is some good fishing to be had on both river and lake during midsummer evenings when species of *sedge* are hatching (see *evening rise*).

At other times during the season, it is to daytime hatches of e.g. *olives* that the fly fisher looks for his sport; on stillwaters, trout sometimes feed heavily on hatches of *midge*, particularly, perhaps, during the early mornings and late evenings of summer.

Further information on the life-cycle and habits of the brown trout may be found under *alevin; parr; redd; sea trout; spawning* etc.

bulging Trout, particularly the *brown trout* of that most blue-blooded milieu, the chalkstream, are said to be *bulging* when they are taking insects or other food underwater in such a fashion as to cause a displacement of the water surface, a 'bulge'. The term seems to apply most frequently to trout feeding on *nymphs* at or just under the surface. Skues, for instance, wrote of his discovery that the Tup's Indispensable was useful as a nymph 'on bulging fish' (*Minor Tactics of the Chalkstream*, 31). A bulging fish may also be referred to as a *bulger*; an early use of this term dates from 1899: 'A moderate performer with the rod...will often...pick up a grubber under the bank, a bulger here, a tailer there' (Buxton, *19th Century*). See also *tailing*.

bull trout A species of sea-running trout, one particularly associated with the river Coquet and other rivers of the north-east coast of Britain. Walton was one of the first to mention the *bull trout*: 'There is also in Northumberland,' he wrote, 'a Trout called a Bull-trout, of a much greater length and bigness, than any in these Southern parts' (74-5). Local anglers believe that the bull trout, or *bullie* (also sp. *bully*), is either a genetic cross between a salmon and a brown trout, or some special breed of sea-running brown. W.E. Davies (*Freshwater Fishing*, 138-9) speaks of the differences between the bull trout and the *sea trout*, chiefly the fact that the bull trout has a rounded tail and gill covers, along with larger and stronger teeth, and a different coloration, being greenish-grey above, dirty silver below. Unfortunately, however, the integrity of the bull trout as a distinct species is hard to prove, and some fishing writers believe that these fish are either salmon running to spawn for a second time, or large sea trout. R.N. Stewart (55-6) records that a number of so-called bull trout were captured, tagged, and released in the river Tay, and returned the next year, to be identified as salmon.

The name may derive from the bullying tactics these fish are said to adopt when on the *redds*. Such aggressive behaviour (which Davies records is directed at salmon) would be consistent with the theory that bull trout are in fact a particular type or local strain of salmon, since sea trout typically spawn in different parts of the river to their larger relatives (and see *sea trout*).

bumble   From ME *boom-, bumme- + -le*. A type of artificial fly, usually with a palmered hackle. Two familiar ranges of dressings are those from Derbyshire, said to have been originated by George James Eaton in the mid-19th century, and those from Ireland, developed by the late T.C. Kingsmill Moore.

The Derbyshire patterns include such useful trout and grayling flies as the Grayling Steel Blue (created by Roger Woolley), and the Honey Dun Bumble. T. Donald Overfield (44) discusses the origins of the Honey Dun Bumble which, whatever the reputation of George James Eaton, must go back at least to the 18th century and probably further. The distant ancestors of the Derbyshire patterns are almost certainly the palmered dressings given in Charles Cotton's list of flies (Part Two of *The Complete Angler*). Palmers were also familiar to Barker, writing in 1651, and to Robert Venables (*The Experienced Angler*, 1662). Venables is one of the first to give detailed instructions on dressing a palmered fly. 'Instead of the silk running thus round the fly,' he wrote,

> you may pluck the feather from one side of those long feathers which grow about a cock or capon's neck or tail, by some called hackle; then run the same round your fly, from head to tail, making both ends fast; but you must be sure to suit the feather answerable to the colour you are to imitate in the fly; and this way you may counterfeit those rough insects, which some call wool-beds [woolly-bear caterpillars], because of their wool-like outside and rings of divers colours, though I take them to be palmer worms, which the fish much delight in. (14-15)

'Palmer worms' are also mentioned by Walton ('in April...the best fishing is with the Palmer-worm ... ; these and the May-flie are the ground of all Flie-angling'); since Walton, however, copied his list of flies from Leonard Mascall (1590), and since Mascall copied from the *Treatise*, we are left with the intriguing possibility that palmered patterns, flies 'tied buzz', had been familiar in England from at least the 15th century. This remains conjecture – there is nothing in the *Treatise* which unambiguously suggests a palmered style of dressing (and for more history of this style of dressing, see *palmer*).

The Irish bumble patterns (see Kingsmill Moore, ch. 10) include the Olive Bumble (a good stillwater brown trout pattern, not least at *mayfly²* time) and two first class sea trout patterns, the Claret Bumble and the Bruiser. These last patterns work well on waters other than the Connemara loughs and rivers for which they were devised, particularly those of the far north and west of Scotland. These bumbles are typically fished as *droppers* on a three-fly loch-fishing *leader*, where their bulk allows them to be fished effectively on the *dibble*.

bushing   See *dibbing*.

bustard   A northern term for a large, night-flying moth or sedge. Courtney Williams (*Dictionary*, 119) records that *bustard fishing* (with an artificial fly) is a method practised on north-country rivers, especially the Eden.

On first thought, bustard might seem to have some relationship with the bird, the bustard (*Otis tarda*, now extinct in the British Isles), whose name derives from OF *bistarde* and *oustarde* (a blend or 'portmanteau word'). But in fact this is not so. Our fishing term derives from the 'buzzard', of which bustard is a local variant. Buzzard, which is related to *buzzer* in its earliest sense meaning 'buzzing insect' (and see *buzzer*), is first attested in English in 1654 ('O owle! hast thou only kept company with bats, buzzards, and beetles...'), but by the nineteenth century, the form spelt <bustard> has developed, as in e.g. the following quote from M.G. Watkins in 1886: 'There are some capital chapters on "bustard" fishing (that is, fishing during the night with a large artificial moth)'.

butt¹   The word is from OE, although just possibly from ON (*butt-r*, 'short'). It is defined in the OED as 'the lower end of a spear-shaft, whip-handle, fishing-rod...', and its first attestation in English comes from Malory's *Morte D'Arthur*: 'Sir Tristram awaked hym with the but of his spere'. In the sense 'butt of fishing rod', the first attestation dates to 1872 ('My only way of working him [a fish] was to project the butt of the rod in the usual manner').

The *butt*, then, is the thickest terminal part of the rod, including the handle; also known as the *butt-section* or *butt-piece*. Two- or three-piece rods have been familiar since the *Treatise*. The rod described there was in two parts, a hollow butt (called 'staff') of hazel, willow, or aspen, and a two-part tip (called 'crop') of hazel spliced with blackthorn, crabtree, medlar or juniper. Both pieces of the rod were around six to eight feet long ('a fadom and an halfe'), and the tip section fitted neatly inside the butt when the rod was not in use. In an intriguing aside, the author added that 'thus shall ye make you a rodde soo preuy [so well disguised] that ye maye walke therwyth, and ther shall noor man wyte where abowte ye goo'. In other words, if you walk from work carrying a rod cunningly camouflaged as a mere six-foot length of wood, no one will realise you are going fishing – a type of 15th century piscatorial absenteeism. (Another possibility is that the rod was disguised so as to keep a good fishing spot secret.)

In Cotton's time the butt of the rod might be made of spliced pieces of hazel or fir, with 'other wood' – probably hazel, again – at the tip. Venables (1662), although apparently not particular about what wood was used for the butt (which he called the 'stock'), seems to favour whole cane, the stiffness of which, he wrote, 'is helped by the length and strength of the top', which was made from spliced blackthorn and hazel, with an extreme tip of whalebone. Venables is also the first writer to detail what we would now call the rod's *action*, and insisted that the whole should be evenly *tapered*, long, and light.

Until the 18th century, the butt, or the pieced and tied wood serving to make up the butt-piece, was commonly spliced to the tip (the jointed rod, as Hills noted [*History*, 86], was mentioned by Lawson in 1620, and in fact the rod of the *Treatise* was jointed and ferruled), but it was only when technical improvements were made to the *ferrule* in the 19th century that jointed rods ousted spliced ones, although salmon rods with spliced tops are still occasionally used. See also *rod*.

Finally, the phrase 'to give (the fish) the butt' (alternatively, 'to show the butt') ought to be noticed. Again according to the OED, this phrase is first attested in 1828 ('Give her [a fish] the butt – or she is gone for ever'), but this late attestation is surprising given the fact that many earlier angling books detail the practice, if not the exact phrase. *Giving the butt* does not mean applying huge (and clumsy) rod pressure to a hooked fish; as Hills explained (*History*, 28), with the early incarnations of fly-fishing tackle – the hair-line affixed directly to the tip of a long, pliable rod – to point the butt at the fish as it was being played was actually to put 'the least strain on the fish, and the greatest on the rod. You are using the rod to its utmost pliability...' Therefore when we see anglers in those 18th and early 19th century prints in their typical poses, the rod thrown over their right shoulders and the butt pointing at the fish, they are not displaying bad '*hands*' but rather, good form. As Hills concluded, 'If the reader thinks it out, he will see that no better rule can be given than to point the butt straight at the fish, for, whatever position he be in, this makes the best use of the elasticity of the rod' (*History*, 28-9) – although of course this comment applies only to the tackle then in use.

butt[2] The thickest portion of the *cast*[1] or *leader* may sometimes be referred to as the *butt* or *leader butt*.

butt spear A light, pointed spike, usually made of aluminium, which screws into the *butt*[1] of a fly rod. Unfortunately, *butt spears* are no longer readily available. If one can be obtained, it proves to be a useful piece of equipment, not for the purpose for which it was intended (which presumably was to enable the angler to stick the rod upright in the ground, see below), but as an extension to the handle which will keep the reel clear of clothing when a big fish is being played. A butt spear also saves the reel from damage, and from contact with sand and mud, when the butt of the rod is put on the ground (e.g. for threading the line through the rod-rings). On single-handed fly rods, the same function is served by an *extension handle*.

One editor of *The Compleat Angler* (the 1815 edition), used a rather novel butt spear. He made the assumption that at that date most of his readers would still be fishing with a line fixed directly to the tip of the rod, rather than with a 'winch' (see *reel*). Therefore in playing a fish, he wrote, 'you will find great convenience in a spike made of a piece of the greater end of a sword-blade, screwed into the hither end of the butt of your rod. When you have struck a fish, retire backwards from the river and, by means of the spike, stick the rod perpendicularly in the ground; you may then lay hold on the line and draw the fish to you' (cited in Trench, 63). See also *play; reel* etc.

buzzer The angler's colloquial term for the *midges* or *Chironomids* which hatch through the summer on stillwaters (and also on rivers). In Ireland, *buzzers* are also known as *duck-flies*, and the summer-hatching species as *racehorses* (Harris, 124). Strictly speaking, the term should apply just to the adult midges, which gain the name partly from their habit of flying rapidly over the water ('buzzing' – according to Harris), partly from the high-pitched whine the adult females emit when they return to the water to lay their eggs (Goddard, *Trout Flies of Stillwater*, 93; Roberts, *Illust. Dictionary*, 113; and see below). It is therefore inaccurate to speak of the *midge pupae* as 'buzzers', although many fly fishers use the term as a convenient way of referring to the pupae and adults alike (e.g. 'They're taking buzzers a foot down').

The modern usage of the word develops from the earliest recorded use, where 'buzzer' meant any buzzing insect (the first attestation, in 1606, spoke of 'Swarms of busie Buzzers').

It is only during this century that the importance of buzzers (both pupae and adults) to the trout has been recognised, largely owing to the development of stillwater trout fishing in England (on this history, see *pupa*). In particular, the work of C.F. Walker (*Lake Flies and their Imitation*, 1960) and Brian Clarke (*The Pursuit of Stillwater Trout*, 1975) should be mentioned, since this writing and analysis brought the humble buzzer to the attention of a growing band of stillwater anglers. Many patterns, of course, are currently available, ranging from the ultra-representative to the recklessly impressionistic; an excellent survey of the natural insects, and of fishing methods, is given by Goddard, *Trout Flies of Stillwater*, 87-105, while a comprehensive list of dressings, including those for larva, pupa, and adult, can be found in Roberts, *Illust. Dictionary*, 113-18.

Caddis   Also referred to as *caddis-grub(s)*. The term is of uncertain origin. The *caddis* is the larva of the adult *sedge*, found on both stillwaters and rivers. Caddis (especially the *Limnephilus* species, the Cinnamon Sedge) typically build a case from twigs, gravel, sand or other matter, and live in it for a year before pupating and making the hazardous journey to the water surface. Trout, both brown and rainbow, often feed avidly on caddis on rain-fed rivers and during the early part of the season on certain lakes. There are several artificial patterns of the caddis, although a large weighted Hare's Ear seems as effective as any specific dressing.

The importance of the caddis was recognised as early as the *Treatise*, which gave the caddis ('the codworme') as a bait for trout (used in conjunction with either the 'redde worme' – the gilt-tail, or the brandling? – or 'the grete redde worme' – presumably the lobworm?) in June and July. That angling on the bottom with a caddis had long been a killing method is attested by Cotton, who wrote of 'angling at the bottom . . . with a Cork or float . . . with a Worm, or, with a Grub or Caddis' (*Angler*, 312). He rated the caddis highly. 'The Caddis, or Cod-bait,' he wrote, '. . . is a sure killing bait . . . and is for all times of the year, the most holding bait of all other whatever, both for Trout, and Grayling' (p.311). As in the *Treatise*, Cotton suggested using the caddis together with a worm, or even with an artificial fly.

Walton was less perceptive. As the trout (which, Walton claimed in one of his most celebrated clauses, 'is not like the *Crocodile*') recovers from spawning, so he gets him 'into swifter and swifter streams, and there lies at the watch for any flie or Minnow, that comes near to him; and he especially loves the *May-flie*, which is bred of the *Cod-worm*, or *Caddis*' (*Angler*, 76). Whether by 'may-flie' Walton meant the true *mayfly[1]*, or just any upwinged fly, is immaterial; his knowledge of fly-fishing was certainly limited. Strangely, though, Walton's error was repeated in Cotton, who claimed explicitly that the *greendrake (Ephemera danica)* was bred of the 'Caddis or Cod-bait which lye under stones' (290). See *larva; pupa; sedge*.

caenis   Also, not unreasonably, called the 'Angler's Curse', or the 'White Curse' (Courtney Williams) but has many less temperate names applied to it. The *caenis* (various species including

Caenis horaria and *C. moesta*) is the smallest of the *upwinged* flies, and hatches on both rivers and lakes during calm evenings in high summer, often in enormous numbers. The adults are instantly recognisable by their pale white colour, their small size, and by the fact that they crawl in hundreds over the angler's clothing, even into his ears. On lakes, the presence of caenis may lead to the trout becoming preoccupied with emerging *nymphs*, *duns* and *spinners* (the last lying characteristically *spent*[2], with spread wings, hence perhaps the colloquial name for the caenis, 'broadwing'). This preoccupation means effectively that, although trout may be rising in numbers, they are almost impossible to catch, at least on stillwaters, although river anglers have reported more success (e.g. Sawyer, and Oliver Kite; see *dry fly; nymph fishing*). Another problem is the size of *artificial* necessary to represent the natural (size 20, particularly where *C. moesta* is concerned). Patterns have been devised for use on larger (size 16) hooks, including Goddard's tellingly-named Last Hope, but, confronted with a hatch of caenis, most fly fishermen resort to the hipflask, or the pub, or both.

The OED has no entry.

calm Fly-fishermen have ambivalent attitudes to calm water on the lake. Traditionally, *calms*, especially *flat calms*, were seen as trying conditions in which to present the fly (or flies). In calm water, trout are too much aware of the fall of the leader and line, any disturbance caused by the *retrieve*, and preternaturally aware of the fly as a deception and a trap (largely because in calm water they can see the fly so clearly). As A.A. Luce put it in 1959, 'In a long-continued flat calm on a sunny lifeless day in June, July and August all angling is unproductive, trolling included' (p.142).

On the other hand, recent improvements in tackle – particularly the development of different densities of *fly line*, and the introduction of double-strength *nylon* – have made flat calms rather easier for the fisher. Another feature has been the development of innovative fishing techniques, such as presenting tiny *dry flies* 'in' (rather than on) the surface from a becalmed boat. As Chris Ogborne puts it, 'The Bristol style is well-suited to dealing with flat calms' (*T & S*, June 1987, 35); the 'Bristol style' here involves fishing *buzzer* patterns static or near-static, or small dry flies in the surface film, both on fine *points* and correspondingly light tackle.

The word *calm*, from F. *calme*, begins life in English as a noun meaning 'stillness, quiet, tranquillity', a sense first attested in 1393 (Gower: 'As the ... rage Of windes maketh the see salvage And that was calme bringth into wawe'). But the word later develops a sense specific to wind and water (1517: 'We . . . fonde the wynde agens vs or ellys . . . calmys' – fishermen will know the feeling). It is noteworthy that the second attestation in this sense modifies the word *calm* with an adjective which describes what sort of calm it was: 'When there is not a breath of wind stirring, it is a calm or starke calme' (1627 Capt. Smith, *Seaman's Gram.*). Despite the improvements in present-day tackle, fly-fishermen are still disconcerted, perhaps, by a 'stark calm' – especially where *sea trout* are concerned.

cane   From F. *cane*, ME *can(n)e*, ultimately from L. *canna*, 'reed'. Defined by the OED as 'the hollow jointed ligneous stem of various giant reeds or grasses, as Bamboo or Sugar Cane', the word is first attested in English in 1398 ('A noyse as it were wyth a canne other a grete reyd'). The OED, however, defines no fishing sense (nor with such compound adjectives as *split-cane* or *whole-cane*).

Cane is a material used to build *rods*. It was used for the *butt* of the rod, at least by fishermen such as Venables, during the 17th century, and mention of the whole-cane rod is found in John Dennys' poem, *The Secrets of Angling*, published in 1613 (Hills, *History*, 40). The split-cane rod, made of bamboo split into sections, planed, and then glued together, dates from the early nineteenth century. As Hills pointed out, early split-cane rods were made up of three or four glued sections; they were superseded by *greenheart* rods, which were cheaper and easier to work; greenheart in turn was superseded by six-sectioned split cane, a method of rod-building which, Hills noted (*History*, 94), was invented in America during the mid 19th century.

The chief advantage of the six-sectioned split-cane rod is that it offers relative lightness with considerable power. Unlike, say, a tubular rod, the sectional method of construction means that the rod retains its strength under pressure. The chief disadvantages of cane are that it can warp (fishing literature has stories of anglers battling epically with enormous salmon in heavy rain, after which – and the fish is invariably lost – the cane rod warps in wooden sympathy with the struggle, and is thereafter unusable); it is fragile; and, compared with modern materials such as *fibreglass* or *carbon-fibre*, it is heavy: a day with a twelve-foot cane rod could be hard work. The six-sectioned split-cane rod is still available, however, and many fishermen, particularly those of a nostalgic or classical temperament, prefer split-cane rods, particularly for river fishing (especially the chalk streams). It should also be noted that the sectional, or at least the hexagonal, method of construction has recently spread to rods made of carbon-fibre. See also *rod*.

cannibal   *Cannibal* trout are large *brown trout* (usually those of
the deep fastnesses of remote Scottish lochs) which have turned
to an exclusively fish-eating diet, usually smaller trout (or *charr*).
They are typically caught by *trolling* (or *trailing*). During the 19th
century, these fish were classified as a separate species, and termed
Salmo ferox, as in the following instructive passage from Scrope:

> When we see a fish quivering upon dry land, he looks so help-
> less without arms or legs, and so demure in expression, adding
> hypocrisy to his other sins, that we naturally pity him; then
> kill and eat him with Harvey sauce, perhaps. Our pity is mis-
> placed... There is an immense trout in Loch Awe in Scotland,
> which is so voracious, and swallows his own species with such
> avidity, that he has obtained the name of *Salmo ferox*. I pull
> about this unnatural monster till he is tired, land him, and
> give him the *coup de grace*. Is this cruel? Cruelty "should be
> made of sterner stuff". (From *Days and Nights of Salmon Fish-
> ing in the Tweed* (1843); cited in Arnold Gingrich, 119.)

cape   A term from fly-tying, meaning the skin and *hackle* feathers
from the neck of a cock or hen. The term is evidently related to
'cap', but in our sense is probably most directly related to *cape*
in the earlier sense 'a kind of short loose sleeveless cloak, fitting
round the neck and falling over the shoulders' (first attestation
1611: 'a cape of veluet'). From this sense a new, transferred meaning, 'short feathers on a fowl's back' develops, this being first
attested in English in 1899 (A.H. Evans, *Birds*: '...a cape of
hackled plumes').

Cock capes are used for *dry flies*, *hen capes* (which have softer
hackles) for *wet flies*. Good quality cock capes (where the hackle
fibres are short, glossy, and springy) can be expensive. Capes
also need careful storage, especially protection against moths.

carbon-fibre   A rod-building material (see also *cane, boron, fibreglass*). Strands of carbon, interwoven with a small amount of
fibreglass, are wrapped round a mandril, and treated to form a
light, strong *blank[1]*. *Carbon-fibre* rods were developed during the
1970s, and are now in extensive use. They are lighter and stronger
than the fibreglass rods which preceded them, are thinner (therefore offering less resistance to the wind), and, in the right hands,
are capable of casting great distances, particularly when used in
conjunction with a *shooting-head*. See *rod; cast[2]*.

carotene   Also sp. **carotin**.   Walton was one of the first to have
observed the difference between white-fleshed and pink-fleshed
trout: '...if I catch a Trout in one Meadow,' he wrote, 'he shall
be white and faint, and very like to be lowsie; and, as certainly,
if I catch a Trout in the next meadow, he shall be strong, and

red, and lusty, and much better meat...' (p.123). Although the distinction between 'lusty' pink-fleshed trout, and 'lowsie' white-fleshed ones, is not as hard and fast as Walton implied, nevertheless many anglers hold pink-fleshed trout in esteem. Pink-fleshed trout are particularly prevalent in *alkaline waters*. The pink coloration is due to the ingestion of carotenoid substances by the fish, substances that are either already present in the food chain, or which have been artificially fed in pellets to stock fish. One specific carotenoid is the pigment Canthaxanthin, which is present in snails and shrimp (Jacques, 77). Carotene-containing pellets are now almost universally used. This argues a demand for pink-fleshed trout. It is not necessarily the case, however, that white-fleshed trout are 'lowsie'; many waters produce white-fleshed trout naturally (the Dales rivers for example), and these trout are often excellent eating. Perhaps the anglers' preference for red flesh is primarily aesthetic, or related to the fact that salmon and sea trout have red flesh owing to the presence of carotene in their high-protein, sea-feeding diet. See also T.C. Bell, *T&S*, December 1982.

carrier A term associated with chalk streams and water meadows. A *carrier* is – or was – part of the system of artificial irrigation which watered the meadows. The water entering the carrier is – or was – controlled by a sluice or *hatch²*. The sluice would be opened in winter, and shut in late spring to allow the meadows to dry. Past tense qualification is needed because in many parts of the south of England, this system of irrigation has been abandoned. Frank Sawyer wrote that 'The carriers, which in bygone years brought life-giving water to the meadow vegetation, are now dried-up ditches...In these circumstances it is inevitable that there are fewer trout and less insect life to-day...' (*Keeper of the Stream*, 19). That carriers could provide good fishing is noted by Skues (*Minor Tactics*, 74): 'Be it known unto you, O angler, that the trout of ditches and carriers are far less affected by the rise of duns, and far readier to feed at all times or any time, than those fish of the main river'.

cast¹ The BrE word for the *leader* (originally an Americanism), which is the less ambiguous, and therefore preferable, term. A leader is made from a *tapered* or level stretch of *nylon monofilament*, nine feet or more long, attached to the end of the *fly line* (see *knots*). In *dry fly* fishing, and *nymph fishing* on rivers, a single fly on a tapered leader is customarily used, since this promotes accurate and gentle fly presentation. For *wet fly* fishing on rivers and lakes for brown, rainbow and sea trout, the leader usually has one or more (commonly two) *droppers* attached to it; untapered (i.e. level) leaders are more often used in these forms of fishing, since accuracy of presentation is not at a premium. Three-dropper leaders (i.e. four flies) are more often employed in Scotland, especially on the Clyde, Loch Leven etc.

The last twenty years have seen advances in leader design, partly owing to the development of new types of monofilament, and partly because of the influence of stillwater fishing. Particularly striking has been the fact that leaders have become steadily longer, especially on lakes: leaders of sixteen feet are now common, and have the advantage that they distance the thick fly line (and the shadow of the fly line) from the fish. Leaders longer than the customary nine feet are also used more often on rivers, especially for the presentation of weighted nymphs, bugs etc. at depth (see Clarke & Goddard, 113-17 for example). For all forms of fly fishing, there has been a general recognition that the leader is not only an essential, but must also be a well-constructed, link between angler and fish.

Historically, the development of leaders cannot antedate the development of the fly line. Until the time of Cotton, and even beyond, the fly was *cast²* using a line made of horsehair, tapered from perhaps twenty hairs twisted, and fixed to the rod tip (the *reel* did not come into systematic use until later), down to a 'casting line' (i.e. the horsehair links nearest the fly) of two or three twisted hairs. A single horsehair tip (and see *point*) was used only for small flies. As Hills (*History*, 68) recorded, the hair lines employed for fly fishing in the 17th century were constructed specially thick to make casting easier. In the later 17th and 18th centuries, silk came into use for the main line, while a mysterious substance called Indian Grass or Indian Weed began to be used nearest the fly (Hills, *History*, 70: Indian Weed defied even his magnificent research). 'Indian weed' must have persisted into the early 19th century, because Ronalds (*The Fly-fisher's Entomology*, 1st edn 1836) wrote that 'For making a good *End* or *Casting-line* [i.e. a leader], gut is recommended in preference to weed, or hair' (10th edn, 29). Once silk lines began to develop, the way was then clear for the development of the 'casting line', the leader proper. In the 18th and 19th centuries, the leader came to be made of silkworm gut. As rods developed, the silk fly line came to be heavier, steeply tapered and dressed with linseed oil. Silk fly lines were common from the early 19th century until the 1960s, when they were almost wholly replaced by plastic-coated lines. *Gut*, which had to be soaked before use, and had a tendency to fray, was eventually replaced by the more convenient nylon monofilament.

cast²   The action of throwing the fly. *Casting* is comprehensively covered in many standard handbooks, and I shall do little more here than attempt to reconstruct some history of casting the fly.

Unfortunately we do not know how the earliest trout flies were cast; the *Treatise* gives no explicit instructions on this, although it is possible that, since the line was tapered horsehair, and fixed directly to the tip of the rod, little more was possible than to allow the fly to drift out on the wind, a kind of modified *dapping*. In addition, it seems likely that the fly was fished downstream (see *wet fly*), although again this is conjectural.

The 17th century is more promising. The first mention of casting in fishing literature dates from the second edition of John Dennys' poem, *Secrets of Angling*, published in 1620 and edited by William Lawson. In one of his notes to Dennys, Lawson explained that '[the trout] gives the most gentlemanly and readiest sport of all, if you fish with an artificial fly, a line twice your rod's length of three hairs' thickness . . . and if you have learned the cast of the fly' (Hills, *History*, 42).

Moving on, we know from his comments that Cotton, for example, typically fished downstream, although in one significant passage he urges Viator to 'angle up the still deep', a mode of presentation which at least implies some casting. Elsewhere, however, Cotton noted that artificial flies 'are to be angled with, with a short line, not much more than half the length of your Rod, if the air be still; or with a longer very near, or all out as long as your Rod, if you have any wind to carry it from you' (*Angler*, 264). Cotton also added that 'not an Inch of your Line being to be suffered to touch the water' – which again argues a kind of dapping (and see *dibbling*).

Venables (1662), however, did explicitly mention casting: 'Be sure in casting, that your fly fall first onto the water, for if the line fall first, it scares or frightens the fish; therefore draw it back, and cast it again, that the fly may fall first' (facsimile, 20). But again, we do not know exactly what this casting entailed. It would have been possible to throw a fly with 17th-century tackle, but it is surely significant that no angling writer of the time, to my knowledge, goes into detail on how this should be done. And it is also significant that all angling writers mention the strength of the wind; perhaps the casting invoked by Venables was really a kind of wind-assisted swing – what Ronalds would later describe as a 'sweep' (see below).

Then come many inventions, not least of which is the invention of the *reel*. Once the reel is developed in the 18th century, the way is clear for the development of a 'reel line', *tapered* and made

of hair (we would now call this a 'single-taper' line), knotted to
a 'casting line' (see *cast¹*). And once this happens, we begin to
hear instructions. Ronalds, for example, devoted a section of his
Fly-Fisher's Entomology (1836) to 'throwing':

> In order to acquire the art of throwing a fly, it may be advisable
> to practise, previously to visiting the stream, in a space free
> from trees, where a piece of paper may represent the spot
> required to be thrown to. Taking the wind in his back, the
> tyro, with a short line, at first may attempt to cast within an
> inch or two of the paper...
>
> He should endeavour to impart to the end of the line a
> uniform sweep or curve round his head; for if it returns too
> quickly or sharply from behind him, a crack will be heard and
> the fly whipped off (10th edn, 44-5).

This sounds very modern. But notice that by this time, throwing
a fly is described an 'art'; elsewhere, Ronalds wrote that '[a]n
attempt to describe *all* the precautions and manipulations requis-
ite for throwing a fly...would be as hopeless a task as that of
trying to teach dancing by words' (45) – a comment which hints,
at least, that other modes of casting may have been being
developed alongside that of the basic overhead cast.

Today, of course, and with the refinements in rod and fly-line
design experienced over the last fifty years, there are several ways
of casting with a single handed trout rod: the basic *overhead cast*,
where the line is back-cast with an accelerating lift, the rod being
stopped at the vertical and the line being allowed to straighten
behind before the forward cast is made; the *roll cast*, where the
line is extended on the water then drawn towards the angler by
raising the rod, the line being switched forward when the rod is
a little past the vertical (this – also known as the *switch cast*, and
employed in a variant form in salmon fishing – is a useful cast
for *boat fishing*, also on rivers where there are trees etc. behind
the casting arm); and also the *steeple cast*, where the line is thrown
vertically behind the angler (wrist and forearm being kept stiff)
– this is another useful cast in places where high banks, trees and
so on would impede a normal back-cast.

The overhead cast and the roll cast are admirably discussed
and illustrated in *To Cast a Trout Fly* (published by House of
Hardy); the steeple cast is very clearly described and photographed in Hugh Falkus, *Sea Trout Fishing* (revised 2nd edn,
91-5).

Lastly, at least as far as the single-handed trout rod is concerned, there are those distance casts made by *double-hauling*,
where additional line-speed is imparted to the back-cast by a

'haul' (a subtly-timed pull) on the line, and where extra velocity is imparted to the forward cast with another subtly-timed pull. Used in conjunction with a *weight forward fly line*, or a *shooting head*, the double-haul technique can be used to put out perhaps thirty yards of line.

Casting a salmon fly is another subject in itself. It seems, though, that until the 19th century, the usual procedure was to present the fly across and downstream, casting in the basic overhead manner. (And it is at least likely that the overhead cast was used, since anglers did not use separate sets of fly-tackle for trout and salmon fishing until the late 18th century – or even the early 19th.)

Then come two more recondite casts, the single and double *Spey casts*. These seem to have been wholly products of the 19th century, and possibly, of the single- or double-tapered silk fly lines that were then becoming prevalent. These casts defy my ability to describe them in print, although someone who did try was Francis Francis (he is here describing, I think, the easier of the two casts, the single Spey):

> Having got a certain length of line out, somehow or anyhow, and being desirous of making a new cast, he raises his hands well up and carries the rod up to his shoulder pretty smartly; but he does not send the rod back over the shoulder, but rather fetches it in towards his feet . . . (cited in Trench, 141).

Perhaps we should leave Francis there, fetching the rod 'in towards his feet', whatever that means. Both the single and double Spey are, however, well described (in prose less convoluted than the casts) in Taverner & Scott (pp.85-90), and in Falkus, (*Salmon Fishing*, 230-33). It is also worth noting that in the 1980s there has been a movement back towards the long rod, the full-length line, and Spey casting (as opposed to the brief flirtation with shorter rods and shooting-heads that took place during the 1970s): as Crawford Little puts it, 'most able and experienced salmon fisherman [have] learned to prefer roll- and Spey-casting a full-length line . . . Having once mastered the ease and delights of the Spey cast, shooting-heads and yard upon yard of backing line [hold] about as much appeal as darning socks' (*T&S*, January 1990, 67). On salmon fishing, see also *greased line; sunk line*.

catch Once in a while every fisherman likes to make *a good catch*, a *brace*, two brace or more of fish. A good catch keeps the Black Dog at bay, inspires confidence and helps concentration.

The word comes from Norman French *cachier* (verb, whose 3sg. present tense form is *cache*). In its verbal sense 'to capture', the word is first attested in English in 1205 (Layamon: 'Monie scipen he ther cahte'). But a nominal sense is quick to develop, where *catch* means 'the catching of fish' or 'the number of fish caught at one time, or during the season'. The first attestation in this sense dates from 1465: 'To axe [ask] of my lorde of Duram in yifte [gift] the kache of Hangeford'. By 1875, the word has developed its familiar sense of 'day's catch'; 'The catch depends very much upon the weather' (Buckland). Any sea trout or salmon fisherman would agree.

It is possible that the marital desideratum, 'a good catch', is derived from the fishing usage. OED defines this sense of *good catch* as 'a person matrimonially desirable on account of wealth or position', and dates the first attestation to 1722, and Defoe's *Colonel Jack*: 'She intended to have me, if she could catch, and it was indeed a kind of catch'. Here Defoe seems to be punning on two senses of *catch*, as 'capture' ('if she could catch'), and as 'success' ('kind of catch').

catch and release   Some fisheries are now run on the basis of *catch and release*, i.e. any fish caught (or taken subsequent to the catching of a *limit*) may be released, and returned alive to the water (usually via barbless hooks, see *barb*). Likewise, some fishermen, mindful of the necessity to conserve wild brown trout stocks, habitually practice catch and release wherever it is reasonable to do so.

Catch and release, which originated as a 'movement' in the USA, poses an ethical problem (see 'The ethics of angling' in A.A. Luce, chapter XII). Should fly-fishermen fish largely if not solely for the pot? If not, how can fishermen justify causing pain and suffering to wild creatures? What constitutes 'sport'?

This ethical unease is put into focus by a recent editorial in *Trout and Salmon*:

> Proponents of the argument for catch-and-release . . . claim that the returning of wild trout is the only way to ensure that such stock will be there for future generations. One wild trout killed, they say, is one wild trout less for the river . . . I would only reply by saying that one wild trout caught and returned is still one wild trout less for the river because, once returned, it is no longer wild . . .
>
> I do not want to visit a "wild-trout water", buy my ticket and then spend the day fishing for trout that have been caught once, twice or ten times before. Even if the outcome of that day were successful – if, say, I caught and put back a dozen fish – I should feel little satisfaction: in fact I should feel that I had harrassed those fish unnecessarily (Sandy Leventon in *T&S*, January 1990, 2).

The debate will continue.

caudal fin From L. *cauda*: the tail fin. The function of this fin is primarily one of propulsion. The shape of the caudal fin can also be diagnostic in differentiating between e.g. salmon and sea trout. Salmon have a concave tail fin (trailing edge); sea trout, especially the larger, adult fish of 2lbs upwards, have square, or even convex tails. See Falkus, *Sea Trout Fishing*, 22-4.

charr Also sp. **char**. *Salvelinus alpinus*, the native British charr, cf. *brook trout*. The charr is distinguished by its red belly and pinkish fins, some of which have a distinct white leading edge.

The charr is a fascinating fish. It is one of the oldest, perhaps the oldest, of our game fish, and its name reflects this. The word *charr* is probably, like the word *loch*, of Celtic origin. Gaelic, for example, has the words *ceara*, meaning 'red, blood-coloured', and *cear*, 'blood'; the Welsh name for the charr, *torgoch*, evidently means 'red-bellied'.

The antiquity of the name is not surprising given the fact that the charr was one of the first salmonids present in the British Isles. Originally, the charr was a sea-running fish like the salmon. The coming of the Ice Age changed that, because when the ice eventually retreated, the charr became stranded in lakes where access to the sea was no longer possible. This geographical fact helps to explain the present distribution of the fish in the mountainous areas of the north and west. In addition, the charr – presumably because of its Arctic origins – is a fish which is commonly found in cold waters, and it prefers (and is probably restricted to) lakes that have deep yet well-oxygenated water.

Because the charr is a land-locked species living in isolated lakes, it is therefore to be expected that, during the passage of time, charr in individual lakes should have developed particular characteristics. The *Observer's Book of Freshwater Fishes*, for example, lists thirteen varieties of charr. Distinguishing between these sub-species is of small importance to the angler.

The life-cycle of the charr is broadly similar to that of brown trout living under similar conditions, i.e. the fish spawn in the winter months, either in the shallows of the lake or in a feeder stream, making *redds* in the same way as other salmonids. The fish is slow-growing, reaching maturity after 3-6 years; it seldom grows bigger than 1lb, and the average size of charr in Britain must be nearer 6ozs. The diet of the charr is primarily, although not exclusively, planktonic (see *daphnia*); this is consistent with the deep-water habits of the fish. Fly fishing for charr is consequently seldom practised systematically, although fish are sometimes caught during hatches of e.g. *midges* or other flies during midsummer evenings, where the availability of a high concentration of insect food attracts them to the surface.

Charr are more consistently caught on heavy, weighted lines trailing spinners or other lures. This form of fishing is practised commercially at Lake Windermere, which has been renowned for its charr since at least the 17th century: in 1662 Phillips defined the 'Chare' as 'a kind of fish which breeds most peculiarly in Winandermere in Lancashire'; in 1674, Ray wrote 'There are two sorts taken in Winandermere: The greater having a red belly they call the red Charre: and the lesser having a white belly which they call the Gilt or Gelt Charre'. (It seems probable that this distinction refers to the male and female charr respectively.)

cheeks From fly-dressing. Small, whole feathers, usually of jungle-cock, tied in behind the eye of the hook, one on either side of the wing, especially on sea trout or salmon flies. They are supposed to represent, perhaps, the eyes of a small bait-fish.

Dressing flies in this manner (such flies are sometimes referred to as *fully-dressed*) seems to have begun with Irish influence on fly-dressing in the 19th century: Trench, for example, speaking of salmon flies, writes of the 'new Irish creations [of the mid-19th century], complete with... topping, cheek, and head' (136).

The OED records a fishing sense from 1867 ('Cheek feathers') and the word seems to derive from OE original *cēce* ('jaw, jawbone', later 'chaps'), which gives rise to a number of subsequent senses, including a general sense 'side(s)' from the 16th century on. By the 17th century, a mechanical sense had developed, where *cheeks* was a 'general name for those parts of machines which resemble cheeks in being arranged in lateral pairs'; it is possible that our fly-dressing term derives from this usage. See also *tinsel; topping*.

chironomids Also, pedantically, *chironomidae* (on the *-idae* suffix see *ephemeroptera*). The L. term for the various species of *midge*, sometimes abbr. 'C.' (for *Chironomus*, the genus) in definitions, e.g. *C. anthracinus*, the Black Midge, and *C. plumosus*, various species of summer-hatching midge including the Large Red Midge (the 'Grenadier') and the Golden Dun Midge. Goddard (*Trout Flies of Stillwater*, 88) notes that the famous Dr Bell of Blagdon was the first to derive an artificial pattern to represent the midge pupa early this century. For further information on midges see *bloodworm; buzzer;* and especially, *pupa*.

chuck and chance it A phrase used to describe careless or thoughtless fishing, or indiscriminate 'fishing the water' with an inappropriate fly or flies. The definition given in the OED is entirely accurate ('a derisive phrase used attrib. to describe wet-fly fishing'); it dates the phrase to 1886, and an edition of *Longman's Magazine* ('So let us return to the good Northern plan of "chuck and chance it", wet.

The use of the dry fly is a utopian dream') – although why chucking and chancing it was held to be specifically northern is mysterious (perhaps because the use of the *wet fly* had long been associated with the north?). In 1899 the *Westminster Gazette* stated that 'A large proportion of anglers regard with unmerited contempt that which they are pleased to miscall the "Chuck-and-chance-it system".' These citations are interesting in so far as in content and dating they suggest that 'chucking and chancing' (with a wet fly) was regarded as contemptible only when the use of the *dry fly* had become seen as somehow superior (see also *purist*) – a distinctly late 19th century view, derived from Halford and his followers. There has to be the suspicion, however, that many anglers were fonder of chucking and chancing than they cared to admit; the practice has certainly continued to the present day.

clegs   The North-country term for *horseflies*, deriving from ON *kleggi* (cf. Mod. Norwegian *klegg*), and being first attested in English in 1449 ('The unlatit woman...pungis as the cleg').

Horseflies are ugly, vicious, bloated, biting insects which suck blood from the exposed parts of fishermen, usually in Scotland or Ireland. They are impossible to deter with insect repellent; insect repellent attracts them. They should be smacked dead before they bite, if possible. Cleg-smacking is an alternative pursuit to fishing during long, hot, sweaty and windless days when the fish are as sulky as the weather.

coch-y-bondhu   Also sp. *cocky-bundy* (and variants); under *cock-a-bundy*, OED notes that this is a corruption of Welsh *coch a bon ddu*, and dates the first attestation of the word in English to 1852 ('Who can trim a cockabundy, turn a rod with him?'), although this is certainly too late, since Ronalds (1836) referred to the fly, giving 'Coch-a-bonddu' as an alternative name for his 'Marlow Buzz' (1901 edn, 104).

However it is spelt, the *coch-y-bondhu* is a type of *beetle*. Courtney Williams records that the prototype Welsh natural fly is *Phyllopertha horticola*, a half-inch long beetle whose predominant colours are 'reddish-brown with a dark peacock green thorax' (*Dictionary*, 146); this appears in June, and is common in bracken and heather country (Wales, Scotland and Ireland).

cock   From OE *cocc*, ON *kokkr*. The male fish, distinguished from the female (the *hen*), particularly at spawning-time, by its red or dark colour. Some *cock fish* develop a *kype* (a hooked underjaw) close to spawning. The dark body colour, and the presence of the kype, are particularly noticeable in cock salmon. Cock fish near spawning should be returned, since they are unpleasant to eat and touch, and full of *milt*.

Some anglers and gastronomes claim that hen fish are preferable to cocks for the table. Walton was again one of the first to have recorded this. 'It is a note observable,' he wrote, 'that the female *Trout* hath usually a less head, and a deeper body than the male *Trout*; and is usually the better meat' (*Angler*, 76).

Also *cock hackle (see* **hackle***)*.

cocking   A term applied to the *dry fly* which, when it lands correctly on the water with its wings upright, is said to have *cocked*. The word derives from a verb, *to cock*, meaning 'to stick or turn up', first attested in English in 1600 ('Peacock's feathers cock't upon a Raven') – thus also *to cock one's eye, to cock one's hat* etc. *Cocking* itself is first attested in 1678 ('. . . cocking of their noses'); OED records no fly-fishing sense.

Many writers have emphasised the desirability of having the fly 'nicely cocked' when fishing for trout rising to natural *duns* (not *spinners*, since these flies lie flat in, rather than on, the water surface; see *spent²*). Cocking the fly is partly a matter of presentation (i.e. a clumsy cast may tend to land the fly on its side), and partly a matter of fly design. Cocking is only an issue with conventional winged patterns; perhaps for this reason, many dry-fly fishermen prefer *spider* patterns (i.e. hackled, but with no wings), or upside-down flies (Clarke & Goddard), or *Funnelduns* (Neil Patterson; see Roberts, *Illust. Dictionary*, 67-9), rather than the older type of heavily-hackled fly with feather-fibre *wings*.

coleoptera   The entomologist's name for the Order of *beetles*, see e.g. Goddard, *Trout Flies of Stillwater*, 153-6. See also *coch-y-bondhu*.

corixa(e)   The various species of Lesser Water Boatman. On many stillwaters, the corixa is an important item of the trout's diet, especially in high summer and the autumn months. The *natural* is particularly prolific in and around weed beds. It makes journeys to the surface for air, at which times it is vulnerable to the trout. Its overall shape is beetle-like, but it has a long pair of hind legs (oar-like, thus the name, 'boatman'). There are various artificial patterns (see e.g. Goddard, *Trout Flies of Stillwater*, 160-62, and Roberts, *Illust. Dictionary*, 42-3). A small (size 14) White Chomper seems as effective as anything.

There is no entry under *corixa* in the OED.

cowdung   A fly. Every fly-dressing dictionary and handbook seems to include a reference to the Cowdung Fly *(Scatophaga stercoraria)*; Cotton (1676), for example, gave a dressing of the 'Cow-turd flie' in his list of patterns under May, and Ronalds (*The Fly-fisher's Entomology*, 1836) gave a good illustration of the *natural*, which he said 'is to be seen throughout the year. It is very abundant about the middle of March, when vast quantities are seen upon the water if there be a high wind' (10th edn, 70). The naturals occur commonly on pasture around water, but artificial patterns are of doubtful utility, largely because the trout seem to take the naturals so infrequently.

crane fly   The Daddy-long-legs. There are many species, but all have the similar characteristics and therefore the differences are irrelevant to the fly-tier or fisherman. The crane fly is only semi-aquatic, hatching in damp areas close to water (Goddard, *Trout Flies of Stillwater*, 108); its importance to the fisherman derives from the fact that on breezy autumn days the adults are blown out across the lake, where they are greedily taken by the trout (see also *daddy-long-legs*; a further note on etymology is given there).

There are many artificial patterns (see Goddard, Roberts, Courtney Williams; also *parachute*), nearly all of which incorporate knotted, trailing legs made of feather fibre. These patterns, both the dry and the wet, are also useful (if not essential) when fishing for *sea trout* in the west of Scotland or Ireland during the autumn. In Ireland, the natural crane fly is often used alone, or in conjunction with a grasshopper, as a dap (see *dapping*).

The word is first attested in English in 1658; the entry refers to a 'Water-fly, which men call from the length of the feet or shanks . . . *Gruinam*; called therefore in English a Crane Fly'. This is interesting in so far as *gruinam* derives from L. *grus* or *gruis*, a crane – the long-legged bird 'regarded by the Romans as a delicacy' (Lewis and Short, *A Latin Dictionary*, 1879).

creel   A term for a particular type of wicker fishing-basket, shaped like the top of a sliced mushroom. Wicker is light; woven, it admits air. Therefore the creel is – or was – suitable both for carrying tackle, and retaining the catch. It often figures in early angling paintings and prints, as well as in literature, e.g. W.G.M. Dobie, 'The Monster of the Pool' (in *Game-bag and Creel*, 1927):

Deep pool, flecked with foam, I your lover
Return now that April is here;
What secrets am I to discover?
What trout will you yield me this year?
The monster that broke me last Autumn
When the net and the creel loomed so near?

The fisherman's creel, Hills noted, was first mentioned in English by John Dennys in his poem, *Secrets of Angling*, published in 1613 (Hills, *History*, 40).

creeper   A term for the nymph of the *stone-fly*, especially of the larger species. It is of less importance as an angler's fly than as a natural bait, much employed in North-Country rivers during the appropriate season (early summer), where fishermen also speak of the stone-fly as the 'mayfly' (see *mayfly³*). At least one species of stone-fly was known to the author of the *Treatise*, who wrote that for April you should use (among other flies) 'The stone fly: the body of black wull, and yelowe under the wynge and under the tayle'. Harris (*Angler's Entomology*, 110) notes that the stone-fly is unique 'in that it is the oldest known artificial fly which has retained its original name'. The fly was also, not unexpectedly, known to Cotton, who also had words to say on the term 'mayfly'; 'here it is [i.e. in May],' he says to his travelling companion, Viator,

> that you are to expect an account of the Green Drake and stone-flie...and some others that are peculiar to this Month ...and that (though not so great either in bulk, or name) do yet stand in competition with the two before named, and so, that it is yet undecided amongst the Anglers to which of the pretenders to the title of the May-flie, it does properly, and truly, belong, neither dare I (where so many of the learned in this Art of Angling are got in dispute about the controversie) take upon me to determine...(*Angler*, 287)

Cotton also gave a very full and accurate description of the habits of the stone-fly, (except for his belief that the stone-fly – along with the *greendrake* – is 'bred of a Caddis'); he is one of the first, if not the first, to detail the crawling, creeping habits of the stone-fly nymph; and he gives a good dressing for an artificial adult, although he also 'dapped and dibbled' with the natural fly. On other species, see *stone-fly;* also *mayfly³*.

Our term *creeper* derives from the earlier sense 'an animal that creeps, a creeping thing, an insect or reptile' (e.g. 1577 Googe: 'You shall be sure to have neither Mite nor Creeper in your Cheese'); the fishing sense develops by 1867, which allowed Francis Francis to write that '[t]he crab or creeper is the larva of the Stone fly'.

croneen Large Irish lake trout (*brown trout*), especially those of the River Shannon and its tributaries, which gather in the late summer in order to run *spawning* streams. Croneen are fished for like *sea trout* (which in their habits they resemble), with largish flies fished at dusk or at night. See Fallon, *Irish Trout*, 139; also *dollaghan*.

The etymology of the word is difficult to trace. None of the English dictionaries appear to know the word, and there is apparently no entry in the *Dictionary of the Irish Language* (Royal Irish Academy, 1913-76). Combing through the last, however, it is possible that there may be a relationship between *croneen* and Ir. *crón*, 'brown, reddish-brown, dark yellow, red'; *-een* is an Ir. diminutive suffix (cf. Irish *boneen*, 'little pig', and *boreen*, 'lane' etc). If this etymology is correct, it follows logically that *croneen* would be glossed as 'the little reddish-brown (ones)' – but this is odd given that croneen are pretty large fish. Another possibility is that the word is etymologically related to *crone* in its sense 'old woman', but why trout should be likened to old women is difficult to imagine.

Daddy-long-legs   Also known as the 'daddy', or, in Ireland, as the 'Harry-long-legs' ('harry'). Cotton is perhaps the first to give a dressing for the *artificial*: 'a Harry-long-leggs, the body made of Bears dun, and blew wool mixt, and a brown hackle Feather over all' (*Angler*, 299). He fished it in August. According to the OED (which is not at all helpful on the etymology of the term, simply noting that the daddy gets its name 'from its very slender legs') the specific name 'daddy-long-legs' is first attested in 1814, leaving 'harry-long-legs' as the older word. See also *crane fly*.

damsel fly   From Fr. *demoiselle*; the word is first attested in 1815. There are various species, including *Agrion splendens* and *A. virgo*. The adult insects are familiar to most stillwater fishermen, being instantly recognisable by the striking blue bodies of the males. The adult flies are less useful to the angler than the *nymphs*, which are long, drab brown or green in colour, and which hatch in considerable numbers during the summer, especially around weedbeds, where they feed on other insects. There are several artificial patterns, all of which comprise some kind of olive-brown body tied up on a longshank size 10 or 12 hook.

daphnia   From L. *daphne*; the first attestation dates from 1847. Zooplankton, including these tiny crustaceans, is an important food source for trout in stillwaters, especially on rich, *eutrophic* lakes. Unfortunately, *daphnia* are so small that they are impossible to imitate; fish feeding on daphnia will, however, sometimes accept a large orange, white, or fluorescent green *lure*.

One characteristic of daphnia is their sensitivity to light. On hot, sunny days the daphnia migrate to deeper water; as evening falls, daphnia rise in the water, until around midnight they are found en masse at the surface (T. Macan & E. Worthington, 115). Evidently the daphnia try to maintain themselves in a particular band of light intensity. Daphnia migration provides one reason why, in hot spells in high summer, fishing is difficult during the day, but easier at night: during the day, the trout have followed the daphnia into the deeps, and may therefore not see the angler's fly; in the evening, the trout are following the daphnia to the surface, and come within range of the artificial. One obvious solution to these conditions is to experiment during the day with *sinking lines*, persisting until the appropriate depth has been found.

dapping The word is etymologically related both to *dabbing* and *dibbling*. The ancestor of all these terms is apparently *dab*. *Dab* makes a sudden appearance in the language around 1300; it is perhaps mimetic, although there may be some connection with *dub*, a verb meaning 'moderately firm blunt thrust or poke' (OED; *dubbing* a fly has a different source). Once *dab* has appeared, its final consonant was devoiced, and pronounced 'p' (/p/), possibly under the influence of words like *sip, snip*, and *skip*, to indicate 'a lighter or slighter touch' (OED). The word is apparently first recorded in Walton; he wrote of how trout will take hawthorn flies: 'with these and a short Line...you may dape or dop, and also with a *Grasshopper* behind a tree, or in any deep hole, still making it to move on the top of the water, as if it were alive, and still keeping your self out of sight, you shall certainly have sport if there be *Trouts*' (*Angler*, 110). It is significant that the essential gentleness and delicacy of the art of dapping is captured in the linguistic history of the term.

Dapping – or 'fishing the dap' – has become primarily associated with stillwater fishing for brown, rainbow, and sea trout. It is invariably practised from a boat, with the angler allowing the wind to catch the *dapping line* or *blowline*, bellying it out downwind. To the end of the blowline is attached a short piece of nylon, carrying the natural or artificial fly (the latter is also called 'the dap').

Kingsmill Moore wrote of dapping as 'the lugubrious art...[I]t is, next to trolling, the dullest and least skilful of all methods' (*A Man May Fish*, 64). Many fishermen do not seem to share this low opinion: dapping can have a certain hypnotic quality; it is also, in the right conditions, very effective. Dapping is particularly associated with the *mayfly*[2], the *Daddy*, and with sea trout in the northern and western lochs and loughs. Sea trout perhaps take the dap because the skittering, waking motion of the fly is reminiscent of a fleeing bait fish in the sea, or perhaps reminiscent of a *sedge*, familiar to the sea trout from its river life as a *parr*.

The essence of the affair lies in a sufficiency of wind. Typically, a long rod is used (there are some purpose-made telescopic rods currently on the market), although given the excellence of modern synthetic *blowlines*, an 11-foot rod can also be employed. The *reel* should be filled with *nylon*, either braided or *monofilament*; this line is attached to the several yards of blowline by forming a small loop in the blowline, then joining the nylon by a Tucked Half-blood Knot, or by a loop-to-loop attachment (see *knots*). The same knots are also used at the terminal end of the rig, and about 6' (minimum) of nylon monofilament attached as a *leader*. The fly is then tied on, and the rod raised. The line is fed out through the rings, and the rod is lowered until the fly touches the water. Thereafter, the fly is kept skimming along the surface by altering the angle at which the rod is held in response to the strength of the wind. The aim must be to keep just the fly on the surface on the surface (i.e. no part of the line), and in motion.

Perhaps the biggest problem with dapping is timing the *strike*. It is generally fatal to strike too soon. The fish must be given time to take the fly, and to turn down with it. Anglers have devised various strategies. One is to wait after a fish has taken the fly until the terminal end of the green blowline disappears underwater; another, perhaps more popular, is to recite some formula, and to strike on the last word – *'God-Save-the-Queen'* is the cliché. The present writer, for reasons entirely unknown, declaims *'The-King-of-France-is-Bald'*. This works just as badly as other formulas. Hooking fish on the dap is difficult. See also *blowline; dibbing; dibbling; flying treble*.

degreaser   One of a number of proprietary or home-made substances used to take grease off a *leader*, especially in *wet fly* fishing, where it is desirable to sink the flies, or to sink the leader so that it does not cause a fish-scaring wake. A popular mixture is *Fuller's Earth*, washing-up liquid, and glycerine, made up into a small ball the consistency of soft putty. Mud is equally effective. Fish slime is also good, but using this entails first catching a fish.

dibbing   A variant term for *dapping*, sometimes used specifically of river-fishing, e.g. *'dibbing* a grasshopper from a tree'. This mode of fishing is also sometimes referred to as 'bushing'. Hills (*History*, 43) recorded that 'bushing' is a term first used by Lawson in the 1620s, in his notes to Dennys' *Secrets of Angling* (and see *cast²*). In a more recent reference, Baverstock (in Mansfield, 241-2) gives a discussion of the technique, which consists of using bankside cover to creep directly above an exactly-located fish, then swinging the line and fly over the position.

dibbling   Charles Cotton dapped and *dibbled* the natural fly. 'This way of fishing,' he wrote, 'we call Daping or Dabing, or Dibling wherein you are always to have your line flying before you up or down the River as the wind serves' (*Angler*, 264; and see *cast²*). Cotton's line was braided horsehair; it caught the wind. His description of dibbling is really a description of *dibbing* – 'if you are pretty well out of sight, either by kneeling, or the Interposition of a bank, or bush, you may be almost sure to raise, and take him too' (*Angler*, 265).

Dibbling is now more often used to refer to the action of the *bob fly* when fished from a boat. The fly is cast, the line *retrieved*; simultaneously, the rod is raised; at the end of the process, the rod is held high, with the top dropper 'on the dibble', i.e. furrowing the surface, causing an attractive wake. The rod may be still further raised, and the middle dropper dibbled. Then another cast is made, and the process repeated. Once again, a sufficiency of wind is necessary to hold the flies on the dibble at a reasonable distance from the boat. Wind / dapping / dibbling are inextricably intertwingled.

Dibbling is effective because it attracts the fishes' attention. In trout fishing, it simulates the minute furrowing of the surface made by hatching insects, and is particular effective in simulating the scuttering of adult *sedges*. In *sea trout* fishing, the dibbled fly may be taken for the same reasons as the *dap*. It also may attract *grilse*, although on the loch or lough salmon are more likely to take a point fly rather than a *dropper*.

Palmered patterns, or patterns treated with *floatant*, or palmered patterns dressed with a Muddler-type head, are sometimes used as droppers and fished on the dibble, so maximising the wake effect. Zulus, the Soldier Palmer, the Bibio, the Claret Bumble, and the Olive Bumble are a representative, though by no means complete, list. See *bob fly; bumble*.

diploid A term associated with fish-breeding. The word is distinctly 20th-century, dating from 1908 and, in its second attested use, from 1914 ('Each has the number of chromosomes characteristic of the species (in modern terminology the diploid number)': G.N. Calkins, *Biol*. ix, p.204). As Greenhalgh explains, 'All animals normally have a double set of chromosomes in each body cell, and are therefore termed *diploid*. Man, for example, has two sets of 23 chromosomes (=46). These chromosomes carry the genes that control growth and development of the body...The new individual obtains its diploid number of chromosomes as one set from its mother (in the egg) and one set from its father (in the sperm)...' (*Lake, Loch and Reservoir Trout Fishing*, 55). Greenhalgh also explains that *triploid rainbow trout*, now reared by some fish-breeders, are fish with an extra set of chromosomes. Since animals without the usual diploid complement cannot make sperm or eggs, and cannot become sexually mature, triploid rainbows are sterile and can never come into breeding condition. Such fish are available to provide year-round fishing.

diptera From L. and Gk; a catch-all term for the flat-winged flies (etymologically, *diptera* = 'two-winged') cf. the upwinged flies such as the *olives*. The word is first attested in 1819 (OED). The flat-winged flies include the *midges*, *black gnats*, and *smuts*. See also *terrestrials*.

dollaghan Large Irish brown trout, especially those of Lough

Neagh, which gather towards the mouths of feeder streams during the latter summer. Fly-fishing tactics resemble those employed for *sea trout* (and see here 'Glensman', writing in *T&S* in the May 1990 issue, 42-3, who gives fly-patterns equally useful for sea trout and dollaghan). Niall Fallon (*Fly-fishing for Irish Trout*, 139) records that the term is the Northern Irish equivalent of the *croneen* of the Shannon system.

As with 'croneen', the etymology of *dollaghan* is hard to trace. It is not given, to my knowledge, in any English dictionary, and the *Dictionary of the Irish Language* does not appear to include the term. The last does, however, give an entry to Ir. *dulach*, meaning 'moving, swift-running', and I hazard that our word *dollaghan* represents an Englishing of that Irish word, in such a way that dollaghan means 'the swift-running one'. But perhaps this is merely fairy-tale etymology (see also *sewin*).

dorsal From L. *dorsum*, used in English in the sense 'of or pertaining to the back' from the 18th century onwards. Specifically, the word is used to refer to the fin in the middle of a fish's back. All game fish have just one dorsal fin, in contrast to e.g. the perch, which has two. The function of this fin is to act as a stabiliser to prevent the fish rolling while swimming.

In all the game fish bar one, the dorsal fin is not particularly large. The exception is the *grayling*, whose huge dorsal fin makes the fish instantly recognisable. One interesting feature is the local variations which exist in the dorsal fins of grayling; these may have an angular trailing edge, a lobe-like edge, or even a scalloped edge, like the perch (see R. Righyni, *Grayling*, 10). The grayling seems to be the only game fish which exhibits such variation in fin shape.

double Also *double hook, double iron, wee double*; a type of *hook* used in fishing for sea trout and, especially, salmon. Hills (*History*, 38) noted that Mascall (*A Booke of Fishing with Hooke and Line*, 1590) was the first English writer to describe the double hook, followed by Venables (1662), who recommended double hooks 'for tender mouthed fish such as grilse or grayling' (Hills, *History*, 72-3).

The OED has nothing in a fishing sense, while noting that as a noun, 'double' has a number of other technical senses in e.g. bell-ringing, printing, dominoes and tennis.

In Northern English and Scots, the phrase *wee double* has some currency ('I changed down to a wee double in the afternoon, and soon had a fish'). *Wee* derives from Northern ME *wei*, and was originally a noun ('a little wee', cf. in Scots' idiom *a bit thing* = a bit (of a) thing), although an adjectival sense develops from the 15th century onwards.

double haul A technique used in distance casting with a single-handed fly rod; see *cast²; shooting head*.

double-taper A type of *fly line*, used especially in *dry fly* and *nymph fishing*, since its profile ensures accurate and gentle presentation of the fly. Another advantage of the *double-tapered* line is longevity; at the end of the season, the line may be reversed on the *reel*, and the back-end *taper* of the line may then be used for another season's fishing.

Double-tapered fly lines are now almost universally made from a plastic-coated braid, although some traditionalists still prefer dressed silk lines.

As far as can be determined, it seems that double-tapered lines first came into use during the 19th century, replacing the single-tapered lines of horsehair, or silk and horsehair, that had been used in the preceding centuries. See also *AFTM; cast²; forward taper; shooting head*.

down Also *gone down*. If the fish (usually on stillwater) are *down*, or if the fish *go down* after rising well, times can be hard for the fisherman. A *rise¹*, for example, may peter out when there are no longer sufficient quantities of hatching fly to keep the fish at the surface. Alternatively, fish may begin to feed on other food-forms, such as *daphnia*, which, being sensitive to light, migrate into the depths during the heat of a summer's day. If the trout follow the daphnia, feeding as they go, this may provide another explanation of the fish going down.

Sea trout on loch and lough are notoriously fickle in this respect; they are often down, and only their habitual *taking time* redeems the day. Such patterns of dour disinclination, followed by taking activity, are not here related to the availability of food, however.

The word 'down' derives ultimately from OE *of dūne*, literally, 'off the hill'. This weakens to *adūne* by the late OE period, and weakens still further to *dune* in ME. It is possible that the phrase 'the fish are down' is related to sinking shipping – the first references to ships 'going down' ('below the surface or to the bottom of the water; into the depths of the sea') date from the mid-17th century; another possibility is to relate our fishing sense of 'down' to the phrase 'to be down', i.e. to be in low spirits. Ben Jonson is the first to use the word in this depressive sense (1610, *Alchemist*: 'Thou art so downe vpon the least disaster!'). See also *put down*.

drag¹ The check on the *reel*, formed by an adjustable sprung lever which, tightened, acts as a brake on the drum and therefore makes it more difficult for a fish to take line during the *play*. A good adjustable *drag* or check is necessary when large fish, e.g. stillwater trout, sea trout and salmon, are the quarry.

The word is etymologically related to *drag²*; in the sense 'to put a drag upon (wheels or vehicles); to retard as by a drag' the word is first used by the poet Southey in 1829. Curiously (since the word is obviously earlier), the OED dates the specific use of 'drag' ('a device in a fishing reel') to 1937 and Ernest Hemingway ('I felt his drag. He had it screwed down tight...', from *To Have and Have Not*).

drag²   From OE *dragan*, ON *dræga*, 'to draw', thus 'to draw slowly ... to trail (anything) along the ground or other surface'. In this sense the word dates from 1440 ('Draggyn or drawyn'). In a specific fishing sense ('a dragging motion on a fishing-line') the term dates from the *dry fly* era ('The drag cannot be overcome' – *Westminster Gazette*, 1907); the word is currently used to mean a fly, particularly a dry fly, which is acted upon by the current in such a way as to behave unnaturally in relation to the stream, e.g. by causing a wake, and which is therefore said to have dragged. Drag is (usually) undesirable since it alerts a potentially taking fish to the fact that the fly is a counterfeit. Unfortunately, some of the best trout in a river are commonly found in places where drag is inevitable, e.g. in an eddy on the far side of the current. In these situations, a fly cast into the eddy will drag almost immediately, because the current will act on the fly line by bellying it downstream; the bellying line will drag the fly with it. River trout know all about these places, and take advantage of them, making life even more than usually difficult for the fisherman.

Certain game fish are more tolerant of drag than others. Righyni wrote of the *grayling*, for example: 'The novice will regard drag as an unforgivable sin in all circumstances. He will remember how, at the last moment when a trout was going to take his fly, the slightest bit of drag developed, and the fish immediately turned away. He will quickly find that he can take a much more light-hearted view of drag when grayling fishing' (*Grayling Fishing*, 23). *Sea trout* on stillwaters are also fairly tolerant of drag; Kingsmill Moore wrote that 'White trout take a dry fly much better if it dragging, and in a lake it is a good plan to twitch it along the surface in short jerks. Pattern I have found to be unimportant – a small bumble is as good as anything' (*A Man May Fish*, 155-6). Fishing the dry fly for sea trout on stillwaters is, however, usually confined to calm conditions; in better fishing weather (i.e. more wind) the *wet fly* is used, and drag is less of an issue.

Recently, there has been a recognition that imparting 'deliberate drag' to the dry fly may be a killing ploy for river trout (Clarke

& Goddard): sometimes, they write, river trout appear to feed on natural flies that have 'self-selected' themselves by movement. 'If the fish,' they continue, 'is selecting only flies that move, then *your* fly must move. Throw upstream of him, wait until the artificial is somewhere just behind his shoulder, and twitch the fly a couple of inches. Sometimes (though not always) the fish will turn and take...' (*The Trout and the Fly*, 132). Interestingly, this view of the dry-fly and deliberate drag is anticipated by Skues, who devoted a passage in *Minor Tactics* (first edn 1910) to 'the deliberate drag'.

Finally here, there is *drag* on the underwater fly, especially the fly presented downstream in trout and salmon fishing. Salmon fishermen, in particular, are aware that a fly dragging unnaturally fast across the stream against the current is unattractive, and have developed several strategies to control (and slow) the passage of the fly, such as *mending the line*: 'At any time when you see that the fly is going to drag or the line is getting below the fly, lift your line off the water to a point beyond where the drag starts and place it again upstream of the fly' (A.H.E. Wood writing of *greased-line* fishing for salmon, cited in Taverner & Scott, 142-3).

drift   In the sense 'the fact or condition of being driven, as by a current; the action of drifting', the word dates from 1562 and Heywood's 'Beware dryft to the woorst shore' – good advice for fishermen. It is now applied to the action of a boat on stillwater, drifting downwind over likely ground, thus also to the fishing ground that boat covers. For example, stony shallows on a sea trout loch would be a good drift, as would underwater shoals, or the shallowing water around mid-loch islands. Drifts (see *boat-fishing*) are usually carried out over roughly parallel 'strips' of water (so that the water covered on the first drift is not fished twice), with the boat being rowed or motored upwind between drifts. The action of beginning a drift is sometimes referred to as 'setting a drift', in which the downwind strip of water is scanned, and the boat, oars, and *drogue* (if any) disposed so that the drift takes place precisely over the targeted strip of water. In the absence of a *gillie*, drifts may be controlled by the oars alone (some fishermen tuck an upwind oar under their arm in order to control the boat), by a drogue (an underwater parachute which slows the speed of the drifting boat in a stiff breeze), or by a *leeboard* (a rudder clamped to the gunwale by a G-clamp), which last allows curved drifts to be made (see e.g. Greenhalgh, 149-50). See also *Northampton style*.

drift-netting   A means of exploiting sea-running or sea-feeding salmon commercially, by catching them in a net set from a trawler. During the 1960s, drift-netting off the Scottish coast posed a threat to British salmon stocks, and was eventually regulated by government legislation. In addition, and during the same decade, drift-netting began off Greenland once the situation of the salmon's feeding grounds had been discovered. In 1972, Eric Taverner and Jock Scott wrote that 'These high seas fisheries have resulted in a "free for all" without any apparent thought to regulations governing type of gear, size of net mesh or quota to insure an adequate escapement of stock for breeding...' (*Salmon Fishing*, 32). Since then, international agreement has gone some way to protecting salmon stocks.

drogue   From *drag*, or perhaps from Scots dialect *drug*, 'to pull forcibly, to drag' (OED). An underwater parachute attached, usually by clamp, to the gunwale (or seat) of a boat by strong cord, and allowed to trail behind the drifting boat so that the speed of the *drift* is slowed. In very high winds, two drogues are sometimes set, one from the bow, and one from the stern. The drogue may also be trailed from the bow or stern of the boat so that the boat drifts end-on, rather than broadside in the traditional fashion, this mode of drift allowing the angler(s) to fish across-wind (see *boat-fishing; Northampton style*).

The use of drogues dates, somewhat surprisingly, from the 19th century. The word is first attested as a nautical term in 1875 (Bedford's *Sailor's Pocket Book* spoke of 'Towing astern a pig of ballast... or canvas bag termed a "drogue" or drag'), and in 1878 the *Boston Mercury* wrote of 'a novel kind of anchor (the drogue)...' Fly-fishermen seem to have used purpose-made drogues only relatively recently, the practice dating perhaps from the 1960s and the development of stillwater trout fishing in the British Isles which followed the opening of Grafham Water. In earlier times, a boatman (or *gillie*) could be employed to control the drift while the anglers fished; alternatively, a makeshift drogue could be made by trailing e.g. a bucket behind the boat from a rope.

One disadvantage of a drogue is that during the *play* of a hooked trout, the line or *leader* may foul the drogue rope, or the drogue itself, unless it is swiftly removed from the water by the angler's boat-partner after the fish has been hooked. This disadvantage can lead to bad language or worse. In general, however, the advantages of a drogue, especially in strong breezes, outweigh those disadvantages entailing the loss of the occasional fish.

Traditional wooden clinker-built boats, which tended to drift slowly, are being replaced on many stillwaters by lighter plastic skiffs, which drift absurdly fast in even a light air. In this last set of circumstances, a drogue is extremely useful since it allows the flies to be fished at a convincingly slow speed.

dropper   A term applied in *wet-fly* fishing, both to the strand of nylon on which a second or third fly is fished, and to those flies themselves. A typical wet-fly *leader* for stillwater boat-fishing would, for example, consist of a *top dropper* (the *bob-fly*), a middle dropper, and a *point fly*. Dropper patterns, at least in stillwater fishing for trout and sea trout, are usually fairly bulky in construction (see *bumble; palmer*) so that they may be *dibbled* in the water surface at the end of the retrieve, causing a fish-attracting wake.

So many angling authors up to the early 19th century wrote of fishing the single fly that it is tempting to suppose that the use of droppered leaders dates from *c*.1800 (when gut was coming into use as a leader material). But in fact this is not so. The first reference I know to the use of droppers comes in Richard (?Robert) Howlett's *The Angler's Sure Guide* (1706); he used as many as three droppers (see Trench, 61; and see *cast[1]; bob fly*). Bowlker used the term *dropper* in 1746. The OED, on the other hand, records the word *drop-fly* as first attested only in 1870, from Blaine's *Encyclopaedia of Rural Sports*: 'When more than one fly is used...the additional one is called a drop-fly, and by some a bob...'. The record for droppers must surely be held by David Webster (*The Angler and the Loop Rod*, 1885); he used no fewer than eight.

The knots used to form droppers on a leader are usually the Blood Knot or the Water Knot (see *knots*). If the last is employed, the downward-pointing strand of nylon should be used to attach the dropper (fly); to attach the fly to the upward-pointing strand (i.e. the strand pointing back to the fly-line) is to invite smashes (see *smash take*).

drop-takes   A phenomenon of both river and stillwater trout fishing, in which a trout takes the fly as it is sinking after being cast, without any additional motion being imparted by the angler. These takes, also known as takes 'on the drop', are generally indicated by a subtle heaviness on the line, rather than, for example, any more overt visual indication; consequently, many takes on the drop are missed.

Drop-takes seem to occur most frequently when the trout are '*on the fin*', actively searching for food in or near the water surface, for example during a *hatch[1]* of *buzzers*. Consequently it pays the angler to be specially vigilant for drop-takes under these circumstances, particularly since many takes on the drop may indicate that the trout require the fly or flies to be fished in a more naturalistic fashion, i.e. more slowly, rather than being pulled or stripped on the *retrieve*.

dry fly   A term applied to an artificial fly, commonly fished singly and upstream, which is dressed and cast so as to float on the water surface, thus also 'fishing the *dry fly*'. Dry flies are usually representative of what the trout are then eating (see *matching the hatch*). They may be used both on rivers and stillwaters. They may also be employed, although in a less specific role, for sea trout (see *drag²*), and even salmon, although this last technique is not common in Britain.

The dry fly is commonly associated with fishing for brown trout on chalkstreams, since it is in this environment that the technique of the dry fly was originally developed. John Waller Hills, a historian of the dry fly (see Chapter 8 of the *History*), ascribed the evolution of the dry fly to the early or mid-19th century, explaining that when earlier writers, such as Mascall (late 16th century) and Barker (mid-17th century) refer to fishing flies 'aloft on the water' (Mascall), or to a particular fly which 'floateth best' (Barker), they are not actually referring to patterns which unambiguously float on the surface, or to a practice which enables flies to be so fished. Rather, Hills thought, these authors were referring to fishing 'At the Top', as Cotton called it – fishing just subsurface, with the artificial cast downstream and allowed to fall on the water before the line. In Hills's view, the first mention of the genuine dry fly, and genuine dry fly presentation (which meant the deliberate drying of the fly by *false casting*), comes in Scotcher's *Fly-Fisher's Legacy*, published in 1800, and thereafter in Pulman's *Vade Mecum of Fly Fishing for Trout*, first published in 1841 and thereafter reappearing in editions of 1846 and 1851, the last of which explicitly mentions the deliberate drying of the fly ('Let a *dry* fly be substituted for the wet one, the line switched a few times through the air to throw off its suberabundant moisture, a judicious cast made... and the fly allowed to float...'). Hills tentatively suggested that Pulman, a tackle-maker at Axminster, gained his knowledge of the dry fly from Hampshire and thus from the chalkstreams.

There are other theories, however, as to the origins of the dry fly. James Ogden, writing in 1879, claimed to have invented the dry fly some forty years earlier, and this was not, Hills thought, totally implausible; Ogden was certainly one of the first fly-tiers to market floating artificials, deliberately dressed as such. Another claim is that of Stoddart who, writing in 1853 in *The Angler's Companion to the Rivers and Lochs of Scotland*, described both how a first cast may be successful because the fly floats, and how the line may be false-cast in order to dry the fly (or flies, in Stoddart's case).

By the mid-19th century, then, the dry fly was established,

although its use was not widespread (Hills noted that Charles Kingsley, whose famous *Chalk Stream Studies* appeared in 1858, had never heard of the dry fly); by the 1860s Francis, in *A Book of Angling* (1867), was able to claim that the dry fly was being systematically, although not exclusively, used in the south. In other parts of the country the dry fly was less well known. Writing as late as 1899, Grey recorded having used the dry fly to good effect on the Dart during his fisherman's apprenticeship; a local angler, seeing Grey's catch, was suspicious when told the fish had been taken on a dry fly ('"Dry fly," he said very sternly, "we know nothing about a dry fly here." Then he went on his way, with thoughts, I fear, that were not very kind.' *Fly Fishing*, 1st edn, 268).

The late 19th century was the era of Halford, a historian and prophet (but not a pioneer) of the 'dry fly cult', a cult which tended to think, with excessive zeal, that the dry fly was the right, the proper, indeed the only way of taking trout, especially on the chalkstreams (see *purist*). Halford's books, especially *Floating Flies and How to Dress Them* (1886) and *Dry-Fly Fishing in Theory and Practice* (1891), were the prime sources for the zealous – even Grey, a liberal in fishing as in much else, stated that those who know and practice dry fly fishing 'are the epicures amongst anglers ... carr[ying] both the skill and pleasure of angling to a height of exquisite refinement' (*Fly Fishing*, 32) and pointed aspirants towards Halford's *Dry Fly Fishing*, which gives instruction of both 'value and completeness'.

Halford propounded and systematised. His conception of the dry fly debarred 'fishing the water' indiscriminately; a rising trout had to be found, its food established by observation, a close copy of the natural (preferably one of Halford's own patterns) tied on and oiled, and finally, the cast had to be made upstream of the trout's position, so that the fly floated back without *drag*[2] ... These were the rituals of the cult, of the 'dry fly purist'. In essentials, they are still good practice when dry fly fishing on rivers, and Halford's legacy (or that of his followers) can still be found today on streams where fishing is 'dry fly only'. On the other hand, there were those who saw the Halfordian enthusiasm as rather too exclusive (indeed, a certain amount of snobbery attached itself to the 'dray flay', although this, perhaps, was hardly Halford's fault), and whose conception of fishing was more catholic and eclectic, not excluding those casts made at a venture, nor even the despised *wet-fly* and *nymph*. Chief among the critics of Halfordiana was G.E.M. Skues. If Halford can be said to be in some sense the 'father' (but not the only begetter) of the dry fly, then Skues can equally fairly be said to be the *fons et origo* of *nymph* fishing (although hardly, again, its only begetter, since nymph-suggesting wet flies had been fished for centuries). It is a comment on the magnitude of both these men's achievements (and advocacy) that today both dry fly and nymph fishing are practiced complementarily, even on the chalkstreams, as occasion and the trout's mood dictate.

Use of the dry fly spread during this century not only to other types of water and other species of game fish, but worldwide: on some hard-fished streams in America, for instance, dry fly fishing has been developed still further, and American fishermen may use the tiniest of artificials (far smaller than Halford ever conceived) on the very lightest leaders and 'toothpick' rods. In Britain, these techniques are in their infancy, but the dry fly is certainly widely used (and that use has been much refined) on stillwaters, especially for brown and rainbow trout during hatches of *midge* or *sedge*, but also for sea trout, who may sometimes be tempted, during times of calm and low water, by a dry fly cast from a boat and trickled along the water surface in the evenings. In this last role, because sea trout seldom feed on natural flies in freshwater, the dry fly has ceased to be strictly 'imitative', and is fished more as an attractor pattern or *lure*, albeit a floating one.

dub[1] A verb, from OF *aduber*, etymologically related to both 'dab' and *dap*, but used in a sense specific to fly-tying to refer to the action of dressing strands of fur or wool onto the silk thread used to construct the fly's body. At the appropriate stage of the tie, the silk is waxed so as to become tacky, then a pinch of the relevant body material (e.g. seal's fur or substitute) is taken between the fingers and offered to the silk by being rolled onto it between the finger-tips, forming a slimly tapered body (see *abdomen*). The word is first attested in the 15th-century *Treatise* ('Thyse ben the xij flyes wyth whyche ye shall angle to þe trought & grayllyng, and dubbe lyke as ye shall now here me tell'), although there the word was perhaps intended as a synonym for 'dress'. The first unambiguous description of *dubbing* a body (in our modern sense) that I know comes from Venables' *The Experienced Angler* (1662, p.14): one way of making a body, he wrote, is to 'wax a small slender silk thread, and lay wool, fur, &c. upon it, and then twist, and the material will stick to it . . .'

Seal's fur and wool are useful dubbing materials because of their translucence when wet, and many patterns of trout, sea trout and salmon fly are dressed with dubbed bodies. Other dubbings include mole's fur (as in the Waterhen Bloa, a copy of a drowned olive *dun*, or alternatively, a stylised copy of a Large Dark Olive *nymph*), hare's ear fur (as in the universally-known Gold-ribbed

Hare's Ear), squirrel fur (as in the Grey Wulff, a *mayfly²* pattern),
and others. Some nymph- or *pupa*-suggesting flies have a *thorax*
formed from dubbed fur, e.g. as in those *buzzer* patterns which
have a body of silk or stripped quill and a thorax of natural or
dyed mole's fur.

dub² Of uncertain origin (but perhaps from Celtic or Gaelic *dubh*,
'dark'?); a term for a deep pool on a rain-fed river or chalkstream,
as in the following: 'There was was all the evidence needed that
this small dub – if I dare call a little, deepish hole on a chalk
stream by that name – was densely populated with very hungry
grayling' (Righyni, *Grayling*, 80-1). In the sense 'deep, dark pool'
the word is first attested in 1535 ('mony dubbis that war bayth
deip and wyde'). Many of the attestations of the word are northern
or Scots, lending support to the idea of a Gaelic origin.

duck fly The Irish term for the *midges* or *buzzers* of spring. Harris
writes, for example, that anglers 'have bestowed many names on
[*Chironomids*] . . . In Ireland the forms appearing in the spring are
called Duck-flies or Black Flies and the large summer species are
called Racehorses or Buzzers' (*Angler's Entomology*, 124).

The origin of the term is puzzling: perhaps ducks are as fond
of these insects as trout? See also *blae; pupa*.

duffer's fortnight When brown trout – especially the fish of chalk
streams – are feeding on *mayflies²*, they are traditionally held to
be easy to catch, a view perhaps deriving from Cotton, who wrote
that with 'the green Drake and the Stone-flie, I do verily believe
I could some daies in my life . . . [have] given over upon the meer
account of satiety of sport' (*Angler*, 300-301). Therefore the relevant fortnight in late May / early June is sometimes termed the
duffer's fortnight. There is, however, another view, which is that
when trout are feeding on mayflies they are sometimes difficult
to catch, as in the following quote from Frank Sawyer: 'Time
and again the Mayfly season has proved wrong the old saying that
it is the duffer's fortnight' (*Keeper of the Stream*, 73).

dun A term for the stage in the life-cycle of an upwinged (*ephemeropteran*) fly between *nymph* and *spinner* (the adult fly). A spinner
is sometimes termed the *imago*, so the dun may be referred to as
the *sub-imago*, and groups of duns as sub-imagines. The term
seems to be derived from the appearance of the naturals – Harris
notes that 'duns are dull and generally sober coloured, whilst
spinners are more brightly coloured and shining and their wings
are clear and transparent' (*Angler's Entomology*, 16). The etymology of the word supports this: OED notes the word is perhaps
from Irish and Gaelic *donn*, 'brown', and/or Welsh *dwn*, '. . . [o]f
a dull or dingy brown colour'.

The OED gives the first attestation of the word, in its strictly angling sense ('a name for various dusky-coloured flies . . . and for artificial flies imitating them') to Chetham in his *Angler's Vade Mecum* (1681) – 'Angle with the smallest gnats, Browns and Duns you can find' – but this is surely too late. To take two examples, the *Treatise* referred to that mysterious fly, the Dun Cut, and Cotton, whose 'Instructions How to Angle for a Trout or Grayling in a Clear Stream' were added to Walton's great work in its fifth edition (1676), gave many references to duns, including the following advice for fly-fishing in February: 'in case of a frost and snow, you are to Angle only with the smallest Gnats, Browns and Duns you can make'. (Not for the first time in the literature of fishing, plagiarism is the issue; it seems clear that Chetham was merely copying Cotton; consequently, the OED's dating of the word is dubious.)

Duns are important to the fly-fisher on rivers, since hatches of these flies provide, along with other flies (notably *midges* and *terrestrials*), the bulk of his daytime sport, beginning in March and April with hatches of the Large Dark Olive *Baëtis rhodani*), and continuing with hatches of the Iron Blue *(B. pumilus)*, the Olive Upright *(Rhithrogena semicolorata)*, the Blue-winged Olive *(Ephemerella ignita)* and others – the last-named are merely some important river flies (for further information, see e.g. *olive*). Still-water fishermen may also see hatches of Lake or Pond Olives *(Cloëon simile* and *C. dipterum)* in early summer. The most spectacular of all upwinged flies, the *mayfly*[2], hatches on both river and stillwater (usually *Ephemera danica*, although hatches of *E. vulgata* may occur in some parts of the country); mayfly duns are sometimes termed *greendrakes*.

The term has understandably been applied to artificial patterns representing naturals, thus August Dun, Claret Dun, Large Summer Dun, Olive Dun, Sepia Dun and so on.

E**closion** From Fr., ultimately from L. *claudere*, 'to shut', and first attested in 1889, this is another term for 'hatching', applied both to the *nymph* hatching from the egg ('After eclosion, or hatching from the eggs, nymphs are so small that they are scarcely visible...' Harris, *Angler's Entomology*, 22), to the *dun* hatching from the nymph, and to the adult (e.g. *midge* or *sedge*) hatching from the *pupa* ('It's the rise to the surface for hatching (eclosion) that makes the pupa susceptible to the trout', Fraser, 54). The word is rather pedantic.

entry Recorded in Courtney Williams (6th edn), Appendix IV: 'An artificial fly (wet) which swims naturally without skirting or offering undue resistance to the water, is said to have a "good entry".' The term now seems to be used chiefly to describe the pitching of a (weighted or unweighted) *nymph* into the water; Oliver Kite, for example, wrote that 'the artificial nymph should be pitched...to arc over and into the water with the minimum of surface disturbance to interfere with vision – an otter's entry' in Walker, *The Complete Fly-Fisher* (revised edn, 1984, 143).

ephemeroptera From L., ultimately from Gk. *ephemeros* (< epi + hemera, 'day'), the original meaning 'existing only for a day or a very short time', cf. ModE. 'ephemeral' etc. The term 'ephemeral' was first used in the 16th century, but it is worthwhile noting that the system of naming natural flies derives from work by the Swedish naturalist Linnaeus; as Harris notes, 'The giving of names under his system in zoology is taken to start in...1758 when the tenth edition of his book [*Systema Naturae*] was published' (*Angler's Entomology*, 10).

In fly-fishing, *ephemeroptera* is the generic name applied to the upwinged flies ('*olives*'), although the word *ephemera* was used in the same sense until well into the 19th century (Bacon was one of the first to use this term; in 1626 he wrote of 'certain Flies... called Ephemera that live but a day'). Where more than one species of the genus is being distinguished, it is common to abbreviate the generic name, especially in its second use, thus *Ephemera danica* (the most common species of *mayfly*) may be contrasted with *E. vulgata*; *Baëtis rhodani*, the Large Dark Olive, may be contrasted with *B. pumilus* (the Iron Blue), and so on.

The word is sometimes used adjectivally ('Conditions during the summer of 1948 were very unfavourable for all ephemerop-

67

teran flies', Sawyer, *Keeper of the Stream*, 67); the term 'ephemerid'
is also sometimes used to describe groups of olive *nymphs* or *duns*
– this is a shortening of the term 'ephemeridae' (the suffix '-idae'
denotes the name of a family).

The ephemeroptera have long been held important to trout
fishermen, particularly since the classifying work done by Halford
(see *dry fly*). But the olives were well known as fishing flies even
at the time of the *Treatise* – Hills believed, surely correctly, that
the 'second Dun fly' of that work is in fact a (rather dark) copy
of the Blue Dun or Large Dark Olive – and Cotton gave several
dressings for olives, the most important being his 'blew Dun' (a
Dark Olive) and his 'Dun-Cut' (also known by that name in the
Treatise), which represents a Pale Watery (at least, this is the
inference from Hills).

Perhaps the most important ephemeroptera to the fly-fisherman
are the Large Dark Olive, the Iron Blue (see above), the Olive
Upright (*Rhithrogena semicolorata*, common on rain-fed rivers),
the *Mayfly*[2], the Blue-winged Olive, and the various Pale
Wateries. On stillwaters, the Pond Olive and Lake Olive may
occur in sufficient numbers to merit attention, and the Claret
Dun may also occur, particularly on *acidic* upland lakes and lochs.
Artificial patterns representing these naturals may of course be
found in any of the standard handbooks, but those of a reductive
and simplifying tendency may note that some of the most successful trout fishermen of this past century – the late Frank Sawyer,
and the late Oliver Kite are but two – have used just three flies
(although in different sizes) to represent olive nymphs, duns, and
spinners respectively, these being the Pheasant Tail nymph, Kite's
Imperial (for the duns), and the Pheasant Tail spinner. (For
further classification of the natural flies, see *olive*).

epilimnion   From Gk. OED defines this as 'the upper, uniformly
warm layer of water in a stratified lake'. The term was first used
in a paper by E.A. Birge (*Transactions of the Wisconsin Academy
of Sciences, Arts and Letters* XVI, 1910). The word occurs rarely
in fishing terminology, and is applied to fly-fishing in those relatively deep, upland lochs which stratify during long periods of
settled summer weather (because colder water is heavier than
sun-warmed water, it therefore sinks until wind- and wave-action
mixes the strata once again). In such places, trout will commonly
be found in the *epilimnion* during the high summer, feeding on
the organisms found at that depth, whereas the lowest levels of
the lake (the *hypolimnion*) will be devoid of food organisms (and
thus all but devoid of trout). On these waters, therefore, one of
the primary tasks of the fisherman during the summer will be

locating the depth at which the trout are lying, that is, locating
the epilimnion (usually by trial and error with a sinking line).
For an interesting discussion of the epilimnion's importance to
the stillwater trout fisherman, see Greenhalgh, 37ff. See also *daphnia, thermocline*.

ethafoam   A recent introduction, *ethafoam* is a closed-cell foam
used to line fly-boxes. Because of ethafoam's properties, tiny balls
of the material are used in the construction of some buoyant
nymphs (notably the '*Suspender*' types) and *fry* patterns.

Ethafoam-lined fly-boxes are both convenient and attractive,
but have one drawback. Since ethafoam repels water, flies should
be returned to the fly-box in a dry condition. If flies are returned
still damp from fishing, moisture collects round the bend of the
hook where it is caught in the foam, causing rust. This weakens
the temper of the hook, with potentially disastrous consequences.

eutrophication   The word *eutrophic* is from Gk, meaning literally
'tending to promote nutrition'. The word is first attested in a
medical sense in the 18th and 19th centuries. The terms have
only been applied in a fishing sense relatively recently (mid-20th
century); see OED, which defines *eutrophic* as 'Of a lake . . . (over-)
rich in organic or mineral nutrients . . . Hence *eutrophication*, the
process of becoming eutrophic'.

Eutrophic lakes are invariably *alkaline waters*, rich in nutrients
and thus in phytoplankton. Algae also thrive; all stillwater anglers
will be familiar with the green algal bloom that occurs on rich
lakes during the summer. Fishing under these conditions is sometimes like casting into a clear pea-soup.

In recent years, however, eutrophication has become a problem
in certain lakes, notably the Irish midland waters such as Sheelin
and Ennell. The reason such lakes became unhealthy was that
the naturally-produced algae did not die off; they continued to
reproduce since the lakes were over-nourished. This state of
affairs was (and is) often brought about by fertilisers (in Ireland
and elsewhere, pig-slurry) applied to the farmland on which the
water lies. This fertiliser percolates into the lake, enriching it still
further; ultimately – since plant and algal growth takes up oxygen
– the waters become saturated with carbon dioxide, causing, in
the worst cases, loss of insect life and fish.

Eutrophication, although a natural process, thus needs to be
monitored carefully. Remedial treatment, which has been attempted with some success in Ireland, is very expensive.

evening rise   During the summer months, trout fishermen look
forward to the *evening rise*, to fish moving in the last hour of
daylight to hatches of fly or falls of *spinners*. On rivers, the most

important evening rise is that to the Blue-winged Olive, followed closely by the rise to the various species of *sedge*, which hatch in the cooler conditions of twilight. On stillwaters, *buzzers* may hatch (see *pupa*), or adult buzzers return to the water to lay eggs; trout often rise well under these circumstances, but owing to their preoccupation, they are sometimes difficult to catch. Sedges also hatch on stillwaters during summer evenings, as do those most disastrous of flies, the *caenis*.

The problem with the evening rise is that first, it is unpredictable; second, it can be very short-lived; and last, it can be hair-tearingly frustrating. Although anglers do anticipate the event with some keenness, confidence can be misplaced. Grey understood this well; writing of the evening rise on chalk streams, he noted that

> the *look* of the evening rise is so often the best of it. Numbers of trout appear to be rising frequently and steadily and confidently, but when the angler puts them to the test, they disappoint him. On some evenings the trout cease to rise after an artificial fly has once been floated over them; on others they continue to rise freely, but will take nothing artificial, and the angler exhausts himself in efforts and changes of fly, working harder and more rapidly as he becomes conscious of the approaching end of day (*Fly Fishing*, 1984, 42).

See also *rise¹*.

extension handle   A short handle attached to the *butt* of a single-handed *fly rod*, usually by a screw-thread fitting. Extension handles are particularly useful when fishing for large trout or sea trout, since the extended leverage makes heavy fish easier to play (the rod butt can be braced against the lower part of the forearm). Like *butt spears*, extension handles also keep the *reel* off the ground (e.g. when the *rod rings* are being threaded) and away from the angler's clothing when a fish is being played.

eye   The tiny circle of tempered steel at the front of the *hook*, through which the nylon is threaded (see *knots*). As Hills made clear, the first illustration of the eyed hook is found in a work by Frère François Fortin (the 'Inventive Solitary') called *Les Ruses Innocentes*, published in 1660. The English were slower to adopt the eyed hook: the admirable illustrations of hooks in the *Treatise* (15th century) do not show eyes. Cotton used hooks whipped direct to the line, as did Venables ('When you set on your hook, do it with strong but small silk...' *The Experienced Angler*, 1662). In fact flies continued to be made in this way for a further two hundred years: even in the late 19th century (and into the early 20th), flies were 'tied to gut' directly. Possibly the first reference to the eyed hook comes in O'Gorman's *The Practice of Angling* (Vol. 2, 1845), who wrote 'OF A NEWLY INVENTED HOOK: This is a hook with an eye in the shank. It is another Scotch invention, and as to its usefulness may be placed on a par with the newly invented mode of breeding salmon' (cited in Falkus, *Sea Trout Fishing*, 113). O'Gorman was evidently not an enthusiast; but with improvements in the drawing of gut, and eventually, the introduction of *nylon monofilament*, eyed hooks were bound to become common. Some match anglers, however, still prefer (or did until recently) 'spade-end' hooks to which the line is knotted directly: the *Hardy Book of Fishermen's Knots* (1987), for example, gives instructions for two knots used to whip on spade-end hooks, so it seems unlikely that eyed hooks are universally used.

False casting   False casts are casts made so that the fly does not fall on the water, but is whisked back and forth so as either to lengthen line (see *cast²*), or to dry the fly (see *dry fly*). As Hills noted, *false casting* is diagnostic in determining the history of the dry fly; he dated the earliest mention of the deliberate drying of the fly by false casting to Pulman's *Vade Mecum of Fly Fishing for Trout* (1851 edition). Gingrich (*The Fishing in Print*, 199) concurs with Hills's judgment, but emphasises the point that it was Francis Francis who, as Gingrich puts it, 'gave it [the dry fly] its first big push' in an 1857 article for *The Field*.

False casting can, however, become a fetish. In the early years of this century, before *floatants* had reached their current excellence, dry flies were either left untreated, or treated with paraffin; it was then necessary to false cast so that the fly would remain dry. Nowadays, flies treated with Permaflote or some other agent are virtually unsinkable, even after continued use, and false casting is less necessary. In terms of distance casting (particularly with a sinking line), it is clearly the case that one or two false casts will have to be made in order (a) to bring the line up onto the surface, and (b) so that distance may be obtained. Weight-forward lines (see *fly lines*) help in keeping the number of false casts to a minimum. Trout, especially the fish lying close to the surface, may be disturbed by a fly line whisking continually above their heads.

fancy fly   See *fly*.

fan wing   A style of dressing wings on artificial flies, used especially in *mayfly²* patterns. Typically, small whole feathers are tied in and 'set' upright, their quills at 90° to the hook shank. Courtney Williams mentions that this style of dressing is 'popular in parts of the U.S.A.' (*Dictionary*, Appendix IV, 419). Fan wing mayflies now seem to have been superseded, at least in Britain, by hackled patterns (especially the Grey Wulff), possibly because flies of a fan wing construction are apt to twist the *leader* (rather as a hooked leaf does), leading to kinks and taffles.

ferox   See *brown trout; cannibal; trolling*.

ferrule   The fitting at the joint of a sectioned rod. A two-piece rod, for example, has two ferrules, a male ferrule (on the *butt*) and a female, into which the male is fitted. O *carbon-fibre* and *fibreglass* rods, spigot ferrules are the most reliable (and the neatest) types for most kinds of fishing. *Cane* rods necessarily have metal ferrules.

The earliest fishing rods, as described in the *Treatise*, were ferruled ('Thenne vyxell [sic. *?vyrrell* = ferrule] the staffe at bothe endes wyth longe hopis of yren or laton [brass]...' – this is the first recorded use of the word as a verb in English). Ferrules, however, seem to have fallen out of favour, for most rods up to the 18th century were spliced; because of the crudity of metalwork at that time, ferrules would have been heavy, and would also have hindered the *action* of the rod. As Hills pointed out, ferruled rods only reappear in the 19th century, when spliced rods fell into disfavour as ferrule workmanship improved (*History*, 86).

fibreglass   Also *glass fibre*. A rod-building material, which largely superseded *cane* in the 1960s, but which has been ousted in turn by *carbon-fibre* or *boron*, which are still lighter and stronger materials. Carbon-fibre rods, however, include small amounts of fibreglass in the weave.

fine and far off   Sometimes, in low water or when trout and sea trout are otherwise being particularly shy, it is necessary to fish 'fine' (i.e. with a fine *leader* and leader *point*) and 'far off' (i.e. by long and gentle casting). The phrase is sometimes used in a general adjectival way, e.g. 'this river needs *fine-and-far-off* presentation' etc.

To my knowledge, the first person to use the phrase was Charles Cotton: the length of line, he told Viator, 'is a mighty advantage to the fishing at distance; and to fish *fine, and far off* is the first and principal Rule for Trout Angling' (his italics; 267). Cotton's admirable advice is, however, anticipated in the *Treatise*, which with supreme clarity gave the following instruction:

And for the fyrste and pryncypall poynt in anglynge kepe ye euer fro the water, fro the sighte of the fysshe, other ferre on the londe or ellys behynde a busshe that the fysshe se you not. For yf they doo, they wol not byte.

finnock   Also sp. *phinnoc(k)*, although this spelling is now obsolete. A *finnock* is an immature sea trout, on its first return to freshwater after descending to the sea as a *smolt* (see also *sea trout; herling; whitling*). Interestingly, as with other terms for small sea trout (*whitling, white trout*, and possibly *peal*), the word emphasises the silvery-whiteness of the fish, since 'finnock' is an Englishing of Gaelic *fionnag* (fr. *fionn*, 'white'). The word is first attested in 1771 ('Phinocs are taken here in great numbers...'). The OED definition is, however, misleading, since it identifies the finnock as 'A white trout, a variety of the Salmo fario'. *Salmo fario* is commonly used to refer to the *brown trout*. It would be sensible if future compilers were to adopt Hugh Falkus's useful distinction (*Sea Trout Fishing*, 19) between *Salmo trutta fario* (the brown trout) and *Salmo trutta trutta* (the sea trout); whatever the taxonomic and genetic niceties involved in making a distinction between the two fish – since sea trout may be considered, in fact, sea-running brown trout – Falkus's distinction is based on commonsense and clarity.

fins The *dorsal, adipose, caudal* (tail) fins (etc.), used to propel and/or stabilise the fish. The tail fin supplies propulsion; the dorsal fin maintains the fish's position in the water; the adipose fin is of no apparent use to the fish, but is used by anglers to identify 'game' as opposed to 'coarse' fishes; the *anal* and *ventral* fins act like the dorsal, while the *pectoral* fins 'slow forward or backward propulsion' or help in 'sideways stabilisation' (Maclean, 19).

When a trout can be seen feeding, it is apparent that the fish is more than usually active and alert, its fins agitated so as to hold it in the current or move it swiftly towards hatching nymphs or other food. This alertness and agitation – very different from the behaviour of non-feeding fish, which tend to lie still and almost sullen – has given rise to the expression 'on the fin'. Hills pointed out that this phrase is perhaps first used in print by John Worlidge, whose *Systema Agriculturae* appeared in 1669; Worlidge wrote that if you 'cast your Fly up against the Stream, the Trout that lies upon the Fin in such strong Currents, and discerns you not, being behind him, presently takes your bait' (cited in *A Summer on the Test*, 1983, 15). Worlidge's comment is also significant in that it implies that upstream fishing was common in Hampshire during the 17th century. This historical aside should not, however, detract from the observation that a trout *on the fin* is a taking trout.

See also *tailing*.

fishing The word *fish* stems from OE *fiscian*, 'to fish', which first occurs in a phrase of King Alfred's (*c*.900 'Ðonne gē fiscian willaþ' – when you intend to fish). Alfred clearly meant fishing with either a net, or with set lines. The word seems first to be used to mean 'fish with a rod and line' in the 15th century, by the copiously and monumentally bad poet, John Lydgate (1440): 'Like hym that . . . fyssheth a bareyn pool').

The term *fishing* is first used in 1300, in the *Cursor Mundi* ('Petre and andreu . . . wit þair fissing war þei fedd' – Peter and Andrew were fed by their fishing); again, to mean 'fishing with rod and line' the term is 15th century.

As an incidental note, the word *fishy*, as in the phrases 'that looks / smells fishy', possibly derives from the idea 'slippery as a fish', or perhaps stems from an allusion to meat with a 'fishy taste' (OED). The phrase is relatively recent, first recorded in use by Disraeli (*Coningsby*, 1844: 'The most fishy thing I ever saw'). See also *angling; fly*.

fishing the water   A phrase, sometimes if not typically used pejoratively, to describe a form of downstream *wet-fly* fishing, or random upstream casting with a *dry fly*. *Fishing the water* is often unfavourably contrasted with more specific fishing for trout lying in known positions, or for trout which have been seen to rise. It is therefore a form of fishing 'at a venture', or by a series of educated guesses as to where trout are likely to lie. It is not to be altogether despised, particularly in the high waters of spring, or when grayling fishing, or on any occasion when fish-location is at a premium.

I have been unable to trace the first recorded use of this phrase, although it seems like that, as with *chuck and chance it*, the phrase gained currency after the emergence of the dry fly cult (see *purist*) at the beginning of the 20th century. I may be wrong.

fish vision   Fish see outwards and upwards through an inverted cone, the tip of which is in the fish's eye, the upturned base of which is the water surface. This roughly circular hole is sometimes referred to as the *fish's window*. The fish can see objects in and through the window directly, whether these objects are under water, or above it. Outside the window, and as seen from underwater, the water surface mirrors whatever is below it. Window and *mirror* are practically useful to fly fishermen, since the theory of optics they entail helps to explain what the trout sees of the fly. The best accounts are those in Clarke & Goddard, *The Trout and the Fly*, chapter 6 (a work that also contains many fascinating photographs), and in Kingsmill Moore, *A Man May Fish* (revised edn, Appendix – which includes an account of how fish see in water disturbed by wave action or stained by peat). Another useful reference work is Sosin & Clark's *Through the Fish's Eye* (especially chapter 3).

flat calm   See *calm*.

floatant   Also sp. *flotant*; ultimately from OE *flōtian*, 'to float'. A proprietary agent applied to *dry flies* (and some *dropper* patterns) so as to aid flotation. There are currently some excellent floatants on the market (see also *false casting*). They work best when applied to dry flies soon after the flies have been tied (or bought), rather than being applied to the artificials at the last minute while fishing. Flies so treated should be allowed to dry thoroughly before being placed in the *fly box*. If an *artificial* is treated hastily at the waterside, not only is the treatment less effective (since the floatant has not been allowed sufficient time to dry), but also after the cast the fly may float in the centre of a tiny rainbow slick, and this unnatural film may cause a shy fish to refuse the fly.

Grey, who resented 'the intrusion of the odious little bottle and oil among my ... tackle' (1984, 175), used untreated flies, stating that 'Well-made dry flies used to float very well before paraffin was adopted'. This suggests that floatant was not common (perhaps not used at all) before the mid-19th century – a hypothesis which tallies nicely with the origins of the dry fly method.

fly The artificial, the 'winged lure', the 'feathered Judas'; a fly is a fly is a fly ... except when it is a *lure*. The terminology is difficult, because *fly*, as well as referring to the artificial copy of a natural insect, also refers to an artificial copy of a small fish (a 'lure'). Therefore all flies are lures, some flies as 'lures', and all lures are not 'flies'. Another way of putting this is to say that all flies (*artificials*) are lures (i.e. traps and artful deceptions); some flies are 'lures', i.e. represent – or purport to represent – small fish, or leeches, or other non-insecty creatures (there is a 'lure' called the 'Christmas Tree'); and all 'lures' are not flies (since they represent fish etc.).

If this seems confusing, consider now the question of whether a 'general *wet fly*' (say, a Mallard and Claret) is a fly or a lure. Clearly, it is a lure; but is it a 'lure', banned on those waters that stipulate 'No lures'? It does not represent a small fish (to us), therefore it is not a 'lure'. But neither does it recognisably represent a 'fly' (a large midge? a dark-bodied sedge?); therefore it must be a 'lure', if not a lure.

Matters are further complicated by the use of the term 'fancy fly' to describe frankly non-representational patterns, such as, for example, the Dunkeld (tinsel-bodied wet flies are particularly often slandered as 'fancy flies'). The problem here is that the Dunkeld may be fished slowly, in sunlit water, so that the overall effect, to a watching trout, would be not unlike that of a small *fry*. Under these circumstances, it is difficult to charge the innocent Dunkeld with non-representation, and therefore the term 'fancy fly' is something of a misnomer. As the angling cliché has it, 'It's not what you fish, it's the way that you fish it.'

However the word 'fly' is defined, what is extraordinary is how fly-fishing in England emerged complete, as it were ('compleat'?), in the 15th century, as the *Treatise* indicates. In that work there is no fumbling towards fly-fishing, nor any trumpeting of new discovery. The instructions on how to fish the fly are quiet, confident, and detailed: you can angle for a trout, said the author, 'wyth a grounde lyne lyenge or rennynge, sauyng in lepynge

tyme' and 'in leaping time' you must fish with an artificial fly,
and not just with any fly, but with a fly 'acordynge to the moneth'.
Then dressings – and relatively accurate ones – are given. All this
suggests that fly-fishing in England must have had a history of
some hundred or two hundred years, or more, before the author
of the *Treatise* came to set down the basic principles of the sport
(which, the author was careful to point out, is 'principally for
your solace . . . to procure the health of your body and, especially,
of your soul'; see Introduction).

It seems not unlikely that fly-fishing was imported from the
Continent after the Norman incursion of 1066. Several factors
point towards this. First, the *Treatise* is aristocratic in tone; fishing
is set contextually among those other aristocratic pastimes of hunting, fowling, and (particularly) hawking. The author was writing,
by his own testimony, for 'all those that are virtuous, gentle, and
freeborn'. 'Gentle' here does not mean that those invoked spirits
are somehow mild-mannered milksops; it means they are aristocrats. 'Gentle' comes from Fr. *gentil*, meaning 'high-born' or
'noble' (a semantic echo persists in the English phrase 'of gentle
birth'). The milieu of the *Treatise* is thoroughly blue-blooded.

Second, Hills argued that the text(s) of the *Treatise* may be a
copy of a lost, probably a French, original. As Hills put it, the
Treatise 'came into the world against a background which was
entirely French. It arose out of, and is deeply moulded and conditioned by, French writings; it is their offspring, and could be
that of none other' (*History*, 3). Hills pointed out that one possible
source for the layout and tone of the *Treatise* may be Edward,
Duke of York's *Master of Game* (*c*.1405); this is an English translation of a Norman French original.

Third, if fly-fishing was a Norman import, and has therefore
a Continental history, then this would be consistent with the fact
that the first mention of fly-fishing in European literature comes
in Aelian's *Natural History* (Aelian: AD 170-230), where he
described

> a Macedonian way of catching fish . . . They fasten red (crimson
> red) wool round a hook, and fix on to the wool two feathers
> which grow under a cock's wattles, and which in colour are
> like wax. Their rod is six feet long, and their line is the same
> length. Then they throw their snare, and the fish, attracted
> and maddened by the colour, comes straight at it . . . (cited in
> Radcliffe, 185ff.).

It is curious and heartening to think that anglers fished something
very like a Soldier Palmer to trout ('fish with speckled skins') in
Macedonia while Rome still had its Empire.

It takes a stretch of the imagination to believe that fly-fishing (which Radcliffe suggested was still older than 'the Macedonian device') existed in Europe invisible to literature for one thousand years, before the lineaments of fishing can once more be discerned in the pages of medieval French and English texts; but this is what the scant references suggest. The theory of unbroken descent is, surely, more plausible than to posit that fly-fishing was somehow forgotten, then rediscovered (perhaps more than once) during the Dark Ages. As Radcliffe put it, the artificial fly 'seems to me to have been for a long time in more or less regular use' (p.190).

Whatever we believe about the matter, it is salutary to think that behind the definitions of 'fly', and what constitutes 'fly-fishing', there is a pale ghost fishing for speckled trout with an imitative fly in a clear river in Macedonia.

fly box   A box lined with clips, or foam (see *ethafoam*) for holding flies. Some *dry fly* boxes hold the flies in compartments with clear plastic lids; this prevents *hackles* from being crushed. Hills noted that the earliest reference to carrying flies in some purpose-made receptacle is found in Barker's *Art of Angling* (1651); Barker carried his flies in a parchment fly book (Hills, *History*, 70).

flying treble   A treble hook whipped to, and trailing from, a single hook, especially on *dapping* flies (as in the 'Loch Ordie' patterns). Fish are sometimes difficult to hook securely when they move to the dapped fly, and a flying treble gives more chance of hooking a *short-taking* (or simply a clumsy) fish. The use of such a device may be considered unsporting (since some fish are not fairly hooked in the mouth, see *foul hooking*). An alternative is to use a small tube fly for the dap, backed with a treble hook. See also *treble; tube fly*.

fly lines   The earliest lines used for fly-fishing were of tapered horsehair; the line was fixed directly to the tip of the rod. These lines were superseded by hair and silk (mentioned in Markham's *Second Book of the English Husbandman*, 1614), although horsehair continued to be used alone. Hair lines were in use until as late as the 19th century, but were gradually replaced by silk lines, first mentioned in Nobbes' *Compleat Troller* (1682; see Hills, *History*, 87). In the later 19th century the heavily-tapered silk line came into more general use for fly-fishing. Such lines survive until the present day, but have been largely replaced by lines made of plastic round a fibrous core.

Double-tapered lines (abbr. DT followed by the line number, thus a line marked 'DT6' is a size 6 double-taper) are rightly popular, since they allow gentle presentation of the fly, and are long-lasting (the line can be reversed on the reel after a season, and the unused part of the line pressed into service for the following spring). *Weight-forward* (or *forward-taper*) fly lines, which consist of a thin running line and a steeply-tapered tip section, are distance-casting lines, and are also useful for throwing into a wind. *Shooting-heads* permit still further distance; they consist of a thin running line made of either monofilament or braided material spliced onto a section of tapered fly line. The running line gives very little resistance to the rod-rings, and so enables long casts to be made. In this instance, however, distance may be achieved at the expense of gentleness, although this depends on the skill of the caster.

The above lines are naturally available as both floating and sinking. Floating lines carry the abbreviation F. following the line size, thus 'DT6F' etc. Sinking lines carry the abbreviation S, occasionally FS (= fast-sinking) or SS (= slow-sinking). It is important for the line to match the line-rating given for the rod, and for the line to be suitable for the type of fishing intended. At the risk of sounding simple, it is unwise for anglers to persist in attempting to fish a *dry fly* on a sinking line; it is folly to attempt to fish a lure twenty feet down with a lightly-rated floating line. Correct line choice means more efficient, and therefore more effective, fishing.

Many anglers carry more than one line, loading alternative lines onto spare spools carried in the fishing bag. This is a practical way to cover different potential fishing situations. Another, although a more expensive, alternative, is to carry two rods, each loaded with a different line.

forward-taper   See *fly line*.

foul hooking   A fish hooked elsewhere than in the mouth is said to be *foul hooked*. There can be a number of reasons why a fish is accidentally foul hooked. First, it may have missed the fly; second, it may have turned away from the fly at the last instant, but the *strike* may still catch the hook in e.g. a fin. Third, the hook may fall out of the mouth during the *play*, but lodge luckily (or unluckily) somewhere else in the body of the fish. Strangely enough, my own two largest brown trout, which took the fly conclusively into their mouths (I know this since on each occasion I saw the take), were each subsequently landed with the hook in a ventral fin.

But to land a foul-hooked fish is always rather a dismal experience, shadowed by the suspicion of ill-luck, bad form, even foul play, and many anglers return foul-hooked fish to the water as a matter of course (some local regulations enforce this).

Of the baleful practice of deliberately foul-hooking e.g. salmon ('stroke-hauling' using a fast-sinking fly line, a thick leader, and a treble hook), I refuse to write.

fry   Tiny fish just produced from spawn; also *pinhead fry*, *needle fry*. OED records that the term is applied specially to 'the young of salmon in the second year, more fully salmon fry'. While this last usage persists (some rivers, for instance, have been stocked with salmon fry as part of angling improvement programmes), for many fly-fishermen the word 'fry' conjures up mental images of the reservoirs, and large brown and rainbow trout feeding heavily and spectacularly on fry during the later part of the season. The prey are usually either roach or perch fry; the latter, which are on the increase (especially on the English lakes) since the perch have been recovering from the disease which affected stocks several years ago, seem particularly common.

During July and early August, when the fry are small, trout may feed quietly on them along the margins of the water. Fishing with small, silver-bodied *wet flies* can then be excellent; a good pattern is the famous Silver Invicta. Another good general representation is the ubiquitous Pheasant Tail Nymph, here employed, and adorned with a white *thorax*, as a fry pattern. Later in the season, as the fry grow, relatively larger flies may be used (*lures* – see *fly*) to copy the size and movement of the natural fish: White Lures, Baby Dolls, and Appetizers are popular artificials (especially when the trout are feeding on roach fry), although silver-bodied artificials may still take fish, as may floating fry patterns. Trout at this time of year sometimes feed heavily on fry (and are referred to as 'fry-feeders'), ambushing shoals of them in savage attacks which can make the fry skitter in fear. These attacks usually take place in shallow water; an artificial cast into the centre of the disturbance, and left static, will often attract the attacking trout. Skittering fry, or the presence of diving seagulls (which feed on the dead or maimed fry), almost invariably indicate that trout are fry-feeding. This form of fishing is extremely exciting, not least because the larger fish feed in this manner, often voraciously.

The word derives from OF *frai*, and is first attested in Anglo-French in 1389, then in English in 1462 ('Grete carpes and... myche ffrye'). A new phrase, 'small fry', then develops (as a collective term for young or insignificant beings, OED); it is first attested in 1697. Fortunately, small fry are not insignificant to the fly fisher.

Fuller's earth   Available from most chemists, *Fuller's Earth* (usually so capitalised to indicate its origins) is a proprietary powder, one use of which was to make babies' bottoms more comfortable, now put to an alternative use by being mixed with washing-up liquid (and glycerine) until it becomes the consistency of putty, when it is ideal for removing any trace of grease from the *leader*, and so assisting the leader to sink. Also called 'magic mud'.

Fuller's Earth itself, which is a powder composed of hydrated aluminium, magnesium, and calcium silicates, and the washing-up liquid, are powerful *degreasers*; rolled into a Fuller's Earth ball (kept in a plastic film container, for example), the mixture should be applied liberally to the leader, especially around the knots. (The leader is simply drawn once or twice through the 'putty'.) When fishing the *dry fly*, careful attention should be given to the last one or two foot of leader nearest to the fly, since a floating leader *point* may deter a taking fish because of its visibility in calm conditions.

A 'fuller' was someone who 'fulled' cloth; fulling was a process of treating and/or beating cloth to clean and thicken it (OED), so presumably the treatment involved taking out the natural grease of wool, say, by application of fuller's earth (also referred to as 'fuller's clay'). Adam Smith's (*Wealth of Nations*, 1776) is the first attested use of the term.

full open bridge A type of *rod ring* (abbr. FOB) with a double foot (as opposed to the single-leg rings now current) and a 'brace'. FOB rings are particularly strong, and may be fitted to rods intended to fish e.g. a *lure* on a heavy *fly line*.

Funneldun A type of *dry fly*, first invented by Neil Patterson during the early 1980s. The term derives from 'funnel', which indicates the manner of tying and also the approximate shape of the finished *hackle*, plus *dun*. Such flies are constructed with their hackles (which should be rather larger than usual for the size of the hook) 'funnelled' towards, and over, the hook's eye; a ball of *dubbing* is tied in at the eye to represent the thorax of the natural; a small 'V' of hackle fibre is then cut out on the top side of the fly (as it is seen in the vice). The bodies and tails of Funnelduns are also modified: the bodies are taken slightly round the bend of the hook, and the tails tied in with a downward list. Flies so constructed float very well, and also fish 'upside down' (i.e. with the bend of the hook pointing skywards, rather than penetrating the water surface as in conventional dry flies). Details of the dressing technique can be found in John Roberts (*Illust. Dictionary*, 67-9). Roberts quotes Dave Collyer's enthusiastic comment about Funnelduns: 'this Funneldun method of tying dry flies could well be the biggest advance in dry-fly design and improvement since the advent of the eyed hook'. It is a splendid form of tying.

fur   From OF *forre, fuerre,* or *fourrure,* the word is first attested
in English in 1430, again by that McGonagall of the 15th century,
John Lydgate ('The shepe...berythe furres blake and whyte', he
wrote, with his usual gift of stating the obvious). Most artificial
flies are constructed of 'fur and feather', where the fur is *dubbed*
onto the tying silk. Hare's ear fur and seal's fur (or a substitute
of the last) are perhaps the most used dubbings, although synthetic materials (such as Antron) are now available in a wide variety
of colours, and perform well.

G **aff** A large, barbless, stainless steel hook, mounted on a long, rigid (sometimes telescopic) handle, and used to land fresh-run salmon. The qualifying adjective 'fresh-run' is inserted because it would be both pointless and cruel to use a gaff on a salmon – a *baggot* or *kelt*, for example – which one wished to return to the water.

Because of their potential for misuse by the less than scrupulous, gaffs are nowadays banned on some salmon rivers. Other methods of landing salmon (*netting, tailing* by hand or by mechanical *tailer*) are reliable, and do less damage to the fish.

If a gaff must be used, the procedure is as follows:

The accepted method is to gaff the fish across the back, about level with the dorsal fin. This is certainly the safest way, but not the best from the culinary point of view. The Norwegians tend to gaff their fish in the head and so retain its full commercial value, but it is not so prevalent a method in this country. I have never gaffed a salmon in the belly, having been told from an early age that this was the likeliest way of losing it ...

So with the fish well played out, the gaff is put across its back, and a firm, even pull, accelerating into a lift, will land it on the bank beside you. That is not the moment to relax, but to turn and carry it well away from the water ... (Alastair Perry, *T&S*, May 1972).

The word derives from F. *gaffe* (first attested in English *c.*1300, in the phrase 'crokid as a gaffe'). In a general fishing sense, the word is first recorded in 1656 ('Gaffe: an iron hook where-with Seamen pull great Fishes into their ships'). As a verb, the word is first recorded in 1844 ('the moment I gaffed him'). Sea fishermen still use gaffs, as do some pike fishermen, although the practice of gaffing pike is, for humane reasons, less common than it was.

gallows tool An attachment to a fly-tying vice whereby *parachute* hackles may be more easily tied. The gallows tool consists of a cross-member from which a small hook is suspended; this hook catches the nylon loop around the base of which the parachute hackle is wound.

A makeshift gallows tool may be easily made from a bent coat-hanger, two clothes pegs, an elastic band and a paper-clip. The coat-hanger is bent to shape (so that a cross-piece is formed above

83

the vice), then clipped to the vice stem with the pegs. The elastic band is now slipped onto the end of the cross-piece, and a paper-clip, formed into a hooked shape, slipped onto the elastic.

The compound is not recorded in the OED in this specific sense, but as a device used in clock-making (first attestation in 1884).

garden fly A euphemism used by shamefaced salmon fishermen who have taken their salmon from fly-only water on a worm or bunch of worms, perhaps at the *gillie*'s prompting. The words *Garden Fly* in a hotel fishing book therefore indicate something covert, illicit, and difficult to admit; users of the Garden Fly are usually found hiding in the bar, mumbling inconclusively about high water and Hairy Marys. See also *travelling fly*.

gill(s) The fish's breathing apparatus. *Gills*, located behind the gill-cover(s), consist of filaments which contain tiny blood-vessels. Oxygen, from the water which the fish actively pumps over the gills, passes through the filament membrane and is absorbed into the blood-vessels. Oxygen is then carried around the fish's body by the red blood cells, specifically, by the haemoglobin. For a good account of the fish's respiratory system, see Norman Maclean, *Trout and Grayling*, p.40ff.

gillaroo A kind of *brown trout*, held to be a sub-species, or perhaps merely a local variant, of *Salmo trutta fario*. This is specifically an Irish term, deriving from Ir. *giolla ruadh* (*giolla*, 'lad, fellow' + *ruadh*, 'red'). Both Kingsmill Moore (in *A Man May Fish*) and Niall Fallon *(Fly-fishing for Irish Trout)* record that the *gillaroo* is found in (and perhaps is localised to) Lough Melvin; Kingsmill Moore called it 'the panther of the water, the loveliest of your fish' (p.66). Fallon calls it 'a brightly-coloured and hard fighting trout, and a free taker of the fly' (p.139).

The word is first attested in 1773 (obscurely: 'The poke of the Gillaroo seems to perform the office of a gizzard'), then in 1776 (R. Twiss, *Tour of Ireland*: 'a species of trout, called gilderoy, are caught here'), and then in 1833, in one J. Rennie's *Alphabet of Angling*: 'Trouts, which are called gillaroos, are found in Loch Melvin...' Interestingly, Rennie claimed that gillaroos differ from 'normal' trout in having more red spots, a claim which is corroborated in the etymology, which stresses the fish's redness.

gillie Also sp. *ghillie, gille, gilly*, although the last two spellings are now infrequent. The term is now used to mean an angler's attendant or boatman, although many gillies are rather presiding spirits than 'attendants', and many are excellent and knowledgeable fishermen (more excellent and knowledgeable than most of their 'clients').

The word is originally from Gaelic, and meant 'man-servant,

young man, lad' (see also *gillaroo*). There are cognate forms in
Irish, *gilla* and *giolla*. M'Alpine's *Gaelic Dictionary* gives the spelling *gille*, while John Jamieson, in *An Etymological Dictionary of
the Scottish Language*, Vol. 2, gives the spelling(s) as GILLIE, Gilly,
and in support of the last cites: 'It is very disagreeable to an
Englishman, over a bottle with the highlanders, to see every one
of them have his Gilly, that is, his servant standing behind him
all the while, let what will be the subject of the conversation'.
The 'gentleman' was one tender Sassenach, a Mr Burt; the quote
dates from 1730.

The OED gives the same information, cataloguing the first
attested use of the word (in English) in 1596, and Spenser's *State
of Ireland*: 'Next after the Irish Kearne, me seemes the Irish
Horse-Boyes or Cuilles (as they call them) would come well in
order'. Further, however, the OED gives the spelling *ghillie* as a
variant. As John Yuille (*T&S*, Correspondence, June 1983)
notes, the orthographic <h> is due to misuse: in Gaelic, [g] is
aspirated after a preposition, or when used in the vocative case
(and then is spelt <gh>). Therefore it is orthographically wrong
in English to spell *ghillie* (unless in the vocative – 'Oh, ghillie!');
gillie is correct. See also *boat fishing*.

glass fibre   See *fibreglass*.

gnat   The OED records that this word (fr. OE *gnætt*, 'a small two-
winged fly') refers to *Culex pipiens*, the mosquito (and see John
Goddard, *Trout Flies of Stillwater*, 112-13). The most commonly
referred-to *gnats*, however, are the *black gnats*, a name which
refers to several species of small black flies including *Bibio johannis*
(perhaps the commonest), as well as the various species of
Simulium (the *reed smuts*; see also *smutting*). As Goddard puts it,
small black flies of various species are common throughout the
angler's year, and all may be referred to as 'black gnats' (see also
black curse). Their importance has long been recognised: Cotton
gave at least four different dressings of small black flies, his 'little
black Gnat, the dubbing of black mohair, and a light grey wing'
(*Angler*, 297), which he fished in June, perhaps being a true Black
Gnat, *Bibio johannis*.

grannom   A kind of *sedge*, *Brachycentrus subnubilus*, found only
on running water and fairly widely distributed. Roberts, *Illust.
Dictionary* (161) notes that this is an early-season species. As
Thomas Best accurately noted, writing as early as 1787, when
the *grannom* is on the water 'its wings lie flat on its back, it has a
small bunch of eggs of a green colour which gives it the name of
the Green-tail-fly'. This is not, however, the first mention of the
grannom; the first unambiguous reference dates from Chetham's

Angler's Vade Mecum (1681), where it is called the Greentail. The presence in the female of the green egg-sac is noted by every writer, and artificial dressings typically incorporate this feature, mimicking it by either a tip of fluorescent green wool, or by *dubbing* of the appropriate colour.

Hills, *History* (147ff.), considered the history of the artificial, noting that the *Treatise* possibly gives a dressing under the title 'Shell Fly'. The problem here is that the *Treatise* stated that the fly was to be fished at St Thomas' Day (7 July), which is far too late for the true grannom; but Ronalds, on the other hand, recorded that he had taken 'many of these flies out of the stomachs of Trout, even in August, which had a green colour at the tail of their bodies, and were nearly as possible of the same size and general tint as those of April' (10th edn, 81). This mystery has not, I think, been solved.

graphite   Often used erroneously to mean *carbon fibre*. Graphite, properly so-called, is 'a finely crystalline form of carbon, used in the manufacture of pencil leads and blacklead for grates, as well as many other things' (Pearson, 93-4). As Pearson points out, 'It is about as possible to make a fly rod out of graphite as it is to make one out of soot.'

gravid   From L. *gravidus*, 'burdened, heavy', thus in English, 'pregnant, heavy with young' (1597: 'Woemen when they are gravide with Childe'). The word then develops a sense in which any female of the species may be referred to as *gravid*, e.g. 'the gravid salmon are on the redds'. See also *baggot; rawner; redd; spawning*.

grayling   From *grey* + the diminutive suffix, *-ling*; the word is first attested in the *Treatise*: 'The grayllynge by a nother name callyd Vmber is a delycyous fysshe to mannys mouthe'.

The grayling, with its huge *dorsal fin*, is possibly the most immediately recognisable of game fish. Another term for the fish, and one which persisted until the late 18th century, was 'umber', the shadow (Best, 1787, spoke of the 'Gragling, Grayling or Umber'). Cotton thought that since 'a grayling is very black about his head, guills, and down his back, and has his belly of dark grey...' then 'I am apt to conclude that from thence he derives his name of *Umber*' (*Angler*, 276). Alternatively, those who have observed the grayling will know that the fish is indeed a shadow ('umbra' in L.) of the stream, haunting the river bed in small shoals. Another and more recent term for the grayling is 'lady of the stream', which derives directly from Francis Francis (*Angling*, 1867): 'If the trout be the gentleman of the streams, the grayling is certainly the lady' – but, the late Frank Sawyer added, 'a very greedy lady, and a flirt'.

Grayling are a river fish. They are found in the northern lakes of Sweden and Lapland, but there are to my knowledge only two stillwaters in the British Isles which contain grayling in any numbers; these are Bala Lake in Wales, and Gouthwaite Reservoir in the Yorkshire Dales. In rivers, grayling prefer highly-oxygenated water, and water that is *alkaline* in character – they thrive in chalkstreams. They are less tolerant of pollution than the trout.

These factors can be linked with the distribution of the fish. As well as preferring well-oxygenated, unpolluted and alkaline water, grayling also require the 'right' water temperature, and a particular type of riverbed. They do not, for example, appear to favour a hard rock riverbed, thus the headwaters of rain-fed rivers will contain few if any grayling. Further downstream, where silt and waterplants are established (see *ranunculus*), and where the current slows, grayling may be found in numbers. Where conditions permit (as in Tweed, where the water remains relatively cold and pure), grayling may be found in an entire river as far as the river mouth.

There are many rivers answering to this description in Britain, along with many chalkstreams which contain stocks. The fish is not, however, found much north of the Highland line, and is entirely absent from Ireland. In England, good stocks are found in the Dales rivers, in the Welsh and Scottish border country (especially the Cheviots), in the Eden and Ribble, and in many chalkstreams. In Scotland, the fish is present in the rivers Tweed (and its tributaries), Tay (and tributaries), Nith and Annan. These are the main centres; for further information on grayling distribution, the Grayling Society produce an excellent handbook which lists occurrence of stocks; there is also a list given in Roberts, *The Grayling Angler* (33-5).

The life-cycle of the grayling is curious since, unlike most other game fish, it spawns in the spring (April or May), sharing this affinity with the coarse fishes. Spawning takes place in a *redd* lying over gravel or sand, between 3000-8000 eggs are laid by each female, and the eggs hatch after 3-4 weeks. At this time, male grayling (usually the darker-coloured of the fish on the redds) may be aggressive, and will attack any intruders (including trout) onto the spawning territories.

Like all small fish, grayling *fry* are vulnerable to predation, and the survival rate is not, on balance, as good as that of the trout. This trend continues throughout the grayling's life; it is a relatively short-lived fish, seldom surviving beyond five winters. Typically, a two-year-old grayling will measure 9-10″, although chalkstream fish are heavier (owing to better feeding); male fish mature at 2-3 years, females at 3-5 years (Roberts, *The Grayling Angler*, 41).

The grayling has an underslung mouth (i.e. the upper jaw is longer than the lower), and this makes the fish adept at bottom feeding: *shrimp, snail, caddis,* and *midge larvae* form the commonest items of food, and these are all bottom-dwelling fauna. In addition, however, grayling will feed on the *nymphs* and *duns* of upwinged flies, for example in October, when the last big hatches of L.D.O. are on the water, and there can be good fishing at this time with both *dry fly* and wet. By November, these hatches of fly are dwindling, and the grayling return to their customary bottom feeding; then the angler searches for them with leaded nymphs or shrimps, or turns to bait-fishing (the trotted red worm is a favourite method).

There are still fly-fishermen who despise the grayling (Skues was one), asserting that their presence in a stream is a threat to trout stocks. This is difficult to prove, largely because grayling lie in different parts of the river to trout, are actively feeding at a different time of the year (i.e. in autumn and winter, when the trout are torpid), and do not compete with trout for spawning sites. While some control over grayling stocks is necessary – as is control over other fish stocks – the eradication of the fish from a river or river system is not to be encouraged: the grayling extends the fly-fisherman's season, is both gullible and capricious in turn (and therefore a fascinating angling proposition), and is 'a delicious fish to man's mouth'. The grayling should need no apologists.

greased line *Greased line fishing* is a form of fishing for salmon. It was developed during the early part of this century by A.H.E. Wood of Cairnton, and revolutionised the sport, making controlled presentation of the fly possible during conditions of low water formerly held to be at best difficult and at worst hopeless. Perhaps it should not be forgotten, however, that at least two salmon fishermen – Percy Laming and Alexander Grant – had experimented with floating (or semi-buoyant) lines at the end of the 19th century, before Wood subsequently popularised the method.

Wood discovered the technique almost by accident. Fishing an Irish river in the summer of 1903, Wood landed six salmon by *dibbing* a White Moth trout fly over them. Following this hint, and developing the use of a floating line in order to keep the fly just under the surface, Wood evolved the greased-line method (see Wood's own summary of his method in Taverner & Scott, *Salmon Fishing*, 134ff).

This he employed whenever the air was warmer than the water

(a point on which he put special emphasis). The fly was cast across the stream, or across and downstream, and the travel of the fly was slowed by one or more well-timed 'mends' of the line (see *mending line*); this meant that the fly was fishing realistically (for its size) in the current. In addition, Wood radically simplified his choice of fly patterns, favouring smallish, very sparsely-dressed artificials (sizes 6 to 12 in late spring and summer). These flies were very different from the fully-dressed salmon flies that had been preferred during the middle and late 19th century (see e.g. *cheeks; tag; tinsel*).

Wood's legacy to the sport therefore involves three factors: he made systematic summer fishing for salmon possible (i.e. in times of low water); his technique brought a further excitement to the sport in that it was possible to see the fish take the fly; and he had developed a useful way of slowing the travel of the fly – a way which, moreover, would be subsequently adopted in *wet fly* fishing for *brown trout* and *sea trout*.

greenback   A winter-running salmon, see e.g. Taverner & Scott, *Salmon Fishing*, 20: 'on the Rivers Taw and Torridge in Devonshire there is a run of winter fish known as "greenbacks".' See also *greyback*.

greenheart   A rod-building material, the wood being from the West Indies. *Greenheart* rods are now obsolete, having been superseded by *cane*, later by *fibreglass* and *carbon-fibre*.

The OED's first attestation of the word is dated to 1884, and *Blackwood's Magazine* ('It was an Irish greenheart'), but Hills dates the first occurrence earlier, to one Edward Chitty's *Fly-Fisher's Text Book* (1841; Chitty's pseudonym was 'Theophilus South'), which stated that Liverpool rod-makers used greenheart imported from British Guiana (Hills, *History*, 91). As noted above, greenheart rods, which were heavy to use, were gradually replaced by built-cane ones through the end of the 19th century, although some greenheart rods were still in use much later (see e.g. Ruthven Todd's 'Trout Flies' (1961), cited under *Greenwell*). See also *rod*.

Greenwell   The Greenwell's Glory is the only artificial fishing fly that has warranted a separate entry in the OED, so deserves an exclusive entry here.

The Greenwell started life in 1854 as a wet fly. Canon Greenwell, a prelate of Durham Cathedral, was fishing unsuccessfully on Tweed, despite a good hatch of natural fly; he carried one of the naturals back to James Wright's house (Wright was a famous Tweedside fly-tier); Wright constructed a few artificial copies. Next day, the Canon caught many trout; and thereafter, the fame of the Greenwell's Glory spread to every continent on earth (details from Overfield, 98-9; Courtney Williams, 197ff.).

The Greenwell is now tied as a *dry fly*, a *wet fly*, and as a *nymph*. The original dressing had a body of waxed yellow tying silk ribbed with fine gold wire, wings of blackbird, and a *coch-y-bondhu hackle*. Today, some fly-dressers tie in tails, use primrose silk, and substitute starling wings for blackbird; the 'Greenwell's nymph' sports a tail of yellow wool and a thorax of blue-grey fur. In fact the fly has been thoroughly adulterated – a testimony, perhaps, to the excellence of the original, even if the original story is hard to believe. (Did the good Canon not recognise what was plainly some common variety of olive *dun*? Is Wright the only begetter of the Greenwell, or was he merely tying a fly known on Tweedside for centuries before?) Still, the Greenwell, and most of its variants, are uncommonly good patterns both for trout and grayling on running water, and for stillwater trout during hatches of olive-coloured *midges*, or Lake or Pond Olives.

The excellence of the pattern has even been sung in verse. The following is an excerpt from Ruthven Todd's 'Trout Flies' (in *A Garland for the Winter Solstice*, 1961):

Ten years of age and intent upon a tea-brown burn
Across a moor in Lanarkshire, brass reel and greenheart
Rod, my first, I tried them out and came to learn
These magic names, from which I now can never part.

The insignificant ones were best, so ran the story
Of the old man who slowly taught me how to cast:
Dark Snipe, perhaps, Cow Dung, or favourite Greenwell's Glory,
Would attract the sleek trout that moved so fast

To attack and suck the right and only fly...

greyback   The OED defines *grey(back)* as possibly a *grilse* (= young salmon on its first return to the river after a year at sea). This is perhaps incorrect; the word 'greyback' is explained by Bill Currie (*The Fishing Waters of Scotland*, 50-1) as being a local Solway name for the big autumn salmon that run the rivers Annan and Nith during October and November.

It is difficult to be certain of the OED's accuracy or lack of it, since the various attestations of the word's usage (dating from 1686) do indicate that a grilse is what is being referred to (e.g. in 1818 Todd defines the 'Gray' as 'a kind of salmon...probably the same as the gilse' [*sic*]). It seems, therefore, as if the word is now obsolete in that specific sense, and is now used solely to refer to the big autumn salmon that run from the Solway.

grilse A salmon on its first return to the river after spending little over a year at sea. (Salmon returning after two or more years' sea-feeding are termed salmon, not *grilse*; the terminology depends on how many *sea-winters* the fish has spent.) Grilse are typically summer-running fish, and weigh up to eight or nine pounds, or may weigh as little as four. They are the fish the salmon fisherman looks to for the bulk of his summer sport. Since the fish do not run large, relatively light tackle is used – on most rivers, a single-handed rod is adequate, fished with a light line and smallish flies (between sizes 4 and 12 depending on the height of the water).

The word is of uncertain origin, possibly deriving from ON *gralax*, 'grey salmon' (and cf. *greyback*), or possibly from OF *grisle*, with metathesis (switching) of the word-final consonants. The term is first attested in 1417, then 1469 ('Salmonde grils and trowtis'), and in 1482 the Rolls of Parliament refer to 'Small fyssh called Grilles, not havyng the perfite lenght of a Samon'.

Grinner knot A strong knot, used in its 'double' form for joining two strands of *nylon monofilament* and/or forming *droppers*, and used in its 'single' form for tying on a fly. See *knots*.

gut This word derives from OE *guttas* (as in 'intestines'). Therefore the term was subsequently transferred to mean 'the silken fibre obtained from the intestines of the silkworm...Chiefly used in the making of fishing tackle' (OED). The first attestation of the word in a fishing sense dates from 1834 (Medwin, *Angler in Wales*: '...where I procured some hanks of gut...My fishing companions did not know that each filum of gut is a drawn-out silkworm just before it is about to weave its cocoon'). And see *leader; nylon monofilament* etc.

gut-shy Before the invention of *nylon monofilament*, trout which were particularly wary of the (floating) gut *leader* were sometimes described as *gut shy*, as in the following excerpt: '...the trout were gut-shy, and we fished fine. I was casting from the stern of the boat; my Red Spinner was bobbing attractively in the surface ruffle; a fish rose; there was a short, sharp jerk, and nothing happened. It was a break' (Luce, 61).

An alternative term is 'gut-cunning'. Hills recorded one particular gut-cunning fish:

> I remember once coming on a fish at Driffield, lying on the opposite side of a still pool. I put the fly well to my side of him, showing him no gut: he turned out to take it, but before doing so, he swam round it to see if there was gut on the other side. He saw it and sheered off. I can never get anyone to believe this simple and truthful tale (*A Summer on the Test*, 1983, 110).

Neither *gut-shy* nor *gut-cunning* are apparently recorded in OED.

gwyniad   One of the whitefishes, *Coregonus lavaretus*, related to, and possibly identical with, the *powan* and the *schelly*. It is said to be local to Wales, especially to Bala Lake, where the fish is sometimes taken by bottom-fishing. The name, from Welsh, emphasises the whitness (or the white flesh?) of the fish (Welsh *gwyn*, 'white'), and is first attested in 1611 ('The fish called guinead bred in that meere [Bala lake] never is seene in the... Dee'), and was noted by Daniel Defoe in 1769 (*Tour of Great Britain*: 'A Fish... called Gwiniad or freshwater Whiting').

None of the whitefish are taken frequently on the fly. Their importance to the angler liles more in the fact that they still exist, relics and survivors of the last Ice Age, having spawned all but invisibly through hundreds of generations. In this sense, their situation is not unlike that of the *charr*. On the Continent, the whitefishes are both more commonplace and more highly valued as table fish.

See also *pollan; whitefish*.

Hackle[1]   That part of an artificial fly which represents the legs (or wings) of a natural insect, or which is tied in at the throat (see below) of a *wet fly* to suggest part of the overall shape and/or coloration of a small fish (e.g. as in the Silver Invicta or Dunkeld etc.). The word derives from ME *hakyll, hechele* ('The long shining feathers on the neck of certain birds', OED), and is first attested in this sense in the *Treatise* ('The yelowe flye, the body of yelow wull; the wynges of the redde cock hakyll'). The ME forms point to an unattested OE form, *hacule (OED). The word is used as a verb ('to hackle') from the 19th century, e.g. Francis Francis, *Angling* (1867): 'Blue jay hackled over the wing'.

A *dry fly hackle* is formed by winding several turns of a cock's neck feather (see *hackle[2]*) behind the eye of the hook, and optionally behind and in front of the *wings* of the artificial. Dry or wet flies without wings, and with a 360° hackle of this kind, are sometimes referred to as *spider* patterns. The hackle on *dry fly* patterns represents the legs of the natural being copied.

Wet flies, such as the Waterhen Bloa, which represents a drowned olive *dun* (or possibly an olive *nymph* in the process of hatching), are constructed with a softer hackle from the neck of a hen bird; soft hen hackle fibres sink more easily than cock, have more suggestive mobility, and retain water better, so assisting the sinking of the fly. Here the hackle is again wound at 360° behind the eye, but is tied in more sparsely, and usually with a backward slant. The hackle in this case represents the gauze-like wings of the drowned natural.

Other wet flies, especially those traditional boat-fishing patterns with wings (Peter Ross, Grouse and Claret etc.), are constructed with hackle fibres sparsely tied in (usually on the underside of the hook only), and are sometimes referred to as carrying a *throat hackle, beard hackle*, or *false hackle*. This style of dressing is particularly common on those sea trout and salmon flies tied on single hooks, e.g. as in the Teal, Blue and Silver (sea trout) or the Blue Charm (salmon, usually fished as a low-water fly); and see *low water iron*.

A small group of wet flies are referred to as being dressed with *Stewart-style hackles*. This is a reference to the type of dressing favoured by W.C. Stewart, whose *The Practical Angler* (first published in 1857) ran through many editions and enjoyed enormous success. Stewart's 'spiders' were dressed with a soft hackle *palmered* around the head half of the body, so giving, Stewart felt, a more lifelike impression of a hatching dun. He was insistent, however, that this palmer hackling should be light: 'Every possible advantage is in favour of a lightly-dressed fly; it is more like a natural insect; it falls lighter on the water ...; and also, as the hook is not so much covered with feathers, there is a much better chance of hooking a trout when it rises. We wish to impress very strongly upon the reader the *necessity of avoiding bulky flies*' (his italics; cited in Gingrich, 142).

Some *lures* (e.g. the Jack Frost) are dressed with a *collar hackle*, tied at 360° at the throat of the fly, and so called in order to distinguish this mode of hackling from e.g. the *beard hackle* etc.

Some artificial nymphs carry a small, very sparse hackle below the *thorax* of the fly to suggest the legs of the swimming nymph (or emerging dun).

Palmered hackles are used on both dry and wet flies. On the former, palmered hackles suggest the bulkiness and fuzziness of sedges (e.g. the Wickham's Fancy). On the latter, palmered hackles suggest the activity and minute fuss of emergent insects, or the scuttering of a sedge, and are favoured on *dropper* patterns (e.g. the Zulus and *Bumbles*) where, fished from a boat (see *dibble* etc.), the palmer hackle causes an attractive wake. See also *parachute*.

hackle² The feathers on the neck or *cape* of a cock or hen bird, used for fly-dressing. Cock hackles, which have relatively stiff and springy fibres, are almost invariably used for *dry fly* patterns, hen hackles, which are softer fibred, for *wet flies* (see above). The following list, adapted from Roberts's *Illust. Dictionary* (p.210), gives the natural colours of poultry hackles, along with some well-known flies on which these hackles occur:

Badger: black centre with white or cream tips (Grey Duster)

Black: jet-black; usually dyed (*Black Gnat*)

Blue dun: blue- or smoky-grey (Blue Dun, Quill Gordon; see *dun; olive*)

Brassy dun: similar to blue dun, but with a golden tinge

Cree: alternate bars of black and red (red/ginger – Cree Sedge)

Coch-y-bondhu: black centre with red outer and tips (*Coch-y-bondhu*)

Dun: dingy brown (or dingy brown/olive, as in the Rough Olive)

Furnace: black centre with reddish outer

Greenwell: black centre with ginger outer (*Greenwell's Glory*)

Ginger: ginger, or honey-ginger (Cinnamon Sedge, other *sedge* patterns)

Grizzle: Plymouth Rock, alternate black and white bars (Beacon Beige)

Honey dun: dun coloured with honey tips (Honey Dun *Bumble*, Imperial)

Honey blue dun: blue dun centre with honey tips

Honey: pale gingery buff

Iron blue dun: inky-blue or slate-grey (Steel Blue, Iron Blue)

Plymouth Rock: see grizzle

Red game: Old English game (bright gingery red – Red Tag; see *tag*)

Rhode Island red: red-brown (John Storey; see *advanced wings; wings*)

Rusty dun or rusty blue dun: dun or blue dun centres with honey tips

Other hackle colours, especially the blues, reds, oranges and clarets found on some salmon and sea trout patterns, are obtained by dying white cock or hen hackles the appropriate shade, and packets of the loose hackles are easily available from tackle shops or specialist suppliers. Alternatively, white hackles may be dyed at the bench by marking them with an oil-based felt pen of the desired colour. This is also a cheaper way at arriving at some of the 'natural' shades noted above (certain natural colours of cock cape are very difficult and/or very expensive to buy).

Half Blood knot   A variant of the *Blood Knot*, used – usually 'tucked' – to attach eyed hooks to the *leader*. See *knots*.

hands   If a fisherman is particularly sensitive to the movement of a hooked fish, responding to it with tact and skill, he is said to have *'good hands'*, or simply *hands*. I believe the first use of the word in a fishing context derives from Skues, who defined the term as follows:

> One of the most enviable of the qualities which go to make up the first-rate fly fisherman is that which, in connection with horsemanship, whether in riding or driving, is known as "hands," the combined certainty and delicacy of correspondence between wrist and eye which mean so much, whether in the despatch of the tiny feathered iron to its coveted quarry, or in the skilful restraint of that quarry when hooked, and its ultimate steering to the net (*The Way of a Trout*, 1949, 192).

harling   A method of fishing for salmon in wide, deep and fast-flowing rivers (such as the lower Tay), which involves *trolling* a large fly, spoon, or other *lure* (e.g. sprat) behind a boat. As Taverner & Scott put it (*Salmon Fishing*, 173-4), 'The hooking of salmon by the method of harling depends entirely upon the skill of the boatmen'.

The origin of the word is unknown. The fishing sense of the verb *to harl*, from which the participle derives, is related to the more general sense of 'to drag: usually with the notion of friction or scraping of the ground' (OED), attested in English from the 13th century. The first unambiguous fishing attestation is 19th century, in Francis Francis' *Angling* (1867): 'The fishing...is mostly from a boat, and the style is called "harling".' In 1891 the *Daily News* described the activity as follows: 'You are rowed about...in a stout boat, with a large phantom minnow, blue or brown, let out, by fifty yards of line, behind...This is the process of "harling".' The fact that the term is employed in quotes in both of these excerpts suggests that the practice was then new and/or unfamiliar.

harvester A local term for the *sea trout*, also *harvest cock*, perhaps from the fact that the autumn run of sea trout is sometimes termed the 'harvest run', see e.g. Falkus, *Sea Trout Fishing*, 29: 'the autumn or "harvest" run...comes up during the early part of September'.

The OED records that *harvest-cock* is a term for 'a salmon of a certain age'. This is misleading, as the OED's attestation makes clear: '(1861) All migratory fish of the genus salmon, whether known by the names...harvest cock, sea trout, white trout...or by any other local name'. The reference is almost certainly to *Salmo trutta trutta*, not *S. Salar*.

hatch[1] A noun derived from the verb *to hatch*, which originally meant 'bring birds from the egg' (from OE ?*hæccean*, unrecorded), first attestation 1250 (in the ME poem *The Owl and the Nightingale*), but which came to mean 'bring (anything) from the egg', in an extended sense 'bring about' (e.g. 'they hatched a plot'). In a fishing sense, the verb has been used since the 19th century (Francis Francis, 1867: 'Larvae rising from the bottom to hatch out'); the word was earlier used as a noun ('a good hatch (of fly)'), in a fishing sense first attested in 1629, and current up to the present day (e.g. a typical usage can be found in *The Field*, 1894: 'a good hatch of Mayfly').

Hatches of fly are important to the *brown* and *rainbow trout* fisherman, less so to anglers fly-fishing for migratory fish (since neither *salmon* nor *sea trout* appear to feed systematically in freshwater). On rivers, fishermen look to hatches of upwinged flies (the *ephemeroptera*) and, in summer and autumn, to hatches of *sedge*, for consistent sport, although flat-winged flies, *stone-flies*, and *terrestrial insects* are of considerable, if not equal, importance.

(The fascination and preoccupation with the ephemeroptera is a relatively recent phenomenon, dating perhaps from the later 19th century and the work of Halford and his *purist* followers.) On stillwaters, the fisherman looks mainly to hatches of *midge* (see also *buzzers*) for sport throughout the season, to hatches of *Mayfly* in late May and June, and to hatches of sedge from June onwards. The important point in both forms of fishing is that when trout are feeding on a hatch of fly it is desirable, or perhaps necessary, to copy (a better term is 'caricature') the natural insects in order to bring about consistent success. This practice of caricaturing the natural flies which fish are taking is very old, dating back to Aelian (see *fly¹*) and, in Britain, to at least the 15th century and the *Treatise*, whose author recommended, with laudable practicality, that 'When ye haue take a grete fysshe, vndo the mawe [stomach], and what ye fynde therin make that your bayte, for it is beste' – the first mention of the angling *autopsy* in English. In the 17th century, as Hills noted, 'The fly on the water was always used when it could be ascertained. You are recommended to look on the bushes, or to examine a trout's stomach. Chetham [*Angler's Vade Mecum*, 1681] tells you to use a microscope to examine the flies you find in it, which is wonderfully like to-day' (*History*, 71). Furher, the list of flies in the *Treatise*, and the list in Cotton, are quite clearly copied from nature. Today we would say that our ancestors attempted to 'match the hatch' (a phrase not recorded in OED). See also *rise¹*.

hatch² A flood-gate or sluice used to control the flow of water, especially on chalkstreams and in water-meadows. The word is first attested in this sense from 1531 ('kept...by the said hatches ...out from the...rivers or water-courses') and is still current, e.g. Sawyer, *Keeper of the Stream*, 8: 'I made a short cut to the hatches below so I could open them and let the drifting weeds pass on down the river'. The system of hatches in the watercourse (see also *carrier*) was, however, part of a much larger system of irrigation; in many parts of the country where this system was common until the early or mid-20th century, it has now been allowed to fall into disuse, to the detriment not only of the fishing but to the overall ecology:

> in much of the Upper Avon Valley, and other valleys too numerous to mention..., the irrigation system is a thing of the past, an almost forgotten art. The waterways of the meadow no longer produce trout and trout food and act as nurseries for the main river, for everywhere is a scene of neglect. The carriers...are now dried-up ditches – drains have been trodden flat by the countless hooves of cattle. Bridges, arches and

bunny holes have all collapsed, hatches lie rotting by their structures, or are suspended high and dry in their sockets, while the crumbling wingings of wood and brickwork of the hatchways now rest among the dried mud and other rubbish that once were aerated pools of water... (Sawyer, *Keeper of the Stream*, 18-19).

Also *hatch-pool*, a pool formed by a hatch, usually downstream of the hatch structure (see e.g. the illustration in Walker, *The Complete Fly-Fisher*, which refers to 'Typical lies of chalk-stream trout... above and in a hatch pool'), and with the local reputation of holding larger than average trout. It is not totally insignificant that the great G.E.M. Skues first 'discovered' the *nymph* and its angling potential while fishing 'a bend from which ran, through a hatch, a small current of water which fed a carrier', from which he took a trout on an unintentionally-sunk Dark Olive (see *Minor Tactics*, 1924 edn, 3ff.).

hawthorn fly   The scientific name is *Bibio marci*, probably from the fact that the fly hatches around St Mark's Day, 25 April (see Goddard, *Trout Flies of Stillwater*, 105). The hawthorn is a relatively important insect, occurring for a short season (perhaps a fortnight) on both rivers and stillwaters, where it is blown onto the surface, often in considerable numbers. The natural is easily identifiable by its apparent gangliness, caused by its long, trailing hind legs. There are many artificial dressings, and in fact the fly has been copied since at least the 17th century – Barker (*The Art of Angling*, 1651) was one of the first, if not the first, to give a specific dressing, (see Hills, *History*, 74), followed by Walton ('you may also make the *Hawthorn-flie*: which is all black, and not big, but very small, the smaller the better' – instructions which Walton clearly poached from Barker). Courtney Williams (*Dictionary*, 206) records that 'the natural insect was known to anglers some centuries ago and is mentioned both by Dame Juliana Berners... and Izaak Walton'; it is difficult, however, to see how any of the famous twelve flies of the *Treatise* can refer to the hawthorn (neither Hills nor that other great historian of fly-fishing, John McDonald, refer to any of the *Treatise*'s flies as copying the hawthorn), although the *Treatise* did refer to the 'hawthorn worm' (some kind of larva found in the vicinity of hawthorn bushes? – a good bait for barbel and grayling).

Today there are several dressings, fished both wet and dry, although the dry patterns are perhaps the most popular. Most incorporate a body of ostrich *herl*, a black cock's *hackle[1]*, pale *wings* of starling slips, with optional legs tied in trailing, these usually being formed by the black *quill* of turkey tail feathers (this was Roger Woolley's dressing), alternatively by two black pheasant tail fibres (Taff Price), see Courtney Williams, *Dictionary*, 205-7, and Roberts, *Illust. Dictionary*, 83. See also *black gnat; heather fly*.

head-and-tail   A *head-and-tail* rise is that movement made by a brown or rainbow trout taking creatures trapped in, or just under, the surface film, thus also 'head-and-tailing'. The phrase is not recorded in OED, but probably dates from early this century. This *rise form* is also very common on stillwaters, particularly when trout are taking *midge pupae*. The best description is that of Brian Clarke:

> If the boil is the most common form of rise... then the head-and-tail is the one that sets most adrenalin flowing. The head-and-tail rise always seems to happen in slow motion, frame by cinematic frame in a literal, head-to-tail, porpoising roll: first the top of the head breaks through the surface, then the shoulders, then the dorsal, and finally the tail. This form of rise is frequently seen several times in succession, from a fish travelling more or less in a straight line... [I]t seems most likely that the head-and-tailing fish is taking either spent or drowned fly on the surface, or midge pupae or other creatures (including floating snail) trapped in, or hanging from, the surface film (*The Pursuit of Stillwater Trout*, 114-15).

Also said of other fish, e.g. salmon or sea-trout, behaving in a similar fashion (although not feeding); a head-and-tailing salmon, in particular, may prove to be a taking fish.

heather fly   Related to the *hawthorn fly*, the heather fly, *Bibio pomonae* (also known as the 'Bloody Doctor' in Scotland) is common on upland lakes and lochs during the later part of the season (August-September), and is distinguished from its relative by having crimson colouring on the top part of each leg. The flies may be blown onto the water in some numbers, and the trout may rise avidly. Artificial patterns are similar to those for the hawthorn, see e.g. Goddard (*Trout Flies of Stillwater*, 106), who recommends that the black *hackle* (of the hawthorn) should be 'replaced with a reddish one' when the heather fly is being copied; Courtney Williams (*Dictionary*, 208) recommends a 'rich red coch-y-bondhu' hackle; Roberts (*Illust. Dictionary*, 84) gives a simple fly with black ostrich *herl* body and *coch-y-bondhu* hackle.

hen   Also *hen fish*, a female (cf. *cock*). A hen trout is distinguished from the male, especially in the breeding season, by the absence of a *kype*, and by a smaller head; these characteristics hold for rainbow trout, sea trout, and also salmon. Hen fish which are close to spawning are noticeably soft to the touch, and may release a trickle of eggs when landed. Most anglers properly return such fish to the water (see also *baggot; rawner*).

The hen fish plays a particularly active role in the *spawning* process, which in the case of brown trout, sea trout, and salmon occurs over pebbly or gravelly shallows during October-December, occasionally later in the case of salmon. A good description of spawning trout is given by Maclean (*Trout and Grayling*, 52):

> Brown trout are sexually highly competitive and aggressive and a number of males may...compete for one female. The spawning site or "redd" seems to be selected by the female, and she prepares the site...by moving the pebbles with side-ways thrusts of her tail, often turning on to her side for improved efficiency. When actual spawning is about to commence she opens out a trough in the gravel with her tail and then presses her abdomen down into the shallow valley..., shedding her eggs in amongst the fine stones. Meanwhile one or more males, already in attendance, excrete a cloud of milt from their testes via the genital pore...The male fish are...in close proximity to the female at the moment of shedding their milt, and can often be seen to quiver markedly and sometimes to arch their bodies around that of the female. During the few seconds of spawning both the cock and the hen fish tend to have bellies pressed towards the gravel and mouths widely open. Immediately after one spell of egg shedding, the female makes a few vigorous thrusts with her tail in order to cover the now fertilised eggs with gravel.

The behaviour of salmon is not markedly different, the female selecting the *redd*, depositing the eggs with the cock fish in attendance, and finally covering the redd with gravel again (to protect the eggs from flood or predation). One difference, however, lies in the fact that hen salmon survive spawning better than the males. Most cock salmon die after spawning: 'The cock fish of the salmon is more delicate than the hen. He is less able to withstand the rigours of spawning than is his mate. If you wander down the shores of any of our great salmon rivers in January or February you will see scores of dead fish stranded on the banks, and nine out of ten of them will be cock fish' (R.N. Stewart, *Salmon and Trout*, 84). With brown trout, on the other hand, cock fish appear to survive spawning relatively well, and afterwards retire to the quieter reaches of the river to 'mend' and to begin feeding again as the days grow longer.

herl A fibre or hair taken from a quill feather. In the sense 'fibre or filament', the word is apparently Germanic in origin, although the first English attestation is found relatively late (late 14th century, *Gawain and the Green Knight:* 'Ðe mane of þat mayn hors . . . Ay a herle of þe here'). In an angling sense, referring to flies constructed with *herl* bodies, the first attestation comes in the *Treatise*: 'The blacke louper: the body of blacke wull and lappyd abowte wyth the herle of ye pecock tayle, and the wynges of ye redde capon with a blewe heed'. The 'black louper' is an obscure fly. Hills noted that 'it corresponds to our Black Palmer or Coch-y-Bonddhu, but cannot be identified exactly' (*History*, 26). Since it is a palmered fly, it may just possibly be a crude copy of the *hawthorn fly*, although the reddish colour of the hackle argues against this. *Louper* meant 'leaper'; the fly was fished in May.

Herl is an important constituent part of many trout flies, especially peacock herl (as in the Black and Peacock Spider, John Storey and many more), ostrich herl (*Black Gnat* patterns, many sea trout and salmon flies, on which last patterns it is sometimes used as a 'butt'), and the herl of the pheasant tail (Pheasant Tail Nymph, some *sedges*, many *spinner* patterns). Its advantage is that herl is both easy to work, and very mobile in the water, giving a good impression of filamentous 'life'; its disadvantage is that herl breaks easily, especially when ravished by trouts' teeth. One solution here is to wind the herl over an underbody of varnished, tacky silk, which makes a slightly stronger body. It could be argued, however, that a disadvantage of this kind makes herl a victim of its own success; many anglers happily put up with this kind of problem.

herling A common term, especially in Scotland, for young *sea trout* or sea trout *grilse*, that is, those fish returning to the river for the first time after descending as *smolts*. *Herling* are therefore relatively small fish, weighing not more than a pound, and occasionally, when a run of herling is freshly come into a river or loch, they take the fly in a tediously suicidal fashion. Great restraint is then needed; in these circumstances – which typically occur in the later part of the season, herling being summer- and autumn-running fish – the angler should return most of the herling he catches, since some (although by no means all, see below) may be sexually mature, and will spawn if allowed to continue their journey upriver (and see *spawning*).

The OED states that the word is 'the name, on the Scottish shore of the Solway, for the fish *Salmo albus*', giving the first attestation in 1684 ('quie Dumfrisiensibus nostris *Hirling* dicitur'), and thereafter in the later 18th and (particularly) in the 19th century, a distribution consistent with the fact that the sea trout was only identified and fished for as a separate species relatively late in the history of British fly-fishing. The identification of the fish with 'S. albus' would today, however, be considered incorrect; herling are certainly the grilse of *S. trutta trutta*. The term is also more widely distributed than the OED implies, being used both in other parts of Scotland (where the word is invading the lexical territory formerly occupied by *finnock* and *whitling*) and in Ireland. As Fallon says (*Fly-fishing for Irish Trout*, 89): 'Many white trout may be very small indeed, often down to half a pound or so. These are the fish which having left the river in early spring as young fish, return again later in the year, usually in late August and early September; because they are immature fish, not many spawn. To the serious white trout angler, these herling are an inveterate nuisance, since they are really too small to keep...'

hook¹   The bent piece of metal used to catch fish, which are snared on the *bend* and *barb*. Typically, a fly hook consists of an *eye* of tapered metal bent to a small circle, to which the *leader* is knotted; a *shank* (the straight part of the hook, onto which the body of the fly is dressed); a bend (the curve of the hook); a barb; and a *point*. The distance between the barbed point, and the shank, is known as the *gape*: wide-gape hooks are effective, and are used specifically on some types of trout fly (such as leaded *shrimp* patterns). The strongest hooks have *forged bends*, i.e. the metal is flattened in section, not circular; these hooks are particularly suitable for larger trout, sea trout and salmon (although salmon hooks are a special case, and will be dealt with below).

Hooks are available as *singles* (i.e. just one single hook; the vast majority of flies for trout and grayling are dressed on single irons), *doubles* (or 'wee doubles' in Scotland; double irons are used on some stillwater trout flies – especially flies fished on the *point* of the leader – and on some sea trout patterns), and *trebles* (treble hooks, especially 'outpoint trebles', are favoured for some types of salmon and sea trout fly, where the fly is dressed directly onto the shank; trebles are also used on *tube flies* for salmon, and also on certain *dapping* flies).

The word is native, and derives from OE *hōc*, first attested in Alfred's translation of Bede's *Ecclesiastical History* (*c*.900): 'thā worhton him hōcas...' – then they made hooks for him/themselves. The two other OE references, one *c*.950 from the *Lindisfarne Gospels*, another in 1000 ('Ic eom...swā swā fisc on hōce' – I am like a fish on a hook), suggest not hooks fished on rod and line, but hooks attached to set lines.

Detailed instructions are given in the *Treatise* on how to make your own hooks (the author calls this 'the moost subtyll and hardyste crafte in makynge of your harnays [tackle]'), and some illustrations are also given. For small fish, hooks were made of the smallest square steel needles, heated until they were red hot, allowed to cool, and then filed and barbed with a knife; thereafter the needle was put into the fire again ('elles he well breke in the bendyng'), and subsequently bent to shape. For larger fish, continued the author, use thicker needles – embroiderers' needles, or tailors' or shoemakers' needles especially ('the best for grete fysshe'). The author made a special point of checking that the needles were well-tempered: they should 'bende atte the poynt when they ben assayed [tried, tested], for elles they ben no good'. This is still sound advice; hooks should be tested in the fly-tying vice by being twanged briefly, which sorts out soft-tempered or brittle hooks.

According to Hills (*History*, 41), hooks could be commercially bought by the early 17th century, but some anglers preferred to make their own: William Lawson's notes to the second section of Dennys' poem, *Secrets of Angling*, recommended hooks made from Spanish and Milan needles, bent so as to form 'a little compasse [gape]', since a hook is weak if it has too large a 'compas'. Lawson's point about the bend is well-taken: today there are variety of types of bend, the plain *round bend*, the *crystal bend*, and the *limerick bend* (known since the 19th century, and particularly good for *nymphs* and *wet flies*) are representative. Earlier this century, 'square-bend' hooks (if this is not a contradiction in terms) were sometimes favoured for underwater trout flies (see *sneck*).

The eyed hook, invented in the East, had been used for centuries (see *eye*), but in Britain, at least, it was not rediscovered until the 19th century: hooks up until that time were attached directly to the line by whipping (in the 19th century, and even into this present one, hooks could be 'tied to gut').

Recently there has been some controversy about how sharp the point of the hook should be (and see *hook stone* below). Some authorities used to claim that a hook should be filed until the point, drawn across a finger-nail, made a thin score-line. In the 1980s Arthur Oglesby and Hugh Falkus, eminent opinions both, have claimed that hooks can be made too sharp; the theory is to the effect that a highly-sharpened (and long) point penetrates gristle only so far, and that this precarious hold will give when a fish jumps. Falkus goes so far as to say that a hook stone 'should be used to take some of the sharpness off, not put it on' (*Sea Trout Fishing*, 115). The ideal is therefore a hook with a short, strong, and not too sharp point.

During the 1980s (in Britain, although earlier in America) there has been a general recognition that *barbless hooks* are useful when trout are to be returned to the water, particularly so when small trout take the fly intended for their larger fellows (see also *barb*). In this circumstance, the trout is played to the bank (or the side of the boat), and the left hand then run down the leader until it can grasp the shank of the barbless hook; a slight twist, and the fish is free. This procedure avoids handling the fish, or damaging it by inadvertent removal of the protective slime in which every fish is covered. Barbless hooks may be bought commercially, but a good alternative is to flatten the barb of the hook with a small pair of pliers, leaving merely a hump of metal; these barbless (or 'de-barbed') hooks are very easy to remove from a fish's mouth.

Hook sizes, after a period of confusion, have now been standardised on the 'Old Scale', on which hook sizes run from size 22 (very tiny indeed, although still smaller hooks are available) to 2 (a big single salmon iron), larger hooks being affixed with '/0', thus 2/0, 4/0 etc. (again, very large salmon hooks). The most useful range of hook sizes for trout are perhaps sizes 10 (larger nymphs, *shrimps* etc.) through the middle-ranging 12s and 14s (medium-sized insects, *duns*, *pupae* etc.) to 16s (midge pupae, small duns). Up-eyed hooks are generally used for dry flies, down-eyed for wet. *Grayling* flies are tied small (the fish has a relatively small mouth), sizes 14 to 18 being most useful. Sea trout flies are tied on hook sizes 4 (large single flies, such as Falkus's Medicine) up to 10 and, occasionally, 12; as noted above, outpoint *trebles* (sizes 12 and 14) are also popular sea trout hooks, and give a good hold. Salmon flies may also be tied on treble hooks (the 'Esmond Drury' hooks are a reliable brand) as well as single irons (sizes 4/0, the largest, down to size 10, used during the low-water conditions of summer). Tube flies (for salmon, also, less frequently, for sea trout) are backed by a treble, the size to match the overall length (and weight) of the fly. See also *tandem; hook-hold*.

hook² A verb, derived from the noun, used as a verb since the 17th century. See *hook¹* above.

hook-hold The purchase of a hook inside a fish's mouth. The best hook-holds are generally in the fish's *maxillary* (the '*scissors*'), or around the gristle of the lower jaw. Elsewhere, because of poor penetration, or because of torn flesh, or both, the hook can work loose, or tear out, during the *play*.

Of all the game fish, the *grayling* has the reputation for being the most tender-mouthed. Walton started this hare: The grayling 'has so tender a mouth,' he wrote, 'that he is oftener lost after an Angler has hooked him, than any other fish' (*Angler*, 126). Walton in this case is wrong; as Roberts (*The Grayling Angler*, 177) puts it, 'In reality the lip of the grayling is extremely tough and leathery'. Perhaps Walton missed so many grayling because his hooks were too big? (His more accurate contemporary and 'adopted son', Cotton, remarked on 'the littleness of that Fishes mouth', in which he was right, as usual.)

hook stone A carborundum stone used to sharpen hooks (but see *hook[1]* above). To my knowledge, the first mention of the use of a hook stone in angling literature comes in Robert Venables' *The Experienc'd Angler* (1662). Running through the tackle an 'experienc'd' angler required, Venables instructed, 'Have . . . a little whetstone about two inches long, and one quarter square; it's much better to sharpen your hooks than a file, which either will not touch a well-tempered hook, or leave it rough but not sharp' (facsimile, 7). This is typically good advice; many anglers carry a hook stone today.

horse fly This nuisance the OED defines as 'one of the various [insects] troublesome to horses, as the horse-tick (family *Hippoboscidae*), the breeze or gadfly *(Tabanidae)*, the bot-fly *(Oestridae)* . . .'. These creatures are also troublesome to anglers, being identical to those scourges of the loch, the *clegs*. If anyone needs to be shown why these vile pests should be smacked dead at once (preferably before they land on exposed flesh), they should study a close-up film of these insects' mouth-parts, which are equipped with serrated edges for better insertion of the blood-sucking probe (the 'sting'). Wycliffe was right: he translated (1382) the *crabrones* of the Latin Vulgate as 'horse fleeʒis' (Joshua XXIV, 12: 'I sa[n]te before ʒou horse fleeʒis'). The later Authorised Version translates as 'And I sent the hornet before you, which drave them out from before you, even the two kings of the Amorites . . .'. Wycliffe's is the first recorded use of the term in English. Horse flies, or hornets? The angler is unfortunate; both are what the *Treatise* would have called 'Impediments'.

houting *Coregonus oxyrinchus*, a form of *whitefish*, very rarely caught with the fly in this country, but classed as one of the game fishes because of the presence of the *adipose fin*.

The whitefishes (see also *pollan*, *powan* etc.) are in an analogous situation to that of the *charr*: despite the fact that the *charr*(s) and the whitefish(es) became landlocked after the last Ice Age, there still exist migratory forms of the two species. The *houting*, at least in Britain (see below), can be considered a migratory form of whitefish.

Very little is known about it. It is thought that the distribution of the fish is confined to 'Northern Europe and Northern Asia.

Also a migratory form along the North Sea coast, from which it wanders up the rivers. Also found in Alpine and Swedish lakes.' But the fish is seldom seen in Britain, and still more rarely caught. It would seem plausible that, like the migratory charr, the houting does not ascend far up the river, running into, and spawning in, the lower reaches during the autumn. It is a small fish: Muus notes that its maximum size is 50 cm, although it is thought that British houting are in general much smaller, making them vulnerable to predation both in the sea and in the river. Like the rest of the whitefishes, the houting is reported to feed on plankton and small crustaceans.

The fish may be identified by its elongated, downward-turning snout, the adipose fin, and by the 35-44 gill-rakers behind the first gill arch.

hypolimnion   The cold, barren water in the deeps of a stratified lake. See *epilimnion; thermocline*.

I **mago** From L. *imago*, 'image'. The adult form of an insect, i.e. of an *ephemeropteran*. The *imago* is colloquially known as the *spinner*: 'The process of moulting...consists in the shedding of the outer skin which covers all portions of the dun, the fly then emerging as an imago or spinner. The spinners are the adult flies, and the Ephemeroptera are the only Order of insects in which moulting occurs after the winged form has been assumed. It is only as spinners that the flies are able to breed' (Harris, *Angler's Entomology*, 19). See also *quill*.

induced take A term from fishing the artificial nymph, popularised by Frank Sawyer and Oliver Kite – Kite wrote, for example, that 'a fish may take the artificial nymph voluntarily, in which case we call it a *voluntary take*, or it may be induced to take by calculated action on the part of the nymph fisherman, in which case it is known as an *induced take*' (his italics; in Mansfield, *Trout Fishing*, 1974, 61).

The essence of the *induced take* is that the nymph is cast upstream of the feeding fish, and allowed to sink and drift inertly until it is just in front of the fish's eyes. At that precise moment, the rod is quietly raised, causing the nymph to rise in the water. In theory, at least, the trout is attracted by such life-like movement, and is induced (or seduced) into a firm take. See *nymph fishing*.

Keeper ring   Also known as a *fly-ring*, this is a small ring whipped to the fly rod, invariably just above the rod handle, into which the fly is hitched for convenience, primarily so that the fly does not dangle and/or become taffled in bankside herbage etc.

There are good and bad designs of this accessory. The worst is the tiny floppy ring fitted to many makers' rods. A large, rigid ring is better. Falkus (*Sea Trout Fishing*, 128) comments that there is – or was – a certain kind of brassière that contained a ring just right for this purpose.

kelt   Etymology unknown, but perhaps from ON (?); the word is recorded from the 14th century (1340 *Durham Rolls*: 'In playces et [ate?] kelts emp. 6s.'). Any game fishes, but especially the salmon, which have just completed *spawning*, and are consequently in poor condition, may be termed *kelts*. Kelts are usually recognisable by their overall lean appearance, the fact that the head looks particularly big in relation to the body, their relative softness to the touch, and their sluggish resistance to the rod; these characteristics are shared by both salmon and trout. In the case of salmon, gill maggots may also be present.

Salmon, unlike brown trout, return to the sea to feed. Some confusion may arise as to which salmon are truly kelted owing to the fact that certain fish 'mend' quickly after spawning. Some fish, for example (rather like the *smolts* running to sea for the first time), may don a silvery coat on their sea-ward river journey, and may even be relatively firm to the touch. These are referred to as '(well-) mended kelts'; they should be returned carefully to the river.

Kelts are troublesome during the early months of the season (typically, January through to March), although odd specimens may be taken later. On occasion, they seize both fly and bait avidly, since the feeding instinct, which is suppressed during the fishes' spawning run, is triggered again once spawning is complete.

Curiously, most salmon kelts are hen fish (see *cock*; *hen*). This fact is recorded by e.g. Muus and Dahlstrom:

> After spawning, the spent salmon, which are known as kelts, are...exhausted – they may have lost up to 40% of their body weight since they left the sea. Many, especially the males, die

after spawning, or are infested with fungus...or in their feeble
state are stranded. Others winter in deep holes or drift towards
the sea. The spawning colouration is gradually replaced by
silvery colours, and the kype disappears. Few spawn a second
time – in some rivers only 4-6% of the spawning fish are mended
kelts...Those kelts that survive recover quickly in the sea...
(*Freshwater Fish*, 54).

The behaviour of *sea trout* kelts is not radically different to that
of salmon, although it may be that sea trout, after spawning,
begin to feed in freshwater more systematically than their larger
relatives. As Stuart (*Book of the Sea Trout*, 8) put it:

> the fact that sea trout feed in fresh water when nominally
> in the kelt condition, makes the kelt sea-trout quite different
> in all respects from the kelt salmon. A sea-trout that has
> spawned, but is still in a river or lake, is in strict law, and
> perhaps also in strict science, a kelt, and will not lose that
> character in either sense until it has sojourned in the sea or
> estuary. But such sea-trout, before they have reached the sea
> or estuary, may recover their full condition and be, except in
> name, as good fish from the edible point of view, from the
> point of view of symmetry and, almost, if not quite, of colour-
> ing, as the sea-trout that has been in the sea; while their sport-
> giving qualities compare favourably with those of fish that are
> just up from the sea, even if they never show quite the same
> sea-born strength, stamina, and wonderful activity as when
> fresh-run.

On the other hand, my experience of sea trout kelts suggests that
they are altogether a poorer fish; nor is it easy to believe that the
type of river favoured by sea trout (typically, upland, relatively
acidic streams) could yield sufficient food to support hundreds,
if not thousands, of kelted sea trout on their way to the sea.
Perhaps the quote from Stuart suggests that our Edwardian
forebears took a more liberal view of the matter (and perhaps, a
more liberal view of what constitutes 'sport'), regarding kelted
sea trout as legitimate fish. It is doubtful whether any fly-fisherman today could or should take a similar stance. See also *kipper;
kype*.

kipper Another term relating to the salmon, this is a local (Tweedside) name which refers to what seems to be a very late-running
fish, an 'autumn' runner which has delayed its entry into the river
until the early spring. In the following passage about the identification of *kelts*, Currie & McLaren mention the *kipper*:

> real perplexity...can...result from landing a Tweed "kip-
> per". The fish may be of twelve pounds, and silvery and clean,

although it may have a distinctly larger head than the springer. There may be a bit of a kype showing. It is not emaciated, may have no gill-parasites, and in some cases may even have sea-lice on its flanks, indicating that the fish has recently run up from salt water. But the fish is heavy with spawn. It is clearly making a spawning run, and given a month or so might well have spawned and become a kelt. But as an unbroken fish, fresh from the sea when caught, it has not spawned. Some anglers return these fish as a matter of course; others kill them, for they are fresh, admirable salmon. We cannot debate the finer legal points of this situation; we merely note that, on the scale of freshness, this anomalous fish is a common catch in early spring. (*The Fishing Waters of Scotland*, 19-20)

The term is etymologically noteworthy. There may be some connection between the terms *kipper* (perhaps 'kype + er'?) and *kype*, but this is difficult to prove – although Walton, for example, wrote that if salmon are prevented from returning to the sea after spawning, then 'those so left behind, by degrees grow *sick*, and *lean*, and *unseasonable*, and *kipper*; that is to say, have bony gristles grow out of their lower chaps' (*Angler*, 127). More certain it is that the word's first attestation in English dates from 1376; as an incidental point, the female equivalent is – or used to be – *shedder*, as evidenced by this quote from 1848: 'the male fish is sometimes also called a kipper, and the female a shedder or baggit'. See also *baggot*.

knots Knots for joining nylon are legion, as are knots for joining nylon to the *eye* of a *hook*, but perhaps the most useful knots are the following:

(a) for joining nylon to nylon, and/or for forming *droppers*: the *Blood Knot*, the (double) *Grinner Knot*, and the (four-turn) *Water Knot*. The Blood Knot was used for joining strands of gut before the knot was adapted to nylon; Scott & Taverner (*Salmon Fishing*, 63) claim that the Blood Knot was first described in print by Chaytor (*Letters to a Salmon Fisher's Sons*, 1919). It is a secure knot, particularly for heavier gauges of nylon (say, 8lb. b.s. and upwards).

The Grinner Knot (also in this use called the *Double Grinner*) was popularised during the 1960s and 1970s by Richard Walker. It is similar to the Blood Knot (also to the old Fisherman's Knot), but even stronger, since the nylon is whipped doubly over the standing part of the knot (see illus.). As with the Blood Knot, one strand of the finished knot may be left long to form a dropper (6″ is a standard length, and one which allows for several subsequent changes of fly before the knot has to be re-tied).

A. For joining hook to leader

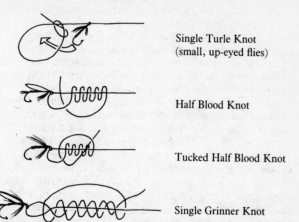

Single Turle Knot
(small, up-eyed flies)

Half Blood Knot

Tucked Half Blood Knot

Single Grinner Knot

Each of these knots should be moistened with saliva before tightening.

B. For joining nylon to nylon

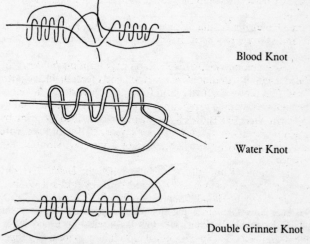

Blood Knot

Water Knot

Double Grinner Knot

Knots should be moistened with saliva, then slowly drawn tight. Use point-end of knot strands to form droppers.

A. For joining fly-line to leader and/or backing

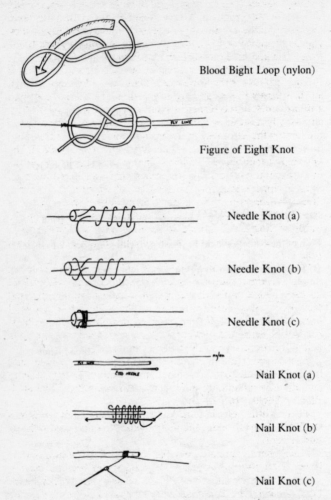

Blood Bight Loop (nylon)

Figure of Eight Knot

Needle Knot (a)

Needle Knot (b)

Needle Knot (c)

Nail Knot (a)

Nail Knot (b)

Nail Knot (c)

This knot is suitable for joining monofilament backing to fly-line; also suitable for braided backing, although the finished knot tends to be bulky.

Both Needle Knot and Nail Knot may be dabbed with 'Superglue' for added security.

The Water Knot is fly-fishing's oldest knot, dating from the *Treatise*: 'When ye have as many of the lynkys as ye suppose wol suffyse for the length of a lyne: thenne must ye knytte them togyder with a water knotte or elles a duchys knotte. And when your knotte is knytte, kytte of ye voyde short endes a straw brede f[rom] the knotte. Thus shal ye make youre lynes fayr and fyne, and also ryght sure for ony manere fysshe'. Falkus (*Sea Trout Fishing*, 107) notes that the *Treatise* knot was tied with two turns, all that horsehair required. Nylon, a slippier material, required a minimum of three turns (in small gauges of nylon, e.g. 2lb), and usually, four or even five turns. One particular advantage of the knot is that it is easy to tie, even in the dark. It is less sure, however, than the Grinner, especially when one strand of the knot is left long for the *dropper*. The usual advice is to use the upward-pointing strand (i.e. the strand pointing towards the rod) as the dropper, since this has the effect of strutting the fly from the main *leader*, but this tactic is dangerous and may lead to smashes (see *smash take*). It seems much better to use the downward-pointing strand (the strand pointing to the tail fly) as a dropper. (See also 'Water-knot warning', Jon Beer, *T&S* Letters, June 1989).

(b) for joining nylon to an eyed hook: the Turle Knot, the (Single) Grinner, and the Tucked Half-Blood Knot. The Turle has been in use for decades, and, in its 'single' form, may be used to tie down- or up-eyed trout flies to the leader; in its 'double' form, the knot is useful for tying on down-eyed salmon flies, particularly since the turns of the knot are lapped over the hook behind the eye, causing the fly to swim on an even keel.

There seems little to choose between the Single Grinner and the Tucked Half-Blood; both are 'sure for any manner of fish', and either is suitable for both trout and salmon flies. The Half-Blood is slightly easier to tie.

There is little point in tying knots carelessly or clumsily. Knots should be neatly formed, and moistened (with saliva) before being pulled tight.

Finally here, there are knots for joining either *backing*, or the leader (butt), to the main line. Monofilament backing may be joined to the line by the Needle Knot, while braided backing may be so joined by the Nail Knot; both knots are made totally secure by completing the finished knot with a dab or two of 'Superglue'. The leader butt may be joined to the tip of the fly line by a Needle Knot, which has the advantage of being very slim, and so passing easily through the tip ring of the rod when required (e.g. as in landing a fish). Alternatively, but more bulkily, there is the old-

fashioned method of joining the leader to the line: a Blood-bight
Loop is formed in the leader butt, and is attached to the line tip
by a Figure-of-Eight Knot (see illus.).

kype A large cartilaginous 'hook' which develops on the lower
jaw of a male salmon, sea trout, or brown trout as the time for
spawning approaches. The precise function of the kype, however,
remains a mystery:

> Why do the cock fish of all the salmonidae grow kypes? This
> particular protuberance at the point of the lower jaw seems to
> serve no useful purpose. When leaving the sea the cock salmon
> has only a modified kype, but it develops in fresh water and
> by spawning time it is a formidable growth. When fully grown
> it must be something of a nuisance to its owner, because it
> prevents him from being able to close his mouth and in a few
> cases it makes a hole right through his upper mandible.
>
> Since the kype is useless as a weapon or tool, why is it there?
> The only plausible suggestion is that it is a decoration and
> grown to please the hen fish. To some extent the change in
> colour, from silver to brownish red, that salmon undergo while
> in the river is, I think, a change made for the same purpose.
> Neither adornment appears attractive to us, but perhaps the
> hen fish like it. (R.N. Stewart, *Salmon and Trout*, 83-4)

Notwithstanding Stewart's remarks, the suggestion has been
made that the kype is used as a weapon 'when two or more [males]
fight for the same female' (OED; see *kipper*); Henry Williamson
(*Salar the Salmon*, 359ff.) describes the cock fish fighting on the
redds, gripping each other, their huge kyped jaws locked across
the waists of rivals' tails. That the kype is in fact a weapon remains
a possibility, as the OED claims.

The origin of the word is uncertain, perhaps deriving from a
Germanic base form *kip* (cf. German *kippe*) meaning 'anything
that is beaked'. Whether from *kipper* or *kip*, the word dates from
the early medieval period.

L **anding net** A circular- or triangular-headed net used for landing fish, usually attached by a screw-thread fitting to a wooden, or tubular metal handle. For trout fishing, meshes of the net are increasingly made of knotless material (knotless-mesh nets are compulsory in some part of the country), the theory being that this kind of mesh does less damage to those fish the angler wishes to return, i.e. less damage to the protective mucous with which the fish are covered. Nets for salmon fishing are, however, still typically constructed of knotted mesh (salmon are less frequently returned alive to the water than trout).

Some fishermen use the landing net handle as a makeshift *wading staff*, weighting the bottom end of the handle with e.g. lead, and fixing the extreme tip with a rubber button for quietness – metal bumping on stones or gravel causes underwater noise which may frighten fish (see *lateral line*). These dual-purpose nets are usually carried over the angler's back on a sling.

Although the landing net was known in Europe from at least the 3rd century AD (as a floor mosaic from the Nile Villa – now in Tripoli Museum – testifies; see Trench, *Hist. Angling* 20-1), it is first mentioned in English in John Dennys' *Secrets of Angling* (1613). Venables, too, instructs his reader to 'Have a small pole . . . to which must be fastened a small net, to land great fish . . .' (*The Experienced Angler*, 1662). The triangular-headed net, Hills noted, was first illustrated in Frère François Fortin's *Ruses Innocentes* (1660; Hills, *History*, 79).

As Skues pointed out, there is more to the landing net than merely landing fish; it can also be used, in Skues' words and with his fine discrimination, 'to assist in the capture of fish' (*Minor Tactics*, 109): the handle, for example, can be used to prod a weed-bed into which a hooked trout has run; the mesh, offered to a fish heading determinedly for a snag, a weed bed, or worse, can frighten the fish away from the obstruction; and so on (see 'Of the Use of the Landing-net' in *Minor Tactics*, 109-14).

Large Dark Olive Abbr. LDO; this is one of the most important flies of the river fisher's early season (April). See *bloa; dun; ephemeroptera; olive; quill; spinner* etc.

larva A term for the larval stage of an insect (the stage between egg and *pupa*), esp. the *caddis* and the various species of *midge*. Our term derives from an earlier meaning of *larva*, that of 'ghost,

115

disembodied spirit, mask' (OED); the adult fly or perfect insect is not recognisable in the larval 'mask'. The word is first attested in English during the 17th century, although the first attested use of the term in an unambiguously scientific sense dates from 1768 and Gilbert White's *Natural History of Selborne* ('the larvae of insects are full of eggs').

Both caddis larvae and midge larvae are of considerable importance to the trout fisherman. Brown and rainbow trout may feed heavily on caddis larvae in certain circumstances (particularly during the early part of the season, when other fly-life is not plentiful; see e.g. Fraser, *Mastering the Nymph*, 65), and they may be tempted with the relevant artificial pattern (a heavily-leaded Hare's Ear seems adequate, although there are more specific patterns, such as the well-known Stick Fly etc.). The caddis, or 'cod-bait', has always been recognised as being of signal importance (see e.g. Cotton's comments under *caddis*).

Midge larvae, or *bloodworms*, are of significance to stillwater trout fishermen, since trout sometimes feed avidly on them, especially where wind- and wave-action disturbs the silt in which these larvae make their burrows. As Fraser puts it, the blood worm must emerge from its burrow, or be washed out, 'sufficiently often for [the trout] to know all about it; and in its bright, almost fluorescent red form, it must be pretty distinctive. Certainly I regularly spoon bloodworm from trout' (*Mastering the Nymph*, 54).

Very occasionally, one finds the term *larva* used erroneously for 'nymph' or 'pupa'. Halford (of all people) was guilty of this misuse, writing of a cold May day on the Test in 1885:

It was a day on which a fresh breeze from the north-west was blowing; and so cold was it that, to an idler on the river-bank, it was a difficult matter to keep his hands warm; and yet the number of flies hatching was, even to one accustomed to the plentiful supply on chalk streams, something astonishing. The trout seemed to have appetites which could not be appeased, rushing about in all directions, making heavy bulges under water as they took the larvae rising from the bed of the river, or here and there just breaking the surface as they seized the fly at the very instant of its casting off the envelope in which it has passed pupa state . . . (*Dry Fly Fishing*, 1889; cited in Gingrich, 232-3).

Given the potential for ambiguity, it seems best to keep the terms *larva*, *nymph*, and *pupa* separate.

lateral line   From L. *lateralis*, 'side'. The word is first attested in 1600 (Ben Jonson wrote of 'a lateral view'), although the word is not used specifically in an angling or fish-related sense until later (1870 and Rolleston's *Animal Life*, which spoke of 'The sensory organs developed in Fish, in connection with the "lateral line"' – the quotes are perhaps indicative of the phrase's novelty at this date).

A fish actually possesses two *lateral lines*, one on each side of its body; these lines, which are formed by canals carrying neuromasts, detect underwater sound vibrations and carry these messages or danger-signals to the brain via nerve fibres. Effectively the lateral line functions as a fish's sense of 'hearing', although fish also possess inner ears, which are sensitive to more distant sounds (see Sosin & Clark, *Through the Fish's Eye*, 74).

The significance of the fish's lateral line to the angler is that the sensitivity of the fish's subaqueous hearing compels a careful approach. Although normal talking, reel-noises and rod-swishings may be undetectable by fish, wader-studs grinding on stones, or on the clinkers of a boat, will certainly be heard, and alarm fish in the vicinity. As Maclean puts it, 'both trout and grayling are very skilled at detecting vibration [via the lateral line] so a stealthy approach is vital' (*Trout and Grayling*, 31). Needless to say, that remark is also pertinent to the salmon and to that wariest of fish, the sea trout.

lead core line   Also simply *lead core*, this is a kind of *fly line*, usually of a level-tapered construction, but also used as a *shooting head*, employed specifically to fish deep water *lies[1]* inaccessible to the usual fly fishing techniques. Such lines were developed during the 1970s, and found some favour with stillwater fishermen, and also some salmon fishermen (although in this last capacity lead cored lines can become poaching accessories used, for example, in stroke-hauling, see *foul hooking*). Lead cored lines were particularly useful for *boat fishing* at anchor on the larger stillwaters ('fishing on the lead').

Given the recent and current improvements in fly-line design, lead cored lines seem to have been rather less used of late, being superseded by lines of a more conventional construction ('ultra-fast sinking lines' or variants of these). Perhaps this is all to the good; lead cored lines were the devil to cast. See also *cast[2]*.

leader   Originally an Americanism, the *leader* is synonymous with the British angler's *cast[1]*, although 'leader' is perhaps the preferable term since it is less ambiguous.

legs   The legs of insects (especially the adults, as in the *spinners* and *sedges*) are quite noticeable, and some anglers believe that the *hackle[1]* (on a *dry* or *wet fly*) gives a stylised impression of legs, although Kingsmill Moore made a good case for the hackle representing the bedraggled gauziness of the *wings* of a drowned *dun* ('In a back eddy I found what I was looking for, several drowned duns, their bruised limp wings very like the soft hackles of the North Country dressing', *A Man May Fish*, 45).

There are some insects whose legs are unmistakable, being so prominent as to perhaps act as 'trigger features' to a potentially-taking fish; these are the *Hawthorn fly* and the *Daddy-long-legs*. Representation of the legs of these insects is usually effected by tying in knotted fibres of *herl* (natural or dyed pheasant tail fibres are most useful), although knotting each individual strand (sometimes twice) is a tedious affair.

lie[1] Every fly-fisherman likes to come across 'a good lie' once in a while, that is, a place which is a sure haunt of, and a sure cast for, a fish. In this sense ('the place where an animal, etc., is accustomed to lie' OED) the word was first attested in 1869, and Blackmore's *Lorna Doone* ('There were very fine loaches here, having more lie and harbourage than in the rough...stream'), although the word is related both to *lie* in the sense 'manner of lying', and *lie* as in the lie of the ball (e.g. golf), as well as to the much older OE verb *licgan*, 'to lie'.

Part of the art of fishing for trout in flowing water is to understand where fish will lie – and where they will not. After some (relatively fishless) practice, it becomes easier to tell the good lies – failure is a great teacher. The cheeks of streams, hollowed-out banks, scoops of water between weed-beds, bridge pools (every river should have a Bridge Pool, home of uncatchable monsters), those purling flats where fish will rise to Blue-winged *Olives* during the long midsummer evenings, the quiet water by the rushes where fish will rise to a well-cast *sedge*...all these, and more, are likely places, taking less time to cast over than to list.

On stillwaters, although there is no current (or appears to be no current) to help the prospective fisher orientate himself towards the trout, one looks for underwater banks, roads, ditches, inflowing and outflowing streams, snags, shallows where fish will cruise at dusk...all these places, similarly, have a kind of eloquence and hold a kind of hope.

Finding salmon and sea trout lies is a more complicated business, and on unfamiliar waters it pays to invest in the advice of a *gillie*. On the other hand, there are certain places which are surer than others: for sea trout in rivers, pool-tails at dusk are the classic (and usually the most productive) casts, those glides where the sea trout make quietly splashing circles during their late-evening movement in the pool. For salmon, the head of a

pool is always a likely cast, as are the cheeks of streams, those
slacks in the current where salmon (and sea trout, too) will rest
for minutes, or hours, or days, or even weeks during their upriver
spawning run (thus, 'a resting lie'). But it is almost impossible to
generalise here; the best way to learn where fish will lie, and
where they will not, is to fish, and fish persistently, and fail a
little; and watch; and learn.

lie² Fishermen are supposed by the less fortunate to be either
congenital or pathological liars (as Byron put it, 'No angler can
be a good man'), and the Fisherman's Lie has passed into the
popular mythology of fishing in clichéd phrases such as 'It was
thi-i-is big . . . really' or 'the one (or two, or three) that got away'.
The Fisherman's Lie has even passed into some typically atro-
cious, although happily anonymous, verse: 'God grant that I may
catch a fish / So large that even I / When talking of it afterwards /
May have no need to lie'. Arthur Ransome (*Rod and Line*, 1980,
114) wrote that 'For at least 275 years the honesty of fishermen
has been something questionable. It should be noted that Izaak
Walton, whose book was published in 1653, spoke not of "anglers
and" but of "anglers *or* very honest men"' (Ransome's emphasis).
The idea that anglers are liars has, then, a long and a literary, if
a faintly disreputable history.

But what is the truth about the Fisherman's Lie? Ransome,
with typical accuracy, casts to, hooks, lands and kills the Fisherman's Lie, and then inspects his catch:

> You will find that the more noted liars among your fishing
> aquaintance are men with a marked lack of nimbleness of mind,
> no splitters of hairs, the sort of men who apply particular names
> in a general sense, who call, for example, everyone a Bolshevik
> who does not vote for the Conservative party. They are not
> romancers but simply dull fellows and probably bad fishermen.
> They are likely even to lie to themselves in their own fishing
> diaries . . .

Ransome concluded this splendid passage as follows: 'Good
fishermen know that in talking about fishing nothing is interesting
except the truth' (*Rod and Line*, 115).

Still, the popular mythology holds, and it is possible (although
not recorded in the OED) that the Fisherman's Lie has passed
more subtly into the common currency in phrases like 'he told a
whopper', or even 'a fishy story'.

Limerick Also *Limerick-bend hook*; a kind of *hook¹* used in fly-
fishing.

The first proprietary hooks for fishing seem to have been made
during the 17th century; Walton, for example, recommended

Charles Kirby (of Harp Alley, Shoe Lane, London) as 'the most exact and best Hook-maker this nation affords' (and see Hurum, 41). As Hurum suggests,

It is likely that considerable numbers of hook-makers moved away from London after the catastrophic fire in 1666. What became of Charles Kirby, no one seems to know. Either the plague or the fire might have killed him. One thing is certain however – that the making of hooks was decentralized, a fact that is apparent from the many varieties of hooks that still bear British place names. Leading centres were Dublin and Limerick ...Carlisle and Kendal...(*A History of the Fish Hook*, 51-2).

Limerick therefore becomes a centre for hook-making during the 18th century. The Limerick-bend hook there developed had a 'very gentle curve at [the] weak point [the further end of the shank], and a sharper bend immediately behind the barb. In the best Limerick hooks the point and barb were angled as in the Kirby bend, but the point was not offset' (Trench, *Hist. Angling*, 283). Because of their relative strength, then, Limerick hooks became popular, and remain so today. Ronalds, for example, noted that the 'Limerick is...a good hook for large flies' (*An Angler's Entomology* [1836], 31) – although Bainbridge, writing in 1816, had compared the Limerick and Kirby forms of hook. Towards the end of the 19th century, Francis noted that the 'Limerick at its best was a good hook for salmon and large trout-flies' (Trench, *Hist. Angling*, 283). But it did have defects, chief of which was that the body dressing had perforce to be rather short, having to end where the shank started to curve gently down into the bend. To correct this, the *sneck bend* hook was developed.

limit   Also *limit bag*; the specified total of fish an angler is able to catch and/or kill according to the rules of the water he is fishing. The term, although elderly (bag-limits have been in force since the 19th century at least) seems to gain ground during the 1960s, with the opening of public reservoirs for fly-fishing: clearly, if a stillwater is to be run as a commercially viable fishery it is necessary that the stock of trout it contains is sensibly exploited. Unfortunately, the taking of a limit bag may become something of a fetish with the more gullible and greedy of the angling fraternity, so that 'Oh yes, I took my limit by lunchtime' becomes a phrase redolent of (an entirely spurious) skill and success. In acute cases, these fishermen suffer from a derivative *limititis*, a disease which entails the unscrupulous pursuit of a limit bag by any fair (or, alas, unfair) means. This last term is more recent, dating as far as I am aware from 1982: '"Limititis" is symptomised by a constant pre-occupation with reaching for that "Holy Grail" – the maximum number of fish allowed by the rules' (Peter Lapsley, *T&S*, April 1982, 51).

Disquiet about limit bags has run deep of late:
Fishing is a wonderful thing, and fly fishing is an arm of the sport that has a long and proud tradition. It is continually developing and expanding its popularity, as more and more participants discover its pleasures. But if fisheries are to survive in their current form, offering sport to all people with a variety of bank balances, then we need less of a preoccupation with limit bags, and "making fishing pay". Rather, we should encourage a return to traditional values, albeit with the benefit of modern technology' (Chris Ogborne, *T&S*, December 1984, 15).

line   See *cast¹; fly line; nylon monofilament* etc.

lined   Another rueful term from the angling lexicon. Say a fish is rising ten yards upstream, and the intention is to offer it the appropriate *dry fly*. The angler should cast so that the fish sees only the fly, and perhaps the extreme end of the *leader* (depending on the angle of attack). If the angler overcasts, however, the thick fly line will land on the water over the fish's head, and the fish will have been *put down* by such clumsiness. In short, that fish will have been *lined*.

A dismal variant of lining occurs when the fish sees the lengthened fly-line whisking to and fro in the air above it. The result will be swift departure of the trout. The lesson is: beware of too much badly-executed *false casting*; and never overcast.

line-tray   Some bank fishermen on stillwaters adopt the use of a *line-tray*, into which loose coils of line are allowed to fall during the *retrieve*. Such loose coils are then shot easily through the rod-rings on a subsequent cast (see *shooting line*). Line-trays, which are belted around the waist (or conveniently round the thigh) seem particularly useful when sinking *fly-lines* are being used, since they prevent the loose, retrieved line from sinking at the angler's feet.

Trench (*Hist. Angling*, 54) notes that the line-tray, made of net and with an iron prong to stick into the belt, was invented in France during the 17th century.

loch-style   Contemporary fishing literature has many references to *loch-style* fishing, referring to the techniques of presenting a fly or flies to stillwater trout from a drifting boat (see *boat-fishing*; *drift*). The phrase is sometimes contrasted with e.g. bank-fishing, fishing at anchor, or *trolling*. The essence of the method is that the fly or flies are cast out on a short line and then *retrieved* so that the *droppers* furrow the surface film (see *dibble*), although a great variety of supplementary tactics are also possible within the broad label 'loch-style'. The central concepts of cast – retrieve – lift – roll – repeat are, however, relatively traditional, and it is proper that the phrase includes one of the oldest fishing-related words, 'loch'.

Loch (and see *machair*) derives from Gaelic and Irish *loch* (compare Anglo-Irish *lough*), first attested in English in 1375 (Barbour's *Bruce* – significantly, a Northern work: 'Cummyn owt our [over] the louch ar thai'), although the word is recorded in Northumbrian OE as *luh*. The distribution of the word – principally from Irish Gaelic, though also with possible Celtic origins – helps to explain why it is that *loughs* (rather than 'lakes') are found in Cumbria and Northumberland as well as in Scotland and Ireland: the term is a survival from early usage in these dialect areas, whereas over the rest of England the word has been supplanted by the borrowed French word *lake* (MF *lac*).

One still sometimes hears the phrase *loch-fishing*, now virtually synonymous with loch-style fishing. This was first attested in English in 1860, although the practice had clearly been developing for some time before this date.

low-water iron   A type of lightweight, black anodised hook used in summer salmon fishing (especially on rivers, see *greased-line fishing*), also occasionally for the larger *sea trout* flies, e.g. the famous Medicine, which, Falkus writes, 'should be tied in sizes: 2, 4, 6, on the lightest low-water salmon hook procurable' (*Sea Trout Fishing*, 55).

The advantages of this type of hook are that, fished on a floating or intermediate *fly line* with a relatively fine *leader*, the fly swims well, and the light dressing involved does not hold the water: the aim should be to present an attractively-moving fly just below the surface of the stream, see e.g. Scott & Taverner (*Salmon Fishing*, 1433ff.): 'In really warm weather…I…use summer flies tied for me with an extremely sparse dressing; no part of it going beyond the point of the hook. The hooks have a long shank and are made of very fine oval wire… The older the fly and the thinner the dressing becomes through wear, the better the fish seem to like it…' See also *hook*.

lunker   Originally an American term, deriving from ?*lunkhead* (first attestation 1889, meaning 'thick-headed, stupid'), OED defines a *lunker* as 'An animal, esp. a fish, which is an exceptionally large example of its species; a "whopper"'. The term seems to be used particularly of big, old, possibly *cannibal brown trout*, maybe because such fish have very large heads in relation to their bodies. See also *ferox*.

lure   The word enters English from French (OF *leurre*, 'bait'), and is first attested in 1440, in falconry ('Lure for hawkys'); thereafter the word extends its semantic range. A lure is now a 'means of alluring animals to be captured, in *Angling* a more general term than *bait*, which strictly denotes only something fishes can eat' (OED; the first attestation of the term in this specific angling sense is 1700).

Once more we face the semantic difficulties of *fly* and *lure*: 'all flies are lures...but only some lures are flies' and so on. But perhaps *lure* is best taken to mean a non-specific, non-representative pattern designed to attract a fish through a general combination of shape, colour and movement. It is a kind of fly which excites the fish's curiosity, rather than its appetite (on curiosity and trout fishing, see especially Brian Clarke, *The Pursuit of Stillwater Trout*, 49-52). The problem here is that an alternative phrase for *lure* is 'fancy fly' (the Butcher, Dunkeld etc.), which certainly appears to bear no resemblance to any natural food form – yet these 'fancy flies' may be fished suggestively slowly, even 'imitatively'. Perhaps these traditional patterns should be abstracted from the analysis, and the term *lure* left to cover e.g. stillwater trout flies such as the (in)famous Dog Nobblers, the Jack Frosts, Baby Dolls and Christmas Trees, along with sea trout flies, and salmon patterns. One further classificational difficulty, however, lies in the fact that these lures bear an indirect relationship to natural food forms, i.e. the Jack Frost may be seen as a stylised representation of a small roach; many if not most sea trout flies are stylised copies of the small fish sea trout may have recently been feeding on; and many salmon flies are reminiscent either of those bait fish, or those crustaceans (shrimps, prawns), which the salmon may have encountered while at sea.

Perhaps the best way of putting the entire issue of representation is to see it not in terms of *types* of artificial fly, but in terms of a representational *scale*. Flies 'imitating' natural food forms closely would be placed at one end of the scale (most *dry flies*, most artificial *nymphs*, many soft-hackled *wet flies*), and flies of a deliberately or crudely suggestive construction at the other end (Dog Nobblers, Poppers, Hoppers, Drunken Experiments and Frank Disasters). In between are the 'traditional patterns' (e.g. Bibio, Mallard and Claret), the 'slow deceivers' (Black and Peacock Spider), and the fancy flies. Sea trout and salmon flies, since they are general stylisations (rather than specific copies) of natural food forms, would occupy a place in the scale tending towards 'lure'.

A scale of this kind would reflect most fishermen's perception of what a lure is: a non-specific, non-representational pattern designed to be visible, to attract the fish's attention, to incite its curiosity. It is this perception of the term invoked in the following:

> I would also put in a good word for the Straddlebug, an old Lough Erne pattern, as ungainly in appearance as in name. Tied with a large hackle from the Egyptian goose, dyed yellow, and attached so that the natural curve of the fibres is forward, it resembles nothing except a baby octopus. When fished in short jerks, the soft feathers work backwards and forwards in a way that suggests a living thing of some kind, and fish do not bother to enquire what. Though classed as a wet pattern of the May-fly, it is a shameless lure (Kingsmill Moore, *A Man May Fish*, 66).

M **achair** From Gaelic, first attested in English is 1684 ('Machirrs, as I am informed, imports white ground'), then 1878 (*Q. Jrnl. Geol. Soc.* XXXIV: 'Benbecula... has only one hill; and if we except the "Machair", as the "good land" along the west coast is called, all the rest of the island consists of low-lying moor, bog, and lake...').

Moray McLaren describes *machair lochs* as follows:

The machair loch is usually a low-lying water, set on a raised beach...They are lochs on a rich soil in a calcareous material made from the sea shells pounded into sand by the waves. This shelly sand gives the water an alkaline character, and in such environments shrimps grow big, snails thrive with hard shells, and there are good colonies of fly larvae for the trout to feed on. Oddly enough, these conditions are usually poor for trout spawning, with the excellent result that you get smaller numbers of really fine trout...By smaller numbers I mean plenty for the angler, but not so many that the loch becomes infested with tiddlers, as so often happens in a Highland or Island acid loch where there is perhaps a good spawning burn and a poorish food supply (Currie & McLaren, *The Fishing Waters of Scotland*, 213-14).

These lochs are particularly characteristic of the Islands; McLaren gives as typical examples Loch a'Phuill on Tiree, and Loch Bornish on South Uist. As the above passage implies, these lochs are very clear, and very rich in food and fish. It is consequently necessary to fish (relatively) fine, and with food-suggesting artificials (more representative, or 'traditional' flies; cf. *lure*); McLaren (p.227) suggests a three-fly *leader* made up with Teal and Red, Butcher, and *Greenwell's Glory*. See also *acid and alkaline waters*.

march brown The natural fly *Rhithrogena haarupi*, and its corresponding artificial. The March Brown is a fly of flowing water: Harris writes that 'Trout feed keenly on the ascending and hatching nymphs, and less eagerly on the duns. The flies are seen in late March, April and early May...emerging in sudden swarms ...The flies are found on rivers such as the Tees and Tweed in northern England and Scotland, and the Usk in Wales as well as on several other rivers in Britain. In Ireland they occur on the Liffey ...also on the Slaney and the Nore' (*Angler's Entomology*, 83).

Given the fairly widespread distribution of the natural, it is strange that the March Brown appears to be unknown to the author of the *Treatise*, and to Cotton (Hills, *History*, 155; although Courtney Williams suggests that Cotton did in fact give a dressing, see *Dictionary*, 229). Hills stated that the fly is first mentioned in Chetham (*The Angler's Vade Mecum*, 1681), where it is called the Moorish Brown, and a further more detailed account of the fly is given in *The Art of Angling* by Richard Bowlker (1747), which gave a dressing not superseded for a hundred years (Body: hare's fur ribbed with yellow silk; Hackle: partridge; Wings: pheasant or partridge). Both these works considerably antedate the first attestation the OED gives for the term *March Brown*, which is a reference to 'Stonehenge' writing in *British Rural Sports* in 1856.

Courtney Williams records that the natural has 'several local names, including *brown drake, cob fly, dun drake,* and *caughlan* (Ireland)' (*Dictionary*, 227). He also points out that the March Brown is a much-used artificial since it is a good general pattern of fly (the kind of fly which Plunket-Greene in his classic *Where the Bright Waters Meet* so memorably described as 'a-dog-of-no-particular-breed-but-nevertheless-an-excellent-ratter'), suggesting not only *R. haarupi* but also dark-bodied *sedges*, or the *grannom*, or even, when fished well-sunk, the freshwater *shrimp* (*Dictionary*, 229). He gives several dressings of the fly: typically, these include a body of hare or rabbit fur dubbed onto orange or yellow silk, a partridge hackle, and optional wings of pheasant, partridge or snipe. We have not, it seems, come so very far from Bowlker.

marrow-spoon   Also simply *spoon* (sometimes used as a verb: 'to spoon the trout, use . . .'); or *marrow-scoop* (see below). This item of tackle is a long, thin, dished implement which is inserted into the gullet and stomach of a recently-killed brown or rainbow trout, then withdrawn so that the stomach contents of the fish may be examined. A marrow spoon is a particularly useful implement for those fishing representative patterns on rivers or still-waters. It is also useful in grayling fishing.

Copying the food found in the stomach of a recently-caught fish is no new angling practice. As recorded under *autopsy*, the author of the *Treatise*, with admirable simplicity, gave this instruction: 'For baytes for grete fyssh kepe specyally this rule: Whan ye haue take a grete fysshe, undo the mawe [stomach], and what ye fynde therin make that your bayte, for it is beste'.

In this century, however, it was G.E.M. Skues who as it were systematised the practice of inspecting the stomach contents of fish with a marrow spoon; he subsequently and famously turned these minutiae into a baby plate for inspection at the water's edge, so that the appropriate artificial could be put up.

More recently, others have testified to the near-indispensable nature of this simple implement. Brian Clarke, for instance, writes that

> There is no need...for the rather gruesomely-named "autopsy" to be a messy business. I get all the information I need from my trout with the aid of a piece of plastic tubing, with a rubber bulb at one end. All that is necessary is to push the tubing down the fish's gullet, press and release the bulb, and then withdraw the tube again. As the tube comes out, the stomach contents are sucked into it, for ready identification. Other methods of achieving the same end, rather less well, are the marrow spoon – ...of chalk stream fame – and a dessert spoon handle (*Pursuit of Stillwater Trout*, 83).

And Gordon Fraser writes that 'Having killed his trout, the good nymph angler will take the chance to use a spoon to test the stomach contents' (*Mastering the Nymph*, 23).

Marrow-spoon is the earlier of the terms. It is defined in the OED as 'a spoon for extracting the marrow from bones' – *marrow* (from OE *mærg, mearh*) is 'the soft vascular fatty substance usually contained in the cavities of bones'. The first attestation dates to the *London Gazette* of 1693 ('Sweat-meat Spoon..., Marrow Spoon..., Ladle..., and...Skillet') although, as noted, the word *marrow* is much older. The term *marrow-scoop* is first attested in 1969 ('The marrow scoop and toothpick are missing').

matching the hatch   A trout angler copying the natural flies which are hatching, and on which the fish are feeding, is said to be *matching the hatch*. To match the hatch is particularly desirable when *nymphs* and *duns* of the *upwinged flies* are coming off the water (see *dry fly*; *nymph fishing*), and also in heavy falls of *spinners*, although it is also useful to copy the naturals during e.g. hatches of *midge* or *sedge* on stillwaters.

Although the term is not recorded in the OED, the practice was first described by Venables (1662): 'When you come first to the river in the morning, with your rod beat upon the bushes or boughs which hang over the water, and by their falling upon the water you will see what sorts of flies there are in greatest numbers; if divers sorts, and equal in number, try them all, and you will quickly find which they [the fish] most desire' (*The Experienced Angler*, facs., 11).

In this century, an unambiguous reference is given in e.g. John Goddard, whose Ch. 13 of *Trout Fly Recognition* details 'Match the hatch charts...to enable the fly fisher to narrow quickly the choice of patterns to be used in any particular month' (p.165). See also *hatch*[1].

maxillary From F. *maxillaire*. OED dates the first attestation to
1626 and Bacon's *Sylva*: 'There is the Skull of one Entire Bone;
there are...the Maxillary Bones...'. OED defines the term as
'Belonging to, or connected with, or forming part of the jaw or
jaw-bone, esp. of the upper jaw of vertebrate animals'. In a fishing
sense, the term is used to indicate the bone and cartilage found
on the outside upper jaw of all salmonids. A *hook-hold* in this
cartilage, particularly in the angle of the jaw (the *scissors*), is usually very firm.

mayfly[1] Any insect of the family Ephemeridae, i.e. any upwinged
dun or *spinner*, thus including e.g. the *Large Dark Olive*, *Iron
Blue*, *Blue-winged Olive* etc. (see *olives*), as well as the true
mayflies, *Ephemera danica* and *E. vulgata* (see *mayfly[2]*). W.G.
Bainbridge classified the fly-fisher's natural flies into three major
groupings, 'May-flies, Caddis-flies and Stone-flies' (meaning
upwinged flies, *sedges*, and hard- or flat-winged flies), although
later in the same work he wrote 'A point which needs clearing
up...is in respect to the word May-fly. Anglers usually regard
the word as meaning the large May-fly (Green and Grey Drake),
whereas naturalists term the whole family of the Ephemeridae,
May-flies'. As Courtney Williams (*Dictionary*, 241) points out,
however, the use of the term '"may-flies" as a generic name for
all flies of the Ephemeroptera family... seems to be a most illogical
procedure', since it breeds confusion. In terms of nomenclature,
it seems better for anglers to reserve the term *mayfly* for *E. danica*
and *E. vulgata*, and to refer to other upwinged flies by their individual names. Perhaps, if some catch-all term is required, 'upwinged flies' is preferable in this context.

mayfly[2] The angler's name for the true mayfly (cf. *mayfly[1]*), of
which two virtually identical species are found in the British Isles,
Ephemera danica (the most common) and *E. vulgata* (the less
common).

As Hills points out, the *Treatise* does not mention the mayfly
by name, although he conjectures that two dressings given in that
work, for the 'Maure fly' (where 'maure' = 'mulberry-coloured')
and for the 'Tandy fly' (where 'tandy' = 'tan-coloured'), may be
patterns for light and dark versions of the mayfly (*History*, 159).
More certain it is that Barker (1651), Cotton, and other 17th-
century writers knew the fly well. Cotton, not altogether unexpectedly given his gifts as a naturalist and keen observer, gave an
excellent description not only of an artificial dressing for the
Greendrake (the *dun*), but of the life-cycle of the natural, being
perhaps the first to note that the newly-emerged dun is unable to
fly until its wings have dried, and is thus uniquely vulnerable to

a waiting fish ('he then lies upon the surface of the water like a Ship at Hull... until his wings have got stiffness to fly with, if by some Trout, or Grayling he be not taken in the interim (which ten to one he is)...' *Angler*, 290-91). Cotton also gave a dressing for the Greydrake (the female *spinner*). Notably, these terms, Greendrake and Greydrake, are still widely in use: Harris (*Angler's Entomology*, 190) identifies large or very large flies having greenish-grey wings with dark brown or black markings as Greendrakes; and Goddard (*Trout Flies of Stillwater*, 67) writes that 'the female spinner will often alight on the water for short periods and at this stage she is referred to as a Grey Drake, the artificial pattern of which is particularly good...' Otherwise, the common term for the (female) mayfly spinner is the *Spent Gnat*.

The life history of the mayfly is of note. The mayfly *nymph*, which is about 1-1½" long, is a bottom-burrower, making its home in a tunnel in the silt or mud of the river or lake bed. (Mayflies are for this reason particularly common in these muddy or silty environments, including e.g. flooded workings that have been opened for trout fishing.) It lives in this tunnel for up to two years (although Courtney Williams records that the nymph lives underwater for up to three years, see *Dictionary*, 235), where its food consists largely of microscopic organic matter. After the fly's wings and other organs have developed inside the nymphal *shuck*, the nymph, which is at this time a dirty cream colour, swims to the surface in order to hatch into the *sub-imago* or *dun*; peak emergence is from mid-May (when the first mayfly hatches begin on the western lakes, e.g. Lough Derg in Ireland) until mid-June (the English midlands and north). At this time, trout may be relatively easy to catch on a corresponding artificial pattern: Richard Walker's Mayfly Nymph is justifiably popular.

At the surface, and after a short period of time, the nymphal shuck splits open and the dun emerges onto the surface. As Cotton put it, 'the Green-Drake never discloses from his husk, till he be first there grown to full maturity, body, wings, and all, and then he creeps out of his cell, but with his wings so crimpt, and ruffled, by being prest together in that narrow room, that they are for some hours totally useless to him...' (*Angler*, 290). Again, because of its resting state, the newly-hatched dun – which is, as the name Greendrake implies, a greeny-yellow colour – is vulnerable to trout. Many anglers use artificial *dry flies* during this time; one good artificial is the Grey Wulff. Alternatively, and especially on the Irish loughs, *dapping* a natural Greendrake (or more than one) from a boat is an effective method.

The dun then flies off into the bankside foliage, where after a further period of up to a day (hence the Latin name – these almost-adult insects are truly ephemeral), the dun transforms into a *spinner*: 'the sub-imago pulls and kicks itself out of its body covering and also out of the very skin of its wings, when (if all goes well) it emerges as an imago or fully developed insect' (Courtney Williams, *Dictionary*, 238).

It is these adults or spinners which then return to the water in the evening; the prelude to this return is the well-known rising and falling dance of the male flies (also known as 'Blackdrakes'), which attracts the female spinners (more prosaically, it is the pattern of their dance which enables the males to maximise their opportunities of seeing females, which typically fly above them). Mating takes place in the air, after which the females, 'gracefully rising and dipping over the water . . . expel batches of eggs which slowly sink to the bottom . . .' (Courtney Williams, 239). Once more, however, the spent gnats are vulnerable to trout, and anglers capitalise on this by using dry representations of the spent fly: Neil Patterson's Deerstalker is a useful pattern.

The courtship and mating of the mayfly is an extraordinarily beautiful thing to watch, and the process it entails is of more than merely local or piscatorial significance. Hills' description is perhaps the one that does the mayfly most justice:

> The coming of the mayfly is more than an incident in the fisherman's year. It is an event of nature. The sight of it carries the mind to other countries and throws it back to earlier times. Few of us are lucky enough to have seen the great movements of wild animals which still take place even on our restricted globe. The migration of the caribou in the Barren Lands of Labrador, the herds of antelopes described by the old African hunters, even the incursion of swarms of the little lemming into Norway, are sights which not many can witness. But though, as continent after continent gets enclosed and cultivated, the range of animal life gets restricted, and many species languish or die, the air is still free to all. Its inhabitants can range at will. The air has no oceans and no continents, and it remains unfenced and unharvested. Even now, in this populous land of ours and this civilised century, the migrations of bird life which occur every spring and autumn are nearly as great as ever they were. It is still possible for a slender bird like the chiff-chaff to pass the winter in Persia and the spring in Hampshire, and for the willow wren to travel every year the long road to and from Cape Colony. And in a humbler plane there still occur, every year, the birth, the life, the mating and the death of innumerable mayfly; and though it sounds a

fanciful confession, I never look at the process without compar-
ing it to those larger movements of more important creatures
which I have not been so fortunate as to see (*A Summer on the
Test*, 57-8).

mayfly[3]   Several writers record that, especially in the North of
England, the term *mayfly* is also used to refer to either *sedges* or
(more usually) *stone-flies*. This is consistent with the OED's definition: 'mayfly: (1) an insect of the family Ephemeridae; esp. as an
angler's name for *Ephemera vulgata* or *E. dania* [sic]...(2) an
insect of the family *Phryganeidae*...; the caddis-fly' – although of
mayfly meaning stone-fly the OED makes no mention. OED gives the
first attestation of this last sense ('mayfly = sedge/stonefly') to
Kirby's *Entomology*, 1816 ('*Phryganeae* [in their imago state are
called] may-flies...'). This last attestation is, however, surely too
late. As already noted, Cotton mentioned the confusion in terminology: 'here it is that you are to expect an account of the Green
Drake and stone-flie...and some others that are peculiar to this
Month [May]...and that...do yet stand in competition with the
two before named, and so, that it is yet undecided amongst the
Anglers to which of the pretenders to the Title of the May-flie,
it does properly, and duly belong...' (*Angler*, 287). Cotton's note
clearly indicates that the term *mayfly* was used of both the mayfly
proper, and the stone-fly. The confusion persists: Courtney Williams records that 'in Scotland, the border counties, and throughout Yorkshire and Lancashire, the name mayfly is commonly
used for the stone-fly *(Perla maxima)*...' (*Dictionary*, 241 – he also
records that *mayfly* is also used in the West Country to denote the
hawthorn fly). Harris (*Angler's Entomology*, 169) records the same:

> The important Stone-fly, or Large Stone-fly, of the fast-flowing
> stony rivers of the north of England, Scotland and parts of
> Ireland, represents two different species of *Perla*...The larvae
> or creepers are easily found under stones in fast-flowing water,
> and they are an excellent bait for trout during April and early
> May. During late May and early June the adult flies, particu-
> larly the females, which are noticeably larger, are used in pre-
> ference to the creepers. In the north of England these flies are
> called the Mayfly, and provide some of the best fishing of the
> year.

It may be, however, that this usage is becoming sporadic, or
even dying out entirely. It is some years since I have heard a
Yorkshire angler speak of the 'Mayfly' (meaning stone-fly).
See also *creeper*.

mending line   Also known simply as *mending*, this is a technique
used by those fishing the sunk fly downstream (or across-and-

downstream) for trout and salmon on flowing water, the purpose of the 'mend' being to slow the travel of the fly, and so presenting the artificial at a more natural speed relative to the draw of the current.

Since *mending line* depends on the casting line being extended on the water downstream of the angler, the technique could not have existed much before the 18th century, before which date the line was held rather more aloft, out of the water. Thus the technique seems to have become popular relatively late in the development of the *wet fly* and its presentation: neither Grey (*Fly Fishing*, 1st edn, 1899) nor, for example, Tod (*Wet Fly Fishing*, 1918) explicitly mentions mending the line in downstream fishing, although Grey, who was brought up on the wet fly, did note that in fishing the fly downstream it was (and is) best to keep the line relatively straight, while at the same time allowing the flies to 'float down and sweep round with such movement as the stream may give them' (*Fly Fishing*, 128) – a practice which at least implies a relatively slow and naturalistic presentation.

In fact mending the line seems, as far as I can tell, to have become commonplace in wet fly trout fishing only after the technique had been promoted as a constituent part of presenting the wet fly to salmon in the method which became known as *greased-line fishing*. Greased-line fishing for salmon was popularised by A.H.E. Wood, of Cairnton on the Dee, who fished and wrote during the early years of this century. As Taverner & Scott put it, 'Wood's technique consisted of a small, single-hooked fly fished just below the surface, and supported by the floating line ... He added a new interest to fishing the fly by developing the *mend* and the *lead*, so making control of the line on the water a very real thing' (*Salmon Fishing*, 132; their italics).

Wood's own description of mending runs as follows:

The lifting-over of a line is done to correct a fault, namely, to take the downstream belly out of a line and thus relieve the pull or pressure of the current on the line, which is communicated to the fly and exhibits itself as *drag*. But if the line is proceeding at an even pace and shows no sign of going to drag, there is no need to mend the cast. On the other hand, if the current continues to belly the line, but before it gets a drag, lift again and continue to do so as often as you can see a drag forming ...

This mending or lifting is effected by the raising of the elbow and by a turn of the wrist, which makes the rod follow evenly a semicircular path, point and butt moving in unison. It is a lift, not a back-cast, and its direction should be across stream as well as up. The line should be removed from the surface of the water by raising the rod almost horizontally and keeping the arm stiff, that is, the point of the rod should usually be no higher than the butt. It should then be swung right or left with a gentle circular sweeping movement and put down where desired . . . (in *Salmon Fishing*, eds. Taverner & Scott, 139-40).

The main point is to avoid *drag²*, which in this instance causes the fly to fish unrealistically (a small fly fished sub-surface cannot, for example, behave in such a fashion as to appear to hold its position in a fast current, nor, worse, can it appear – to the fish – to swim upstream against such a current); the aim is to present the fly naturally – 'naturally', in this instance, meaning that the angler has to remain sensitive not only to the brute fact of drag, which is easy enough to detect, but also to fly size and current speed. These points also hold good for both sea trout and trout fishing (on flowing water). The best description of mending in this context comes from Kingsmill Moore (and notice that he claims that trout anglers borrowed the technique from salmon fishermen):

Some modern wet-fly fishermen have borrowed a hint from salmon anglers. They grease all except the last yard or two of their line and defeat the drag by small well-timed "mends". "Mending" a line means lifting it off the water and putting it down in a fresh place without moving the fly. With a long two-handed salmon rod this is difficult to do, but with a trout rod it is easy. Suppose a fast current, intervening between rod and fly, has started to put a down-stream belly into the line. This curve has to be reversed and put up-stream. Hold the rod out with a straight arm at shoulder level, parallel with the water, and imagine there is a blackboard just in front of the point and facing you. Now with a fairly stiff arm try to trace a circle about four feet in diameter on the blackboard with the point. Do this smoothly and slowly. You will find that the line comes up from the water and is put down again with an up-stream belly which will defeat the drag till the fly has travelled down another two or three yards . . . (*A Man May Fish*, 39).

Interestingly, Wood's point about mending being a technique to 'correct a fault' exemplifies the etymology of the term well. The term *mending* stems from a verb, *mend*, itself from *amend* (< Fr. *mender*) meaning 'To improve by correction or alteration'. In this sense the verb is fairly old, being first attested in *c*.1300 (*Cursor Mundi*: 'Leuedi, sco said, for drightin dere, þou mend þi mode and turn þi chere' – Lady, she said, for (the sake of) the dear Lord, you (should) improve your spirit(s) and be more cheerful).

midge   From OE *mycg* or *mycge*, a word first attested in a glossary of 725 ('*Culix*, mygg'). Also *chironomid(s/ae)*, the various species of midge, one of the chief food forms of brown and rainbow trout on stillwaters, and extremely important to fishermen. OED records that the term is first attested in the sense 'artificial fly for fishing' in 1799 (G. Smith, *Laboratory*: 'Black-midge, or gnat. Dubbing, of the down of a mole'), although it is impossible to believe that some of the small gnats of Cotton and others are not intended to represent midges.

The real impetus behind fishing small, representative, midge-suggesting patterns in the stillwater context seems to have come from Brian Clarke's pioneering study *The Pursuit of Stillwater Trout* (1975) – although on Dr Bell of Blagdon, see *pupa*. Of the most important stage in the midge's life-cycle, the pupa, Clarke writes as follows:

> the midge pupa is the star of the piece. It is immensely vulnerable to trout, because it has to make the perilous journey from the lower depths (where it lived as a larva, and pupated) to the top (where it will, if it is lucky enough, hatch into the adult fly). Not only, however, is it extremely accessible to the trout; but trout eat pupae in immense numbers (which is unlucky for the pupae); and the pupae are easy to imitate on hooks (which is unlucky for the trout). So great, indeed, are the numbers in which pupae are eaten that it is comparatively rare for a trout to be caught with food in it, and for that food to include no pupae at all. At the other end of the scale, it is by no means uncommon to find trout packed to the gills with midge pupae alone. They are . . . one of the few creatures with which trout can become totally "preoccupied" – that is to say, they can on occasion be eaten to the exclusion of all other foods (*Pursuit of Stillwater Trout*, 67-8).

Consequently, most stillwater anglers' fly-boxes will contain many representations of midges, from the larval form (*bloodworm*), through the various sizes and colours of pupae (*buzzers*), to the adult midges. These last are not insignificant as anglers' flies: adults return to the water, usually in the evenings (the females to lay their eggs), and this mass movement may provoke a *rise*. At these times, *dry fly¹* fishing with an appropriate artificial can be very productive.

Of artificial patterns, and as a very rough guide, the following seems to be particularly successful: the Cove Pheasant Tail (a general pupa-suggesting pattern); artificial pupae in the following colours and in a variety of hook-sizes (12-16 seem most usual) – black, brown, grass-green, red; and dry flies such as the *Black*

Gnat or Grey Duster. In addition, there are many patterns which stylise hatching buzzers: of these, perhaps the famous Grenadier (designed early this century by the renowned Dr Bell of Blagdon) is the most well-known; it imitates the Large Red Midge, which hatches in quantity on Blagdon and, especially, Chew Lake, prestigious waters both. See also *hatch[1], rainbow trout*; and for a brief history of 'imitative' fishing on stillwaters, see *pupa*.

Lastly here, there are those Other Midges, not our sprightly chironomids but those evil whisperers of tartan twilights, the biting midges, they of the semi-aquatic habits and tubes of repellant. But 'midge repellant' is too optimistic a phrase. Nothing really deters these midges. Cigar smoke is reputed to be good, but producing it in sufficient quantity is expensive and damaging to the health. Since the biting midges are bankside creatures, rowing into the middle of the nearest lake may be advisable, but inevitably, the angler takes his own resident supply of midges with him – the Hat Brim Midge is particularly tenacious. Another alternative is to pray for a gale which will disperse the midge swarms. If the gale is whistled up, however, the angler is by now far from home, and either (a) has to abandon the boat miles from the boathouse, or (b) sinks. The last course is drastic, but will repel midges. Another alternative is to seek solace in a car or bar. The last is preferable, but biting midges are intrepid and have been known to reach parts that other beers can't reach. They also taste vile.

Midge repellant at least creates the illusion of repellancy. A further alternative is to wear a stocking over the face (and hat, if possible). If this alternative is chosen in conjunction with the bar (see above), it is best to remove the stocking before seeking that ultimate sanctuary. The arrival of masked fishermen has been known to cause some consternation.

Notably vicious biting midges include the Skye Midge of Glen Brittle, the Kielder Midge, and the Connemara Jungle Midge (and on this last, see Kingsmill Moore, *A Man May Fish*, 145).

milt The spawn of the male fish, the sperm; in this sense first attested in English in 1483 (Caxton: 'Open the fysshe and take to the herte the galle and the mylte'). The word derives from OE *milte*, 'spleen'. OED explains: 'The sense "spawn of fish" may have been adopted from Du. [*milt*]; as the milt of a fish is of soft substance like the spleen, the transferred use was not unnatural, but it was no doubt helped to gain currency by the resemblance in sound between *milt* and *milk*, ... the older name for the soft roe of fish'.

A good description of the behaviour of *cock* trout on the *redds* is given in Norman Maclean (*Trout and Grayling*, 52):

[The female trout] opens out a trough in the gravel with her tail and then presses her abdomen down into the shallow valley in the gravel, shedding her eggs in amongst the fine stones. Meanwhile one or more males, already in attendance, excrete a cloud of milt from their testes via the genital pore. Milt is simply a mass of motile sperm and fertilisation is completely external, so no actual copulation takes place. The male fish are, however, in close proximity to the female at the moment of shedding the milt . . .

mirror   Part of the fish's system of sight-perception (see *fish vision*), the *mirror* is what the fish sees outside its *window*, i.e. outside that circular hole, through which the fish can see into the outside world, the water surface mirrors back whatever is below it. In practical terms this means that a fish seeing an underwater fly may in fact see a double image, one being the 'real' fly, the other being the reflected fly. It has been conjectured (by Kingsmill Moore, for example, in *A Man May Fish*, revised and enlarged edition, Appendix) that the glimpses of the fly perceived by the fish in a water disturbed by wave action may in fact be tantalising glimpses of the mirrored image – glimpses sufficiently tantalising for the fish to formate onto the 'real' fly . . . and take it.

The fish's system of sight-perception was to my knowledge first described in print by Ronalds (*The Fly-Fisher's Entomology*, 1st edn, 1836), although Ronalds did not use the terms mirror and window.

The term has a respectable literary pedigree; it is first attested in the sense 'polished surface which reflects images of objects' in 1225, but attested first in the sense 'water surface' in 1595 and Spenser's *Epithalamion* ('And in his waters, which your mirror make, behold your faces').

monofilament   Also *monofil*. See *nylon monofilament*.

mort   A local term (specifically N-W) for the *sea trout*, as in e.g. Falkus, *Sea Trout Fishing* (p.436) who, publishing entries from the fishing diary of Walter Caddy (entries spanning the years 1893-1913), writes that 'for the uninitiated, I should explain that Smelt = Small = Herling. Mort = Big = Sea trout. (Both Cumbrian terms.)' The term *mort* (meaning sea trout) is also used by Arthur Ransome: 'I estimated that departed mort at about a couple of pounds' (*Rod and Line*, 113).

The OED states that the origin of the word is unknown (but see below); the given definition – 'A name for the salmon in its third year' – is misleading. The attestations of the word are most interesting, however. It is first recorded in 1530, where *morte* is rather unhelpfully glossed as 'a fysshe'. In 1584 the mort is defined as 'the young salmon'. In 1672 it is recorded (in Latin) that on the River Ribble 'salmon of the first year of their lives are called "smelts", of the second year "sprods", and of the third year "morts"'. There is apparent confusion here between salmon and sea trout; it is also difficult to interpret what the word 'year' means in this context – the first year of the fish's return from the sea? Or (more unlikely) the first year of the fish's life? Nor are the terms *smelt* and *sprod* of much help. Even though Falkus records that smelt means *herling*, the etymological relationship may well be with *smolt*. Moreover, a quote from the *Westmorland Gazette* in 1884 suggests that *sprod* means *herling*: 'A good many morts and sprods have been landed from the lower reaches of the Kent'. It is all rather perplexing. But I am inclined to believe the OED when it suggests that *mort* may derive from ON *mergö*, Northern dial. *murth*, meaning 'great': a Norse derivation for the term would be consistent with the pattern of Scandinavian migration into England during the later Anglo-Saxon period, since Vikings colonised the NW from Ireland. The very localised nature of the term makes such a connection at least plausible. If so, *mort* is our oldest word for the sea trout.

murrough   Also sp. *murragh* (and variants), this is the Irish term for a species of *sedge*, the Great Red Sedge, *Phryganea grandis* or *P. striata*. As the Latin name implies, the natural is very large, and rapacious in its habits (Harris, 109, records that the larvae will attack and eat small fish). The adults' peak emergence occurs during late May and June, typically during the evening and into the darkness.

I have been unable to trace the origin of the term. It is possibly Gaelic, but also, possibly, from ON *mó-r*, 'moor, heath' + *rauö-r*, 'red', thus, 'heather-brown, reddish brown'. This gives E. dialectal *murrit*, first attested in 1809 ('a dusky brown called moorit'). A final possibility is that the word is from Fr. *morée* ('murrey'), meaning 'dark red'.

Nail knot   A knot used to join e.g. *backing* to the *fly line*, or, less frequently, to join the *leader* (or the butt part of the leader) to the tip of the fly line. Taverner & Scott (*Salmon Fishing*, 69) speak of 'the attachment known as the Needle Knot and Nail Knot', implying that the same knot has two interchangeable names. Today, the two knots seem to be distinct in tying as in nomenclature. In the *nail knot*, a nail (or needle) is laid alongside the tip of the fly line, and turns of *nylon monofilament* are then taken around the nail, and the standing part of the knot, the knot being finished when the tip of the nylon is threaded through the formed coils, and the knot drawn tight. In this knot, then, no part of the nylon is passed through the core of the fly line; the knot is formed wholly outside the braid. In the *needle knot*, however, a hole is made in the tip of the fly line (usually by inserting a heated needle into the core), and the nylon (or butt-piece of nylon) is then passed through this hole, exiting from the fly line core perhaps a quarter inch from the tip; the nylon is then looped back on itself, and turns of monofil are subsequently taken over this loop, the nylon tip being finally inserted into the loop, and the knot drawn tight. Fortunately, both knots are easier to see than to describe. See *knots*.

natural   Some anglers speak of *the natural* (fly or flies) as opposed to the *artificial*, thus e.g. 'there was a good hatch of naturals between two o'clock and four'.

The word comes from OF *naturel*, and in English is first attested as an adjective, but a substantive sense – 'natural things or objects; matters having their basis in the natural world' – quickly develops (1541: 'Than come vnto the naturalles...').

neb   The extreme forward part of the fish's mouth (the 'nose'), from OE *nebb*, cf. e.g. the *nib* of a pen. In angling literature, the surface of, for example, a placidly-flowing chalk stream is often broken by 'the large neb of a rising trout' (usually some Leviathan the author has stalked for months). Here is an instance from the writings of the great G.E.M. Skues: 'Where duns are floating in eddies one often sees trout sailing gently under and sipping them softly. Occasionally in these positions one sees a succession of head-and-tail rises – first the neb appears and then descends, then the back fin, and then the upper portion of the tail fin' (*The Way of a Trout with a Fly*, 62).

Norman Maclean (*Trout and Grayling*, 50) records that the term *neb* is also used to mean *kype*: 'As the breeding season advances cock fish develop a distinct upturn to the point of the lower jaw, known as a neb or kype . . .'. Perhaps in this sense the term means 'any extreme projection'.

needle-fly Also simply *needle(s)*. Needle-flies are small *stone-flies*; they are widely distributed, and are indeed abundant on fast-flowing rain-fed rivers. I cannot do better than to quote Courtney Williams on the nomenclature: 'Strictly speaking, this name [needle fly] should be applied . . . only to three species of the Leuctra family, although in practice, it is used by anglers to denote any of those small thin brown flies, with long narrow flat wings, which are so typical of the smaller perlidae' (*Dictionary*, 258). The three species of flies referred to are *Leuctra geniculata* (the *Willow Fly*, common from April to late autumn), *L. hippopus* (an early-hatching species, common in spring), and *L. fusca* (an autumn-hatching species, common until late October). Both Goddard (*Trout Fly Recognition*) and Roberts (*Illust. Dictionary*) record that the two last-named species are virtually identical in appearance.

Being so abundant, these flies are of some importance to trout fishers. In fact stone-flies, as a family, have always been held in high esteem: the *Treatise* gives good dressings of the large stone-fly and the February Red, and Cotton, too, gives dressings for these, and possibly other stone-flies, although it is difficult to be precise because of Cotton's habit of referring to e.g. 'a small bright-brown [fly] . . . a little dark brown [fly]' etc. Perhaps the best-known modern pattern (but one whose history goes back into the 19th century at least: Overfield, p.57, notes that this dressing is found in Pritt's *Yorkshire Trout Flies*, 1885) is the Dark Needle or Dark Spanish Needle favoured by Yorkshire fishermen. This has a body formed of orange silk, hackle from a dark brown owl's wing feather (or dark starling), and a head made of a turn of peacock herl. A lighter fly (imaginatively called the Light Needle), has an almost identical dressing, save that the body is made of yellow silk; possibly this represents the Small Yellow Sally (*Chloroperla torrentium*). Matters are complicated, however, by the fact that e.g. Roberts (*Dictionary*, 126) gives two other dressings for the 'Light (Spanish) Needle', dressings which clearly indicate other Small Browns (and see e.g. Goddard, *Trout Fly Recognition*, 127).

needle knot See *nail knot; knots*.

net See *landing net*.

Netheravon school See *nymph fishing*.

Northampton style A style of *boat fishing* for brown and rainbow trout originated on the many good stillwaters around Northampton during the 1960s, and still evolving. I have heard (and read of) the phrase being used to describe a wide variety of boat-fishing techniques, but perhaps the phrase is most commonly used to describe side-casting from a slowly drifting boat with a quick-sinking fly-line. The line is then retrieved in a slow, deep curve. The fly is typically a large *lure*. Alternatively, a rudder-board may be fixed to the downwind gunwale of the boat, whereupon the boat will drift across-wind. These methods are suspiciously close to *trailing*, which is banned on some fisheries.

nylon monofilament   Also *nylon*; *monofil*. Nylon monofilament ('a single strand of man-made fibre') was developed in the early years of the present century. OED gives the first attestation as 1916, in Cross and Bevan's *Text-book of Paper Making*: 'The [cellulose] solution has been extensively applied to the production of artificial threads of high lustre, so-called "artificial silk" and various grades of monofil'; it dates the next attestation to 1940, and the next to 1972 and an entry in *T&S* (June, 58): 'Nylon monofil slips more easily through the rod-rings'.

As noted elsewhere (see *leader* etc.), fishing line was first made of tapered, braided horsehair; then 'Indian Weed' (whatever that was, see Hills, *History*, 70) was used for the casting line, then silkworm gut. *Fly lines* of tapered, dressed silk, and gut leaders, were used until well into this century (dressed silk fly lines are still commercially available). Angling writers tended to attach much importance to the gut:

> As for silk-worm gut, and the gut collars that are made from it, I do not think I can do better than advise the learner to place himself unreservedly in the hands of any first-rate fishing-tackle maker, in order to insure getting reliable hanks of gut, either as it comes from Spain, or, after it has been drawn through the machine.
>
> In the early spring months, the very finest whole-gut, may at times be used. As a rule, I use drawn gut.
>
> Three yards is the usual length of the fine fly casts . . . (E.M. Tod, *Wet-fly Fishing*, 161-2).

Lord Hardinge of Penshurst, writing in 1976 but recalling his boyhood between the wars, gives some interesting detail on gut casts:

> These of course were the days of gut casts, nylon not having been invented [at least in a fishing context – Ed.]. The casts were expensive, about two shillings (if I recall) for a trout 3X and twelve shillings and sixpence for a salmon cast. You have to multiply these sums by about five to obtain equivalent prices in 1976, so that the loss of a cast by a schoolboy was a serious

matter. It was extremely easy to lose them too. They had to
be soaked and gently ironed out straight before you could use
them at all, or they fell like wire coil on the water. They had
also to be kept damp in round tin boxes in which each cast
was separated from the next one by a round piece of damp
felt; but if the felt was *too* damp they quickly went rotten.
Worst of all, they easily got into the most staggering tangles
when casting in a wind, and since they did not have the smooth-
ness of nylon they did not disentangle half so easily. Nylon
can usually be disentangled, but if the tangle looks bad it is
cheap and simple to throw the cast away and replace it. No
schoolboy could afford to do that with gut, though even if you
could sort it out it was apt to have sharp bends and corners in
it for a long time afterwards.

   Gut has one advantage only in that it is heavier. For this
reason a few perfectionist salmon fishermen still carry one or
two such casts with them... (*An Incompleat Angler*, 12-13).
Given the disadvantages of gut (cost, labour, kinking and vile
fankles) it is hardly surprising that nylon had virtually ousted gut
by the (late?) 1950s. As Kingsmill Moore put it (*A Man May
Fish*, 145), nylon is 'stronger and less visible... and... so reliable
that testing is more a routine than a necessity'. Its use is now
universal, although there is a reminder of the gut-old days in the
labelling of some shop-bought leaders, which, despite being
nylon, are still marked as e.g. '2X' (roughly-speaking, a 6lb b.s.
point), '4X' (roughly a 4lb point), '6X' (roughly a 2lb point) and
so on.

   Of late, nylon has been developed so that 'double strength'
monofil is available, i.e. nylon which has twice the strength for
its thickness. Although it is too early to tell whether this kind of
line will supersede the conventional kind, there have been good
reports of its performance, although extra care has to be taken
when forming *droppers*, *knots* etc. (see Chris Ogborne, 'Fine,
strong, but handle with care', *T&S*, March 1989, 52-3. He claims
that the introduction of this new nylon is 'one of the greatest
advances in fishing for a decade').

nymph The subaquaeous stage in the life-cycle of an *upwinged
fly* (ephemerid or *ephemeropteran*) between *larva* and *dun*. As
Courtney Williams notes, 'the immature ephemerids are called
larvae and only become nymphs when their rudimentary wings
become visible, but... fishermen have long found it more convenient to use the term nymph to designate all the sub-surface stages
of its life' (*Dictionary*, 259).

   The term is also used nowaday to refer to *midge pupae*, but this usage ('they're feeding on buzzer nymphs') is inaccurate and incorrect. The pedant in me tells me that the word should really be reserved for the nymphs of upwinged flies (and *stone-flies*).

Most fly-fishing handbooks give details of the four different basic types of ephemeropteran nymphs (see e.g. Courtney Williams, 259; C.F. Walker in *The Complete Fly-Fisher*, 251-2; Harris, 66-83; etc.). These are (a) burrowing nymphs; (b) crawling nymphs; (c) swimming nymphs; and (d) flat nymphs. These different types may be distinguished largely on the grounds of their habitat. For example, flat nymphs (*Ecdyonurus* spp., and nymphs of the true *March Brown*, *Rhithrogena haarupi*) are found in torrential currents; burrowing nymphs (most famous of which must be the *Mayfly*[2] nymph) are found in the slower reaches of rivers, and in lakes (i.e. wherever the slackness of current has allowed sand or silt to build up). Other nymphs (Harris mentions e.g. the *Baetis* species, and especially the *Caenis*) are less particular in their chosen habitats, and can occur in weeds or among the bottom stones of fast-flowing rivers, as well as in stillwaters. (It is something of a pity that the Caenis nymph should be so catholic; the fact that it is at home anywhere accounts for the abundance of those frustrating millions of summer snowflakes, the duns.)

As noted, the burrowing nymphs comprise the two species of Mayfly, *Ephemera danica* and *E. vulgata* (see *mayfly*[2]).

The crawling nymphs comprise the various species of Caenis, the Blue-winged Olive (one of the most important summer flies, especially on chalk streams, where it hatches in numbers during summer evenings), and the Claret Dun (common on peaty, upland waters).

The swimming nymphs include those two aristocrats, the *Large Dark Olive* and the Iron Blue, as well as the common Medium Olives and Pale Wateries. The Lake Olive and Pond Olive also belong in this group.

The flat nymphs include the March Brown, along with the Dark Dun (a stillwater species common in the English Lake District and elsewhere in upland country).

Clearly, the trout have several opportunities of feeding on these nymphs, either by rooting among the stones, or among weeds, or by intercepting the nymphs as they swim (or crawl) to the surface to hatch, or by feeding on the nymphs as they are emergent, i.e. trapped briefly in the surface film prior to the dun's emergence from the nymphal *shuck*. It is the second and third of these types of feeding that the nymph fisherman looks to for his classic sport (see *nymph fishing*, below).

As may be imagined, there are many different dressings of

artificial nymphs. Perhaps the most important are the Mayfly Nymph, as designed by the late Richard Walker; the Pheasant Tail Nymph (or PTN), which does duty in representing (when tied in different sizes) nearly all the swimming nymphs; and the Gold-ribbed Hare's Ear which, when fished small, sunk, and sparsely dressed, may imitate the flat nymphs as well as the tiny Caenis nymphs.

Along with these nymph-suggesting patterns (which, it should be noted, have no proper hackle), there are also many nymph-suggesting *wet flies* (sparsely-dressed hackled flies fished down-and-across, or upstream). Some of the most important of these are the Waterhen *Bloa* (representing a Large Dark Olive nymph, or perhaps a drowned dun), the Snipe and Purple (a stylisation of the small Iron Blue nymph), and the Partridge series of wet flies – all of which are good, tried Yorkshire patterns, particularly useful on the North-country streams for which they were devised.

nymph fishing A method of presenting the artificial nymph, which is usually fished singly (especially on rivers), or, as in *wet fly* fishing, in a team of flies. Chalk stream fishermen almost invariably fish a single fly on a light *point*. Clarke & Goddard (*The Trout and the Fly*, 106) give a helpful definition of nymph fishing on chalk streams: 'The casting to a specific, sizeable fish, of an artificial representation of the insect food upon which it is either feeding below the surface, or can reasonably be expected to be feeding upon, below the surface.'

Revolutions, in angling as in all things, do not begin with answers but in the discovery of new questions. Although nymph-suggesting wet flies had been fished for centuries, and although great advances had been made in upstream fishing (notably by W.C. Stewart), it was G.E.M. Skues (*fl*.1880-1940) who, it can be truly said, pioneered nymph fishing as we know it today. Skues, a solicitor by profession, was above all a great questioner. But for some years, by his own testimony, this was not so: 'I look back upon many years,' he wrote, 'when it was my sole ambition to follow in the footsteps of the masters of chalk stream angling, and to do what was laid down for me – that, and no other' (*Minor Tactics*, p.2).

For many years, that is, Skues fished the Hampshire chalk-streams (especially the Itchen) and followed the 'masters'. These masters fished the *dry fly* exclusively. The master himself was F.M. Halford, a man of acute observation and painstaking accuracy. Halford's disciples – and they were many and vociferous – followed his doctrines of the dry fly with an unfailing enthusiasm that ultimately tended to dogmatism. The bible of this group was

Halford's classic *Dry Fly Fishing in Theory and Practice* (1889). After the publication of this work, Skues wrote that 'the dry fly on chalk streams became at first a rage and then a religion' (*Nymph Fishing*, p.5).

In retrospect it is easy to see why this should be so. The chalk streams held many fine wild trout, trout that were more than prepared to rise to hatches of prolific insect life, trout that were manifestly feeding on the *duns* and *spinners* of *ephemeroptera*, or on the adult *sedges*. Given this, and the fact that at the turn of the century, at least (when the dry fly cult was at its height), the fish would generally rise at some period during every day of the fishing season, it is little wonder that the dry fly became popular. (Things are not the same now; pollution and abstraction have done their work; the wild trout are gone from the lowlands and the hatches of fly are much diminished.)

In addition to the practicalities of fishing the dry fly to fish feeding on the surface, there was also the excitement of seeing the fish rise to a floating artificial – a matchless moment of sheer deception. And the dry fly was (and of course still is, under the right conditions) very successful – after all, it was not invented to make the capture of trout more difficult.

Halford clarified, codified, propounded. The cult of the dry fly prospered. The disciples – as is usual with disciples – were even more vehement than their mentor (see *purist*). The representation of upwinged flies became more exact, the methods of presentation more refined. So successful was the dry fly, and in such good voice were its practitioners, that it seemed as if the dry fly were the only way to fish a chalk stream.

It had not always been so; and Skues emerged from his impeccable dry fly background to ask the most provoking questions.

He owed his 'discovery' of nymph fishing to a kind of accident, or more correctly, to a series of accidents which set him thinking. He recorded his first experience of what he called 'the efficacy of the wet fly on the Itchen' as follows:

It was a September day, at once blazing and muggy. Black gnats were thick upon the water, and from 9.30 a.m. or so the trout were smutting freely.

In those days, with *Dry Fly Fishing in Theory and Practice* at my fingers' ends, I began with the prescription, "Pink Wickham on 00 hook," followed it with "Silver Sedge on 00 hook, Red Quill on 00 hook, orange bumble, and furnace". I also tried two or three varieties of smut, and I rang the changes more than once. My gut was gossamer, and, honestly, I don't think I made more mistakes than usual; but three o'clock

arrived, and my creel was still "clean", when I came to a bend
from which ran, through a hatch, a small current of water
which fed a carrier. Against the grating which protected the
hatch-hole was generally a large pile of weed, and to-day was
no exception. Against it lay collected a film of scum, alive with
black gnats, and among them I saw a single dark olive dun
lying spent. I had seen no others of his kind during the day,
but I knotted on a Dark Olive Quill on a single cipher hook,
and laid siege to a trout which was smutting steadily in the
next little bay. The fly was a shop-tied one, beautiful to look
at when new, but as a floater it was no success. The hackle
was a hen's, and the dye only accentuated its natural inclination
to sop up water. The oil tip had not yet arrived, and so it came
about that, after the wetting it got in the first recovery, it no
sooner lit on the water on the second cast than it went under.
A moment later I became aware of a sort of crinkling little
swirl in the water, ascending from the place where I conceived
my fly might be. I was somewhat too quick in putting matters
to the proof, and when my line came back to me there was no
fly. I mounted another, and assailed the next fish, and to my
delight exactly the same thing occurred, except that this time
I did not strike too hard.

The trout's belly contained a solid ball of black gnats, and
not a dun of any kind. The same was the case with all the four
brace more which I secured in the next hour or so by precisely
the same methods. Yet each took the Dark Olive at once when
offered under water, while all day trout had been steadily refus-
ing the recognized floating lures recommended by the highest
authority. It was a lesson which ought to have set me thinking
and experimenting, but it didn't (*Minor Tactics*, 2-4).

There was to be another 'accident' of the same kind two or three
years later. But

still I did not realize that I was on the edge of an adventure,
nor yet did I realize whither I was tending when Mr. F.M.
Halford told me how a well-known Yorkshire angler had been
fishing with him on the Test, and, by means of a wet fly admirably fished without the slightest drag, had contrived to basket
some trout on a difficult water.

Indeed, it was several years later that, after fluking upon a
successful experience of the wet fly on a German river which
in general was a distinctively dry-fly stream, I began to specu-
late seriously upon the possibility of a systematic use of the
wet fly in aid of the dry fly upon chalk streams. In conversation
with the late Mr. Godwin ... who had seen the very beginnings

of the dry fly on the Itchen, and remembered well and had practised the methods which preceded it, I learned how, fishing downstream with long and flexible rods (thirteen or fourteen feet long), and keeping the light hair reel-line off the water as much as possible, these early fathers of the craft had drifted their wet flies over the tails of weeds, where the trout lay in open gravel patches, and caught baskets of which the modern dry-fly man might well be proud.

I gathered, however, that a downstream ruffle of wind was a practical necessity; and as I could not pick my days, and such as I could take were few and far between, I realized that, even if they appealed to me – which they did not – these methods would not do for me, as I might, and often did, find the river glassy smooth, but that, if I were to succeed, it must be by a wet fly modification of the dry-fly method of upstream casting to individual fish (*Minor Tactics*, 5-6).

'...a wet fly modification of the dry-fly method of upstream casting to individual fish'. In that single significant clause lies the beginning of Skues' exploration of nymph fishing on the chalk streams. However, use of the wet fly on the chalk was by no means 'new', as Skues was the first to admit. The 'early fathers' had used wet flies with some success, fishing by means of a hair reel-line carried out by the wind, a manner of presentation detailed by Cotton (see e.g. *dapping*; *dibbing*; *dibbling*). There is no reason to suppose that a similar method was not used on the chalk streams – with minor modifications – in the early and middle years of the nineteenth century:

In the days preceding the advent of the dry-fly there were no doubt exceptional fishermen who did some at least of their fishing to individual rising fish; but, taking it by and large, I infer that most of the chalk stream wet-fly fishing was done in rough windy weather with flies which searched the water, being fished dragging across and down. The diary of the Rev. Richard Durnford, 1809 to 1819, published in 1911 by Henry Nicoll under the title *Diary of a Test Fisherman*, speaks constantly of "a whistling wind", "a sufficient wind" and so on, and he used "a bob fly to steady the cast". In those times the angler stayed at home on still days...(Skues, *Nymph Fishing*, 67).

Not to be forgotten in this context is another Test fisherman, Peter Hawker, whose diary runs from 1802 to 1853 (Hills, *A Summer on the Test*, 11). Hawker was 'a great character – conceited, obstinate, opinionated and passionate; but eager, vital, enthusiastic and tireless' (Hills, 17). He, like Durnford, fished his fly (or flies) downstream; he even fished them from horseback.

But none of this was any good to Skues. It contained a hint, no more. In particular, the great improvements in the design of tackle made during the 19th century – the replacements of hair lines by dressed silk lines, the corresponding improvement in fly rods, the development of the eyed fly *hook*, and advances in dressing artificials (e.g. the development of split-winged dry flies, see *wing*) – had made earlier methods outmoded. Fishing the fly was no longer so much dependent on the presence or absence of the wind. It is a paradox perhaps that Skues was to use the improved tackle, and the upstream cast, of the dry-fly man, and modify them and the dry-fly style of presentation to his own advantage, and to the advantage of fly-fishing history.

Nymph fishing, as defined by Skues, consisted of presenting a nymph representation upstream to a visible, feeding fish (the nymph-fisher's equivalent, perhaps, of Halford's trout 'in position'). Skues did not advocate, and indeed totally deprecated, the haphazard fishing of the water, or the persistent flogging of a visible trout that was manifestly not feeding, not *on the fin* (see *fins*). His was a specific method of presentation – just as was the theory of the dry fly – and over the years he evolved an approach, and a range of artificial nymph patterns, that reflected his preoccupation with the trout feeding on natural nymphs at or near the surface. But Skues never claimed that his method was a replacement of the dry fly; obviously, there were times when the dry fly would succeed better than the nymph, and Skues saw nymph fishing very much as a complement and supplement to the dry fly. (Today, perhaps, we see the dry fly as a supplement and complement to the presentation of the nymph.) Skues quotes with approval the famous words of Francis Francis: 'The judicious and perfect application of dry, wet, and mid-water fishing stamps the finished fly fisher with the hall-mark of efficiency' (cited in *The Way of a Trout*, 140).

These are wise words; but the dry fly disciples did not heed them. Some were doubtful, others openly antagonistic, towards what they saw as a kind of iconoclasm. They invented arguments purporting to show how misguided (and how damaging) was the presentation of the nymph to the trout. Skues, with admirable logic, set out the pros and cons of the debate between himself and the dry fly purists as follows:

> The dry-fly man, after the long innings he has had, is often not of an open mind, and is unwilling to give up the exclusive doctrine of the dry fly, and he therefore seeks for arguments to justify it.
>
> If he insists that trout will not look at the nymph and I prove the contrary, then he claims:

(1) That nymph fishing is easier than the dry-fly, mainly because of the matter of drag;

(2) That it kills more fish, i.e. is too deadly and leaves too few fish for the relatively finer art of the dry fly;

(3) That persistence in the use of the nymph drives the fish to feed deep by killing off those which feed just under the surface;

(4) That trout feed mainly on nymphs and only take floating flies as a sort of sport or delicacy and that it is right that there should be one part of their habitat where they can feed with confidence and need have no fear of the angler's wiles;

(5) That for all or some of these reasons the use of the nymph on chalk streams is ethically wrong.

To all this the nymph fisher replies:

(1) If it is so much easier than the dry-fly, why do so few relatively practise it – and still fewer competently? As a matter of fact it has difficulties of its own, not excluding the matter of drag. Moreover many anglers refuse to try it as being beyond them. Indeed there must be hundreds of chalk stream anglers who are unable to distinguish between the rise of a trout to the floating natural insect and his rise to a nymph, and so go on despairingly and vainly hammering nymphing trout with floating flies.

(2) If it kills more fish, is that an objection? Why, pray, was the dry fly advocated but because it provided a method of killing fish not amenable to the previous practice of the wet fly? Well, nymph fishing provides a method of taking trout when they are not amenable to the attractions of the dry fly.

(3) I am afraid the answer to the dry-fly man's third point is the rude one – "Skittles". As well say that the persistent presentation of the dry fly has driven trout to nymphing...

(4) If one analyses the contents of the stomach of a trout, and finds, as he consistently will find, that it consists almost entirely of nymphs, it will be obvious that in confining himself to the floating fly the angler will either be condemning himself to inactivity for the greater part if not all of his fishing day or be casting floating flies to trout which are feeding exclusively below the surface. If and when trout will not feed on the surface, the only way to get them is to fish them where they are feeding...(Skues, *Nymph Fishing*, 85-7).

So Skues answered his critics, with the kind of methodological arguments that seemed to be second nature to him. The dedicated dry fly man was enraged; Skues was politely damned; a public debate was held. But Skues was not to be deterred, and he lived to see the presentation of the nymph to the trout become a widely used method on many streams.

But to further understand Skues' aims and methods, a closer look must be taken at his technique of presenting the nymph.

It must be already clear that Skues' methods involve a 'modification' of dry fly presentation. In particular, Skues was concerned with the actively feeding fish, and he approached it from downstream. Trout feeding near the surface in this way are easy to identify: as Oliver Kite later wrote,

> [a] nymphing trout is recognisable by the little movements it makes in the water as it intercepts natural nymphs, larvae, freshwater shrimps and other small food creatures borne to it by the current...Nymphing trout, to use a convenient term, look lively in the water, with their tails and fins moving to enable them quickly to cut off drifting food creatures, real or artificial...(in *Trout Fishing*, ed. Mansfield, 56).

But for Skues, unlike some later practitioners, a nymphing fish was a fish feeding within a couple of feet or so of the surface, a trout actively intercepting natural nymphs, or *bulging*; of the trout of the lower depths Skues had comparatively little to say. He quotes with approval Halford's words – 'When a trout has poised itself *near the surface* and is steadily taking duns or other flies without any great movement laterally or up and down the stream, it is said to be "in position"' (my emphasis), and he goes on to state that then 'the angler has found a fish in ideal conditions for the dry fly or the nymph, according to what the fish may be taking at the moment' (*Nymph Fishing*, 16).

That Skues' main preoccupation was with fish feeding near or at the surface no one will be tempted to deny who has studied Skues' artificial nymph patterns. Almost without exception they are tied on light wire (mainly Pennell *sneck*) *hooks*, employ *fur* or wool for *abdomen* and/or *thorax*, and are sparsely hackled with short-fibred *hen hackles*. They are thus designed to fish just under the surface. This is a point of some historical importance.

Later modifications to Skues' basic methods came about through the fishing and writings of Frank Sawyer, water keeper on the Netheravon stretch of the Hampshire Avon, and of Oliver Kite. Between the 1940s and 1960s these men were to extend the application of the principles Skues had established.

There was, for example, the design of the artificial nymph. Skues advocated the use of several different 'imitative' patterns of nymph, and concentrated on presenting them to trout near the surface. Moreover, despite his disclaimers, Skues' nymphs can be improved with respect to their sinking qualities; a hackle, for instance, on a light artificial nymph can impair the efficient sinking of the artificial to the required depth.

Sawyer and Kite were to change this. At first obsessed by 'the idea of making exact copies', Sawyer soon simplified his range of nymph representations to two or three key patterns – the Pheasant Tail nymph, the Grey Goose nymph, and (although this is not strictly a nymph pattern) the Killer Bug. The Grey Goose nymph, Sawyer wrote, 'is a blending of dressings to bring about a general representation of the pale wateries... This same pattern, tied in various sizes from 00 to size 1 can meet the requirements at all times when the pale watery group is hatching or active' (*Nymphs and the Trout*, 55). The world-famous Pheasant Tail Nymph (abbr. PTN) is a similar simplification: 'I feel the success of the pheasant tail is indeed due to the fact that it might well, in the different sizes, be mistaken by fish, for one or another of at least a dozen nymphs, of various genus and species... [S]implicity is an aim to be desired' (*Nymphs and the Trout*, 55).

But not only was there simplification in reduction of the number of artificial dressings required, there was a corresponding simplification in the style of dressing: Sawyer's artificials are constructed with wire and *herl* – the wire is used in place of tying silk (very fine red or gold wire is necessary), and the herls are used to form tails, body, and thorax. The result is a quick-sinking, streamlined nymph – not a hangover from the 'exact imitation' days of Halford, but a stylisation of features in which wings and hackle were extra to requirements:

> Baetid [olive] nymphs all share a common and basically similar structure: a small head, humped thorax, tapering abdomen and tails. Logically, therefore, the artificial nymph should be constructed in such a way as to reflect these physical characteristics.
>
> Natural nymphs do not have wings nor, when they swim, do their legs stick out as they do when arranged for examination on an entomologist's slide. It is unnecessary, indeed wholly illogical, to incorporate either wings or hackle in the dressing ...(Oliver Kite, 'Elements of nymph fishing' in *Trout Fishing*, ed. Mansfield, 46).

The artificial nymphs of the 'Netheravon school', as Sawyer/Kite nymphing became known, were simple to tie. They had good *entry*, sunk immediately and deeply where required; and they were constructed from the trout's point of view. In particular, such nymphs made it possible to fish for deeper-lying trout, and especially, for trout not directly visible to the fisherman.

One innovation made by Sawyer must be stressed. In many cases, the Netheravon school were not content (as was Skues) to let their nymph patterns fish dead drift. Trout would and will, of course, take an artificial presented in this way, but on the whole Sawyer and Kite found it more productive to induce a fish to take (see *induced take*). The induced take involves 'calculated action on the part of the fisherman':

> The induced take is used when the fish disregards the artificial until attention is drawn to it by some deliberate action by the angler, usually with a short sideways movement of the rod-tip causing the nymph to lift or swim in the water in a lifelike manner, impelling the fish to react by taking it, perhaps involuntarily (Kite, in *Trout Fishing*, ed. Mansfield, 61).

The movement of induction is not a large one; the aim is not to *drag*[2] the nymph in the water unnaturally, rather, to draw the trout's attention to the fly. An analogy may be useful: assume there is a mouse in the room where you are sitting; that mouse is rarely visible *until it moves*. Just so, the induced take moves the nymph so it becomes conspicuous. This manner of presentation is also useful when fishing the artificial *shrimp*.

Another issue raised by consideration of the induced take is again that of fly design. Kite, for example, must have taken hundreds if not thousands of trout on the PTN dressed according to Sawyer's recipe. But he found that when the dressing of the artificial had been destroyed by the ravages of trout teeth, the pattern would continue to catch fish, providing the basic structural outline of the fly was unimpaired. Kite caught many trout on what was effectively a bare hook lapped with a few turns of wire (the 'bare hook nymph'). His experiences show that, as far as nymph fishing on rivers is concerned, precise imitation is of only limited importance. What is more important is 1) that the nymph should be presented at the correct depth and at the correct speed (i.e. not dragging unnaturally fast); 2) that the structural outline of the fly be preserved; 3) that the fly behaves as the trout expect to see it behave. Imitation thus gives way to sheer presentation, which is the essence of nymph fishing in rivers (and on stillwaters).

Nor did Sawyer and Kite stop there. As well as fishing for visible, feeding trout, their techniques, and particularly the induced take, made it possible to cover deep-lying and/or invisible trout. This did not mean that they and their followers *fished the water*, flogging every reach of the river with nymphs indiscriminately; they did, however, fish for trout assumed to be present:

> Both trout and grayling...can be taken with nymphs if you cannot see them...[B]lind fishing calls for considerable

concentration and precision in action and a skill which surpasses the high art of the dry fly. Though I refer to it as blind fishing it is not with any intention of conveying the idea that one can go indiscriminately flogging the water in a sink and draw method just hoping a fish will take...(Sawyer, *Nymphs and the Trout*, 93).

This technique is useful in reflected light, when the fish cannot be directly seen, and in depths of water inaccessible to clear vision – hatch-holes (see *hatch²*), weirs, the hole under a bridge. It is particularly appropriate when fishing for grayling, which generally lie deep.

Sawyer and Kite consequently opened the way for the technique known as the 'deep nymph'. Sawyer's Killer Bug, for example, tied with a wire underbody, could be fished effectively in water up to six to eight feet deep, providing the current was moderate. At these depths, neither trout nor grayling are easily visible, and yet the deep waters of chalk streams, and of other rivers, hold many fine fish. In these places, and at those times when fish are not active on or near the surface, the 'deep nymph' comes into its own.

The phrase 'deep nymph' is put into inverted commas since what is usually presented is not a nymph, but a shrimp pattern. An artificial shrimp, suitably weighted (with e.g. strips of wine-bottle foil, or with lead wire) and fished on a long leader, may be fished at depths of 10 feet and more. (And as Skues wrote, 'If and when trout will not feed on the surface, the only way to get them is to fish them where they are feeding.')

The late Richard Walker, whose shrimp dressing is probably one of the most effective ever devised, wrote of the deep nymph as follows:

The development by...Sawyer of the weighted nymph was an important step in the progress of nymph fishing. It did, however, take place mainly in the upper reaches of the Hampshire Avon, where the depth is mostly modest and the current speed is moderate. In such conditions, a nymph of size 14 or 16, tied as Mr. Sawyer advises, will usually go as deep as is necessary.

However, such a nymph may prove quite inadequate in rivers that are much deeper and faster flowing. In recent years I have done a good deal of fishing for both trout and grayling on the middle and lower Test and some of its carriers. Since a day's fishing there involves me in a round trip of about 300 miles, and also because, at any rate in my opinion, surface fly is far less profuse than it was when I first fished the Test nearly

40 years ago, I am not inclined to sit waiting in vain for opportunities to fish a dry fly.

When the opportunity to do so occurs, I take it, but there
are so many occasions when there is not a rise to be seen all
day, that catches would be very meagre indeed without
recourse to the nymph or shrimp...(*Dick Walker's Trout Fishing*, 176).

As noted above, the use of a leaded shrimp pattern is also useful
when grayling are the quarry. Many of the grayling I have taken
during the winter months have contained a high proportion of
shrimps, and it would seem feasible to present a corresponding
artificial. As John Roberts writes

> Bug fishing is in its infancy. We have been schooled in our
> trout and grayling fishing to imitate the ephemeroptera nymphs
> and little else. But deep-sunken bugs similar to Sawyer's Killer
> Bug and heavily weighted shrimps are being developed to take
> those deep lying bigger trout and grayling that refuse to move
> to small nymph copies (*The Grayling Angler*, 118-19).

In conclusion, these remarks on nymph fishing have served to
show something of its history and development through Skues,
Sawyer and Kite, to modern techniques of fishing the shrimp in
deep water. It is a fascinating development, moving as it does
from the 'imitative', near-surface patterns of Skues to the stylised,
sparse patterns of Sawyer, to the heavily-weighted 'bugs' many
fishers now carry as supplement to the first two types of pattern.
Versatility has taken the place of dogma; careful thought has
replaced blind adherence to one particular method. In this context
it is also salutary to consider 'nymph fishing' on stillwaters, where
many advances in technique and presentation have been made.
But since this form of fishing typically involves presenting an
artificial *pupa*, rather than a nymph, properly so-called, further
comments may be found under e.g. *buzzer; midge; pupa; sedge*.

Offer   An *offer* is the movement of a trout, grayling or other salmonid to an artificial fly, a movement which may either be conclusive (i.e. the fish takes the fly; see *take¹*) or inconclusive (see also *short-taking*), but which has been definitely instigated by the presence of the angler's fly or flies in the fish's immediate vicinity. The following example is taken from Greenhalgh, here writing of presenting a fly on a sinking line, and is entirely typical of the word's usage:

> Cast your normal length of line and count as the lure sinks: "One...two...three..." and so on. By doing a series of retrieves at, say, 10, 20, 30, 45 and 60 seconds sinking times you know that all depths have been carefully fished...If you catch a fish or have an offer following a particular sinking time, you have discovered the depth of the fish and...can put your lure again at that depth precisely (*Lake, Loch and Reservoir*, 123-4).

oligotrophic   *Oligotrophic* waters, in contrast to *eutrophic* ones, are waters poor in nutrients. Greenhalgh writes of oligotrophic lakes as follows:

> the word *oligotrophic* is derived from Greek and means, literally, "little food"...Such waters have catchments of hard rock with little soil cover and, consequently, little agriculture... Rainfall percolates through the catchment drainage system into the lake and adds very little in the way of mineral salts...Due to the low salt content of such lakes the population of plant plankton...drifting in the surface layers of the open water is relatively low...In the lake margins the sparsity of nutrient salts and the rocky shore, so characteristic of oligotrophic lakes, means that only small beds of rooted water plants...can be supported (*Lake, Loch and Reservoir*, 34-5).

Such waters provide an inhospitable environment for *brown trout*; native populations tend to be small, stunted, and starving. The acidic character of many of these waters has been intensified in recent years owing to *acid rain*. On the other hand, where acid rain is absent, and where such waters lie on the western sea-board, runs of migratory fish such as salmon and esp. sea trout may be present during the summer months.

olive   Pl. *olives*, these flies are also referred to as '*upwinged flies*', also (in older literature) as *mayflies¹*. The term *upwinged flies*, however, is a term for an order (the order *ephemeroptera*, which includes all upwinged flies including the family *Baëtidae*), rather than a family or genus. Properly-speaking, therefore, *olives* are the flies of the genus *Baëtis*, the much-mentioned (and possibly overrated) aristocrats of the chalk streams and (the lowland reaches of) rain-fed rivers. Thus the two commonest true olives are *Baëtis rhodani*, the Large Dark Olive (also referred to simply as the Olive Dun and, in older literature, as the Blue Dun) and *B. vernus*, the Medium Olive; the other important flies within this family are *B. pumilus*, the Iron Blue; *B. scambus*, the Small Dark Olive; and *B. bioculatus*, the Pale Watery. (There are several other flies belonging to the family, including the Spurwings and the Pale Evening Dun, but these are arguably of less importance.) Finally, within the family *Baëtidae*, but of a different genus (see e.g. C.F. Walker, *Lake Flies and their Imitation*, 98), are two stillwater species, *Cloëon dipterum*, the Pond Olive, and *C. simile*, the Lake Olive.

There is one other ephemeropteran dubbed an *olive*: that is the Olive Upright; it is classified as *Rhithrogena semicolorata*, and is not properly a baëtid.

The olives have always been understood to be important fly-fisher's insects. Chief among them is surely the Large Dark Olive (abbr. LDO), a fly which, along with the February Red, the March Brown, and on some waters the *grannom*, may truly be said to begin the fisherman's year. It is above all to hatches of the LDO that the fisherman looks in April, from lunchtime and into the forenoon; the hatch of fly is generally over by about 4 p.m. Here, for example, is Skues, opening his Hampshire season:

It was by now ten minutes to eleven summer time (9.50 a.m. by Greenwich) and consequently at least two hours before there was any reasonable hope of the fly beginning to show. But I had my cast soaked and a Rough Olive floater tied on and oiled, and I didn't feel a bit unreasonable. Presently eleven o'clock... chimed, and almost before the echoes of the last stroke had died there appeared a little dark form on the surface at the lower end of the bend. It drifted, fluttering, for a little space, and then there was a cheerful smack and a widening ring, and it was not... [P]romptly I was covering that trout... and at length brought him up to my Dark Olive – short. I then cast across to a fish I had seen rise just by a tussock at the point of the inner corner of the bend. Up he came boldly – and missed. I pondered. I knew my pattern was as good imitation of the dark spring olive as was made... but something was wrong. I caught a fly and had a look at it. It was not the dark spring olive at all, but the large medium olive which usually comes on about mid-April, a fly which experience has taught me indicates Gold-ribbed Hare's Ear. I had only one in my box, but I knotted it on and was presently covering my first riser again. Up he came promptly...a nice plump fish of one pound three ounces, in excellent condition...(*The Way of a Trout*, 93-4).

And here is Grey of Falloden, opening his season with the *wet fly* on a Northern stream:

> ...the real rise must not be expected till eleven o'clock or later ...Presently the signs of life, both of flies and trout, will be evident enough, and then the true test will begin. There are days when the trout will rise everywhere and take badly, but a very short time will show whether this is such a day or not. If the rise is really a good one, and choice of water can be made without interfering with the sport of any one else, the angler should so have arranged matters that he is now, as the rise is beginning, not far from a really good pool...(*Fly Fishing*, 134).

Olives of one sort or another continue to hatch all season through, also into the autumn, and the beginning of the *grayling* fishing, so that they are therefore the standby flies of the river angler's year. This is not to suggest, however, that other flies are not of equal or even more importance; in particular, *terrestrial* flies may be taken season-long (esp. on a well-wooded, upland stream), as may underwater crustacea such as *shrimps* or hoglice (*Asellus*, see *water louse*), and the general attractiveness of the olives, along with their august literary pedigree, should not blind the fisherman to the value of other patterns.

The LDO was for long known as the Blue Dun; it was so in Ronalds (*Fly-Fisher's Entomology*, 1st edn, 1836), and was so in Cotton, although since Cotton gives two dressings for the Blue Dun, and one for a 'Great Dun' – all to be fished in the early spring – he is, as Hills noted (*History*, 151), 'confusing' (Hills takes Cotton's 'Great Dun', tied with dun bear's hair and with grey mallard wings, as his pattern of LDO). Hills further believed that the LDO is represented in the *Treatise*'s second dun fly ('Another Dun Fly: the body of black wool; the wings of the blackest drake; and the jay under the wing and under the tail'), although this dressing is difficult to construe accurately, and, as Hills says, the dressing is dark ('a little dark even for the Dark Olive'). The illustration of the fly in John McDonald's *Quill Gordon* (1972), however, shows a lighter fly, with the black body-wool so lightly dubbed as to be almost grey.

The other olives are again difficult to construe from the *Treatise*, although that work certainly details the spinner of the LDO, the Red Spinner ('In the beginning of May a good fly, the body roddyd wool...the wings of the drake and of the red capons hackle'). The Iron Blue is, according to Hills (*History*, 156ff.), first mentioned by Chetham (*The Angler's Vade Mecum*, 1681) as the 'Little Blue Dun', and is well known by Richard Bowlker (*The Art of Angling*, 1747), who dressed the body with mole's fur (as today). The Snipe and Purple, so effective a wet fly for the Iron Blue nymph, is given by Pritt (*Yorkshire Trout Flies*, 1885 – also the Dark Watchet, see Overfield, 66-7).

The Medium Olive (or rather olives, for there are three species, albeit virtually indistinguishable from one another) is a smaller fly than its spring relative, and hatches during the early to mid summer; it is common; and like the other olives, the fly hatches again in the autumn. I feel strongly that this fly is first identified in Cotton; it is his 'whirling Dun, which is taken every day about the mid time of day all this Month [April] through, and by fits from thence to the end of June, and is commonly made of the down of a Fox Cub, which is an ash colour at the roots, next the skin, and ribb'd about with yellow silk, the wings of the pale grey feather of a Mallard' (*Angler*, 286). Such a fly would be light in tone, corresponding with the fact that the 'duns are an olive colour, but appear to be a creamy colour in flight as they ascend from the surface...due no doubt to the pale yellow-olive colour of the underside of the body' (Goddard, *Trout Fly Recognition*, 88). There exists the bare possibility that the medium Olive is intended by the *Treatise*'s 'Yellow Fly' (for May), but Hills, surely correctly, identified this as the Little Yellow May Dun, *Heptagenia sulphurea* (*History*, 161).

So far, this entry has concentrated almost wholly on the olive duns. They are indeed important flies, but this should not be taken to mean that the olive *nymphs*, or those sparkling adults, the olive *spinners*, are less important. As detailed under *nymph fishing*, however, there seems less need here to look for precisely representative or imitative patterns: the ubiquitous Pheasant Tail Nymph in the appropriate sizes does duty for all olive nymphs (although those of an 'imitative' cast of mind may wish to use Goddard's splendid PVC nymph), and for the spinners, there are no finer patterns than the Pheasant Tail Spinner, or Lunn's Particular, tied in the correct sizes (sizes 14-16). These last are effective when the Red Spinner (the adult LDO, see above) is on the water in the evening. See also *dun*.

on the fin   See *fin*.

on the reel   See *reel*.

ova The eggs of a female (*hen*) salmonid. Norman Maclean writes:

> The ovaries of the female fish and testes of the male are paired, and lie along with the gut in the body cavity. For much of the year both are soft opaque organs, but at all times the ovaries may be distinguished by the presence of small bead-like swellings which represent ripening egg follicles. Since the outer membrane of the ovary eventually ruptures as the mass of ripening eggs increases, hen fish which are close to the breeding season will have the body cavity very largely filled with eggs (*Trout and Grayling*, 48-9).

It should be added that hen brown trout, and especially *rainbow trout*, are sometimes common captures on stillwaters, the latter during the early part of the season (when anglers refer to e.g. 'black' – these last usually *cocks* – or 'spawny' fish). Although rainbows do not commonly spawn in British stillwaters, females and males congregate in areas of the lake where spawning would, under different circumstances, take place, e.g. stony shallows around feeder streams. These thwarted fish are unpleasant to catch and still more unpleasant to eat, and should be avoided as far as possible.

All hen salmonids lay several thousand eggs, of which perhaps one hundred, or even less, will survive through the subsequent stages of *alevin*, *fry* and *parr*. Mortality is heavy (although conditions in a hatchery are obviously more conducive to survival than conditions in the wild): even during the egg-laying process it is common to see other fish (such as the *grayling*) eating stray ova. Perhaps for this reason, bait incorporating roe has long been held to be particularly killing. Bait fishing is, however, outside the subject of this book. See also *baggot; rawner; redd; spawning*.

overhead casting The basic fly-fishing cast with both a single- and double-handed fly rod; see *cast*[2].

over the front This phrase seems to have crept into the fly-fishing lexicon very recently. It refers to the practice of 'traditional' *boat-fishing*, i.e. angling downwind with a team of flies from a drifting boat (see also *loch-style*; *drift*). 'Front' here refers to the downwind gunwale, as in the following: 'Far too many people seem to have a simplistic idea that loch-style is just about drifting downwind, and casting and retrieving in front of the boat' (Chris Ogborne, 'Loch-style today', *T&S*, March 1987, 44).

Palmer A type of dressing on an artificial fly in which the *hackle* is wound in open spirals up the *hook shank*; thus also the term is applied to the artificial fly itself, as in Soldier Palmer etc. The origin of the term is of interest: 'The name Palmer arises from the days of the crusades when it was the term used for warriors who had returned from the Holy Land, since it was their custom to bring back branches of palm. It then became applied to the woolly caterpillars from their nomadic habits and subsequently to describe the artificial flies which they were supposed to represent' (Courtney Williams, *Dictionary*, 279).

As Courtney Williams notes, despite the fact that *palmers* are supposed to represent hairy caterpillars according to the old authorities (e.g. Ronalds [1836], who noted that the Red Palmer 'is the caterpillar of *Arctia caja*, or the Garden Tiger Moth'), the theory is 'somewhat far-fetched', largely because one very seldom sees trout eating caterpillars, and the number of the last which find their way onto the water must be very small. Nevertheless, this etymology is supported by e.g. Walton:

> 'Tis endless to tell you what the curious searchers into Natures productions have observed of these Worms and Flies: But yet I shall tell you what *Aldrovandus*, our *Topsel*, and others say of the *Palmer-worm*, or *Caterpillar*, That whereas others content themselves to feed on particular herbs or leaves... yet he observes, that this is called a *pilgrim* or *palmer-worm*, from his very wandering life and various food (*Compleat Angler*, Part 1, 99).

Walton later noted that 'the *Palmer-worm*... and the *May-flie* are the ground of all Flie-angling' (106, and see the verse below). In this instance, Walton did acknowledge his source: 'Mr. *Barker* commends several sorts of the *Palmer* flies, not only those rib'd with silver and gold, but others that have their bodies all made of black, or some with red, and a red hackle...' (109). Hills (*History*, 77) cited the following verse from Barker's *Art of Angling* (1651):

> Once more, my good brother, Ile speak in thy eare,
> Hogs, red Cows & Bears wooll, to float best appear,
> And so doth your fur, if rightly it fall,
> But always remember, make two and make all.

As Hills explained, 'float' in this instance does not mean to float

159

on the surface, but rather, to float 'aloft in the water', near the top (and see *dry fly*); the explanation of the curious phrase 'make two and make all' is that 'Barker considered that if you knew how to dress two flies you knew all, what he calls a Palmer (though it had wings) and a Mayfly' (Hills, *History*, 77).

Was Barker in fact the first to use such flies? The history of the term perhaps suggests this – OED dates the word's first attestation to Barker's *Art of Angling* (1651) – but the context of the Barker entry suggests otherwise. Barker wrote 'There are several kinds of Palmers...' Clearly this implies that palmered dressings were in existence before 1651. It may well be, for instance, that the *Treatise*'s instructions on how to dress a fly could be taken to include instructions on dressing a palmered hackle. Where the *Treatise* wrote, for example, of the 'Ruddy Fly' (for use in May) that its wings are 'of the drake and of the redde capons hackyll', this might be construed to mean that the hackle was palmered. In the admirable illustrations to John McDonald's *Quill Gordon* (1972), palmered dressings are in several cases given as 'alternatives'. Perhaps we can never know for certain, but it seems reasonable to conclude, with Courtney Williams, that the palmers are among the oldest British flies.

More certain it is that palmers are killing flies for brown and rainbow trout, particularly on stillwaters in the summer months, where the Soldier Palmer, and its many variants, are particularly effective during hatches of *sedges*. The palmered hackle gives the fly plenty of kick and life in the water, and such dressings are especially good when fished on a *dibbled* top *dropper*. In larger sizes (sizes 10 and 8), palmered patterns, such as the Soldier Palmer, Zulu, Blue Zulu and Kingsmill Moore's range of Bumbles, are also useful for sea trout on lochs and loughs. See also *bumble*.

parachute Also *parachute hackle* or *parachute fly/flies*. The term is not recorded in the OED in a fishing sense, although it is clearly related to *parachute* ('apparatus used for descending safely from a great height', first attestation in English 1785) and to the same word in its applied or extended form ('any contrivance, natural or artificial, serving to check a fall through the air', first attestation 1796). In its fishing sense, the term seems to be 20th century in origin (see below).

A fly dressed with a *parachute hackle* is a fly in which the hackle is tied not around the *hook shank* but round a piece of nylon, or the root of a nylon loop, or an upwardly-projecting *hackle* stalk, so that it lies 'horizontally across the hook which it covers in the manner of an open umbrella' (Courtney Williams, *Dictionary*,

280). Courtney Williams states that this style of dressing is, or was, 'the speciality of a well-known Scottish tackle firm' (I have been unable to identify this firm), but also notes an 'American account [which] states that it was originated by Mr. William Brush, of Detroit, who applied for a patent for the idea in 1931 ... In this instance, the patent related ... to a projection on the hook and not to the fly itself' (*Dictionary*, 280-81).

The advantage of such flies is that they fall very lightly onto the water and, since all the hackle fibres support the fly, they also float well. Of late there has been renewed interest in this style of dressing, especially in the 'upside-down flies' (abbr. USD) of Clarke & Goddard, who write of their designs that 'they are tied upside down, and stand on a parachute-hackle situated on the reverse side of the hook, (*The Trout and the Fly*, 152). They continue that 'The parachute style of hackling ... spreads the fibres across the surface, dimples it and gives off a sparkling refraction in a manner very similar to that created by the feet of the natural dun when seen in the mirror. *And what is more, keeps the body of the dun aloft from the surface of the water*' (152, their emphasis). There may therefore be good scientific reasons, based on the fish's presumed perception of the fly, for employing such patterns, as well as practical ones (see also *Funneldun*; *mirror*; *window*).

Finally here, it should be noted that there is an excellent artificial *Daddy-long-legs* which is constructed with a large parachute hackle formed from one or two cock pheasant flank feathers (see 'Daddy with a difference', Richard Stephen, *T&S*, August 1987, 48-9).

parr   *Parr* refers to the young *brown trout*, *sea trout* or *salmon* in its second and subsequent years in the river of its birth; a stage of development between *fry* and, in the case of migratory fish, *smolt*. (Non-migratory brown trout pass from being parr to adult fish with no intervening stage of development.) Parr can be easily distinguished since they carry characteristic 'thumb-prints' (also known as 'parr-marks') on their flanks. This is explained by Norman Maclean, who also gives some useful information concerning the distinction between trout and salmon parr:

> Salmon parr have very bluish "thumb prints" with a single red spot between each. Trout parr have more lightly coloured "thumb prints", with many red spots, and most of these spots are surrounded by whitish rings. In salmon parr the little adipose fin ... is greyish green, while in trout it is orange. Parr of rainbow trout are rather similar to those of brown trout (*Trout and Grayling*, 36).

Parr are inexperienced fish and greedy feeders; they will often

take a fly intended for their larger relatives, and need to be carefully handled and released by the fishermen. They feed on *midges*
and *upwinged flies*, and also on underwater food such as *caddis*.
This feeding behaviour may be significant: it is possible, for example, that mature salmon and sea trout, after spending some time
in freshwater after their return from the sea feeding grounds, may
begin (rather mysteriously) to remember their feeding behaviour
in the river as parr, and may consequently be prepared to accept
small fly-suggesting artificial patterns, rather than the larger fish-
suggesting patterns usually employed. But 'may' is here the opera-
tive word; much remains speculative.

Parr also serve a function in terms of breeding. Some male
salmon parr attain early sexual maturity: Jones (1959, reported
in Taverner & Scott, *Salmon Fishing*, 25) found 'that the presence
of ripe male parr on the spawning grounds [of salmon] was to
insure fertilization of the eggs in case of lack of fertilization by
the adult male'. This point is also made in Henry Williamson's
anthropomorphic epic, *Salar the Salmon*:

Gralaks lay above the Fireplay Pool. The roe which had been
growing within her all the summer were now one-fifth the
weight of her body. She was ripe, ready to drop her eggs.
Three male fish, knowing this, were near her, waiting to shed
their milt on her eggs. One of them was Salar.

Behind the three cock-fish lay Garroo the cannibal trout.
Behind Garroo lay two smaller trout who had tasted salmon
eggs before. And lying close beside Gralaks was Grai, a salmon
parr weighing two ounces, who had fallen in love with Gralaks
with all the volume of his milt, which weighed one-tenth of
an ounce. Gralaks was aware of Grai; indeed she was pleased
by his nearness . . . Grai was determined that no other cock-fish
should lie beside Gralaks (chapter 24 of *Salar the Salmon*; from
The Henry Williamson Animal Saga, 1960, 359).

The word is of unknown etymology, although the first attestations are Scots, so perhaps the origin of the word is Scots Gaelic?
The term is first found in the early 18th century (1715-22, Pen-
necuik, *Descr. Tweeddale*: 'Salmo salmulus, Samlet, or Par' –
evidently the little fish was here held to be a separate species) and
thereafter in Smollett's 'Ode to Leven-Water' (1771), in an
entirely characteristic piece of 18th-century bucolic: 'The scaly
brood In myriads cleave thy crystal flood; . . . The Salmon,
monarch of the tide, the ruthless Pike, intent on war; The silver
eel and motled par'.

peal   A West Country term for the *sea trout*; also (but see below)
an Irish term for the *salmon grilse*. OED also gives other fish terms

(all terms for sea trout) in which the word is used combinatively, e.g. *herring peal*; *may peal*; *pugg peal*. The term is of uncertain origin, but I conjecture that it may come from OF *palle* (cf. ModE *pale*), 'of a whitish appearance'. This would be congruent with the many other dialectal terms for the sea trout (see e.g. *finnock*; *herling*; *white trout*; *whitling*) which stem from the fish's silvery-white appearance when newly from the sea.

Peal is first attested in English in 1533, and throughout the 16th and 17th centuries the word seems to have been used indiscriminately for both salmon and sea trout (thus, incidentally, supporting the theory that sea trout fishing was not seen as a pastime in its own right until later). The OED's definition suggests that *peal* means either 'grilse or young salmon (now esp. one under two pounds in weight)' or a 'smaller species of salmon, Salmon Cambricus (or S. trutta)'. There is threefold inaccuracy here. First, the term is nowadays used most frequently to mean sea trout (in the West Country); second, the terms *grilse* and 'young salmon under 2lbs. ...' are not exactly interchangeable (and salmon grilse under that weight are, surely, caught so rarely – and occur so infrequently? – that they would hardly warrant a special name); and third, *Salmo cambricus* (whatever that is – the cited source is Günther's *Study of Fishes* [1880]) is perhaps not the same fish as our familiar *S. trutta*. (Does the OED mean here *S. trutta trutta*, the sea trout, or *S. trutta fario*, the **brown trout**?) The OED seems almost to imply that the local names for sea trout correspond to genetic varieties of the fish; this is not the case, at least as far as the most recent study of the sea trout's life and behaviour suggests (Edward Fahy, *Child of the Tides*, 1985).

pectoral fins The fins situated on either side of a fish's body immediately behind the gills (the term *pectoral* derives from Latin *pectoralis*, 'chest'). Norman Maclean writes that the pectoral fins 'perform many different roles, such as [to] slow forward or backward propulsion, or sideways stabilisation' (*Trout and Grayling*, 19).

Peter This is a shortening of *Green Peter*, a species of *sedge* found in Ireland. Irish anglers sometimes speak of 'Peter fishing' of 'Fishing the Peter' when the trout are feeding on the emerging *pupae* and adults.

plasticiser Also *replasticiser*. An ugly word which refers to the grease-like substance anglers use (usually during the close season) to replace the dressing on today's plastic-coated *fly lines*. My jar of plasticiser bears the following information: 'The coating on fly lines is P.V.C. mixed with a plasticising agent. Plasticiser can escape through high temperatures or by greasing with ordinary line grease, or simply by evaporation. If plasticiser is lost the line becomes stiffer, and the coating may crack'. The makers of this substance recommend dressing the line (or lines, since most fly fishermen carry several) once or twice a year.

The term is transparently from *plastic*, in its sense 'that [which] may be moulded' (cf. L. *plasticus*). The term *plasticizer* is first found in English in 1925 (perhaps from the verb *plasticize*), in the *Paint, Oil and Chemical Review*: 'In order that the film may remain flexible . . . plasticizers . . . are incorporated in the lacquer'. OED defines the word as 'any substance which when added to another makes it (more) plastic or mouldable . . .'

Fly line plasticiser, which sells under the trade name 'Perma-plas', was I think devised by the late Richard Walker, and is marketed by Chubbs Ltd, Amersham. The term is not found in a fishing sense before the 1970s.

play   In one sense this word may be used as a noun, as in e.g. 'the play of a hooked fish', here ultimately deriving from OE *plēga*, 'rapid movement, exercise, sport'. This meaning of the word extended to become *play* in the sense 'free or unimpeded movement' (OED), a usage first found in Walton (*Angler*, 68: 'Give him [the chub] play enough before you offer to take him out of the water'). A typical 20th-century use of the term comes from Sidney Spencer's *Newly from the Sea* (1969, p.128): '. . . my advice was ignored and the play proceeded with the rod hardly flexed'.

Walton's usage gives rise to a new verb, *to play*, i.e. in a specifi-cally angling sense, *to give play to* (a fish). This verb is first attested (although probably in use long before) in Richardson's *Pamela*: 'I . . . soon hooked a lovely carp. Play it, play it, said she; I did, and brought it to the bank' (1741). The second attestation of the verb comes in Best's *Concise Treatise on the Art of Angling* (1787): 'He seldom breaks his hold if your tackle is strong and you play him properly'.

Playing fish is primarily a matter of what some anglers call '*hands*'. Skues, for example (*The Way of a Trout*, 192) defined this enviable quality as 'the combined certainty and delicacy of correspondence between wrist and eye which mean so much, whether in the despatch of the tiny feathered iron . . . or in the skilful restraint of [the] quarry when hooked, and its ultimate steering to the net'. This steering involves not only sensitivity but also a kind of strong tact in knowing when to give line and when to redeem it. It is also a matter of keeping the rod up (see *pointed*) and, of course, of sound tackle. The *Treatise* puts this last point admirably; under the general heading of 'Impediments' ('whyche cause a man to [t]ake noo fysshe'), it listed, as the first impediment, 'yf your harnays [tackle] be not mete nor fetly made'. (As an incidental point, the third impediment listed in the *Treatise* is magnificently inclusive: 'yf that ye angle not in bytynge tyme'.) 'Twas ever thus...

played out   Other things being equal (which of course they seldom are), one might expect this phrase to derive from the sense of *play* (vb.) detailed above. This does not seem to be the case, however. The phrase *play out*, in its meaning 'finish', is first attested in Shakespeare (1596, *HenryIV*, Pt. I: 'Out you Rogue, play out the Play'); in origin it appears to be specifically a dramatic term. This sense then seems to give rise to an extended meaning, 'performed to the end, brought to an end, ended, finished... also exhausted, used up... worn out' (OED). This sense is first attested in 1863 ('One remains... a played-out man').

A *played out fish* is a fish near to the end of the play or fight, a fish beaten by rod pressure, the angler's skill and/or the weight of the current. Fish tend to turn on their sides when exhausted in this way (the gleam of a sea trout's dimly moon-struck flank in the midsummer darkness...), and this is the moment to use the *net* (or *tailer* / *gaff*, perhaps, when fishing for salmon). One example that comes to hand is again from Sidney Spencer, here writing of landing salmon: '... I have never had any trouble when asked... to tail a fish. But I would much sooner do so in suitable circumstances or in the absence of a net. The method has the great merit of simplicity and of having only one restrictive rule – that which dictates that the fish shall be played out before any attempt is made. The net scores highly here, of course...' (*Newly from the Sea*, 129). See also *spent[1]*.

plecoptera   See *creeper; stone-fly*.

point   The end of the *leader*, hence also *point fly* (cf. *dropper*) or tail fly. The OED does not appear to record the term in an angling sense, although *point*, in the usage 'salient or projecting part of anything, of a more or less tapering form... a tip, apex...' is first attested in English in 1391 (Chaucer: 'At the poynt of thy label... set a prikke'). As noted under *cast[1]*, *leader* etc., in trout fishing the leader is usually tapered, and culminates in a relatively long, relatively fine point. The following is advice from the late Oliver Kite on constructing a leader for nymph fishing on a chalk stream:

> I recommend a cast of about nine feet, consisting of four or five links, of which the thickest should be at least three feet and the point at least three feet. The breaking strain of my point is 3.6lb... until after Mayfly, thereafter 2.9lb... Changing the fly and shortening the point to eliminate wind knots and frayed ends soon reduces the length of the point to less

> than a yard...When I am fishing, I always carry a roll of
> point-strength nylon...('Brown trout in chalk streams' in *The
> Complete Fly-Fisher*, ed. C.F. Walker, 129-30).

Nowadays many anglers use shop-bought, tapered leaders,
perhaps adding to the end of the taper their own choice and length
of point nylon. Many anglers also use leaders longer than 9 feet,
particularly on stillwaters, where the point may be 6 feet long or
more. This tendency to use longer leaders is practical in so far as
it distances the point fly from the thicker *fly line*; in calm water,
this means that surface-feeding fish may be approached more
circumspectly. The tendency has also gained ground owing to
the recent availability of braided leaders (properly, leader butts),
which attach to the fly line by means of a sleeve joint; a nylon
point is then knotted to the end of the braid. See also *cast¹*.

pointed   To be *pointed* is one of fly-fishing's many misdemean-
ours; it usually comes about through the careless bungling from
which none is exempt, and involves an unbent rod and taut(ening)
leader being in a straight, direct line between the angler's rod-
hand and a hooked fish. If the rod is not bent, it cannot absorb
the shocks of a hooked fish's head-shaking and running, hence
the advice given to every beginner playing a fish: 'Keep the rod
up!' (and see *play*). The usual result of allowing the rod to drop
during the play is that undue pressure is put on the leader which,
especially if light point material is being used, tends to break at
the *point* (or at the relevant *dropper*). In any case, the fish is lost,
resulting in sick numbness and brutal, quiet self-accusation.

It has long been known that to allow rod and line to be straight
when playing what our ancestors would doubtless have called a
'great trout' was folly. The *Treatise* gave advice on the matter.
Not only did it say 'never oversmite the strength of your line'
(i.e. don't *strike¹* too hard), but also this: 'as moche as ye may
lete hym not come out of your lynes ende streyghte from you.
But kepe hym euer vnder the rodde and euermore holde hym
streyghte, soo that your lyne may susteyne and beere his lepys
and his plungys wyth the helpe of your croppe [rod tip] and of
your honde'. Of course, the 15th-century fisherman had no reel,
and was obliged to 'keep him under the rod'. But the general
advice is still good.

pollan   One of the *whitefishes*, *Coregonus lavaretus* (although OED
defines the pollan as *Coregonus pollan* [?]), closely related to the
powan and the *vendace*. It is (said to be – is it still?) found in
Lough Neagh, Lough Erne and lakes on the Shannon system in
Ireland. Like the other whitefishes, it seems to be very rarely
caught by fly fishermen, largely because it feeds on planktonic

matter, rising seldom to the surface to eat flies.

The first attestation of the word dates to 1713, and one Mr
Nevill's *Lough Neagh*: 'The English call them fresh Water Her-
rings, for want of another Name; for Pollan is an Irish name'.
OED suggests that the word is possibly fr. Irish *poll*, 'inland lake'
+ *-og* or *-an* (derivative suffixes), cf. Gaelic *pollag*.

powan   One of the *whitefishes*, *Coregonus lavaretus* (OED defines
the powan as *Coregonus clupeoides* [?]), very closely related to the
gwyniad and the *schelly*. It is said to live in Loch Lomond (M.E.
Varley, *British Freshwater Fishes*, 41). The *Observer's Book of
Freshwater Fishes* records that the fish is silvery, the back is slate-
blue or grey, and that it is large-scaled. It notes that the fish may
grow up to 16 inches and live to 10 years of age. Powan, like their
immediate relatives, are mainly plankton feeders, and are very
rarely caught by fly fishermen.

The term is first attested in 1633, and the writings of one Mr
Monipennie ('Loch [Lomond], besides an abundance of other
fishes, hath a kind of fish of the owne [sic], named, Powan, very
pleasant to eate'). The second instance of the word comes in Smollett (whose writing has been cited before in this work, see e.g.
parr): 'Powans [are] a delicate kind of fresh-water herring peculiar
to this lake [Lomond]' (*Humphry Clinker*). See also *vendace*.

priest   The term is a euphemism for the implement of the final
kill. A *priest* is a piece of (usually weighted) wood, metal or other
material (e.g. weighted stag's horn) which is used to kill a landed
fish quickly. Two or three taps on the back of the fish's head are
usually sufficient. It is considered bad form, and is unnecessarily
cruel, to allow fish to die gasping on the bank. Most fly fishermen
carry a priest; all should.

The *priest* is so-called because it 'administers the last rites' to
the fish; another theory is that it is called a *priest* because it is the
last thing a fish sees before it dies (this is an Irishism).

In fact the history of the word seems to be thoroughly Irish. OED
defines a *priest* as a 'mallet or other weapon used to kill a fish
when spent. (Chiefly in Ireland.)' The first record of the word
dates to 1851, and a note in Newland's *Erne, Leg[ering?] and
Fly-Fishing*: 'Priest, a short wooden mallet, whose offices are
required when the salmon is *in extremis*'. In 1900, however,
William Senior noted that 'The baton, or short cudgel, used to
perform the last offices for captured fish is still called the "priest",
the name lingering, perhaps, more in Ireland than in England or
Scotland' (*Pike and Perch*). Senior's comment suggests that the
term was not widespread, or was perhaps even dying out, at the
turn of the century. If so, it has certainly recovered since then.

Perhaps the ultimate history of the term is older than the 19th century. In one of its senses, the word *priest* (in its meaning 'minister') could gloss as a verb, 'To be (a person's) priest: to kill him' – in allusion to the function of a priest in performing the last offices to the dying. In this usage, the word is first attested in a medieval romance of 1430 ('The Iren with his hawberk met Right ageyn the self brest; Wel nigh it had been his prest'), again in Kyd's *Spanish Tragedy* ('Who first laies hand on me, ile be his Priest'), and also in Shakespeare's *Henry VI*, Part II: 'And to preserve my sovereign from his foe, say but the word, and I will be his priest'.

pupa   A stage in the life cycle of e.g. the *midges* (*Chironomids*) and the *sedges* between *larva* and adult fly. The term is ultimately from L. (*pūpa*, 'girl, doll', cf. e.g. Dutch *poppe, pop, popje*, 'doll, nymph, chysalis'). Its first attestation in English dates to 1773, and Gilbert White's *Natural History of Selborne*: 'The black shining cases or skins of the *pupae* of these insects...'. Another instance is Kirby's *Entomology* (1815): 'The states through which insects pass are four: the egg; the larva; the pupa; and the imago'.

Midge or sedge pupae are perhaps most important to fly fishermen hunting brown or rainbow trout, especially on stillwaters, although both the sedges and, increasingly, hatches of midges occur commonly on rivers.

Midge pupae emerge from their larvae (see *bloodworm*) after having developed inside the larval case. Goddard (*Trout Flies of Stillwater*, 90) records that the pupae live up to 72 hours (in captivity). During this period, when conditions are suitable for hatching, the pupae swim slowly to the water surface, and there hang in the surface film before transforming into adult flies. The pupae appear to favour calm water for this last process, and so the most spectacular rises of fish on stillwaters tend to occur on calm evenings (see *evening rise*); this is connected with the fact that when the water surface is calm, the surface film is thicker than when the surface is disturbed (as by wind), and consequently the pupae may become trapped in the film for a time before hatching can take place. In this trapped state they represent easy pickings for trout.

The actual hatching process is significant. Some anglers (and angling writers) imply that the pupa hatches 'vertically', i.e. the adult breaks from the nymphal *shuck* when that is hanging vertically in the surface film. This is not the case. At the moment of hatching, the pupa lies horizontally in the film; this point is made by Goddard: 'the pupa, hanging vertically, slowly adopts a... rigid posture and then floats upwards until it is horizontal in the surface...' (*Trout Flies*, 91). Then the skin splits, and the adult insect emerges. At this time, anglers fishing with artificial patterns fished in (rather than on) the surface (some anglers call these 'damp dries', i.e. barely-floating *dry flies*, see e.g. Fraser, *Mastering the Nymph*, 45) may take good bags of fish.

Midge pupa patterns are legion. Most have very slim bodies dressed round the bend of the hook, to represent the curved profile of the *naturals*. *Buzzers* are usually fished in a team of two or three on a long leader, greased if necessary. Alternatively, they may be fished singly. The patterns include the Cove Pheasant Tail Nymph, which is typically fished in sizes 8-12, and sometimes weighted (to represent the pupa near the bottom, or swimming to the surface), a range of naturalistic buzzer patterns, usually tied (in sizes 12-16) with prominent tufts of white hackle-fibres or synthetic material at tail and thorax to represent the natural pupa's 'breathers', and stylised buzzer patterns such as small *bumbles*, *palmers* etc. There is also a range of those 'damp dries' referred to above: a small Grey Duster seems an effective representation of a small, dark pupa hatching from the film. There is also a further range of *suspender* patterns used to represent the pupae just prior to hatching.

From an angler's point of view, hatches of midge tend to fall into seasonal groups. On many waters, the season begins with hatches of large black midges, *Chironomus anthracinus*; these hatch through April and into May, and again at the back-end of the season (September). During the early and mid summer, the green and 'Golden Dun' midges (*C. plumosus* spp.) may put in an appearance, as may the Campto midge; these tend to be smaller than the black midge of spring. On some waters, notably the Bristol lakes, there are good hatches of Large Red midges (again, *C. plumosus* spp.). This diversity means that if an angler intends to fish midge-representing patterns seriously, he should carry a range of sizes and colours (particularly black, green, olive, and red), and be prepared to experiment in presenting them at different depths according to the behaviour of the naturals and the response of the fish. At its best, buzzer fishing is an intense and captivating branch of the art.

Then there is the *sedge pupa*, a larger insect, which typically hatches during the mid to late summer on many lakes (and rivers). As everyone knows, the life cycle of the sedge is *caddis* – pupa – adult (and see *sedge*). The pupae, using strong mandibles, actually cut their way out of the caddis case, having first constructed a cocoon for themselves, in which they pupate (Goddard, *Trout Flies*, 120). They then swim to the surface, or towards the stones of the shore (such variant behaviour apparently depending on species). Goddard adds that those species which hatch in the surface film in open water do so by inflating the pupal case from within until it splits, when the adult emerges (*Trout Flies*, 121). The behavioural pattern is not radically different to that of the midges, in the sense that the pupae are vulnerable to trout both when they are swimming towards the surface to hatch, and when they are emergent.

The commonest sedges are brown, brown/orange, or green in colour; representative here are the Cinnamon Sedge *(Limnephilus lunatus)*, the Medium Sedge *(Goëra pilosa)*, the various Silverhorns *(Athripsodes cinerus* and other spp.), and the Longhorns *(Oecetis lacustris* and others). All these are extremely common and widespread. The largest sedge, and a species which can provide very exciting fishing where it occurs, is the Great Red Sedge *(Phyganea grandis)*; this is called the '*Murragh*' or 'Murrough' in Ireland. Another common river sedge is the Caperer *(Halesus radiatus)*. Finally here, one should not forget the Green Peter *(Phryganea varia)*; this is an Irish fly – Roberts believes it is 'unknown or extremely rare in the U.K.' (*Illust. Dictionary*, 77) – but it is important where it occurs, notably on the Irish midland loughs.

Once again, artificial patterns are legion. Sedge pupae are typically tied on a hook size 10-12, with a bulky (although not fat) body of e.g. dubbed seal's fur of the relevant colour, some sort of *thorax* (e.g. of pheasant fibres or condor herl), and perhaps a sparse *hackle*. One stylised pattern, particularly good when cream-bodied sedges are hatching, is Goddard's Persuader (size 10). Another stylised pattern, and one with a long and august history, is that great traditional fly, the Invicta. This was designed by James Ogden *c.*1870s (Overfield, 102); it is a cracking pattern, and also useful, in smaller sizes, on flowing water.

Until the 20th century very little was known about the flies which hatched on stillwater. Take, for example, the chapter on 'Loch Fishing' by R.C. Bridgett in *Trout Fishing* (ed. Kenneth Mansfield), published as recently as 1970. As C.F. Walker put it, in his introduction to that chapter:

> When this work appeared, every conceivable aspect of the subject was covered with commendable thoroughness. There is, however, one department in which our knowledge has increased since Bridgett's day; namely, the entomology of still water. It was not, in fact, until the publication of J.R. Harris's invaluable work, *An Angler's Entomology*, that the lake fisher had anything to guide him in the recognition of the various

insects he encountered at the water-side...[Bridgett] did not, for example, quite appreciate that many of the flies he found on lakes were not the same species as he had been accustomed to see on rivers, particularly those of the order Ephemeroptera...

Bridgett's chapter makes it clear that he was thinking very much in terms of the *upwinged flies*, the *olives*. Nowadays, although of course olives do hatch on lakes and lochs, stillwater anglers think much more in terms of midge, sedge, and *fry*, and it is this branch of the art which, arguably at least, has seen the greatest advances in understanding and technique this century. How do we trace this development?

Perhaps we ought to begin at Blagdon, which was one of the first artificially-made stillwaters to be stocked with brown and rainbow trout (early 20th century). Before that time, as C.F. Walker made clear (*Lake Flies and their Imitation*, 17ff.), stillwater trout fishing did not exist in any systematic sense, apart, perhaps, from the fishing on the Scottish and Irish lochs (and see *sea trout*). It was the Blagdon experiment which 'set the fashion for stocking newly-made reservoirs with trout' (C.F. Walker, *Lake Flies*, 19). And it is from Blagdon that we can date the first artificial patterns specifically designed to represent pupae. These are two patterns of the famous Dr Bell ('Bell's Bush' at Blagdon is named after him); they are the Amber Nymph, a sedge pupa, and the Blagdon Buzzer. Roberts (*Illust. Dictionary*, 4) writes of Dr H.A. Bell as follows: 'Bell, a nymph-fisher on the Bristol reservoirs during the 1920 and 30s...is very much the father-figure of stillwater nymph fishing. In an era when winged lures were the norm for lake fishing, he devised a series of flies based upon items he found in trouts' stomachs...Most of his patterns were entirely new'. And of the Blagdon Buzzer, Roberts writes that it 'was probably the first stillwater midge-pupa imitation' (p.20).

Thereafter, we might follow C.F. Walker in tracing the development of this branch of the art through Sidney Spencer's *The Art of Lake Fishing with the Sunk Fly* (1934) – a work which argues that 'the angler's objective is the successful imitation of some form of underwater life upon which trout are feeding or may be expected to feed under given conditions' – to *The Art and Craft of Loch Fishing* by H.P. Henzell (1937) – which suggests that 'we can imitate very well, by the use of nymphs and wet flies, the various larvae of flies and freshwater shrimps'. There is then a lacuna, caused by the war. Subsequently, we can trace the development of lake fishing from Tom Ivens' classic *Still Water Fly Fishing* (1953, and subsequent editions) – although Ivens

declared that exactly imitative flies were 'a waste of time' – and
Harris's *Angler's Entomology* (1952; a great work, see above) – to
the opening of many public reservoirs for fly-fishing in the 1960s
and 1970s. It is during this period that perhaps the greatest
advances are made, and chief among the works devoted to 'imitative' fishing was Brian Clarke's magnificent *The Pursuit of Stillwater Trout*, which was serialised in *Trout and Salmon* and first
published in 1975. It is Clarke who writes that 'the midge pupa
is the star of the piece' (p.67); of the sedge pupa, he writes 'As
with the midge, it is the sedge pupa which offers the angler his
best chance of trout...The pupa is the stimulator of many a
joyous evening rise, with the trout hitting it with a smack and a
wallop' (p.70). This work brings us close to home, and the many
refinements in pattern, presentation and overall technique that
have been made during the later 1970s and 1980s. Thankfully,
despite all refinements, midge and sedge pupae will continue to
be eaten as long as trout swim.

purist   A term associated with the *dry fly*, particularly with the
adherents and followers of Halford, who fished the dry fly exclusively and who were later to deride the use of the artificial *nymph*
(see *nymph-fishing*). Thus Skues, for example, in an early use of
the term, dedicated his first book, *Minor Tactics of the Chalk
Stream* (first edn 1910) to 'my friend, the dry-fly purist, and to
my enemies, if I have any'. The term is in sporadic use today,
and perhaps is heard most often around the banks of those streams
which are still 'dry fly only'. I have also heard the term used of
nymph fishermen on stillwaters, i.e. of those who abjure the use
of *lures*; this usage of the term is ironic, considering its dry-fly
origins.

The word *purist*, in its sense 'one who aims at, affects, or insists
on scrupulous or excessive purity, esp. in language or style', is
first attested in English in 1706 (Phillips: '*Purist*, one that affects
to speak or write neatly and properly'); in a more general, non-
stylistic sense it is found first in *Murray's Hand-book of Northern
Italy* (1842): 'The cortile is a fine example of...the architecture
which purists term *impure*...'. The OED does not give any attestations of the term's angling sense, but it is worth noting how
convenient it was that the term developed its last sense mere
decades before the dry fly came to be used systematically on the
chalk streams – a good example of linguistic serendipity.

put-and-take   This phrase is used in a general adjectival sense to
describe stillwaters stocked with brown and (more commonly)
rainbow trout. The stillwaters in question are usually small in
size; some are little more than purpose-built holes in the ground.

In such locations, the fish are stocked *(put)*, and usually *taken* soon after stocking (see also *stockie-bashing*). These waters burgeoned during the 1970s; as Pearson writes: 'the small still-water fisheries have to offer rather more to the angler than do reservoirs, if they are to attract enough custom, so the general tendency is to offer a much higher stocking rate, normally based on high-frequency put-and-take principles, and usually, larger stock is used than in reservoirs' (*Catching Big Trout*, 18). See also *limit*.

put down   An uncomfortable verb, not recorded in a specific fishing sense in the OED. To *put down* a fish, perhaps more often 'to put down a rising (or feeding) fish', is to alarm it by clumsiness in approach, or by a misjudged or heavy initial cast (or by some subsequent cast or other piece of ghastly bungling). It is a term most often associated with fishing the *dry fly*, usually on rivers, but it is also heard on stillwaters ('Damn! I've just put him down') when fish are cruising and feeding near the surface. As an example, here is Skues, casting for four fish taking wind-driven duns in September on the chalk stream: 'Fishing from the west bank, I stuck to four fish which I satisfied myself were good ones, and in over two hours' fishing I never put them down' (*Minor Tactics*, 4).

Some fish, usually those lying in the fast, glass-thin water of pool-tails, are very easy to put down; others seem more happy with the angler's presence. *Grayling*, in particular, seem more difficult to put down than trout (the late Reg Righyni observed that the grayling 'is much more tolerant of the figure of the angler on the bank'; *Grayling Fishing*, 16). A cautious approach, and an accurate first few casts, are, however, good practice whichever fish is the quarry.

Q **uill**[1] OED defines this as the 'tube or barrel of a feather, the part by which it is attached to the skin'. The word is first attested in English in 1555 (Eden, *Decades*: 'suche thinges as they make of fethers and quilles impaled with golde').

In a fishing sense, *quill*, or stripped quill, is a material used in making artificial flies, esp. dry flies. The fibres of, say, peacock quill (the most frequently used form of quill, taken from the peacock's eye feather) are stripped from the quill stalk by e.g. a soft rubber, and the quill is then wound on the hook shank to form the body of the fly. Being light and hollow, quill floats well; wound in neat, touching turns up the hook shank, quill also gives a good effect of the segmentations of a natural insect's body. See also *spinner*.

quill[2] An artificial fly, a *quill* (e.g. the Red Quill) is what earlier writers might have called a *quill gnat* (e.g. Francis Francis, *Angling*, 1867): 'The Quill gnat...makes its appearance late in April' – here meaning the Large Dark Olive *spinner*?). The most famous of all quills is the Red Quill, which represents the olive spinners (cf. the Pheasant Tail spinner), especially perhaps the Red Spinner (LDO, *Baetis rhodani*; see e.g. *dun*). The Red Quill is a 19th-century development of the earlier 'Ruddy Fly' found in the *Treatise*, and many other early dressings: Cotton, Bowlker, Theakston and Jackson, to name but a few, all gave dressings of the LDO spinner (Hills, *History*, pp.162-3).

The Red Quill, tied with an undyed quill body, red-ginger hackle and upright starling's wings, is a redoubtable fly. Halford wrote of it that it is 'one of the sheet anchors of the dry-fly fisherman on a strange river, when in doubt' (Courtney Williams, *Dictionary*, 296). Courtney Williams himself calls it 'invaluable... It will kill on all rivers and is an effective floating pattern for still waters' (p.297). Grey of Falloden agreed: 'In June, or perhaps even in the end of May, a red quill becomes the...successful fly, and a medium size, neither large nor small, is the best. The trout have a tendency to prefer the smaller sizes, and when their appetite has become very delicate in hot summer weather the smallest possible size of red quill...is the most attractive' (*Fly Fishing*, 55). He includes it among his favourite dry-fly patterns.

Grey also attested the usefulness of another quill, the Olive

174

Quill, a killing fly for the dun of the LDO (and Medium Olive dun).

The last quill pattern considered here (although this is far from being an exhaustive list) is the Orange Quill, which has a special claim to fame since Skues discovered (see *Minor Tactics*), not without some reason, that it was particularly effective during hatches of Blue-winged Olive: 'At one time the trout will be nymphing, and the only way to take them will be with a sunk, sparsely-hackled, dark brown olive pattern. At another time, maybe later in the same rise, the trout will be taking the subimago. Then, according to my experience, a large Orange Quill, No.1 size, is fatal' (*The Way of a Trout*, 166 – Skues was here writing of evening fishing during the summer). Courtney Williams agrees with Skues' estimation: 'First and foremost [of all flies to represent the b.-w. o.] is the Orange Quill. It is an outstanding pattern and in my experience when duns are hatching towards night-fall, it can seldom be bettered. All fly-fishermen have reason to be grateful to Mr. Skues for this fly, as although it was not invented by him, he was the first to appreciate, and call attention to, its efficacy' (*Dictionary*, 111).

Rainbow trout Also simply *rainbow(s)*, or *stockie(s)*. Now one of the commonest salmonids, classified as *Salmo gairdneri* and with two sub-species, *Shasta* and *Irideus* (see below), the rainbow is found from Land's End to the Highland Line. It is most commonly stocked into *put-and-take* fisheries, first because of its fast growth, and second because it is relatively short-lived: rainbows may over-winter in stillwaters, but they are only rarely found breeding naturally in Britain (although they have naturalised, and are found wild, in the Derbyshire Wye and some other waters).

The angling history of the rainbow begins in the United States during the 19th century. Early settlers in the USA had discovered the **brook trout**, *S. fontinalis*, but it was only with the opening of the West that other species of trout were discovered: 'the Dolly Varden, a large western variety of the brook trout; the red- or cut-throat and the rainbow-trout of the Rocky Mountains; the steelhead or salmon trout' (Trench, *Hist. Angling*, 103 – *steelheads* are migratory rainbows; they are not found in the UK, although sporadic reports suggest that some rainbow trout may have taken to migrating seawards, see entry).

Of the two sub-species, *S. gairdneri irideus* may be taken to refer to the migratory steelhead (Maclean, *Trout and Grayling*, 8), while *S. gairdneri shasta* can be taken to be 'the non-migratory autumn-spawning rainbow favoured by British fish-farmers'. The shasta rainbows derive their name from Lake Shasta in California. Demand for these fish has been great, and they have largely been interbred with other species (*Trout Fishing*, ed. Mansfield, 144). This interbreeding (of, say, *shasta* with *irideus*) accounts for the occurrence of dark, out-of-condition rainbows on some stillwaters in April: the *irideus* strain are spring spawners. This problem has been countered, however, by the development of *triploid* fish (and see *diploid*; *spawning*), which are sterile since they carry an extra set of chromosomes.

Rainbows were first introduced into Britain during the early 1880s (the precise date differs from writer to writer: Mansfield reports 1884; Greenhalgh suggests 1882); shasta rainbows were also introduced into e.g. Chile, New Zealand, Kenya and elsewhere. In most regions they thrived, and sometimes provided spectacular fishing – Negley Farson wrote of the fishing in Chile

176

(in 1937) that 'I doubt if finer rainbow can be found anywhere else in the world' (*Going Fishing*, 99).

As recorded elsewhere (see e.g. *pupa*), Blagdon was one of the first, if not the first British stillwater to be stocked with rainbows, in 1904. In 1909, rainbows escaped from a lake near Ashford Hall above Bakewell on the Derbyshire Wye, and colonised the river. Since then, the rainbow has been widely cultivated as a sporting fish by fish-farmers and anglers; because it is cheap and available, it has also been developed as a table fish, as a glance in any supermarket freezer will show.

The rainbow can grow large. The world record rod-caught fish is apparently one of 51lbs, and fish between 10 and 20lbs are taken by rod and line in the British Isles each year. The current British record stands at over 22lbs. It is doubtful, however, whether many (or any?) British waters could sustain such fish naturally, and some writers (e.g. Norman Maclean) argue cogently that these 'jumbo stockies' should be differentiated from either truly wild, or naturalised, rainbows. From my own records, it would seem that a rainbow stocked into a medium-sized, rich stillwater (such as Blagdon) at 1½lbs may subsequently attain weights of up to 6lbs, and certainly, a naturalised fish of 4lbs would be considered a good one.

Opinions vary as to the value of the rainbow as a sporting fish. There were early enthusiasts, among them (a crowning irony given his comments on stocking) Plunket-Greene, who wrote of the fishing at Blagdon that 'both brown and rainbow trout always seem in the pink of condition, and I will back a Blagdon 1½lbs rainbow to win the feather-weight championship of the world' (*Where the Bright Waters Meet*, 135). Chevenix Trench writes that 'I am inclined to think that rainbow trout take lures and fancy flies more readily than brown trout. Introduced into rivers like the Test, they provide good sport for the dry-fly and nymph expert...' (*Hist. Angling*, 104). This seems to be a fairly wide-spread view, and it is not entirely groundless: a well-conditioned rainbow feeds keenly, takes a fly purposefully, is a doughty opponent when hooked, and is (usually) excellent eating. It also seems to be the case that rainbows tend to feed more avidly, and perhaps more regularly, than *brown trout*; this pattern is marked in the bigger fish (the very biggest brown trout are apt to be secretive, and feed, I think, largely at night).

Against this, it has to be said that some fishery-owners, and fishing clubs or syndicates, can be less than scrupulous in their stocking policies. There are several, perhaps many stillwaters which are over-stocked with smallish rainbows. These fish cannot be supported by the natural ecology of the water; therefore, unless they are taken by anglers, they quickly starve. After a month in the water, these may be pitiable fish, long and emaciated.

In these islands, the best of the rainbow trout fishing, on stillwaters at least, undoubtedly comes during the months of May – September, when rainbows feed on hatches of *midge* and *sedge*, a diet supplemented, during the late summer, by their often voracious feeding on e.g. roach and perch *fry* (or on sticklebacks where these occur). During these times, fishermen using corresponding artificials from bank or boat may make good catches. On some waters, the season extends into the autumn (some fisheries stocked with triploids remain open all winter); the fishing during these months, like the fishing in the early spring, is usually with sinking lines and *lures*. See also *stockie*.

ranunculus A form of water-weed, the water crowfoot, *Ranunculus fluitans*, common on the swift but steady water of chalk streams and the middle reaches of some rain-fed rivers. Ranunculus roots itself in patches of silt among the gravels, and provides a home for swimming *nymphs*, *shrimps* and other underwater life. The presence of crowfoot usually indicates a healthy stream, rich in food and fish. Ranunculus also has an important role to play in the oxygenation of the stream. It flowers magnificently in the summer, and grows fairly quickly. For this reason, weed-cutting is sometimes necessary, especially on the chalk streams. Interestingly, Sawyer pointed to the fact that weed-cutting also has a secondary purpose, to spread insect life into different reaches of a stream (*The Keeper of the Stream*, 187).

Playing large trout among the ranunculus is always a hazardous business. Fly-fishing literature is full of stories about big fish and weed. Here is John Waller Hills, playing his largest fish:

He played deep and heavy and I had to handle him roughly, but I brought him down without a smash, and I began to breathe again. But then another terror appeared. At the place we had reached the only clear water was a channel under my bank, and the rest of the river was choked with weed. Should I try to pull him down this channel . . . to the open water below? No. It was much too dangerous, for the fish was uncontrollable, and if he really wanted to get to weed he would either get there or break me . . . Well, if he would not come down he must go up, and up he went willingly enough, for when I released pressure he made a long rush up to the higher weed bed, whilst I ran up the meadow after him, and with even greater difficulty turned him once more. This time I thought he was really going right through it, so fast and heavy was his pull, and I think

he was making for a hatch hole above: but once more my
gallant gut stood the strain and, resisting vigorously, he was
led down (*A Summer on the Test*, 194-5).

That fish weighed 4½lbs. Not all contests among the weeds end
so happily.

rawner   Another name for a *baggot*, i.e. an unspawned hen *salmon*
full of eggs. It is evidently a local, specifically Scots, term: 'In
the early part of the...season, a few hen fish are caught whose
shape looks excellent, but whose colour is wrong...These hen
salmon are found to be unspawned...[and] and called *baggots* or
rawners' (R.N. Stewart, *Salmon and Trout*, 84). Taverner & Scott
(*Salmon Fishing*, 22) record that 'baggots or rawners...return to
the sea with eggs or milt unshed' (the terms apply less frequently
to male fish).

The word derives from the noun *rawn*, 'roe' (cf. Da. *ravn*, and
possibly ON. *hrogn*), which is first attested in 1483 ('Rawne of a
fysche...'). *Rawner* is first attested in Jamieson in the early 19th
century.

redd   Usually pl., *redds*, as in 'the fish are on the redds', i.e.
spawning or about to spawn. A *redd* is the fish's chosen breeding-
site, an excavation among stones or finer gravel where the eggs
are laid and fertilised. The term is also applied to the mounds of
gravel which cover the fertilised eggs.

The word is of obscure origin, but possibly derives from a verb,
to redd, meaning 'to clear (a space, the way etc.)' (cf. MLG and
Du. *redden*, and ModE *rid*). This verbal use is first attested in
1425 ('to red a grownde'); *redd* in its nominal sense 'nest' is first
attested in 1808 ('With their snouts they form a hollow in the bed
of the river....This is called the redd').

Among the salmonids, the female does the redd-making. The
following is a good description of *salmon* spawning:

The female starts with an exploration of the gravel and, after
testing it at various places, begins to excavate. This she achieves
by turning on her side and wafting the gravel away by flicks
of her tail. The excavating is periodically interrupted while
the female rests or lies in the hole, apparently testing it to see
if the dimensions are right. The male meanwhile is in close
attendance except when it becomes necessary to drive away
another male that threatens to become a rival. Eventually the
female is satisfied, after hours, sometimes days, of work. She
settles in the hole and the male places himself close alongside.
As she starts to extrude eggs, she opens her mouth, and the
male, quivering violently, ejaculates a stream of milt over them.
The female then starts another excavation upstream, and in

so doing covers her eggs with a pile of gravel and small stones. The depth of each hole varies according to the size of the female, and the speed of the current. A fish weighing 12lb... may excavate a hole 12 inches... deep at the deepest point, and may repeat the process 12 times before shedding all her eggs (Macan & Worthington, *Life in Lakes and Rivers*, 230-31).

Brown trout and *sea trout* spawn in not dissimilar ways, although it is worth noting that where a river contains all three species, they either spawn at slightly different times, or in different parts of the river, so that competition for spawning-sites is minimised. On most of the river-systems of my acquaintance, salmon tend to spawn either in the headwaters of the parent stream, or in relatively large tributaries. Sea trout tend to spawn in tiny streams (perhaps they prefer finer gravel for spawning). The same point is made by R.N. Stewart: 'Sea trout in the river I know best use quite small streams for spawning, burns that are but little bigger than oversized field drains; even big sea trout up to ten pounds will spawn in them... The sea trout that use these very small burns are careful to get their spawning done quickly. As a rule they take twenty-four to forty-eight hours...' (*Salmon and Trout*, 39-40). The same writer also makes the point that both sea trout and salmon almost invariably use the same respective sections of river and stream for spawning, year after year ('On one burn there is... a favourite redd, which has been used yearly for over forty years; this period of time represents many generations of sea trout, so it must be a good redd', 40).

Once the eggs are hatched, the tiny fish of the various salmon species are known as *alevins*. These minute creatures live around the redd for a while, not feeding actively, merely absorbing the nutrients which they carry in an umbilical sac ('yolk sac'). Sawyer wrote of the brown trout alevin that,

> burdened by its ungainly yolk sac, [the alevin] struggles from the shell and takes cover under a nearby stone. There it will remain for the first three weeks of its life, without moving any appreciable distance; just wriggling here and there, from stone to stone and through the interstices of the heap of gravel of which the redd consists (*Keeper of the Stream*, 49).

After the yolk sac has been absorbed, the alevins move to the fringes of the river, where they commence feeding. See also *fry; parr*.

reed smut Also *smut(s)*; another term, less frequently used perhaps, is *blackflies*. Goddard (*Trout Fly Recognition*, 107) notes that the older angling writers used to refer to the *smuts* as the Black Curse.

Reed smuts, properly speaking, are species of *Simulium*, aquatic in the various stages of their life (Harris, *Angler's Entomology*, 121). They are thus to be distinguished from the various **black gnats** (e.g. *Bibio* species such as *Bibio johannis*, the true black gnat, and *B. marci*, the *Hawthorn Fly*). Many anglers, however, do not differentiate between the smuts and the black gnats, calling them all either 'smuts' or 'black gnats'.

Reed smuts are extremely common on flowing waters; Goddard records that they occur only on those stillwaters which are fed by a constant inflow, since the smut larvae require running water (*Trout Flies of Stillwater*, 112). They are small insects, rather like tiny house-flies to look at (Goddard, *Trout Fly Recognition*, 107). Trout are extremely fond of them, and sometimes become preoccupied with these smuts on hot summer days: 'the fish are/have been smutting' is a dismal phrase, since smutting trout are notoriously difficult to tempt with an artificial *dry fly*. A very small Black Gnat pattern can sometimes work, but it is perhaps more profitable to fish in the surface film, because those reed smuts the trout can most easily take are those trapped in the film prior to hatching (see e.g. the comments of the Danish angler Preben Torp Jacobsen in Roberts, *Illust. Dictionary*, 174-5). It is worth experimenting with tiny flies fished in, or just under, the surface (and see *smutting*).

It is difficult to tell when the reed smut makes its first appearance in fly fishing literature. Since it is unlikely to refer to *B. johannis*, it is possible that Charles Cotton's dressing for 'another little black Gnat, the dubbing of black mohair, and a white Grey wing' (*Angler*, 297), a fly which he recommended for use in June, represents a smut. The fly has certainly received attention this century, partly, perhaps, under the influence of the dry fly *purists*: J.C. Mottram gave a dressing in the 1920s, and other eminent fly fishermen and fly-dressers, among them J.W. Dunne, Jacobsen, and Taff Price, have all essayed representations.

reel The early fathers of fly-fishing used no reel; as detailed elsewhere, they used a tapered hair line fastened directly to the top of their *rod*. And although fishing reels had been invented in China centuries before (Trench, *Hist. Angling*, 62, dates their use in China definitely to the 12th century, and notes that it is possible they were in use as early as the 4th), reels are first recorded in England in the mid-17th century. Hills stated (*History*, 70) that the reel is first mentioned by Barker (1651), who used a reel-like device for *trolling* (as well as a hand-winder, perhaps; see below). In the 1655 edition of the *Compleat Angler*, Walton noted that some salmon fishermen 'use a wheel about the middle of their

Rod, or near their hand, which is to be observed better by seeing one of them, than by a large demonstration of words' (p.131). Walton was evidently not impressed by, or knew little about, reels. However, the frontispiece of Venables' *The Experienc'd Angler: or Angling Improved* (1662) shows a good illustration of a reel, and it seems that thereafter the reel was in sporadic use, notably for salmon and pike fishing (see below), until the 19th century when, with developments in the making of *fly lines*, fly reels became more generally employed.

If the earlier term was *wheel*, the word *reel* is first attested (in its sense 'fishing reel') in 1726 (*Gentleman Angler*: 'He must have a Landing-Hook, Reels for his Silk Lines...'). *Reel* derives from OE *hrēol*, 'rotatory implement on which thread is wound'.

It seems to take a long time for the reel to be used systematically. This is possibly because of the influence of Continental practice. In France, for example, it is clear from François Fortin's *Les Ruses Innocentes* (1660), that he used a crude forerunner of the reel, a kind of line-winder not so different from those line-winders used today for handline sea fishing (Hills, *History*, 53-4). This line-winder, and with it, the practice of the 'running line' (i.e. a line allowed to run through one tip ring), represent early attempts to get away from the fixed line, and they survive for centuries. In William Radcliffe's *Fishing from the Earliest Times* (1921), the following passage is of interest:

> It is inconceivable that invention should have soared to a Reel without there having been some intermediate stage between it and the "tight" line. The advantage of extra line for emergencies must have been recognised pretty early, and a wire ring at the top of the Rod, through which the line could run, naturally resulted from such recognition.

> The method of disposing of the "spare" line may be presumed from survival of primitive practice. Not many years ago pike fishers in rustic parts of England often dispensed with a reel. They either let their spare with a cork at its end trail behind on the ground, or wound it on a bobbin or a piece of wood stowed away in a pocket (p.9).

It is not only this 'running line' that survives. Fishing with a 'tight line', a line fixed directly to the tip of the rod, survives until the later 19th century in fly-fishing, and for longer in coarse fishing. Indeed, the fixed line is with us still in the form of the roach pole favoured by coarse fishermen on canals and elsewhere. So it is little wonder that the reel takes so long to develop. Trench, for instance, draws attention to the editor of the 1815 edition of *The Compleat Angler* who still assumes that most of his readers will be fishing with a hair-line tied to a loop attached to the top of the rod. "A winch," he conceded, "will be very useful," but in its absence "you will find great convenience in a spike made of a piece of the greater end of a sword-blade, screwed into the hither end of the butt of your rod. When you have struck a fish, retire backwards from the river and, by means of the spike, stick the rod perpendicularly in the ground; you may then lay hold on the line and draw the fish to you" (*Hist. Angling*, 63).

As Trench points out, this editor must have had a fantastic gift for disaster (and see *butt spear*).

Even as late as 1885, the reel was still viewed with suspicion by some. David Webster, author of the intriguing *The Angler and the Loop Rod* (1885), used a 13½-foot rod with a line fixed to the tip; he also used up to nine flies on the same leader. But by this time the reel was in more general use. This is partly because line-making had improved. As Trench points out,

one reason for reluctance to use the reel was the nature of the hair-line. This was composed of lengths of twisted horse-hair which could not be more than 3 feet long, each length being knotted to the next. However neat the water-knot, however carefully it was lashed over with fine silk, these knots were apt to catch in the rod-rings and check the free running of the reel. So reels were used more by pike- and salmon-anglers who used an undressed silk line rather than a horse-hair line. Undressed silk was prone to tangles, and too light for casting small baits or fly – but good for casting heavy baits (*Hist. Angling*, 65).

By 1918, a variety of fly reels were on the market. E.M. Tod, *Wet-fly Fishing* (1918, 157), mentioned reels made of either bronzed gun-metal, Vulcanite, or aluminium. He preferred a heavy reel placed behind the casting hand, since this helped (in his view) to 'balance the rod'. There was some force in this opinion considering the relatively heavy *greenheart* and built *cane* rods then in use, but the idea that a reel can help to 'balance' today's generation of *carbon-fibre* and *boron* rods is something of a fallacy.

There is one final usage that needs examination: this is the phrase *on the reel*, which refers to the practice of playing fish. A fish is said to be *on the reel* when there is no slack line between fish and reel; the fish can therefore take line directly from the drum, which may be braked by either the angler's hand, or an automatic check (giving rise to the 'my-reel-screamed' paragraphs of angling writing). The other way of playing fish is to play them 'by hand'; this refers to the slack line there may be between reel and fish, a relationship mediated by the angler's hand (left hand, for a right-handed angler), which maintains a taut line to the fish, but which allows any slack to fall between (left) hand and reel. Typically, this loose, spare line stays on the ground, or on the boards of the boat. Unless the fish runs, thus taking the slack, the loose line remains where it is until the end of the *play*, when, for the sake of tidiness as much as anything else, it may be rewound onto the reel before fishing recommences.

There has been much debate as to whether playing fish on the reel, or by hand, is the best method (see e.g. 'Hand or Reel?' by the late Richard Walker, *T&S*, April 1980, 73): 'I am often asked ... whether the angler should attempt ... to play the fish on the reel, or whether it is preferable to control the line by hand ...'). Playing large fish *on the reel* is certainly safe, and many anglers feel more comfortable in this situation. On the other hand, achieving this state of affairs may entail winding in some slack line during the play, and this can sometimes be dangerous. Again, playing fish by hand has its problems: the loose line may catch under bankside stones, or trap on some projection in the boat, or the angler may simply step on the loose fly line (a classic bit of bungling); all these situations are fatal if a large fish then decides to run, since the line is caught. The usual result is that the *leader* breaks at a knot, usually the knot nearest the fly.

retrieve   The *retrieve* is the action of controlling and giving motion to the *fly line*, *leader* and flies after they have been cast, especially when fishing e.g. *nymphs* or *lures* on stillwaters, or the *wet fly* (for sea trout on lochs and elsewhere). The retrieve necessarily involves pulling the fly or flies back towards the angler (see also *working the fly*). This is effected either by raising the rod (as in fishing the wet fly or nymph upstream on flowing water) or, more commonly, by retrieving line in the non-casting hand. (Occasionally, when fishing upstream in fast currents, it is necessary both to raise the rod and to draw in line.) The retrieve serves two chief objects: first, it enables the angler to keep in contact with the flies via a relatively taut line, and second, it serves to give motion to the fly or flies (sometimes referred to as 'working the fly'). This last is particularly important on stillwaters, where an unretrieved wet fly, lure or nymph would simply sink, an inert thing. Therefore a retrieved fly suggests life, something swimming to the surface to hatch (e.g. a *buzzer* or *sedge pupa*) or otherwise living (e.g. a *fry*).

The usual and least complicated method for a trout angler to retrieve line from bank or boat is effected by trapping the line lightly under the forefinger of the rod hand, and then pulling in line with the left hand over the crook made by the right forefinger (for a right-handed angler). The (line and) flies should be retrieved in such a way as to suggest living creatures. A series of slow, quiet, 6-inch draws will, for example, suggest a small fish; a series of smaller pulls may suggest the tiny movements of a pupa trying to break through the surface film. A slow series of 1-inch draws may suggest the erratic course of a *shrimp* or other food form. Again, if adult sedge representations are being fished on the *dibble*, it may pay to retrieve the flies relatively fast, in a series of sweeping draws, simultaneously retrieving line and raising the rod.

The method referred to above will cause the flies to fish in small spurts and starts. Sometimes, fish (especially rainbows on still-waters) will respond better to a fly retrieved continuously. This may be achieved by the following retrieve, described by Kingsmill Moore:

> Another way [of retrieving the flies], which I prefer, gives a continuous as opposed to an intermittent draw, but one which can be varied in pace within wide limits. The hand movement which produces this result is at first rather difficult to learn, but soon becomes quite automatic. With the rod balanced comfortably in the right hand at the correct angle take hold of the line between the reel and the bottom ring with the left forefinger and thumb, palm upwards, and fingers in line with the forearm. Pull the line a little downwards and to the left, till your hand and arm are comfortable and your whole position is balanced... Now you are ready to begin the draw. Bend your left wrist outwards as far as possible, retaining the finger and thumb grip, and keeping the palm upwards. This draws in about four inches of line. Now hook the remaining fingers over the line above your original grip, which relaxes as soon as the fingers have got a hold, and bend your wrist, palm still upwards, as far inwards as you can. This draws in another four inches, and you will find that you will have now about seven or eight inches in a loop in your palm, while your thumb and forefinger are in the correct position to take a fresh hold. As you take your new hold, your other fingers relax and the loop of line drops down. Continue the movements till you have recovered enough line (which is allowed to fall on the floorboards as before) and shoot all the loose line with your next cast (*A Man May Fish*, 111).

There are many variants of this basic procedure, the commonest of which is perhaps the 'figure of eight' retrieve, in which the line is again trapped lightly under the right forefinger, and where the retrieved line is not allowed to fall to the ground, but kept coiled in the angler's left hand, ready to be shot at the next cast (see *shooting line*; the 'Finger Ring' figure of eight is well illustrated in e.g. Falkus, *Sea Trout Fishing*, 86-8). In addition, many anglers develop their own idiosyncratic methods of retrieve (see also *strip-and-hang*).

It seems clear that retrieving line, in the senses detailed above, cannot have developed before the advent of the reel. In earlier centuries, there would have been a fixed length of line beyond the rod tip, and consequently the only way to retrieve line would have been by raising the rod, a practice reminiscent of, and perhaps underlying, *over the front* traditional *boat-fishing* styles of today.

rise[1] A general movement of fish, especially brown trout, rainbow trout or grayling to insects on or near the surface. If sufficient surface food prompts these fish to feed, they are said to be *on the rise* or simply *rising*.

Every trout fisherman likes to see rising fish; they exercise his imagination and talent (even if they subsequently disappoint his skill). The *Treatise* detailed this: 'From Apryll tyll Septembre ye trought lepyth. Thenne angle to hym wyth a dubbyd hoke acordynge to the moneth...'. These two sentences suggest that 'imitative' fishing already, by the 15th century, had a tradition and history, and of course this continues through Cotton, Venables et al. to the ultra-representative techniques of the dry fly *purists* and into the present day.

There are literally thousands of examples of the terms *rise* (in this general sense) and *rising*. Two taken almost a random are the following, from Grey: 'the real rise [of trout in April] must not be expected till eleven o'clock or later...'; 'the angler should so have arranged matters that he is now, as the rise is beginning, not far from a really good pool' (*Fly Fishing*, 99-100). Another is taken from Righyni's *Grayling*: 'Sometimes if there are several fish rising within casting distance from the one stand... it pays to cast once to each in turn, catch all the most willing ones quickly, and then move on and repeat the performance in the next good place' (pp.24-5). And see *evening rise*.

rise[2] A specific movement to the angler's fly, cf. the more general sense noted above; a *take* or *offer* on or near the surface, and thus visible to the fisherman (e.g. when fishing the *dry fly*, or *nymph* patterns). It is this specific sense invoked by Charles Cotton: 'for on my Word if a Fish rise here, he is like to be such a one, as will endanger your tackle' (*Angler*, 279). Also the following examples: 'The tarn was dead. I saw no rise and heard no rise' (Arthur Ransome, 'Fish and the eclipse', in *Rod and Line*, 64); '... I had four chances. One rose and was missed. A second was hooked, but jumped and wriggled off...' (Hills, *A Summer on the Test*, 143).

rise form   Trout taking flies on or near the surface tend to do so in ways characteristic of the size, and relative position in/on the water, of the insect being taken; therefore an angler can speak of the *rise-form*, and even codify the various different types. Thus, for example, the *head-and-tail* rise is typically a movement of a fish to insects trapped in the surface film: 'it seems most likely that the head-and-tailing fish is taking either spent or drowned fly on the surface, or midge pupae or other creatures... trapped in, or hanging from, the surface film' (Clarke, 115). The same author goes on to detail a further eight different types of common rise-form, including the 'boil' or 'whorl' (trout taking underwater *nymphs* or *pupae*), the 'open-mouthed wallow' (trout swimming along the surface, jaws agape, taking pupae or *spent* fly), the 'slashing' rise (trout taking large, relatively fast-swimming or -hatching insects such as adult *sedges*), and the 'kiss' rise (trout sipping down flies in or on the surface) – see *Pursuit of Stillwater Trout*, chapter 6 and photographs.

The 'kiss' rise is interesting in so far as it gains its name from the fact that the trout literally sucks in the surface insect, ingesting it with air, air which the fish then subsequently expels from its gills. The expelled air shows as a bubble or bubbles on the surface. This is significant because it tells the angler that the fish is taking something actually on the surface, not below it.

Clarke and Goddard effectively dispel the myth propagated by Skues, to the effect that trout feeding on Blue-winged Olives rise with a 'kidney-shaped whorl'. They write that although the 'kidney-shaped whorl has become a "classical" [sic] rise-form' (*The Trout and the Fly*, 57), there is no basis for it in fact.

rising short   See *short taking*.

rod   Whole books could be written about the history of the fishing rod. As noted under *angle*, the rod was first referred to as that, the 'angle', as well as by the term *rod* (hence *Treatise of Fishing with an Angle*); by the 17th century, the usual term is *rod*.

The fishing rod was well known in antiquity. The earliest representation of angling dates to *c*.2000 BC, and an Egyptian source, *Beni Hasan*; the picture shows several fishermen, including one with a hand-line, two with some form of net, and one with a rod about five or six feet long. Radcliffe (*Fishing from the Earliest Times*, 314) believed that this was 'the only depictment... of the Rod till we reach Greece about the 6th century B.C.' In Greece, the rod is mentioned by Homer (said to have lived between *c*.1050-

850 BC) in the following passage from the *Odyssey*: 'Even, as when a fisher on some headland lets down with a long rod his baits for a snare to the little fishes below, casting into the deep the horn of an ox of the homestead, and as he catches each flings it writhing, so were they [i.e. the companions of Odysseus] borne upwards to the cliff [i.e. by Scylla]' (Radcliffe, 76; also Trench, *Hist. Angling*, 11 – Trench conjectures that the puzzling 'horn of an ox' refers to the end of the line, which was protected against the fishes' teeth by a tube of hollow horn; see also Radcliffe, 81ff.). There is also a vase-painting of Heracles angling, and several other pictures of fishing rods in the 6th-2nd centuries BC.

As we progress to the centuries after the birth of Christ, there is a very striking mosaic of fishermen angling with rod and line dating from the third century (Trench, 20-1), which depicts the central figure in a familiar pose, rod bent in the left hand, reaching for the fish with a landing net in his right; there are passages in Plutarch and Ausonius detailing not only the rod, but also horse-hair lines; and of course there is the passage from Aelian already cited (see *fly*), dating from the second or third centuries (although Trench gives a different dating). Aelian wrote that fishermen dibbed with a rod six feet long, and with a line the same length (Radcliffe, 188).

Thereafter, the fly fisherman and his tackle are all but lost to European literature for a millennium. It is just possible that fly-fishing was lost, too, but it seems far more plausible to assume that fishing with rod and line continued, particularly given the fact that the text of the *Treatise* implies that its techniques, and its famous list of fly dressings, had been in existence for some considerable time before the mid-15th century. The *Treatise* was not an experimental work; it detailed existing practice. It could not have done so in the way it did if angling with rod and line was in any sense a 'young' pastime in *c*.1450.

The all-purpose rod of the *Treatise* was 12 feet or more long, and in two parts, a 'staffe' (see *butt*) and a two-piece top joint, the 'croppe'. The two pieces of the top (hazel for the lower part, blackthorn, crabtree, medlar or juniper for the extreme tip) were spliced together, and the whole top joint fitted inside the butt, which was hollow, when the rod was not in use. A tapered horse-hair line was fastened to the rod-tip.

One thing that is apparent is the length of the *Treatise*'s rod compared to the rods of antiquity. Can it be conjectured that the need for a long rod had developed alongside, or as a consequence of, the developments that had taken place in fly-fishing? *Pace* Aelian, it would be difficult to fish a fly effectively with a short rod.

There were apparently no great improvements in rod building for almost two hundred years. When the rod reappears in fly-fishing literature, it does so in Cotton's era, when rods are no longer home-made – the first tackle shops seem to date from the early 17th century if not before, see Trench, 38; Gervase Markham (*Country Contentments*, c.1614) wrote that 'there is a great choice of [rods] in every haberdasher's shop'; Venables (1662) also referred to 'those that sell [rods] in London'. The following is Hills' summary:

> In Cotton's day trout were fished for with either a single or doublehanded rod. Both were long, the single rod running up to eighteen feet and the double to twenty-one. Rods were spliced, not jointed. Cotton praises specially Yorkshire rods, with butts of fir, made of six, eight, ten or twelve pieces spliced together, tapering like a switch and playing with a true bent down to the hand. Hazel was however the favourite material, though some used cane with a hazel top; whalebone was generally used for the actual point (*History*, 67-8).

One of those favouring whalebone was Venables (1662), who wrote that a fly-rod should be 'long and light, easy to be managed with one hand', and that its top should be finished 'with a small piece of whalebone, made round, smooth, and taper' (pp.3-4).

This is not to suggest that all rods were similar at this period. As Trench points out, by the mid-17th century anglers had begun to specialise: Walton was primarily what we would call today a coarse fisherman, Cotton and Venables (and perhaps Barker) were primarily game fishers. In fact, the great distinction between 'game' and 'coarse' dates from early in the 17th century, when Lawson saw a particular gentlemanly virtue in fishing for trout: 'The trout makes the angler the most gentlemanly and readiest sport of all other fishes. If you fish with a made fly, this is the chief pleasure in angling' (c.1613; from Trench, 52). And by the later 17th century, angling had ramified into still more specialised areas. In 1682, for instance, Thomas Nobbes published *The Complete Troller*, and, as Trench observes, used a short rod of around 9 feet (indeed, he sometimes used his walking-stick; see Trench, 58).

But the long, spliced fly-rod remains in favour for another 150 years at least. As Hills wrote: 'The one hundred and eighty years which separate Stewart from Cotton are years of advance which, though great, proceeded by hardly perceptible stages. At the beginning men fished with no reel, twisted hair lines, long rods, and a single fly. At the end [c.1850] they used short rods, sometimes of split cane, reels, silk lines, and drawn gut, and, except for those bold adventurers who used the dry fly or on very shy waters, two or three flies' (*History*, 82).

The split-cane rod (see *cane*) dates from the early 19th century. By this time, largely owing to the development of the *reel*, there was a trend in favour of shorter rods. As Hills put it,

> Stewart [*The Practical Angler*, 1857] considered a ten foot rod, if stiff, big enough for any water, and adds that he generally used one from eight to nine feet long. This is a big drop from Cotton's fifteen or eighteen footer. The drop occurred after the reel came into general use, which revolutionised rod making, for it enabled men to fish fine with a short rod, impossible before (*History*, 85).

The long rod was not quite dead, however: Francis Francis used rods of between 11½ feet and 12½ feet for trout fishing, and even Halford stated (in 1886) that a 12 feet rod could be used for dry-fly fishing (Hills, *History*, 86). Skues, though, came to use what he abbreviated as the 'W.B.R.' – the World's Best Rod – a 9½-foot Leonard made of split cane; this he used both for dry-fly and nymph fishing. Skues also observed, with penetrating accuracy, that the factors which made the dry-fly possible were the development of the oil-dressed silk line, and the (American) development of split-cane rods designed to cast such lines (*The Way of a Trout*, 139).

Once shorter rods had developed for dry-fly and nymph fishing, this left the longer rods for further specialised functions, such as the presentation of the wet fly on rivers, and for *boat-fishing* on lakes and lochs. In both these cases, the longer rods allow subtleties of presentation such as *mending* the line on flowing water, and *dibbling* (at some distance from the boat) on still. Grey used a rod of 11 feet for his wet fly work, and a slightly shorter 10½-foot rod for dry fly fishing. He also noted that split-cane was a more reliable material than *greenheart*:

> Every angler . . . must know how impossible it is even with the greatest care to prevent the hook touching or catching in weed now and then, when a line of any length is being lifted off the water quickly. Time after time have greenheart rods snapped most untowardly in this way . . .
>
> Split cane is the most staunch of all materials; like an old and faithful servant, it is incapable of treachery or sudden change, and when it fails it does so gradually . . . (*Fly Fishing*, 168-9).

From its development in the mid-19th century, split cane remained a favourite material for over one hundred years. Even relatively late in this century, cane was still the preferred material for some fishermen. In the second, enlarged edition of *A Man May Fish* (1979), for example, Kingsmill Moore wrote that

> The materials of my fishing years were greenheart and split cane. Greenheart could make a very delightful trout rod and older salmon fishermen were faithful to their Grant Vibrations and Castle Connells. But...[s]plit cane will, literally, last a lifetime...My trout rod, bought in 1928, is still in mint condition though it has had one new top. Split cane had no serious rival.
>
>   Now split cane is giving way to rods made of glass fibre, carbon fibre, or a mixture of both. I have no experience of them but angling friends, on whose skill and judgment I am prepared to rely, tell me that they are as good or better than the best split cane. They are certainly lighter...(148).

Fibreglass, *carbon fibre* and *boron* rods have come to oust cane; these rods offer lightness with considerable power. They have also been developed for more specialised purposes than cane rods (rods for fishing lead-cored or other heavy, sinking fly-lines are a case in point) and give intending fishermen a somewhat wider choice.

Finally here, it is necessary to consider salmon rods. As will be seen, *salmon* fishing – at least, systematic salmon fishing – with a fly took a considerable time to develop. Although salmon had been fished for for centuries (even the *Treatise* mentioned that they could be taken with a fly – but, it added darkly, 'this is seldom seen'), it was only during the 19th century that fishermen sought them out *systematically* with flies. Prior to this, as Trench makes clear (*Hist. Angling*, ch. 6), and despite the fly-fishing skills of e.g. Franck (*Northern Memoirs*, 1694), Venables (*The Experienced Angler*, 1662), and Chetham (*The Angler's Vade Mecum*, 1681) – men who all seriously attempted to catch salmon with flies – the preferred methods were either bait fishing, or *trolling*. As detailed above, in both these forms of fishing, short rods had been developed.

The long, strong rod developed, as we may by now expect, during the second half of the 19th century. During this period, many fishermen took up salmon (fly) fishing as a sport:

> More salmon-fishers meant more ingenious experimenters, and far, far more books on salmon fishing which by the 1830s and 1840s were being churned out at the rate of nearly one a year...
>
>   Successive inventions changed the salmon-fisher's equipment as it had the trout-fisher's. Rods composed of crab, ash, yew, whole cane and whalebone gave way to greenheart rods.

The Castle Connell was a great rod, and is still used. Made of greenheart, rather top-heavy with its slim butt, the joints spliced and bound with tape rather than joined by metal ferrules, it has a singularly sweet action and certainly casts a long line. But it is inconvenient, rather tiring to use, and apt to snap at the butt under sudden great strain. Split cane – split cane with a steel centre – glass fibre – the salmon-fisher tried them all in the course of a century and a half... Lines developed from horse-hair, silk and horse-hair, silk, horse-hair and 'Indian grass' to the oiled silk and cellular nylon lines we use today (Trench, 136-7).

In the last decade of this century, the preferred salmon rods are either fibreglass or carbon fibre, the advantages of which are noted above. But tradition dies hard in fishing: in 1985 I fished (gingerly) with a Castle Connell salmon rod eighty years old. See also *action; AFTM; butt; ferrule* etc.

roll-casting   A form of fly cast used, typically with a single-handed trout rod, when there are bushes, trees, or other obstructions behind the angler. See *cast²*.

Salmon The Atlantic salmon, *Salmo salar*. The fish was known in England in pre-Conquest times: Bede (early 8th century) drew attention to it in his *Ecclesiastical History*, where he noted the abundance of salmon, eels, and pike in these islands. But he did not use the word *salmon*; he used the OE term, *leax*. This word was common to all Germanic tongues, and survives in that form in ModG *lachs*. The original term also survives in place-names such as Laxford (NW Scotland – the ford over the salmon-river) and Leixlip (Ireland – the salmon leap). Our word *salmon* derives from Latin *salmo* via Old French *saumon*. It is first attested in English in *c*.1300 (*King Alisaunder*: 'And of perches, & of salmons, Token & eten grete foysouns').

The life cycle of the salmon is well-known. Fish spawn on *redds* cut from gravel or stones during the late autumn; the female lays between 500-1400 eggs per pound of body weight (Varley, 96). The eggs hatch into *alevins* after 70-120 days (typically, late March / early April). The alevins absorb their yolk sacs after about a month, after which they are termed *fry*. These fry begin to feed actively at the edges of the river, later moving into stronger, deeper currents as they grow. After about one year as a fry, the immature fish are termed *parr*; they remain in this stage for between a further one year, or up to eight years (e.g. in northern Scandinavian rivers, see Taverner & Scott, 25). Typically, in British rivers, the parr become *smolts*, and migrate to the sea, after about two years. As with the *sea trout* parr, the feeding behaviour of the fish at this (pre-smolt) time in their lives may be significant: summer-run, adult *grilse* or salmon may, for example, take relatively small, natural-fly-suggesting artificials fished close to the surface. It may be that after some time in fresh water, the adult fish's behaviour adapts to its new environment, and begins to pattern like that of the parr.

Why do parr become smolts? The overall downstream migration of salmon smolts, like the smolts of sea trout, is not too difficult to explain: it is prompted by competition for food. Parr are aggressive and territorial. As they grow, they need more food; this need, along with their increasing size, drives them into deeper water, i.e. downstream. Migration to the sea could be seen as an ultimate development of this trend. Moreover, it has been long known that a certain size-threshold operates – in other words, once the parr reach a particular size, they will migrate: Elson (1957), reported in Taverner & Scott (*Salmon Fishing*, 25), recorded that 'as a general rule, parr which have reached 10cm. by the end of one growing season are likely to become smolts at the next season of smolt descent'. This pattern appears to be repeated in the case of the sea trout.

Smolts are distinguished from parr by their silvery appearance, their sea-going coats; they descend to the sea in the late spring. Thereafter, the fish begin their sea feeding, migrating to the waters of the north Atlantic (Greenland and elsewhere). Here they feed on fish such as herring, capelin and sandeels, as well as on molluscs. They may remain in the sea for one further winter, or for several further winters. Those that return to their parent river after one sea-winter are terms *grilse*; those that return after two or more sea-winters are termed *salmon*. (Compare the distinction between *herling* and sea trout.)

The salmon's return to freshwater is one of the most intriguing aspects of their lives. Several theories have been put forward as to the salmon's ability to return to its own river-catchment, but perhaps the most persuasive are those that suggest this is achieved by the salmon's awareness of the earth's magnetic field, and/or by sense of smell (i.e. of particular stream odours).

By whatever means the salmon returns, return it does, either as a spring fish (see *springer*), as a summer-running grilse, or as an autumn leviathan of 40lbs or more. Fish running straight off the tide into the river are known as 'fresh' or 'fresh-run'; they are blue-silver, firm-fleshed, and strong. Many still bear *sea lice*; these parasites drop off after a short period (about four days) in fresh water, so their presence indicates a fresh-run fish.

The angling season, on a major salmon river such as Tweed or Tay, therefore lasts from February until November. On rivers of the western seaboard, the season typically lasts from late June until October. Recently there have been signs that autumn runs of fish are increasing, while spring runs seem to be largely decreasing. Whether this is due to some natural cycle of which we know nothing, or whether it is due to some man-made cause, is moot.

After they have entered the river, the salmon run upstream, eventually reaching the spawning beds. How far and how fast they run is controlled (a) by the time of their return from the sea, and (b) by the amount of water in the river. A salmon may, for example, enter the river as a springer in March; it may (if it is not caught or poached) remain in the river for the rest of the summer and autumn, gradually turning darker in colour ('red', 'stale', '*kippered*' or 'potted' – and the males grow *kypes*), running slowly from pool to pool on each small rise of water. Alternatively, a fish may run in on an autumn flood and reach the spawning beds in mere days. Only one thing is vital: that the river contains sufficient water for the salmon to leap any obstructions in its path to the redds. During drought years, therefore, fishermen pray for floods – to bring the fish in off the tide, and to help them to the spawning beds.

All salmon fishermen realise, however, that angling for salmon rests on a paradox. The fish do not feed (or scarcely feed) in freshwater. Their appetite is suppressed during their spawning run. They may take a bunch of worms, but this is perhaps a conditioned reflex rather than active feeding behaviour. They may even rise to hatches of fly on the surface, but again, this may be explicable in terms of instinct rather than hunger. To all intents and purposes (this bears repeating) salmon do not feed in freshwater – and what river is rich enough to feed a big run of salmon, possibly for months? Therefore the salmon fisher seeks to prompt, to cajole, to intrigue, or to anger fish onto his fly, to stimulate a response, to draw a reflex from what the *Treatise* called this 'gentyll fysshe'.

The *Treatise* did not in fact go into much detail. The salmon of the *Treatise* is 'comberous for to take,'

For comynly he is but in depe places of grete ryuers. And for the more parte he holdyth the myddys of it, that a man maye not come at hym. And he is in season from Marche vnto Myghelmas.

In whyche season ye shall angle to hym wyth thyse baytes whan ye maye gete theym. Fyrste wyth a redde worm in the begynnynge and endynge of the season. And also wyth a bobbe that bredyth in an dunghyll. And specyally wyth a souerayn bayte that bredyth on a water docke.

And he bytith not at the grounde but at ye flote. Also ye may take hym, but it is seldoom seen, with a dubbe at such tyme as whan he lepith, in lyke fourme and manere as ye doo take a troughte or a graylynge.

Given the tackle of the 15th century (particularly the fixed length of line beyond the rod tip), it is small wonder that the author appears to be pessimistic, and that the salmon seems so unattainable to him. Likewise it was the tackle which compelled the priority given to bait fishing – as I write I can see that monstrous cable of line, fifteen twisted hairs, plumbing an eddy on the Thames in which our 15th-century salmon rested. How difficult it must have been to have cast or drifted the fly into the 'deep places of great rivers'.

This pattern continued in Walton. The salmon, Walton wrote,
swims in the deep and broad parts of the water, and usually
in the middle, and near the ground; and there you are to fish
for him, and that it is to be caught as the *Trout* is, with a *Worm*,
a *Minnow*...or with a *Flie*. And you are to observe, that he is
very seldom observed to bite at a *Minnow* (yet sometimes he
will) and not usually at a *Flie*, but more usually at a *Worm*,
and then most usually at a *Lob* or *Garden-worm*...(*Angler*,
130).

It is evident, however, that the salmon was more deeply understood in the 17th century than it had been in the 15th. Walton
noted that the salmon 'is accounted the King of fresh-water fish,
and is ever bred in Rivers relating to the sea'. He also had a dim
idea of the salmon's sea feeding: 'if the old *Salmon* gets to the
Sea, then that gristle which shews him to be a *kipper*, wears away,
or is cast off...and he recovers his strength...'. He knew about
the homing instincts of the fish, too: 'every *Salmon* usually returns
to the same River in which it was bred'. And he knew about the
genetic intensity of the salmon's spawning run: 'Next, I shall tell
you, that though they make very hard shift to get out of the fresh
Rivers into the Sea: yet they will make harder shift to get out of
the salt into the fresh Rivers, to spawn, or possess the pleasures
that they have formerly found in them: to which end, they will
force themselves through *Flood-gates*, or over *Weires*, or *hedges*,
or *stops* in the water, even to a height beyond common belief'
(*Angler*, 126-8). About this time, too, the salmon began to be
celebrated in verse, as in Drayton's *Poly-Olbion* (1612-22, cited
in *The Magic Wheel*, eds. Profumo and Swift, 87):

When as the salmon seekes a fresher streame to find
(Which hither from the sea comes yeerely by his kind,
As he in season grows) and stems the watry tract
Where Tivy falling downe, doth make a cataract,
Forc't by the rising rocks that there her course oppose,
As though within their bounds they meant her to inclose;
Heere, when the labouring fish doth at the foote arrive,
And finds that by his strength but vainlie he doth strive,
His taile takes in his teeth: and bending like a bowe,
That's to the compasse drawne, aloft himself doth throwe...

Two of Walton's near-contemporaries understood the fish still
better. One was Venables (*The Experienced Angler*, 1662), who
noted that the salmon was not only found in 'great rivers' but
also in lesser streams 'high up in the country, yet chiefly in the
latter end of the year, when they come thither to spawn' (facsimile,
44). He also stated categorically that the salmon 'takes the artificial

fly very well'. Salmon flies, he noted, 'must be much larger than you use for other fish, the wings very long, two, or four, behind one another, with very long tails' (p.29; and see *wing*). Elsewhere he also hinted that the salmon 'delights in the most gaudy and orient colours' (p.21). Venables' work is perhaps the first to intimate that what the angler is doing in fly-fishing for salmon is stimulating the fish with a stylised representation of their food at sea – hence, for example, Venables' insistence on long-winged flies.

The other writer is the wordy Richard Franck (*Northern Memoirs*, 1694). If anything, he anticipated what a later age would call the *greased-line*: what he called the 'baits or charms' for salmon 'reduce under the classis of two generals, viz. the fly for frolick, to flourish and sport on the surface of the stream; and the ground-bait for diversion'. His artificial flies were for the most part what his age would have called 'sad-coloured': 'obscure, of a gloomy, dark and dusky complexion; fashioned with tufts of bears-hair, blackish or brownish discoloured wool, interwoven sometimes with peacocks feathers, at otherwhiles lap'd about with grey, red, yellow, green or blueish silk, simple colours, or colours sometimes intermingled' (from Trench, 128-9).

But fly-fishing for salmon was still not a particularly favoured method compared with worm or live bait, and this is the status quo until the later eighteenth century. To be sure, there were exceptions (as Trench observes, James Chetham was one), but even when we reach the 18th century,

> most ... salmon-fishers preferred worms, minnows, and cockles as baits, and large trout patterns for artificial flies. There seems [sic] to have been only two patterns, described by successive authors, tied specifically for salmon, the Dragon and the Kingfisher, believed to resemble dragon-flies on which salmon were presumed to feed ... The pattern of fly was supposed to be of little consequence: anglers could use any dressing they fancied, as salmon would rise at any gaudy fly some 2 inches long, and at large trout flies ... None of these early writers gave much advice on *how* to fish for salmon: they simply implied that one cast across and downstream, and let the fly or lure swing round under one's own bank, as in trout-fishing (Trench, 131-2).

But changes in tackle – not least, the development of the *reel* – and changes in the use of leisure time did give rise to developments in salmon fly-fishing during the 19th century. One innovator is Sir Humphrey Davy, whose *Salmonia* appeared in 1828; as Trench points out (p.133), Davy was one of the first to realise that salmon did not feed in freshwater; he also suggested that when they took a fly, they were impelled to do so by memories of their time in the river as a parr. Arnold Gingrich (p.85) goes so far as to call Davy 'the Berners of salmon fishing'. Another important writer from the mid-19th century was William Scrope, whose *Days and Nights of Salmon-Fishing in the Tweed* appeared in 1843. Scrope is a better writer than Davy (whose adoption of the dialogue form reads as somewhat stilted), but, arguably, a lesser theorist. His book, though, contains exciting accounts of epic battles with enormous salmon (the kind of fish he described as '*monstrum horrendum ingens*'), and is a classic of its kind. Salmon fishing was coming of age.

During the 19th century, another development in salmon fishing took place. This was to do with the fly. The 19th century had inherited two theories about the salmon fly. One looked back to Venables, and his large, relatively bright lures; the other looked back to Franck, and 'sad-coloured' flies that were really over-grown trout flies. During the course of the century, and perhaps stimulated by the discovery of salmon fishing in Norway and other waters further afield, the larger 'orient-coloured' patterns were used more systematically. One source of these patterns was Ireland, where a style of dressing had developed which was both ornate and effective. The Irish salmon flies of this period (some are still with us) typically sported *tip* or *tag*, a butt of ostrich herl, a floss body ribbed *palmer*-style with one or more *hackles*, a married, feather-fibre *wing*, a *topping*, and *cheeks* of junglecock. At this time, too, theories were developed that are still current – for example, that a fly had to be used in a size which was sympathetic to the pace of the stream in which it was being fished (thus larger sizes of fly were used in the head of the pool, where the current was fast, than in the quieter draws of the pool body).

And yet the methodology of salmon fishing appears to have changed little. It seems still to have been largely across-and-down *wet fly* (a technique we would today call the *sunk line*), a searching of the water with a long rod and a heavy, sunk line. Of course, this method took fish, particularly in spring or autumn when the rivers were high and the fish lying deep. This technique, it hardly needs pointing out, is still used on Tweed and Tay during spring and autumn, when 'sunk-line fishing' is almost universal practice.

But in the early 20th century, a further revolution took place – perhaps (it is tempting to suppose) in reaction to the methods and fly patterns used in the later 19th century. This revolution involved what is still known as the *greased-line*, a technique pro-moted by the late A.H.E. Wood of Cairnton. (Notably, however, both Percy Laming and Alexander Grant had experimented with similar methods before Wood. Wood adopted the greased-line in 1903; Laming had fished for salmon with a floating line in 1897; and Grant had fished with an 'oiled line' before Laming. Laming and Grant were unusual among anglers, though, in that they 'disliked publicity' – see Taverner & Scott, 131-3).

Wood experimented on his most excellent beat of the Dee with relatively small flies fished not on a sinking line but on a floating one. As noted here, Franck had done something of the same kind some two centuries and more before, but as Taverner & Scott say, this technique had been 'long neglected'. Nor would it have been really possible before the development of tapered, silk fly-lines during the later 18th and 19th centuries.

Wood discovered that during most months of the year, but particularly during the summer, when the waters were warm and the streams small, the salmon would 'rise' to a small fly fished slowly across the river near the surface. He thus introduced new elements into the pursuit: for the first time, salmon could be regularly seen coming for the fly, sometimes with a sullen boil, more often with a *head and tail rise*. Another innovative feature of Wood's approach was the light tackle he used – a rod of a mere 12 feet, and a 3-yard leader tapered to perhaps 8lbs.

The other elements he promoted were more theoretical. He fished the greased-line only if the air was warmer than the water; he controlled the speed of the fly by *mending* the line (insisting that a *dragging* fly would not be taken properly), a technique he used in conjunction with 'leading' the line across the lies. He also (re?)introduced very small flies into salmon fishing, dropping to a fly as small as size 12 if the water was very low; these flies were mere wisps of dressing, indeed Wood recorded that he had caught fish on what was almost a bare hook.

The small fly fished on the floating line allowed anglers to fish for salmon during conditions that might previously have been considered unsuitable, the low waters of summer. Its introduction marks the final stage (thus far) in the history of salmon fishing, since nowadays, salmon fishermen typically use the sunk-line until the water (and air) warms sufficiently to make use of the floating line and small fly realistic, reverting to the sunk-line again in the chill waters of autumn. In practice, there are two uneasy periods in the season when both methods ('slow and deep' vs. 'small and surface') will take fish, in late spring and early autumn; but certain it is that, despite recent interest in more peripheral techniques such as the dry fly for salmon, most salmon anglers think of their fishing largely in terms of these two central methods.

See also *cast²; tube fly*.

scale[1]   The *scales* of a fish are a set of overlapping, bony out-growths of skin which form a protective outer layer of body covering overlaid by a further layer of mucilage ('slime'). Trout (of all species) and salmon have relatively small scales; grayling have much larger ones – a fact of merely gastronomic importance. Of more importance is the fact that the scales of a fish may be damaged, e.g. by clumsy handling; once scale-damage occurs, bacteria can attack the fish's body. Therefore it is good policy, when one intends to return a small fish alive to the water (and where the use of **barbless hooks** is impracticable or has been overlooked), to wet one's hands before removing the hook. As far as I have been able to establish, the first reference to this thoughtful practice comes in Oliver Kite's *A Fisherman's Diary* (1969), which is a collection of that author's writings for *Shooting Times and Country Magazine*. In a small item titled 'When to Kill', Kite recommended that fish to be returned to the water should not be touched more than absolutely necessary, and that such fish could be spared suffering 'if the hands are first damped and cooled in the water'.

Scales are also useful reference-points during a *scale-count* intended to establish e.g. the distinction between a sea trout and a salmon. Close inspection of fish scales under a microscope can also establish the age of a fish, since the 'growth-rings' of that fish show up as a series of roughly circular (typically oval) rings (rather like tightly-packed isobars on a weather-map). In winter, when the fish grows slowly, the rings are closely spaced; in summer, when the fish is actively feeding and therefore putting on weight quickly, the rings are spaced further apart. Therefore the years of a fish's growth can be deduced by the relative spacing of the rings. Scale-reading in this sense dates from the early 20th century. (For an excellent account of scale-reading see Norman Maclean, *Trout and Grayling*, 22ff.; also 'Salmon Scales' in *Salmon Fishing*, eds. Taverner & Scott, ch. 16).

The word *scale*, in the sense 'thin membrane . . . or horny outgrowth . . . of the skin' derives from Old French *escale* (and is aptly related to *shell*), and is first attested in English *c*.1300, where the reference is to the invulnerability of a dragon ('þe smallest scale þat on him is / No wepen may no atane'). In a specifically piscine sense the first recorded use dates to Chaucer's *Parliament of Foules* (a medieval debate-poem *c*.1381), where he wrote of 'Smale fischis lite With fynnys rede & skalis syluyr bryȝte' (probably a reference to roach or dace).

scale[2]   Usually pl. *scales*, an apparatus for weighing (fish). The word derives from Old Norse *skal*, 'bowl' and is first recorded in English in 1375 (although probably in use long before). The etymology suggests that the 'bowl' was the pan, or one of the pans, of a balance.

My impression is that anglers did not carry scales, and did not, in fact, care very much about the exact weight of the fish they had taken, much before the early or even mid 19th century. That is not to suggest that the early fathers were happy to catch tiddlers; on the contrary, the earliest texts speak of 'great fish' with a kind of superstitious hush. But it seems to have been rarely considered necessary to weigh fish to the nearest ounce. I may be wrong.

Grey of Falloden (*Fly Fishing*, first edn, 1899) recorded that he carried two spring balances, small for trout, large for salmon, so it is probable that the practice of weighing fish exactly had originated during the 19th century, when fly-fishing was developing quickly and when more anglers – some, perhaps, of that sadly competitive temperament for which ounces are crucial – were fishing than ever before.

scale-reading   A method of determining the age of a fish by microscopic examination of an individual scale or set of scales, particularly useful (and interesting) in the case of migratory fish such as salmon and sea trout, when the periods the fish has spent in the river (as e.g. a *parr*) and at sea, as well as any previous spawning run(s), can be reconstructed from the growth-rings and ridges on each scale. See *scale[1]*.

schelly   Also sp. *skelly* (and variants). The *schelly* is one of the *whitefish* family, related to the *gwyniad*, *pollan*, *powan* etc. but localised to the Lake District, especially Ullswater and Haweswater (also – reputedly and for anyone who cares for the climb – Red Tarn under the shoulder of Helvellyn). Holgate & Parkinson not that although captures of schelly from Ullswater have been infrequent, some anglers using bait-fishing techniques (i.e. legering) have recorded 'modest catches' of this rare fish.

As with the other whitefishes, the schelly has been landlocked in upland, glacial lakes since the Ice Age. It is reputedly a deep-water species, feeding on plankton and small invertebrates, and spawning in January. The *Observer's Book of Freshwater Fishes* records that the schelly grows up to about 16 inches and may weigh up to 1½lbs (the British rod-caught record is, or used to be, 1lb 10ozs). It also notes that the fish has a distinctive smell of cucumbers, and is delicious eating. But because of the fish's distribution and habits, most fly-fishermen will come into contact with the schelly only rarely or not at all, so will never have the chance to prove the schelly as a table fish.

The fish is defined in the OED as 'the gwyniad, the fresh-water herring, *Coregonus clupeoides*'. The word is first attested in English

in 1740 (R. Brookes, *Art of Angling*: 'The Schelley is bred in...
Ulles-water... In shape it is more like a Herring than a Trout...'),
was noted in J. Clarke's *Survey of the Lakes of Cumberland* (1787:
'The skelly is remarkable for this, no bait has ever been found
which they will take'), and also figured in Dorothy Wordsworth's
Journal (1805: 'Hundreds of fish were leaping in their prison.
They were all of one kind, what are called Skellies'). See also
vendace.

scissors The cartilaginous parts of a fish's mouth at the junction
of upper and lower jaw, the *maxillary*. A fish hooked in the *scissors*
is usually firmly hooked, as in the following quote: 'If the hook
gets a good hold in the "scissors" and comes adrift... there is not
much that [hook] design or sharpness can do to prevent it' (Falkus,
Sea Trout Fishing, 115).

The word is ultimately from Old French *cisoires*, 'shears', and
in the sense 'a cutting implement' is first attested in Chaucer
(1384, *House of Fame*). The sense and meaning of 'maxillary' is
apparently not recorded in the OED.

sea-lice These are parasites (the species is *Lepeophtheirus sal-
monis*) which attach themselves to the skin of salmon and sea trout
during their sojourn in the sea. Their presence is not normally
serious, but injured or diseased fish may be so heavily infested
that death follows (e.g. lice may eat into the fins, or into the back
of the head).

Sea-lice do not live long in freshwater, so their presence on a
newly-caught fish indicates that the fish is fresh-run. They are
usually found on the ventral regions of the fish. Fish straight off
the tide, blue-silver, clean-scaled and bearing sea-lice, haunt the
dreams of sea trout and salmon fishermen.

Defined in the OED as 'a parasitic isopod crustacean', the word
is first attested in 1601 (Holland's *Pliny*: 'Those creepers or insects
which be called sea-lice'), and also occurs in Sir Thomas Browne's
Norfolk Fishes (1682: 'The gills of these fish we found beset with
a kind of sea-louse'), although the reference here may possibly
be to gill-maggots, rather than to sea-lice.

sea trout The *sea trout* is properly *Salmo trutta trutta* (cf. *S. salar*,
the *salmon*, and *S. trutta fario*, the *brown trout*). It is closely related
to the brown trout, but differs in that it is migratory, feeding (as
an adult fish) in the sea and returning to its parent river system
to spawn.

No other game fish has so many local names. Hugh Falkus, in
his epochal *Sea Trout Fishing* (1st edn, 1962), mentions at least
eight terms for the sea trout: *herling, whitling, finnock, smelt, sprod,
scurf* (these terms seem clearly to refer to the smaller fish), along

with *truff* and *mort*. But there are many other terms: *peal* is a West
Country name for the fish. In Ireland, the fish is almost universally
known as the *white trout*. In Wales, it is known as the *sewin*.
Fishmongers, no doubt hoping to capitalise on the *cachet* of the
salmon, call the sea trout the *salmon trout*. And the OED lists many
other terms, among which are *sea truff, grey trout, bull trout, pug-
trout, forktail* (which probably refers to the herling, the sea trout
grilse), *herring peal, may peal, pugg peal, harvest cock* (see *harvester*),
and *yellow-fin*.

Here, entries on the sea trout concentrate on the terms for the
fish in common use today. One set of terms may be taken to refer
to the adult fish, that is, to fish which (and this is merely a rough
working guide) have spent perhaps six months or more at sea and
which may weigh 1lb and upwards; the second set of terms refers
to the juvenile fish, the fish which have spent less than six months
in the sea and which return to the river weighing perhaps ½-1lb.
(Of the river life of the sea trout before its descent to the sea, see
fry, parr, smolt.)

The term *sea trout* itself is first attested in English in 1745 (very
late for a fishing word, and see below), in Egede's *Descr. Greenland*
('Small Salmon or Sea-Trout of different Kinds and Sizes'); but
it is quite possible that the fish was known earlier as a *salmon-trout*,
which term is first attested as early as 1421 (*Rolls Parlt.*: 'Frie de
Salmon-Trought'). My impression is that *S. trutta trutta* went by
many local names before the 19th century (and Francis in particular, see below) fixed it firmly as a sporting fish in its own right.

These notes on terminology and taxonomy imply that the sea
trout has been, from an angling point of view, something of a
problematic fish, difficult to classify (perhaps even difficult to
catch). This was early apparent. The sea trout is not to my knowledge mentioned in angling literature until the 17th century, when
Walton, for example, distinguished not only what he called 'a
Samlet or *Skegger Trout*' (which live 'in divers Rivers, especially
that relate to, or be near to the Sea' – are these parr or herling?)
but also spoke of the 'Fordidge Trout'

> that is accounted the rarest of Fish; many of them near the
> bigness of a *Salmon*, but known by their different colour, and
> in their best season they cut very white; and none of these have
> been known to be caught with an Angle, unless it were one
> that was caught by Sir George Hastings...and he hath told
> me, he thought that *Trout* bit not for hunger but wantonness;
> and it is the rather to be believed, because both he then, and
> many others before him, have been curious to search into their
> bellies, what the food was by which they lived; and have found

out nothing by which they might satisfie their curiosity (*Angler*, 72-3).

The 'Fordidge trout' sounds rather like a sea trout (apart from its flesh which 'cuts very white'). But Walton also wrote of the bull trout, which further stated that 'there are in many Rivers that relate to the Sea, *Salmon-trouts*, as much different from others, both in shape and in their spots, as we see sheep in some Countries differ . . . in their shape and bigness' (*Angler*, 75). These sound like the genuine item, *S. trutta trutta*; but it is difficult to be certain.

The first attestation of the term *sea trout* itself dates from 1745 (see above quote), where the term is defined as 'The salmo trutta = Salmon-trout; also the bull or grey trout, S. eriox'. Leaving aside the difficulty posed by 'S. eriox', the term's rather late entry into the language must be connected with the fact that, before the 18th century, the sea trout must have gone under many local names (as implied in Walton), and/or not been distinguished from the salmon. Contrast this with a quote from Francis Francis, who, writing in the *Encyclopaedia Britannica* in 1875, seemed to have the sea trout and its place in the sporting hierarchy firmly in mind: 'Next to the salmon ranks in value for sport the sea trout. Of these there are two kinds . . .' And of course Grey devoted a whole chapter of his *Fly Fishing* (1899) to sea trout fishing. So historically, it seems to be the case that the sea trout is (apparently) unknown or not distinguished before the 17th century, is indistinctly recognised during the later 17th and 18th centuries, and becomes clearly recognised as a sporting fish, and a species in its own right, during the 19th century.

I believe, although I may be wrong, that the recognition of the sea trout as a sporting fish during the 19th century relates to something that seems, on first thought, altogether peripheral. This is the coming of the railway age. As railways were developed,

> it became the custom for the well-to-do Englishman and his family to migrate to Scotland when the London "season" was over, and although the grouse or the red deer would be his main objective, a bundle of fishing rods would no doubt be included in his voluminous luggage for use on off days from the moor or forest (C.F. Walker, *Lake Flies*, 18).

Walker's next paragraph makes instructive reading:

> In these late summer months, when the rivers are normally at their lowest level except for a short period following a spate, the loch is likely to afford a better prospect of sport, and as it happens this is also the season when sea trout are to be found in lochs with access to the sea. And, human nature being what

it is, our holiday angler would inevitably be attracted by the larger quarry [i.e. to the sea trout], for which a compromise between a salmon fly and a trout fly is the most profitable form of lure. But it must have soon become apparent that this was equally attractive to the brown trout, whereupon the fisherman found himself in the happy position of being able to enjoy the best of both worlds...Whether it actually happened like this or not, the fact remains that this became the standard type of lure for the brown trout of lakes, and to this day the tackle dealers' catalogues invariably treat "lake fly" and "sea trout fly" as synonymous terms. It is, moreover, significant that every well-known lake pattern whose origin I have been able to trace dates from the nineteenth century and that the majority of them hail either from Scotland or from Ireland, where similar considerations would apply (*Lake Flies*, 18).

So the theory is to the effect that sea trout fishing evolves during this leisured age, during escapes from the London season. In other words, it evolves almost by accident, and this evolution is connected, too, with the history of fishing for brown trout in stillwater. Of fishing for sea trout in rivers, very little useful is said until the end of the 19th century.

Such a theory helps to explain the fact that, although the sea trout runs large, and in its habits behaves like a salmon, the flies used for sea trout fishing were, until relatively recently, rather like large trout flies ('fancy flies' – see *fly*). As Walker noted, such flies would help the loch angler to enjoy the best of both brown trout and sea trout fishing. On rivers, too, sea trout could perhaps have been seen moving on the surface (and even feeding, perhaps?), and an apparently logical conclusion to draw would be that such fish could be caught with a trout fly, a fly suggesting some surface food. From this historical position, it is a mere step to assuming that sea trout are not only related to the brown trout, but also behave like them. There are works still in print which make this assumption. F.W. Holiday, for instance, who wrote the 'Sea trout' chapter of *The Complete Fly-Fisher* (ed. C.F. Walker), recommended that the intending sea trout angler should use either simulations of natural flies, or fancy flies. But these fancy flies, he suggested, are taken by the fish as *sedges*; and he went further, advocating that fancy flies should 'bear at least some resemblance' to the sedges which hatch in the evening on the water being fished. He also stated that sea trout would feed on *upwinged flies*, and on their *nymphs*, 'with...gusto' (*Complete Fly-Fisher*, 60-1).

This is how sea trout fishing developed during much of this

century. It was seen, perhaps, as a minor diversion, and although some fairly firm guidelines were established (such as the fact that sea trout in many rivers take the fly best at night), sea trout fishing was generally considered to be a form of trout fishing. It took the pioneering work of Hugh Falkus to change this perception. Falkus was one of the first – perhaps the first – to claim that sea trout could be caught systematically by linking fishing techniques with the sea trout's behaviour. Before looking in brief at those techniques, however, it is necessary to consider the sea trout's distribution and life cycle.

Sea trout are distributed throughout the British Isles. The river systems which they prefer must, of course, be clean, and have fairly easy access to the sea: although the fish can surmount relatively formidable falls, they cannot run barrier falls or dams without some artificial help from e.g. a fish-pass. Such river systems must also be relatively *acidic*. Although the fish will run the more *alkaline rivers*, or rivers where the pH factor is neutral (such as Tweed), in general they turn quickly from these streams into the more acidic hill streams. It is not too much of a falsification to assume that sea trout are largely fish of moorland and torrent, of peat-stained upland lakes and foam-flecked river pools the colour of black tea. The fish also appear to prefer the smaller river catchments. (These distributional facts are relevant to the fish's migration; see below.)

As with the other salmonids, life begins on a *redd* cut from stones or gravel. Sea trout *spawn* in late October-December, although it is significant that on many systems, sea trout may spawn either earlier or later than salmon (thus minimising competition for the redds) and/or spawn in a different part of the catchment. The pattern thereafter is very like that of the salmon, i.e. the egg hatches into an *alevin*; the alevin's yolk-sac is consumed and the tiny fish becomes a *fry* and begins to feed actively; the fry becomes a *parr*; the parr, after feeding in the river for perhaps two years, develops salt-secreting glands in its gills and a silvery coat, and becomes a sea trout *smolt*; the smolt migrates, and the fish begins its sea-feeding, returning to the river after mere months, as a herling, or after a year or more, when the fish returns as a mature adult of 2 to 3lbs and upwards.

The life cycle is familiar, but it can and should be related to the distribution of the fish. First, the upland, acidic hill streams in which the fish spend the first part of their lives are poor in food; the growth of the parr, and their eventual migration as smolts, can be explained (cf. the salmon) by competition for food – that is, the parr tend to drop downstream, looking for more productive water, eventually reaching the sea. Another way of putting this is to say that the fish *require* to migrate. Second, I noted above that sea trout tend to prefer smaller catchments, and acidic streams. In general, limestone catchments flow over a flatter topography than acidic streams, and are therefore larger systems. It therefore seems plausible that sea trout prefer smaller catchments because in such waters they are better physically able to run from the tide to the spawning redds in the hills. In effect, this means that it is no accident that the sea trout is found in largest concentrations westerly – in the upland waters of Scotland and Ireland. The fish also occurs in numbers in Devon and Cornwall, Wales, the Lake District and Galloway.

Of the fish's sea feeding, relatively little is known. The fish do not apparently travel as far as the salmon, but remain in estuarial and coastal waters, rarely going more than sixty miles from the river mouth. Their food appears to consist of fish, such as sprats and sandeels (these have been identified as major components of the fish's sea-feeding diet), as well as small crustaceans such as sand-hoppers and sand-fleas. A link may be made here between sea-feeding and sea trout fishing tactics. On the eastern seaboards, sea trout tend to feed most heavily on small fish; this is also true of the sea trout which feed in the Irish sea (these fish will eventually take the Irish east coast rivers, or the rivers of the English and Welsh west coast). It may not be accidental that fishing tactics on the rivers of these coasts centre on presenting the sea trout with fish-representing flies – typically, large, slim, hair-winged flies with silver or gold bodies. On the other hand, on the Atlantic coasts, sea trout tend to feed most heavily on crustaceans (Fahy, 73). Again, it may not be accidental that on the river systems of the Atlantic coasts (Western Ireland, the far NW of Scotland) sea trout fishing tactics centre on the presentation of smaller flies such as *bumbles* or *palmers*, which may be taken to be representative (albeit crudely so) of the smaller crustaceans the fish has been feeding on in the sea.

These links, however, remain conjectural. But recent work on sea trout fishing does tend to emphasise the links between a sea trout's feeding (in the sea) and angling tactics. Falkus, for instance, revolutionised sea trout fishing by suggesting that to all intents and purposes sea trout should not be understood as actively feeding in freshwater. He therefore proposed that, logically, what the sea trout fisherman should attempt to do is to present the fish with a fly which represents something on which they have been recently feeding in the sea. For many river systems, this means that the sea trout fly should *not* represent natural flies (*pace* F.W.

Holiday), but *should* represent small fish. It is a comment on the magnitude of Falkus's achievement that his Medicines, Sunk Lures and so on, and the method of presentation they entail, are now standard parts of the sea trout fisherman's repertoire. But Falkus did more: he also suggested that these flies could be fished systematically, largely if not wholly at night, when the sea trout are most active. At night, Falkus posited, sea trout would be active and near the surface until the middle watches of the blackness (perhaps this is a relic of their sea-feeding behaviour). At this time, the fisherman could catch sea trout on a floating line in the glides and pool-tails. But there is a period towards or near midnight when the sea trout go *down* and the river seems dead. After this period, Falkus and his friends discovered that sea trout, which retire to the deeps after their dusk activity, could still be caught, providing that a larger fly (typically a Sunk Lure) was presented slowly and at the right depth in the places where the fish were resting.

This fairly changed sea trout fishing. Instead of the smallish, mothy trout flies formerly in use, sea trout fishermen in many parts of the country began to use (and still use) larger, fish-suggesting lures. Nor did fishermen walk home after midnight, thinking that the river was dead. Many stayed on, fishing through the night in the still places of the stream with a fast-sinking line, reverting to the floating line only, perhaps, for a short period before the full dawn.

Of sea trout fishing in stillwaters, however, it has to be said that little has changed since the early years of this century (save that waters are harder-fished than ever before). The favoured tactics on the loch still involve broadside *drifting* (see *boat fishing*; *drogue*; *dibble* etc.) and a two- or three-fly *leader*. The *dap* is also used to some effect, although why sea trout take the dap is still something of a mystery – do they think it is some particularly large fly (the natural or artificial *Daddy-long-legs*, fished in August and September, is one of the deadliest of all daps)? Or does the wake of the dap stimulate the sea trout to some dim memory of fleeing bait-fish in the sea? Perhaps we will never know for sure. This uncertainty, along with many others stemming from the fish's behaviour and response to the artificial fly, reveals the tantalising nature of sea trout fishing, its intellectual excitement and its joy. It is very much to be hoped that recent developments in e.g. salmon-ranching, which takes place in coastal waters where sea trout tend to feed, or in commercial exploitation of sandeels, do not lead to the disappearance of the sea trout from waters in which they were once common. If we lose the sea trout of the west, we have been responsible for a dismal angling future.

sea-winter   A convenient term which refers to the length of time
a *salmon* or *sea trout* has spent in the sea. The number of *sea-winters*
spent by a fish can be deduced from *scale-reading*. Fahy writes,
for example, that a 5lb sea trout might have spent, say, 3 years
in the river as a *parr*, 'followed by three sea winters in the last of
which the fish spawned' (*Child of the Tides*, p.82). This is expres-
sible by the following formula: '3. 2+ S.M.+' – three years as a
parr ('3.) followed by three sea winters ('2+') during the last of
which the fish spawned ('+ S[pawning] M[ark] +').
   The term is apparently not recorded in the OED.

sedge   The *sedges*, also known as *caddis*-flies, are an important
family of flies for the river and stillwater trout fisherman. The
Latin name for the Order is Trichoptera; they are distinguished
in many handbooks as 'Flies with roof-shaped wings', contrasting
with e.g. the *upwinged flies* (*ephemeroptera*) and the *stone-flies*
(Plecoptera). Sedges are immediately recognisable from the dis-
posal of their wings and their *antennae*.
   The term *sedge* is a shortening of *sedge-fly*, and is recorded very
late, its first attestation apparently dating from 1889 and Halford's
Dry-Fly Fishing: 'A small sedge on a No. 0 hook...' (but see
below for possible earlier attestations – the sedges were certainly
recognised as angling flies earlier than 1889). It seems to be related
to the noun *sedge* meaning 'water plant' (especially species of
Carex, and also the wild Iris, *Iris pseudacorus*), perhaps because
the flies hatch out in the vicinity of these plants.
   The life cycle of the sedges is well-known, consisting of the
stages egg – *larva* ('*caddis*') – *pupa* – adult. Trout may feed heavily
on the larvae, especially on stillwaters (but also on many rain-fed
rivers) during the spring; the Stickfly, or Carnill's Cased Caddis,
are popular representations. They also feed on the ascending
pupae, particularly during the evenings of the months of peak
emergence (typically on stillwaters, June-September), and on the
adults, whose fussy, scuttering travels across the water surface
make them tempting targets for trout, which take the adults with
characteristically heavy rises (see *rise-form*).
   On rivers, the most common species of sedge would seem to
be the Cinnamon Sedge *(Limnephilus lunatus)*, the Caperer
(Halesus radiatus), the Medium Sedge *(Goëra pilosa)*, and the Grey
Flag *(Hydropsyche pellucidula)*. The first two species typically
hatch during the evening (Goddard, *Trout Fly Recognition*, 114,
records that the Caperer gets its name from its habit of dancing
and fluttering over the water), while the last two are daytime-
hatching species. The Grey Flag seems particularly common in
Ireland; Harris (*Angler's Entomology*, 139) notes that it gets its

name from the 'flies' habit of resting on the flags which border
many of the limestone rivers'.

Other running-water species include the Welshman's Button
(Sericostoma personatum), the *Grannom (Brachycentus subnubilus)*,
and the various Silverhorns (see below). The grannom is of
interest since on some of the chalkstreams it is one of the flies
which begins the angler's year, hatching in April and May.

Fortunately for the fisherman, the sedges share certain general
characteristics: the adults all have roof-shaped wings, are some
shade of mottled brown ranging from dingy yellow to almost
black, and most hatch in the evenings. This means in practice
that some 'general pattern of sedge' can be useful, rather than
some very specific representation. (The fact that sedge patterns
are usually fished at dusk, when fish tend to be less wary, also
helps here.)

On stillwaters, rather more attention has been paid to this order
of flies. Along with the various species of *midge* (and the various
fry) they are one of the staples of the angler's year. Early in the
season, fish are often found browsing among the caddis larvae on
the lake bottom, when a leaded artificial representation can work
well. From the early to the late summer, evening hatches of the
various species of sedge complement hatches of midge, and it is
not uncommon to find fish feeding at the surface on both midge
and sedge pupae, sometimes switching their attention from one
to the other (this can be unnerving for the fisherman). One very
useful sedge pupa-suggesting pattern is the famous Invicta, a
'traditional' *wet fly* here put to a specifically-representative use;
among the more 'imitative' pupa patterns, Dr Bell's Amber Sedge
Pupa, and the range of artificial pupae devised by John Goddard
(which '*match the hatch*' by being dressed with either cream,
brown, orange or olive-green seal's fur in accordance with the
prevalent colour of the naturals) seem justifiably popular. (On
Dr Bell of Blagdon, see *pupa*.) For the adult fly, there is in my
experience very little to beat the G&H Sedge, another brain-child
of Goddard; this may be fished as a single *dry fly*, or used as a
top dropper or *bob fly* on a three-fly leader fished from a boat. In
this last role the G&H Sedge is sometimes supremely effective.
Another very effective general pattern (on both river and stillwater) is the Wickham's Fancy,

It is a little puzzling that many sedges are apparently not recognised, and perhaps not fished, until relatively late in the history
of fly-fishing. The earliest sedge to have been distinguished seems
to have been the grannom, about which James Chetham gave a
clear account (1681; Hills, *History*, 147, rightly rejected the 'Shell

Fly' of the *Treatise* as a candidate for the grannom because of the date given in the *Treatise* for fishing the fly – July, whereas the naturals hatch in April). It is just possible, though, that the 'Dun Cut' of the *Treatise* was intended to represent the Welshman's Button; Skues evidently thought so (see McDonald, 115), but the overall coloration seems wrong; it is also difficult to interpret the yellow stripes ('yelow lyste') which the *Treatise* incorporated into the body of the fly.

Cotton's list of flies, however, contains a related 'Dun Cut', which he gave as a fly for May. Its dressing (a bear's dun body mixed with yellow and blue, a dun wing, and 'two horns at the head, made of the hairs of a Squirrels tail' – *Angler*, 288; and see *antennae*) looks uncommonly like that of a sedge, and since the Welshman's Button hatches from early May to mid July, Cotton's Dun Cut may well represent this insect. None of the other flies given in his list, however, seem to represent sedges, which is surprising.

Hills noted that the (Great) Red Sedge is first given an account in Theakston (*A List of Natural Flies*, 1853). Ronalds (*The Fly-fisher's Entomology*, 1836) also gave a picture of the Cinnamon Sedge. But it is the later 19th and early 20th century when, possibly owing to the impetus towards 'imitative' fishing brought about by Halford and others (see *dry fly*), the sedges are more closely described and copied.

sewin A Welsh term for the *sea trout*. OED notes that it is of 'obscure origin: apparently not Welsh'. My own theory, picturesque but unprovable, is that the word may derive from Old English *sæ- wynn*, literally 'sea-joy'. However that may be, the definition given in the OED is once again confusing: '[a] fish of the Salmon tribe (Salmo cambricus or eriox), the bull trout, found in Welsh rivers'. The classifications 'cambricus or eriox' date from a time when the minutest differences between local species of sea trout were thought to betoken different species of fish; Walton perhaps started this hare when he commented that 'Salmon Trout' differ widely 'both in shape and in their spots'. The term *bull trout* is today best reserved for those problematic fish which run the river Coquet.

The word's first attestation dates from 1532, when a certain abbot is to be given each year 'x. samones v. gyllynges [grayling?] and xliiij^te suwynges'. He must have liked fish. The term survives widely in Wales today; one example from early this century is from Gallichan:

"I wass seen a fine salmon and many sewins last night," says Dafyd, blowing a puff of Amlwch shag-smoke from his pipe.

"Yes, inteet, there is plenty big fishes in the river now. I shall go in the night with a worm." Dafyd is quite right. Since the floods of the latter end of June there had been a great run of salmon and sea-trout up the Glaslyn . . . (*Fishing in Wales*, 53).

shedder   A term (now obsolete?) for a female salmon or trout full of roe, and thus out of season. The term perhaps derives from the late 16th century, and *An act for the preservation of the spawn and fry of fish, 1599*, attributed to George Clark – this 'act' was one of *The Game Laws* (from King Henry III to the Present Period), published in 1786. This states that no person or persons should 'take or kill any salmons or trouts, not being in season, being kepper salmons, or kepper trouts, shedder salmons, or shedder trouts' (rpr. in Profumo & Swift, *The Magic Wheel*, 59). It is heartening to think that early laws and literature relating to game fish took such care for their preservation. The *Treatise* itself, for example, exhorted anglers not to be 'to ravenous in takyng of your sayd games as to moche at one tyme', and to 'nouryssh the game in all that ye maye'. See also *kipper*.

shooting-head   A type of *fly-line* developed by distance-casters at fly-casting tournaments; see *To Cast a Trout Fly* (published by House of Hardy, 25), which dates the discovery of the shooting-head – there called a 'shooting taper' line – to 1946. Since then, the shooting-head has come into more general use, especially by bank-fishermen on reservoirs.

The shooting-head consists of a length (between 10-15 yards) of conventional fly-line, usually the forward part of a double tapered floating or sinking line, which is attached to either braided or monofilament *backing*. The 'head' is *false-cast* outside the tip ring and then the main cast is made, usually in conjuction with the *double-haul* technique; given the consequent line-speed and velocity of the head, when the cast is made the backing (which, being of relatively fine diameter, slips easily through the rings) shoots out through the rings behind the head. Great distance may be achieved this way: with, say, a 10-foot rod rated for line sizes 8-9, a size 9 or 10 shooting head may be cast well over 30 yards by the proficient.

Some anglers feel that the shooting-head is clumsy, that it lands with more disturbance than is desirable; others feel that the backing is difficult to handle satisfactorily in normal fishing situations. The first set of problems tend to disappear with practice; the second difficulty is eased if some form of *line-tray* is used. See also *cast²*.

shooting line   As implied in the previous entry, fly line is said to 'shoot' as any loose coils of line are pulled through the rings by the impetus of a cast. *Double tapered* and *forward tapered* lines may thus be 'shot' in a similar way to a shooting-head. *To Cast a Trout Fly* describes shooting line as follows (the section is headed 'More Distance'):

> With your regular thirty feet past the rod tip, preferably lying on the grass or water out in front, strip another ten feet of line from the reel. Let it fall at your feet. Now take a back cast in the usual way, holding the line tightly and making the same foot-long pulls with your left hand. All the slack, the extra ten feet, is between your left hand and the reel. Make the forward cast. Just after tipping the rod forward at the peak of the power application, release the line held in your left hand.
> It will shoot out through the rings...(23).

short taking   Fish are said to be *short taking* when, for one or more reasons, they are not taking the fly solidly; an alternative is to say (with a frown) 'the fish are taking short today'.

This behaviour is common, especially on lakes, lochs and reservoirs, and it is, alas, widespread where stillwater sea trout are concerned. It also occurs on rivers; brown trout, sea trout, and salmon may 'come short', and this is usually a sign that the fly is being presented incorrectly. Short taking typically occurs when the *wet fly* is being fished. Although it is rare to hear specifically of short taking on the *dry fly*, a variant of the phrase is there used: *short rising* ('Damn! He rose short'). For some writers, however, the phrases are interchangeable: thus Kingsmill Moore, for example, wrote, with his usual wisdom: 'Short rising! This is a topic which I have been shelving, for I cannot supply the answer...' (*A Man May Fish*, 156). He went on to distinguish two types of this maddening behaviour, the first where the fish do not really want the fly and are merely mouthing it out of caprice, the second where the fish actually rise to but miss the fly. But there are other possibilities: that because of some combination of water condition and light, the fish comes to the fly but at the last minute sees it as a deception and a trap; that the fly is moving too quickly; that the fly is moving too slowly; that the fish merely nip the trailing feather-fibres on the fly (this applies particularly when *lures* incorporating marabou wings are being fished); or that the fly is too big. All these are possible explanations of short taking, and in the course of a fishing day where short taking is prevalent I try most sensible remedies, typically without success.

shoulders   An alternative term for the *thorax* of a natural or artificial fly, as in e.g. Harris, *Angler's Entomology*: 'The body of an adult ephemeropteran is composed of three main regions, namely, a head, a thorax (sometimes known as "chest" or "shoulders") and an abdomen' (15).

shrimp   The freshwater shrimp, *Gammarus pulex*, is one of the most important food-forms to the brown and rainbow trout of alkaline lakes and rivers; it is particularly on common chalk-streams and the waters related to them, and it is also not unusual to find chalk-stream grayling feeding heavily on shrimp during the winter months.

The shrimp is a bottom- and weed-dweller. It grows up to half an inch in length, and varies in colour from translucent fawn, through washed-out dirty green, to a kind of brown-orange during the mating season, which may occur at any time of year (but perhaps most frequently in the high summer). Artificial patterns should mimic these characteristics; there are several good designs current, most popular of which seem to be the late Richard Walker's leaded Shrimp (weighted with strips of wine-bottle foil lapped onto the top of the hook-shank) and John Goddard's Shrimper (weighted with wire). Whichever pattern is chosen, the pattern should be fished slow and deep, and *retrieved* with a series of lifelike sink-and-draw movements (natural shrimps swim in short bursts of activity, usually on their sides). Where the fish can be seen, the *induced take* may be put into operation.

The word *shrimp* itself seems to derive from a verb cognate with MHG *schrimpen*, 'to shrink up'. It is first attested in English in 1327 ('Shrimpis, 3d.'), and subsequently in a cookery book of 1430 ('Take þe Luce, an þe Perche, & þe Schrympe, & seþe hem' – which sounds rather good).

shuck   A term for the skin which covers a natural *nymph* or, especially, *pupa*. When the nymph or pupa hatches, the pupal skin, the *shuck*, splits from the thorax, and the adult emerges, sometimes (e.g. the adult *midges*) resting either on or near the empty shuck.

The presence of insect shucks in the water – and they can sometimes be seen in millions along the calm shorelines of still-waters – is a good indication that fish have been or will be feeding on hatching pupae (typically midge or *sedge*).

These shucks are also significant in another way. Sometimes, midges seem to find great difficulty emerging from their shucks (especially in oily-calm water), and in these conditions, fish sometimes feed exclusively on the pre-emergent pupae trapped in the surface film. At these times, artificial patterns may need to incorporate some suggestion of the shuck, perhaps feather fibres or other material tied in at the tail or thorax of the fly.

Shuck is of unknown etymology, but there may be a relationship to *shuck* in the sense 'something valueless' (i.e. the shuck is of no value to the insect; the first attestation of *shuck* in this last sense dates to 1851, and Mayne Reid's *Scalp Hunters*: 'They'd whip us to shucks on the [prairie]'). Defined in our sense in the OED as '[a] husk, pod, or shell ... The shell-like covering of some larvae', the first attestation of *shuck* in a fishing sense dates to a *Field* of 1886: 'To secure the swiftly darting larvae... before emerging from the "shuck"'.

side-strain   A running fish may be controlled during the *play* by the application of *side-strain*. The rod is held low, and roughly parallel to the direction in which the fish is running; rod-pressure is then applied away from the fish. The fish usually responds by turning its head and body towards the direction of the pressure. Thus snags and other horrors may be negotiated; if a fisherman says, lifting the net under a large brown trout, 'Oh, he ran straight towards that weed-bed but I turned him by side-strain', that fisherman is happy.

Skues devoted a piece in *The Way of a Trout with a Fly* to side-strain, and in it explained why side-strain is such an effective method of controlling a fish:

> ... it was my guest who explained why side-strain was so immediately effective... "You see," he said, "the trout swims with a lateral action, moving his head from side to side, and if, as he goes down-stream, you pull his head round hard sideways, half the time he must be yielding to the strain, and that makes it so hard as to be almost impossible for him to fight against it the other half of the time. So he comes round... (p.179).

The first description of side-strain in fishing literature seems to be that of Thomas Barker (*The Art of Angling*, 1651). As Trench makes clear (*Hist. Angling*, 128), Barker played salmon (which he caught in the Thames) not by 'giving them the butt' (i.e. pointing the butt of the rod at the fish, a common practice with the long rods of the day), still less by throwing the rod into the water and allowing the fish to tow it around until it exhausted itself (as Walton wrote that he 'use always to do when I meet with an overgrown fish' – *Angler*, 119), but by side-strain: 'You must forecast to turn the fish as you do a wild horse, either upon the right or left hand, and wind up your line as you find occasion in guiding the fish to the shore, having a good, large landing-hook to take him up'. (This is also the first mention of the *gaff*.) See also *play*.

single haul   The most common type of overhead fly-casting typically involves a *single haul*, i.e. as the line is back-cast, the left hand pulls ('hauls') the line at the moment of power application so that the line has greater velocity in the air. See *cast²*.

sink and draw   This is a method of presenting the sunk fly, especially e.g. a heavily leaded fly intended for brown and/or rainbow trout, or for grayling. The technique is adaptable to both still and flowing water. The essence of the affair is that the fly is cast in the usual way, and allowed to sink to the relevant depth. At that point, and not before, the fly is drawn smoothly towards the angler, then allowed to sink again. Thereafter, the process is repeated until the cast is fished out. A fly presented in this manner rises and sinks enticingly in the water. In effect, this is a variant of the *induced take*, except that in this instance the process (i.e. the fish taking) is usually unseen by the fisherman.

It is worth pointing out that many boat fishermen employ this technique almost unconsciously when fishing a team of *wet flies* on a promising *drift*. There, the flies are cast downwind (or better, across and downwind), and *retrieved* by a series of slow draws, so that the flies dart then pause in the water. It is this lively movement that the fish seem to find so attractive.

My belief is that this term has been adapted from coarse fishing. In *The Penguin Guide to Fishing* (ed. Willock, 31), for example, *sink-and-draw* is defined as a technique 'used with small dead-bait such as a minnow, and sometimes a worm, for perch or pike. The weighted fish is allowed to plunge to the bottom and is then retrieved in a sink-and-draw movement that often proves irresistible'. More recently, Greenhalgh writes of fishing the natural minnow for trout 'in a slow sink-and-draw manner' (p.180). That the term has long been associated with fishing the minnow in this way is attested by e.g. A.H. Chaytor who wrote that one method of fishing the prawn for salmon is very similar to 'the old system of "sink and draw" fishing, as used with natural minnow' (p.291).

slob trout   A term for a *brown trout* that lives and feeds in the estuary of its parent river (see e.g. Niall Fallon, *Fly-fishing for Irish Trout*, who defines *slob trout* as fish 'which have adapted to brackish water'). It is just possible that there is some etymological connection between the defining adjective *slob* and the word *slob* meaning 'a large soft worm, using in angling'. This last term is first attested in 1815 (*Sporting Magazine*: 'A gentleman was angling with the maiden slob for trout'). On the other hand, it seems much more plausible to assume that the compound derives from Irish *slab*, meaning '[m]ud, esp. soft mud on the sea-shore; ooze; muddy land'. This is first attested in 1780 (Young, *Tour Ireland*: 'Under the slab or sea ooze he dug some very fine blue marle'). See also *voe fishing*.

smash take   A *smash take* usually occurs when a fish seizes an artificial fly which is being fished at speed, a stripped *lure* for example. If the fly is moving quickly, the fish has to move equally quickly to intercept it, and if the moment of the *take* coincides with the angler stripping in more line, that take will be so heavy as to cause a 'smash' as the rod goes up (the *leader* usually breaks at the knot nearest the hook). Smash takes therefore (usually) indicate poor technique: the fly should be retrieved more slowly, and the rod held at a steeper angle to the water as the fly is being fished. Brian Clarke has accurately stated that although we attribute smash takes to a particularly large or fast-moving fish, it is not so much the fish which causes the smash take, but rather, it is the angler who 'smash retrieves' (*Pursuit of Stillwater Trout*, 127).

smolt   The sea-going stage in the life-cycle of a *salmon* or *sea trout* subsequent to those fishes' river-lives as *parr*. This is also how the word is defined in the OED, which dates the first attestation to 1469 ('All myllaris þat slais Smo[l]tis with crelis or ony vthir maner of way' – although why millers, in particular, should 'slay smolts' is unclear). There is possibly some etymological connection with *smelt* ('A small fish . . . allied to the salmon . . . the sparling or spirling'), a native word first attested in English in 725 (where the *Corpus Glossary* defines '*Sardas*, smeltas'). It seems as if all small, silvery fish, especially those found in or related to the sea, were once called 'smelts'.

As noted in the relevant entries, smolts assume a silvery coat during their downstream migration(s); this coat is due to the presence of guanine (sp. 'guanin' in Taverner & Scott, *Salmon Fishing*, 248), which reflects the light (Maclean, *Trout and Grayling*, 20, notes that the tiny crystals of guanine are removed from the scales of some silvery fish, e.g. the bleak, for use in the manufacture of artificial pearls); at the same time, salt-secreting cells develop in the gills of the fish (Falkus, *Sea Trout Fishing*, 22).

In the case of sea trout, recent work has established that there are two runs of smolts each year, a main run, which takes place in the spring, and a later autumn run. The main run of smolts may return to the river later that summer, in which case the fish will have had mere months' sea-feeding and will be termed *herling*, weighing up to 1lb, but individuals from that run may stay at sea for a further year (or more), returning in a subsequent year to the natal river as large fish of 2lbs and upwards.

The autumn run is more problematic. These smolts are evidently not so well-adapted to life in the sea (Fahy, 63), and many seem to perish, while some recruit into the stock of the next spring's smolt run, and return to the river in that subsequent summer. It is a little puzzling as to why such an autumn run of smolts develops at all: some scientists believe they are the harbingers of the next spring's smolt run, but, since they are not apparently adapted to sea-life, why should they run in the autumn, and not the following spring? Another theory, put forward by Fahy (*Child of the Tides*, 64) is that the autumn migration may be a 'tactical withdrawal' in the face of the upstream migrations of returning sea trout which, Fahy writes, 'can be voracious', especially as *kelts*. But this theory is also problematic: first, returning sea trout have suppressed appetites, and it is difficult to imagine fish intent on spawning devouring thousands of pre-smolts; second, although sea trout do feed 'voraciously' as kelts, since the fish spawn in October-December they are properly termed kelts in the later autumn and winter, i.e. after the autumn run of smolts has taken place.

These queries reveal how much we have still to understand about the life-cycles of the migratory fishes.

smutting   Brown and rainbow trout feeding at the surface of rivers during the high summer, delicately taking *reed-smuts* and other minute insects, are said to be *smutting*. Many angling writers list the reed-smut, a species of *Simulium*, under the heading **black gnat**, so fish feeding to any small, tiny, dark fly may be said to be smutting fish. Such fish have a well-deserved reputation for being difficult to catch. This is perhaps because the natural insects on which they are feeding are so tiny as to be all but impossible to represent on a hook.

Smuts, curiously enough, were at the beginning of Skues' discovery of *nymph fishing*. Arriving at the river Itchen one blazing September day in 1892, he found the fish were 'smutting freely' (to some small black flies Skues subsequently called 'black gnats', see *Minor Tactics*, 2ff.). He discovered that the fish would take a wet fly fished just subsurface; it was a lesson he remembered in later years.

A recent article in *T&S* ('Cinderellas of the streams' by Michael Meddings, December 1989, 56-9) goes into some detail on the life of the true reed-smut and its relevance to the trout. The reed-smut is available to the trout at three stages in its life: first, as an adult, crawling underwater encased in an air bubble in order to lay eggs on some piece of vegetation; second, as a larva, clinging worm-like to some underwater support; and third, as a newly-hatched adult. These adults look rather like very tiny house-flies, having dirty-black bodies and small, transparent wings. They swarm in millions over the surface of many streams in summer.

The history of the word *smut* is of interest. Our angling smuts are at least etymologically related to *smut* in the sense 'fungous disease...affecting various plants...which are spoiled by the grain being wholly or partly converted into a blackish powder' –

smut in this sense being first attested in 1665 (*Phil. Trans.*: 'Mel-dew, Blasting, Smut'). Then there develops a transferred sense meaning 'soot, or sooty matter' (1806 Southey, *Letters*: 'That cursed composition of smoke, dust, smuts, human breath, and marsh vapour') – thus, a 'smut in one's eye' – a piece of soot or other black matter. Then our angling sense develops: small black insects come to be known as *smuts*, a usage first attested in the *Daily News* of 1899: 'A trout . . . grubs in the weeds, chases larvae, and revels in almost invisible smuts'.

snail   The snail is another important food-item for the brown and rainbow trout of rivers and lakes. River trout often take snails, along with *caddis*, from the bottom in the early months of the season, and stillwater trout feed on snails either at depth, or during snail-migrations in the summer. That snails migrate seems odd, but, when the oxygen content of the water is reduced, they rise to the surface film, hanging by their 'foot' (a fleshy pad) and drifting over the lake surface (Goddard, *Trout Flies of Stillwater*, 165-6). At these times, trout may feed heavily on them, although their rises may initially be difficult to interpret: it is usually neces-sary to first catch a fish, and then use the *marrow-spoon* to divine that snails, and not, say, *midge* or *sedge pupae*, are the favoured food.

The classic snail-representing artificial is undoubtedly Tom Ivens' Black and Peacock Spider (size 12), although Cliff Henry has developed a cork-bodied pattern which floats nicely in the surface film. If trout are bottom-feeding, a leaded Black and Peacock Spider, or perhaps a leaded, dark-bodied Shrimp or Stickfly, seem suitable.

snake   Also *snake-ring(s)*; a type of rod ring. These used to be fitted as standard when cane rods and silk *fly-lines* were in general use, but have been partly replaced by single-leg or 'Full Open Bridge' rings with today's plastic-coated fly-lines. The choice of ring is largely a matter of personal preference: *snake rings* are relatively hard-wearing, and are less susceptible to bending than light, single-leg rings. But not everyone has agreed: E.M. Tod, for example, wrote that he saw 'no reason for changing the old-fashioned [i.e. upright] ordinary rings and keepers. Indeed, I once had one of my rods fitted with snake rings, and afterwards had them removed . . .' (p.153).

sneck   A *sneck, snecked, sneck-bend* or *snecky-bend hook* is a kind of fish hook with a relatively square bend and an offset point (see also *Limerick*). One does not often find these hooks today, but they were certainly in vogue earlier this century: Skues, for instance, used to tie some of his nymphs on what seem, judging by illustrations, to be sneck-bend hooks (although he also noticed his preference for 'unsnecked square bend' hooks).

The word *sneck* is of obscure origin, but may have some relationship to *snatch* (?OE *snæccan*). Its original sense, still preserved in many Northern English dialects, is 'latch of a door or gate' (1324: 'xxviij snekkes'); the important point here is to note the sense of 'fastening, means or catch by which something may be secured', a sense which surely underlies the later use of the term to mean a kind of hook (1816 Bainbridge: 'The Sneckbend, as it is commonly called, diverges from the parallel lines from the bend upwards' – Bainbridge was clearly referring here to the hook's offset point).

sonaghan An Irish term for what is held to be a variety of *brown trout*, said to be localised to Lough Melvin. Fallon (Appx. VII) writes that the *sonaghan* is a shoaling trout, preferring deep water, and a free-rising fish, although it does not grow to the same size as a brown trout. I would also add that some anglers hold the sonaghan to be recognisable by its very heavy complement of black spots.

The term is apparently not recorded in the OED. See also *gillaroo*.

spawning Most of the information relevant to the spawning of the various game fish can be found under E.G. *brown trout*, *rainbow trout*, *redd*, *salmon*, *sea trout* etc. The only thing necessary here is to add an etymological note. The term *spawn* begins life as a verb (from OF. *espandre*, Anglo-Norman *espaundre*, 'to shed, spill, pour out'). It is first recorded as a verb (participle) in 1400 ('whiche fisshes he putte in the stewe, where they haue spawned and multyplyed'), and as a noun in 1491 ('Grete multitude of Spawne and broode of all maner fysshes of the See', *Act 7 Hen. VII*).

spent[1] A fish exhausted by the *play* will typically turn onto its side as it nears the net (see *landing net*) or *gaff*. It is then said to be a *spent fish* (or 'the fish is/was spent'), rather as in the following: 'By this time the hardy warrior's strength was almost spent . . . as he came again to the surface, lying on his side . . .' (*The Fisherman's Bedside Book*, ed. 'BB' [1985 edn], 56). An alternative is to say the fish is *played out*.

A related use of the word is to describe game fish after spawning, when they are said to be 'spent', i.e. exhausted, by that arduous process, as in the following: 'When spawning has been completed, the fish gradually work downstream to the sea. The spent fish are known as kelts . . .' (Scott, 'The natural history of the salmon', in *The Complete Fly-Fisher*, ed. C.F. Walker, 19).

spent²   *Ephemeropteran* flies lying spread-winged on the surface after egg-laying has taken place (and see *imago*; *spinner*) are said to be *spent* (or 'spent fly'). Trout in rivers often feed on these spent spinners, especially in the evenings (this is when egg-laying typically occurs).

Perhaps the best known use of the word comes in the phrase *spent gnat* (the adult or imago of the *mayfly²*, *Ephemera danica*), although there the term seems to be a general description of the fly, and applies to the adults both before and after egg-laying. Curiously, in some uses the phrase *spent gnat* is also used of the male spinner ('For tying the male Spent Gnat, endeavour to procure a black cock's spade or saddle hackle...' Harris, 161), but it is most correctly used of the female: '*The Spent Gnat*[:] This is the popular name given to the female spinner of the Mayfly as she drifts along, dying, on the surface after laying her eggs...' (Goddard, *Trout Fly Recognition*, 84).

For the more general sense of the word, i.e. that which refers to spent upwinged flies of whatever species, see e.g. Skues: 'All the spinners do not die and fall spent on the water over night...', or 'I ... turned into a glass ... three large greenish-amber spinners, with the distinctive three setae; and next morning ... I tied an imitation of these insects, spent-gnat-wise...' (*Minor Tactics*, 64, 66). See also *quill* (Skues was the first to discover that the Orange Quill is indispensable when the spinners of Blue-Winged Olives are on the water, see ibid.).

The word has also given rise to a direction in fly-dressing. If a pattern is to be constructed with wings 'tied spent', this typically means that the pattern is made with e.g. hackle-point wings dressed so as to be horizontally spread from the body (rather than upright, as on conventional patterns of *dun*), or dressed with a conventional hackle tied into two wing-suggesting bunches by figure-of-eight lashing. An example is that excellent trout fly, Lunn's Particular, which is made with wings formed by two medium blue(-dun) hackle points.

Interestingly, Clarke & Goddard have suggested that the spread-eagled winds of the natural or artificial spinner are an important feature of the fly, since they catch the light of the setting sun and so 'the fly appears to glow like soft fire' (p.101), thus making it easy to see from underneath. Consequently, they suggest that artificial spinners could be profitably constructed using orange hackle-points (or an orange hackle tied spent with figure-of-eight lashing).

Spey casting   The *Spey* and *Double-Spey* casts are used by salmon fishermen. As Barr puts it in *The Haig Guide to Salmon Fishing* *in Scotland* (17): 'Many of the best fishermen in Scotland are Spey casters. Spey casting is the technique of casting a fly off the water without it travelling behind or above the fisherman, a way of casting that is necessary on many of the rivers, not just the Spey. A Spey caster can fish anywhere...'. Since they are described in print by Francis Francis during the later 19th century (see Trench, 141), the techniques of Spey casting must have developed on that river during the mid-19th century, perhaps as a result of developments in tackle (especially the coming of tapered silk lines). See also *cast²*.

spider(s) Also known as *spider-pattern(s)*, these are artificial flies, both dry and wet (but more usually the last), tied with a head tackle but no wing. Although spider patterns had been fished for centuries before, perhaps the most famous spiders are those of W.C. Stewart (*The Practical Angler*, 1st edn 1857). As well as his lucid passion for fishing the *wet fly* upstream, Stewart also had much to say on the subject of fly design, rejecting 'exact imitation' and stating that 'in practice it has been proved beyond doubt, that a black, brown, red, and dun-coloured fly, used together, and varied in size according to circumstances, will at any time kill as well, and even better, than the most elaborate collection arranged for every month in the year' (from *The Practical Angler*, rpr. in Gingrich, 140-1). In fact Stewart went even further than this: 'Never a man to load his fly-box with a multitude of patterns he specifies only three spider types – the Black Spider, the Red Spider, and the Dun Spider' (Overfield, 11).

Stewart's lightly-dressed spiders are still killing wet flies today: the softness of the feather fibres used for the *hackles* ensures that the flies have plenty of life in the water. And as Kingsmill Moore put it, 'The North Country soft-hackled patterns... are often loosely called spiders, but anyone who closely examines the colours and materials will have no doubt that they are meant to represent drowned duns or spinners' (*A Man May Fish*, 45). The flies Kingsmill Moore is referring to are, of course, those York-shire patterns such as the Waterhen Bloa (see *blae*, *bloa*), Dark Watchet, Dotterel and Yellow etc.

When the wingless fly broke out into the then exclusive world of the *dry fly*, however, there was some resistance to it. Although Charles Kingsley, in *Chalk Stream Studies*, described how North Country spiders had been introduced on the Itchen in 1858 (and were fished, successfully, upstream as *nymphs* – see Hills, *A Summer on the Test*, 21), it was the early 20th century, the height of the dry fly cult (see *purist*) before the resistance was felt. The wingless fly was often referred to disparagingly as a 'hackle fly':

I realise – and own up – that I am a fool to stick to the winged fly. All my experience, and that of others, goes to prove that the hackle fly is the more deadly killer. But it all depends what fishing means for you as an individual. To me every separate bit of my tackle has a personality, and I love my winged iron-blue as I love my dog. To me the hackle-fly is a ferret and the winged fly a cocker spaniel (H. Plunket-Greene, rpr. 1983, 83).

But, perhaps because wingless flies are so easy to tie (see *wing*), spider-style dry flies became, and remain, popular. In terms of the way the trout sees the floating fly, however (see *window*), winged flies may have the advantage over hackle-only patterns, particularly in calm or slowly-flowing water, since one of the clues a potentially-taking trout may look for is what Clarke & Goddard call the 'flaring' of the insect's wings at the edge of the *mirror* (and see the photographs in *The Trout and the Fly*, 84-5). See also *hackle[1]*.

spinner   A *spinner* (not to be confused here with a shiny piece of twizzling ironmongery used to attract salmon and other fish) is the common name for the imago (pl. *imagines*) or adult of an upwinged fly, one of the various species of *ephemeroptera*.

In its angling sense, the word is first attested in 1787 (Thomas Best, *A Concise Treatise on the Art of Angling*, 2nd edn: 'The Palmers...The Great Red Spinner') and occurs next in Francis Francis (1867: 'The spinners are only second in the estimation of the trout to the duns'). The etymology of the term is puzzling, however: it may possibly be related to the verb *spin* meaning 'to revolve or gyrate' (first found in this sense in Milton's *Paradise Lost*: 'The Earth...with inoffensive pace that spinning sleepes On her soft axle') – these revolutions and gyrations being applicable in an extended sense to the motion of the spinners over the water.

As noted under *imago*, *quill*, and *spent[2]*, spinners are commonly on or around the water during calm evenings of the later spring and summer. Three particularly common spinners are those of the Large Dark Olive, the Medium Olive, and the Blue-winged Olive. The first two are represented by different sizes of Red Quill (or Pheasant Tail), the last by the Orange Quill. The Red Quill has a famous pedigree: it was Halford's 'sheet anchor...on a strange river' and was included in the list of flies given by Grey of Falloden, who commented that the fly was 'most attractive' in June (possibly in its role representing the spinner of the Medium Olive).

Few river anglers will be unfamiliar with the swarms of spinners which collect around the river during warm evenings. These swarms are formed by the males, whose hovering, dipping dance attracts the females; copulation takes place on the wing (Harris, 20). After mating, the female returns to the river and begins her egg-laying task, which is accomplished in different ways according to the species involved. The *baëtis* species crawl underwater to attach their eggs to some submerged rock, weed, or planking; the Blue-winged Olives *(Ephemerella ignita)* fly upstream, depositing their eggs as they go; while other species, such as the *mayfly*[2], deposit their eggs in batches during their visits to the water surface. After egg-laying has been completed, the females die, and it is then that the trout take full opportunity to feed on them in their *spent*[2], helpless state.

Historically, the first artificial dressing for a spinner is that given in the *Treatise* for use at the beginning of May: 'a good flye: the body of roddyd wull, amd lappid abowte wyth blacke sylke, the wynges of the drake and of the redde capons hackyll'. This clearly represents the spinner of the *Large Dark Olive*. The dressing was repeated in Mascall (1590), and copied by Walton, the rascal, who, like Mascall, called it the Ruddy Fly. As Hills pointed out (*History*, 163), this is the forerunner of today's Red Quill. See also *olive*.

springer   A name for a spring-run *salmon* (also *spring salmon*, *spring fish*). In the sense 'a newly-run salmon' OED dates the first attestation to 1753, but the quote cited seems to bear no relation to the salmon ('Springer in ichthyology a name given by authors to the grampus, or arca'). More promising is the word's second attestation, from the *Field* of 1886: 'Only one succeeded in landing a fish, viz., Tom Murphy, who got a nice springer [sc. salmon], weighing 11½lb.' And an 1893 citation suggests that the word enters the language from Ireland: 'The newly run fish which the Irish fisherman calls a "springer"' *(Daily News)*.

These fish are highly prized where they occur, since they are characteristically perfect fish – silver-blue, firm-fleshed, clean-scaled, and covered in sea lice. The spring runs of fish take place during February-April on rivers such as Tay and Tweed; other rivers have smaller spring runs of fish, and of late, judging by angling reports, the overall trend has been one of declining spring runs – whether the reduction in netting now taking place on some river systems will remedy this problem remains to be seen. Perhaps other sinister factors have been at work to diminish the spring returns. But 'if you were to fish on lower Tweed in February or March to enjoy the spring salmon fishing, you might hook small clean springers of eight or nine pounds... The larger springers are rare...' (McLaren & Currie, 19).

sproat   A kind of bend on a fly-hook, thus 'Sproat-bend hook'. The hook is named after a hook-maker, Mr Sproat of Ambleside near Kendal, who worked in the 19th century. In 1866, for example, Mr Sproat wrote the following: 'I send . . . salmon hooks made by Messrs. Hutchinson and Son, of Kendal. They have affixed my name to them'. (This firm, incidentally, was commended by E.M. Tod in *Wet-fly Fishing*, 200). The sproat-bend hook quickly became popular: in 1871, 'Stonehenge' wrote in *British Rural Sports* that 'The sproat-bend, which is intermediate between the round-bend and the limerick, has . . . come a good deal into use of late for trout'. See also *hook; Limerick* etc.

sprod   A dialectical term, seemingly specific to the NW of England, for a small *sea trout*. The term is first attested in 1617, then in 1672, where it is recorded that on the River Ribble 'salmon of the first year of their lives are called "smelts", of the second year "sprods", and of the third year "morts"'. Although these terms seem to refer to salmon, the term *mort* does, it seems, mean sea trout. But that citation is problematic on other grounds: what is meant by the term 'first year, second year' etc? The first year in which the fish return from the sea?

That the term is NW in provenance, and that it refers specifically to a (small) sea trout, is attested by this more recent quote from Oliver Kite: 'The next two casts brought me a small silver leaping sea-trout, a sprod, as they call it only in Lancashire, and a modest brown . . .' (*A Fisherman's Diary*, 120).

steelhead   This is an American term for the sea-running *rainbow trout*. The first attestation of the word dates from 1882 (Jordan and Gilbert, *Syn. Fishes N. America*: '*Salmo gairdneri*; Steel-head; Hard-head; Salmon Trout').

This word would not be included here were it not for recent reports that some Scottish rivers have developed small runs of migratory rainbow trout, trout which have escaped from fish-farms and subsequently feed at sea, returning to the river principally in order to spawn (or to attempt to spawn). Colin Shedden, in a recent issue of *T&S* ('Steelhead Blues', May 1990, 44-5), writes that these 'steelheads' are potentially 'injurious to the rod interests on salmon rivers' since in his experience they feed actively in freshwater – unlike other anadromous fishes – and so may take every fly 'before any salmon can'. At the time of writing, it is probably fair to say that runs of steelhead would not be particularly welcome in British rivers.

The etymology of the term is puzzling (and none is given in OED). I can only think that well-conditioned steelheads have the characteristically small, compact heads of other well-conditioned, sea-run fish, thus 'hard-head' (see above), leading to a developing sense in 'hard as steel' (= steel-head). Is this possible?

steeple cast A form of overhead fly cast with a single-handed rod, in which the caster's wrist does not break and where the line is thrown almost vertically on the back stroke, high behind the angler. Like the *roll-cast*, it is a useful cast where there are bushes or other obstructions behind the angler. It is well described and photographed by Falkus (*Sea Trout Fishing*, 91-5). See *cast²*.

stockie A diminutive, sometimes used derisively, for the word *stockfish*. It usually applies to newly-stocked *rainbow trout* (on both river and stillwater), but may also apply to *brown trout*. There are examples of both *stockfish* and *stockie* in the recent literature, as in the following: '[Hot orange and pink lures] relate to brilliant sunshine and usually to daphnia. Their use in other circumstances is a good way of catching recently-introduced stockfish – if you like such things' (Parton, *Flies for '87*, 33). Or as here: 'this pre-dilection of stockies for the rapid lure has deceived many anglers ...into relying heavily...on the big lure, usually on a sinking line, stripped back quickly' (Greenhalgh, 84).

The word *stockie* has given rise to a new compound, *stockie-bashing*, an aptly inelegant term which describes the often-indiscriminate capture of recently stocked fish. As Greenhalgh puts it, 'catching huge numbers of stockies can *never* be equated with top-quality fishing. "Stockie-bashing" requires little skill...' (p.84).

The etymology is puzzling. The word *stockfish* is attested quite early (in 1290), but at this date the term refers to 'cod and other gadoid fish cured by splitting open and drying hard in the air without salt'. In other words, stockfish in the 13th century were fish that had been cured, rather than fish introduced into a water by stocking. More promising, then, is to attempt to derive the word from the verb *stock*, meaning 'to fill (a pond, river) with fish', a usage first recorded in 1683 (R. North, *Discourse Fish & Fish-ponds*: 'The fish wherewith you stock the waters'). There may also be some etymological connection with the adjective (or noun) *stock* in its sense 'an animal that is chosen or kept for breeding purposes' (1801 *Farmer's Mag.*: 'The season throughout has been remarkably favourable to stock sheep') – but I suspect that the term now used for e.g. rainbow trout that are kept 'for breeding purposes' is *brood-fish*.

stone-fly Or, more usually in pl., *stone-flies*, the various species of *Plecoptera* or 'hard-winged flies' (the last term derives from Goddard).

OED defines this insect as 'of the family *Perlidae*'; the English name probably derives from the fact that the *larvae* of the fly are commonly found under stones (rather than from the fact that the wings are 'hard'). The word's first attestation dates to the mid-15th century, and the *Treatise* ('In May take a ston flye and þe bub vndur þe cow turde . . .'; it also occurs in that work as a name for an artificial fly). As J.R. Harris truly notes, the large stone-fly 'is unique in that it is the oldest known artificial fly which has retained its original name' (p.110).

This is an important order of flies for the river trout fisherman, since it includes the Large Stone-fly (*Perla bipuncta*, common in the North of England), the Early Brown (also called the Winter Brown – *Protonemura meyeri*), the February Red (*Taeniopteryx nebulosa*), and the various species of Needle-flies (*Leuctra fusca* etc.). All these flies are fairly widely distributed in Britain and Ireland; my experience of them stems from the Yorkshire rivers.

The adult flies are immediately recognisable, if only by a process of rapid elimination: they do not have upright wings (so they are not *ephemerids*), nor roof-shaped wings (so they are not *sedges*); in fact, the wings when at rest lie flat over the body, and usually extend behind the end of the abdomen. In some species, notably the *needles*, the wings when at rest are very thin indeed, and held very close to the body (thus the name).

The *nymphs*, too, are recognisable from their flattened, rather blunt bodies (adapted to stone-clinging and bottom-crawling in swift currents), and only two tails (the nymphs of the upwinged flies have three). They are called *creepers* in the North, and the larger species make very effective baits. Similarly, trout take the medium-sized and smaller species with gusto. Both Goddard and C.F. Walker, however, have written that because the nymphs crawl and labour on the bed of the river, they are of little interest to the fly-fisherman since their movement is difficult to represent. I have not found this to be true: in my experience, a lightly-leaded fly fished upstream (e.g. a Hare's Ear) has taken trout which, when examined, have been found to have been feeding on stone-fly nymphs. This is not entirely conclusive, and I am unable to prove that these trout did not take my artificial for something else; but it seems that the prospects of representing the stone-fly nymphs in fur and feather is not entirely hopeless.

The Large Stone-fly is in evidence in May and June (in the North it is occasionally called the *mayfly*[3]). The nymph lives under large rocks and stones, and when it is ready to hatch, it crawls ashore; it is not uncommon to find the cast skins of the nymphs among the river-bank stones. After two or three days, the adult females return to the river to lay eggs; this is accomplished during a clumsy, fluttering series of visits to the water surface.

The spring-hatching species, the Early Brown and February Red, sometimes bring the fish on (to the adults), but in my view it is the early and later species of Needle-flies which are of greater interest to the angler. The early-hatching species, *Leuctra hippopus*, seems common in April on rain-fed rivers, and it is not unusual to find fish feeding on the adult flies in the late afternoon (perhaps after a hatch of Large Dark Olives has taken place earlier that day). The pattern is not dissimilar to the autumn-hatching species, *L. fusca*, and it is worth noting that grayling also seem very fond of this Needle-fly, sometimes rising to the adults during the short hour of October twilight. As to artificial patterns, that Yorkshire *spider*, the Dark Spanish Needle, seems very effective, as does the Orange Partridge.

strike[1]   The action of raising the rod and pulling home the hook after a fish has taken the fly, thus also *striking*. Some angling writers (rightly) dislike the word, since it implies rather more force than is necessary. Pearson, for example, writes that 'I do not like the term "strike", not only for its connotations of industrial disorder, but also because it appears to have over-tones of violence. The action is really a very firm pull...' (p.37; the author is writing of hooking large brown and rainbow trout).

Striking and how to strike (or, in the case of salmon, how not to strike) are controversial subjects. Some fish, of course, hook themselves, and no 'strike', as such, is necessary. Others may rise so firmly and unproblematically that little is needed to pull the hook home but a firm yet delicate turn of the wrist. But some fish rise more subtly; this is especially the case with *nymphs* or *wet flies* fished on river or stillwater, and there the angler has to be alive to the most evanescent of clues to tell him when to raise the rod and set the hook. Other difficult areas are the *takes* to the *dry fly* and to the *dap*: the problems here centre not so much on discerning that the fly has been taken (this will be obvious enough), but when to strike, to timing. With the dry fly fished on stillwater, it is usually recommended that the angler should leave plenty of time for the fish to turn down with the fly before striking (one clue here is to watch the *leader* after the take), but this does not invariably work. With flies fished in the surface film, for instance (rather than on it, as with conventional dry flies), a take may need a very rapid response.

Another set of problems awaits the grayling angler. Small grayling, in particular, are very difficult to hook (the late Frank Sawyer used to think an angler was doing well if he could hook one in twenty rises), and I can do little better than to quote the following unsurpassable extract on little grayling, with permission of The Grayling Society:

Generally, then, of these little graylings, I will say this. They are the most contemptible of fishes. They are deceivers, raisers of false hopes, liars. They are nincompoops and popinjays and diddings. They are all levity and sham, masqueraders, infirm of purpose, gluttonous, heart-breaking, effervescent, undesired, conspiring, omnipresent, ignorant, unspeakable.

And I will say this...

No, I will say this.

They make good fishing an irritation and they make bad fishing unbearable...

For the little grayling is by nature a darter-about, an uneasy, tattling, common informer, a comer between a man and his amusements, a kill-joy, a spoil-sport, a breeder of mis-trust, a bell-man, a scare-monger, a yellow-journalist, a moor-hen. She is a small-minded fish, a riser-at-nothing, a mere breaker of surfaces, a ring-producer, a maker of deceptive sounds, a frog. A jelly-fish is a better fish...('Of graylings large and small', from *An Angler at Large*, William Caine, 1911; rpr. in *The Grayling Society Newsletter*, Summer 1984).

Another problematic fish to hook is the *sea trout*, especially where it rises to the fly on lochs and loughs. (*Dibbled* flies are notoriously difficult in this respect: fish can be hard to hook on the dibble, especially when the rod is high and the flies are nearing the boat at the end of their travel.) What is needed is a relatively soft, firm lift of the rod (a rod with an easy *action* helps here). As Kingsmill Moore wrote: 'the mouth of a fresh run white trout is very tender...Salmon fishermen find it difficult to appreciate this softness of mouth in a white trout. When they have accustomed themselves to strike, they strike too hard...' (p.131).

As implied in the last quote, the salmon fisherman does not usually strike in any of the forementioned senses. He waits for the fish to take the fly, turn, and then move away with the artificial; he should wait for the loop of line he may hold in his left hand to pull away through the rings; or he may wait for the fish to pull line directly off the check of the *reel*. Above all, he must wait for the pull of the fish. And then the rule is not to 'strike' but to tighten: 'The act ought to be deliberate and determined and its spirit is well expressed by the description I have adopted ['tightening' rather than 'striking']' (Taverner & Scott, 129).

So, timing the strike is, or can be, something of a vexed matter. And there are always days when the timing goes wrong, compared with those times when, for some unknown reason, correct striking seems to be natural and instinctive. Practice, perseverance, sensitivity do bring their reward...eventually.

Unfortunately, the given definition of *strike* in the OED is misleading: '[t]he jerk by which the angler secures a fish that is already hooked'. First, as the above citations make clear, a strike is not a 'jerk'; nor (apart from perhaps in the case of salmon) does one strike to secure a 'fish already hooked'. One strikes in order to hook a fish. Be that as it may, the word is first attested in its angling-related sense in 1840 (J. Younger, *River Angling*: '[This motion is wrongly named: it is] rather a retentive hold than a start, or strike'), and again, and accurately in the context of salmon fishing, in a *Field* of 1892: 'Once the salmon has gone down head foremost with the fly, there is no reason to delay the strike'.

strike² Where a British angler has an *offer*, a *rise*, or a *take*, the American angler has a *strike*. That this is an Americanism is attested by the following, from Skues: 'The American angler seldom uses the term "rise." He has "a strike." And it may be believed that the term is just. A book of American trout flies shows a large majority of them to be fancy flies, appealing to curiosity, rapacity, tyranny, or jealousy, rather than to hunger...' (*The Way of a Trout*, 3).

As a frankly irrelevant note, I would like to add that the German equivalent of 'It was a rise/take/offer' is the phrase 'Es war ein Pflück'.

strip and hang This is a technique used in *boat fishing* for brown and rainbow trout on stillwaters. It seems to have been developed during the late 1980s by a school of anglers who habitually fish the Bristol lakes. The technique involves long, downwind casting, a sinking (usually a fast-sinking) flyline, and a team of flies, where the top *dropper* may be some form of 'disturbance pattern' (e.g. a Muddler, or a Peach Baby Doll). After the cast, the line and flies are allowed to sink, and the angler keeps in touch with the flies by a *retrieve* whose speed will vary according to the strength of the wind. What seems important is that the team of flies will follow a deep, curving path towards the boat. At the end of the retrieve, the rod is raised, and the flies will therefore rise in the water. Then everything is held steady, and the (bow in the) line is watched for the *take* – this is the deadly *hang*, the last phase of the retrieve. The theory is to the effect that the fish will see the disturbance pattern on the top dropper, and be stimulated to follow the path of the flies, eventually taking one of the more 'imitative' flies on middle dropper or point during the 'hang'.

There are many references to this form of retrieve in recent issues of *T&S* (also the sister publication, *Trout Fisherman*), particularly in articles by Chris Ogborne, Jeremy Lucas, and others specialising in stillwater fishing.

sub-imago   The Latinate term for the *dun* of an upwinged fly (see *ephemeroptera*; *olive*), in pl., *sub-imagines*, as in the following: 'Presently, as the swarm of drifting nymphs becomes more numerous, escaping units, first in sparse, then in increasing numbers, reach the surface, burst their swathing envelopes, and spread their canvas to the gales as *subimagines*' (Skues, *Minor Tactics*, 11).

The name clearly derives from the fact that the dun is the stage in the life cycle of an upwinged fly before that of the *imago* or *spinner*. It is a term preferred rather by entomologists than by the majority of anglers.

Sub-imago is first attested in 1861, where Hagen's *Synopsis Neuroptera N. America* wrote of '*Subimago*, a state of Ephemera, &c., wherein the wings, &c., are covered with a membrane, which is cast off when it becomes an Imago'.

sunk line   It is nowadays something of a solecism to speak of *wet-fly* fishing for salmon; rather, one speaks of *greased-line* fishing (when the fly is fished just subsurface in summer), and of *sunk-line* fishing (when the fly is fished more deeply in the colder waters of early spring and autumn). This last is an apt description, because a full sinking fly-line (usually a fast-sinking line) is used for the technique, which consists, crudely speaking, of casting squarely across the current, or across-and-downstream, and then allowing the line and fly to fish deeply and slowly around below one. The relevant fly is today almost invariably a large *tube fly* (say, a 2-inch Willie Gunn). Speaking of this method, Taverner & Scott write as follows:

> Before the advent of floating-line fishing, dry-fly and very fine low-water fishing, the accepted method of fly-fishing for salmon was one which demanded a river flowing at a minimum level, and equipment suitable for these conditions, i.e. all the heavy wet-fly tackle still thought by many to be essential to the sport... In trout-fishing terms, it was wet-fly fishing downstream and largely "chuck-and-chance-it". It is still in wide use today...' (*Salmon Fishing*, 118).

Taverner & Scott do not, however, appear to use the phrase 'sunk-line', tending to use the phrase 'sunk-fly fishing'. A more recent reference comes in the writing of that expert fisher, Crawford Little, here speaking of the importance of water temperature in deciding which tactic to adopt:

> ...I have long regarded the 40-degree mark as being nearly as important as that of 50 degrees. The latter represents the changeover point between sunk and floating line tactics whereas the former, 40 degrees, is the changeover from heavy,

deep and slow tactics with the sunk line, to medium, rather
faster tackle and techniques (*T&S*, April 1988, 60).

Suspender patterns   Also *Suspender nymphs*; these are *nymph* or
pupa patterns recently developed by Clarke & Goddard (*The Trout
and the Fly*, 163ff.; also Goddard, *Trout Flies of Stillwater*, 269-71)
to represent hatching insects. The artificial is suspended from the
surface by a small ball of *ethafoam*, which is incorporated into
the dressing by being wrapped in a piece of nylon stocking, the
'foot' of which is whipped onto the shank at or around the *thorax*
of the fly. These flies can be very effective under the right conditions, e.g. when stillwater trout are taking hatching *midges*.
Perhaps it is unnecessary to point out the pun in the nomenclature,
but these flies gain their name both from the fact they 'suspend'
from the surface, and because nylon stocking is used in the dressing.

Tackle The fly-fisherman's rod, reel, bag, net and other impedimenta are today collectively referred to as his *tackle*, although the older word was *tackling* (Walton: 'I will ... mend my tackling'). The noun derives from a Germanic root (Low German *takel*, Danish *takkel*) meaning 'apparatus, utensils, instruments', and was first recorded in English in 1398: 'Aristotel sayeþ þat fisheres heldeþ hoot water on here instruments and takles ... [The fish] comeþ ofter in to newe tacle þat is set for hem, þan in to olde'. This quote – from the Cornishman, John of Trevisa – antedates the *Treatise* by several decades; the reference, however, may well be to the weakness or otherwise of set lines, rather than to rod-and-line tackle.

A whole set of semantic relationships centres on this word: in addition to the fishing sense, there are also recorded nautical senses (where *tackle* is a verb meaning 'to handle or work the tackle of a ship') and senses in horsemanship. The metaphor, *to tackle a problem* is distantly related to the nautical sense.

The word also combines with the preposition *up* to give the phrasal verb, *to tackle up*, i.e. to set up one's tackle at the start of a fishing session. It is possible that this verb derives straight-forwardly from the extended phrase *to set (or put) the tackle up*, where *tackle up* becomes a new verb in its own right, but it is also just possible that the verb derives from horsemanship, in which context it is first attested in 1869 ('I shall jest tackle up and go over and bring them children home again') – a reference to harnessing a horse for riding.

tag A piece of wool, floss or other material tied in at the bend of a trout fly so as to form a short *tail*. Today's fly-tiers sometimes use fluorescent wool for the *tag*.

In its sense 'the tail-piece of an angler's fly', *tag* is first attested in Chetham in 1681 ('Some Red warp'd in for the tag of the Tail'), although in the sense 'a tail (etc.) tipped with white (or other distinctive colour)' the verbal participle *tagged* is attested much earlier (a Ripon Will of 1458: 'Unum bovem vocatum taggyd ox'). But Chetham's certainly seems to be the earliest angling attestation – and he got the colour right, too. Red-tagged flies have long been known to be useful patterns. In the 19th century, for example, the most famous of all the tagged patterns, the Red Tag, is invented. Courtney Williams (p.298) dates the invention of this fly to *c*.1850, and one Mr Flynn, a Teme angler. (The fly was evidently originally known as the Worcester Gem.) The pattern was subsequently introduced to Yorkshire in 1878 by F.M. Walbran, and it has since achieved renown as a grayling fly, fished both *dry* and as a *wet fly*.

Some fully-dressed salmon flies also incorporate a 'tag', but this is typically formed by oval silver tinsel, wool, floss etc. tied around the *hook shank* behind the tail-proper, which may be formed by e.g. a golden pheasant *topping*. (Some fly-dressers refer to the tag on salmon flies as a *tip*.) The dressing for the Black Doctor given in the *Trout and Salmon Pocket Guide to Hairwing Salmon Flies* (*c*.1985), specifies 'Tag: Oval silver and yellow floss...'

tail   Many artificial trout flies carry *tails* which represent the setae of the living insect; these tails are often formed of *hackle*-fibre strands, golden pheasant *tippets* etc., and may also be referred to as *whisks*.

It is a curious problem to discover when trout fishermen first affixed tails to their artificial flies. Given the fact that the flies of the *Treatise* clearly copied nature, it might be expected that their dressings include tails, but unfortunately the instructions for the flies are difficult to construe. McDonald (pp.105-6) gives a very clear review of this subject, and I paraphrase him here. The arguments to the effect that the flies of the *Treatise* include tails are (i) the work advises the fisherman to copy the naturals, and many naturals have tails; (ii) subsequent works dress certain flies with tails, as in Cotton and Venables; and (iii) the earliest known English illustration of an artificial fly (in John Dennys' *Secrets of Angling*, 2nd edn. 1620) bears a tail – even though the dressing given in the text does not specify it.

The arguments against tails are as follows: first, no directions were given specifically in the *Treatise*; second, Mascall, who clearly copied the *Treatise*, did not apparently dress any of his patterns with tails (and neither did Markham in 1614); and last, even though Cotton dressed some of his patterns with tails, he specified them only three times in a list of sixty-five patterns.

McDonald's conclusion is that when the word *tail* appears in the *Treatise*, it is a reference to the hinder part of the hook, rather than to what he calls a 'tail-appendage'. If McDonald is right, then the invention of tails on trout flies should not be attributed to John Dennys himself (since the 1st edn of *Secrets of Angling* does not mention fly-fishing, see Hills, *History*, 40), but to Dennys's subsequent editor, William Lawson. If that sounds too far-fetched (and Hills did say that the illustration in the 2nd edn of *Secrets* 'resembles a house fly on a hook more than anything'), then we would be justified, I think, in attributing the *systematic* dressing of tails on trout flies to either Cotton or Venables, fine candidates both.

Finally here, there is the question of what the tails of 'fancy flies' represent, if anything. Typically these tails are formed by a few fibres of golden pheasant tippet, as in the Black Pennell or Mallard and Claret. One theory is that these tails represent a stylisation of the *shuck* of an emergent insect, and this may not be too implausible, especially when the flies are fished as 'slow deceivers' during a hatch of *buzzers* and other small insects: the success of the Black Pennell when the black *midge* is hatching is at least suggestive. See also *tag; tip*.

tailer[1] A *tailer* is a device used for landing salmon when other techniques (*beaching*, use of a *landing net*, or hand-*tailing[1]*) prove difficult or impossible because of the fishing situation. The tailer consists of a wire slip-loop which draws tight on the 'wrist' of the salmon's tail. As noted in *The Penguin Guide to Fishing* (p.203), one modern (and still current) tailer consists of a trigger-operated noose 'which works unfailingly'.

The OED dates this sense of *tailer* to 1962 (*The Times*: 'Some fishermen prefer the tailer to the gaff at all times'), but there are certainly earlier attestations of the word, e.g. in Taverner & Scott, *Salmon Fishing* (first edition 1931, and subsequent editions).

tailer[2] When a brown trout, rainbow trout or grayling is actively searching for *shrimps* etc. in the bottom gravels, head down and tail up (the tail perhaps even disturbing the surface), it is said to be a *tailing fish* or *tailer*. The word is perhaps most commonly applied to brown trout feeding on chalk streams, where the word seems to have originated: the dry fly *purist*, on encountering a tailing fish, was and is apt to pass that fish up as a fish which would not look at a fly presented on the surface. As Skues wrote in *Minor Tactics* (see chapter VII, which includes 'Of the negotiation of tailers'): 'Authority [i.e. Halford] hath it that "the best policy is, perhaps, to leave tailing fish alone"'; but Skues, typically, devised a strategy for taking these fish, involving repeated casting of a dry fly (typically the Pink Wickham on a 00 [size 16] hook). In *The Way of a Trout with a Fly* Skues also recorded taking tailing fish on a Pope's Green Nondescript, size 000 [18], but both in that work, and the earlier one, noted that it was possible to catch tailing fish on artificial *nymphs* – this being perhaps the most obvious strategy, and one today's chalk stream angler might favour (using e.g. an artificial shrimp) where the rules of the water allow.

In my experience, grayling on chalk water are great tailers. It is not uncommon to see several members of a shoal tailing hard during the autumn and winter. If a leaded fly (especially Sawyer's Killer Bug, or a weighted shrimp pattern) can be put over these fish, they often take it avidly.

Tailer, in its sense 'a fish that tails', is first attested in 1899 (Buxton, in *19th Century*: 'A moderate performer with the rod . . . wil often . . . pick up a grubber under the bank, a bulger here, a tailer there'), but the verb, *to tail* (i.e. of a fish, to show its tail at the surface), is attested a little earlier, in a *Daily News* of 1892, ('The Man sees there is no fly up. The Man sees the fish are tailing') and again in the *Edinburgh Review* of 1908: 'When trout are "tailing" they break the surface with their caudal fin as they grub with their noses for water shrimp'.

tailing[1]   Also known as *hand-tailing*, this is another reliable way of landing salmon (but it should not be attempted with sea trout as that fish's tail is as it were collapsible and will slide through a finger-and-thumb tailing grip).

Several writers have noted how efficient this method of landing salmon is: Sidney Spencer (*Newly from the Sea*, 129ff.), for example, wrote that in his fishing diaries he had made a note of how he had landed his salmon, and, while he remembered 'a few mishaps with the net and an odd fish scratched by the gaff', he could not recall any disasters when salmon had been either *beached* or hand-tailed.

Tailing a salmon is practised both at the river's edge, and by boat fishermen on lochs (although there the *landing net* is nowadays the usual method). In either circumstance, the essential thing is that the salmon must be *played out*, and that the angler's movements must be thereafter confident and unflurried. Spencer continued, 'If all is well and the fish lies still, I reach out with my bare hand, grasp him firmly by the wrist of the tail and lift him into the boat [sic] or ashore. He will not kick once his tail is clear of the water . . .' (130). Spencer also noted that although fishing literature is full of fairly esoteric advice about tailing salmon (i.e. different hand-grips being advocated etc.) he had not found any special technique necessary. From my own experience of salmon (usually other people's), I would only add that a grip where thumb and forefinger are nearest the tail seems the most secure: the fish's caudal fin then fits securely into the notch of the hand (thumb and index finger). This seems better than the 'handshake grip', where the fist is clenched thumb-forward over the wrist of the fish's tail. See also *gaff*.

tailing[2]   Also *tailing fish*; see *tailer*[2].

tail fly Also known as the *point fly* (see *point*), this is the fly on the end of a *droppered leader*, i.e. the fly 'at the tail of the cast', thus also a fly fished 'on the tail'. The following excerpts (Falkus, *Sea Trout*, 385, 386) are typical of the word's usage: 'a combination of the following tail and bob flies will kill sea trout on most lakes...' (here used in the sense *tail fly*); 'No matter whether the fly was presented on the bob or on the tail the fish took it...' (here used in the sense *tail of the cast*).

Most tail flies for trout and sea trout fishing on stillwater are relatively streamlined affairs, contrasting with the bulkier patterns favoured for the droppers (and see *dibble* etc.). In trout fishing, they often stylise hatching *pupae*, e.g. a small Connemara Black might be used during a hatch of black *midges*, or they could represent small *fry* (a size 10 or 12 Silver Invicta is useful here). The tail flies favoured for sea trout fishing are very broadly fish-suggesting, e.g. the Butcher, Peter Ross etc., although here it is dangerous to generalise as many waters have their own favourite flies (or combinations of flies on the leader), and local advice may be invaluable.

Tail fly, i.e. the fly at the end of the leader, is first attested in 1883, in a quote which indicates that *stretcher* was the earlier word: (*Century Magazine*: 'For a stretcher or tail-fly...').

take¹ A fly-fisherman *has a take* when a fish moves to, intercepts and turns away with the artificial fly, usually where this is being fished underwater (see also *offer*, and compare with *rise*, *strike²*). Therefore the word, and the phrase *(to have a take)*, are most commonly heard where the *wet fly* or *nymph* is being fished, or the sunk fly for salmon. One typical example of the word's usage in a trout-fishing context is the following: 'The type of rise has no relation to the subsequent play of the fish except that in very general terms I would say that the usual firm take of an eager fresh-run fish will be followed by the usual vigorous play' (Spencer, *Game Fishing Tactics*, 28).

See also *rise form; smash take*.

take² Some particular time of day when brown trout, sea trout or salmon are active and willing to take the angler's fly may be referred to as the 'time of the rise' or *time of the take*. The distinction between this use and that of *take¹* is essentially that between the general and the particular: in take¹ the angler says 'I had a take', i.e. a particular fish took my fly at a particular moment; take² on the other hand refers to a general tendency of a group of fish on river or stillwater to be active and responsive rather than dour and sullen, as in e.g. 'Yes, it was a good morning: there was a good take between first light and 6 a.m.'.

Kingsmill Moore, for example, speaking of white trout, wrote that these captivating fish 'have their time of "taking", and if a rise of fly coincides with this time they will not overlook the natural, but a rise of natural will not necessarily bring them on the "take"' (*A Man May Fish*, 128). He went on to give more detail on the time of the take (speaking specifically of the Connemara loughs), writing that it typically occurs between 11 a.m. and about 1.30 p.m., with a revival of activity around 4.30 to 7.30 p.m. This taking activity was, he felt, connected 'with the desire of the fish for a gentle constitutional', a theory supported by a more recent work, Fallon's *Fly-Fishing for Irish Trout* (p.94: 'Mid-morning and late afternoon seem favoured times for this ... pattern'). This has certainly been my experience of the Connemara trout.

Of salmon, too, various authors have written that a particular water-height, or temperature, or, more reasonably, some combination of a set of conditions (including the proportion of dissolved oxygen in the water) may bring the fish 'on': Sidney Spencer, for example, wrote that 'Coming to know salmon we learn beyond any doubt that – *at some time in every day there will be an inclination to take*' (*Newly from the Sea*, 18; his emphasis).

With brown trout, of course, the fish's responsiveness to the artificial (usually) coincides with increased fly-life (see *hatch[1]*), which is sufficient to bring the fish on the take, as in e.g. an *evening rise* to *midges* or to *spinners*.

In this sense, the word *take* is first attested in 1881, and Andrew Lang: 'The "take", as anglers say, is "on" from half-past seven to half-past nine a.m.'. See also next entry.

taking time   The *time of the take* (see previous entry) may also be referred to as the *taking time*. The late and great Reg Righyni, for example, wrote a book significantly titled *Salmon Taking Times* (later revised as *Advanced Salmon Fishing*), in which, following Waddington and others, he theorised that salmon take the fly best when they feel 'unsettled' and lively because the water is high in oxygen content (and when the fish are best able to absorb that oxygen). This theory is particularly attractive since it links with what has long been known about salmon: that they are most inclined to chase and take a fly when the water is relatively warm (i.e. in late spring and summer, when the salmon find it easiest to absorb oxygen from the stream), and most lethargic when the water is very cold (when oxygen is present but the fish find it difficult to absorb).

So far as sea trout are concerned, the taking time(s) may also be related to oxygen-content, but (possibly as with salmon) other factors appear to be at work, such as when the fish have been accustomed to feed at sea, the length of time the fish have been in freshwater etc.

With non-migratory trout, the position is simpler: the taking time usually corresponds to either the availability of certain food-forms (*nymphs* and so on) or to insect activity on the surface.

tandem   Also *tandem-hooked (lure)* etc. This usually refers to a fly with two hooks, one set behind the other (a tandem thus being distinct from the 'wee doubles' used in salmon and sea trout fishing, where the two hooks share a single shank). Tandem flies are used especially in sea trout fishing (particularly, perhaps, when sea trout are being fished for in the sea, see *voe fishing*), but are also used in brown and rainbow trout fishing on stillwaters, where the tandem functions as a large *lure*, often fished at depth (and see *troll*).

Another kind of tandem is that in which two flies are tied on a single long-shank hook (see e.g. Roberts, *Illust. Dictionary*, 214).

The earliest reference to a tandem fly known to me derives from Courtney Williams's *Dictionary*, where he refers to the Worm Fly as being originated by 'William Black, the novelist, who is said to have invented it sometime prior to the year 1880' (p.340). (Like other writers, I have no idea what the Worm Fly is supposed to represent – certainly not a worm. But it is a good fly, especially at the back-end of the season on lochs.)

That tandems are useful in sea trout fishing is brought home by Hugh Falkus, who developed a very successful tandem pattern, the Sunk Lure, for use in the still reaches of the night. This lure represents, in his view, the logical size of pattern to use for fish accustomed to sea-feeding on small fish. He also notes that it is an excellent saltwater fly (*Sea Trout Fishing*, 63; and see the same work, 409ff.).

Tandem derives from the original sense of 'two-wheeled vehicle' (1785: 'a two-wheeled chaise . . . drawn by two horses, one before the other'), which developed an extended sense of any thing in which one (thing) is behind the other.

taper   A *fly line* or *leader* which decreases in thickness towards the end nearest the fly is said to be *tapered*. Most anglers must be familiar with e.g. *double-tapered* fly lines, and shop-bought, tapered leaders, so there is little to add here beyond remarking that early fishing lines were tapered: by the 17th century, for example, it was common for the fly-line itself to taper from twelve or even twenty twisted horsehairs to a 'casting line' (i.e. the links nearest the fly) made of two hairs – or even a single hair. As Cotton put it, 'your Rod and tackle will in a manner be taper from your very hand to the hook; your line will fall much better and straiter, and cast your Flie to any certain place to which the hand and eye shall direct it, with less weight and violence...' (*Angler*, 267). Today we would call Cotton's line 'single-tapered'.

The double-tapered line was developed in the 19th century, relatively late (its appearance clearly relates to the development of the *reel*, some decades before); its invention helped to make the *dry fly* possible. The *forward-tapered* line, and the *shooting-head*, come later still. On tapered leaders, see not only the entry for the head word but also *cast*[1], *point*.

The word is developed from its original sense, *tapur* meaning 'candle' (in OE, 897). Then it develops a sense of 'a spire or slender pyramid, a figure which tapers up to a point', as in Put-tenham's *Arte of English Poesie* (1589: 'Of the Spire or Taper called Pyramis...'). The OED, however, dates the first attestation of the word in its sense 'gradual diminution in width or thickness of an elongated object' to 1793 ('From thence its taper diminishing more slow'), which is too late for fishing lines, as the earlier cita-tion from Cotton suggests.

terrestrial insects Also known simply as *terrestrials*, these, as their name implies, are those insects whose life-cycles are not (wholly) aquatic, but which are nevertheless found on lakes and rivers, usually having been blown there. They are an important, but rather neglected, group of flies which includes not only *beetles*, but also *crane flies*, *hawthorn flies*, *heather flies*, houseflies and other insects which may find their way onto the water from time to time (including ants, caterpillars and sundry creepy-crawlies).

Perhaps our thinking about flies for brown and rainbow trout has been too much conditioned by 'exact imitation' of those great families of flies, the *olives*, *midges*, *sedges*, *stone-flies* and so on. And certainly it is representation of these flies, and of small *fry*, that is the fly-dresser's and -fisher's stock-in-trade. But the fact remains that on some waters, particularly upland brooks and becks overhung with trees, but also on many stillwaters, it is rare to catch a trout that does not contain some sort of terrestrial insect. My suspicion is that trout feed far more often on these terrestrials than we perhaps think, and it is possible that, say, a *Black Gnat* pattern, fished as a *dry fly*, could deceive fish the whole season through, representing as it does a whole range of both aquatic and terrestrial flies.

Our fishing ancestors were perhaps more catholic than we are today, more willing to think about the possibilities of terrestrial insects (against that, of course, one could argue that they knew less about entomology). Cotton, for example, spoke of the 'Thorn

Tree Flie' (March), the 'Cow-turd flie' (May), an 'Owl-Flie' (for use on June evenings, perhaps a kind of moth), a 'Flesh-flie' (again for June, whose dressing strongly suggests a bluebottle), 'the flying Ant' (for June, copying the red ant, although June is early), two different types of grasshopper, a 'Wasp-flie' (for July), the 'Palm-flie' (also for use in July; the dressing and Cotton's comments suggest a caterpillar), and, finally, the 'Harry-long-leggs'. That is a fairly significant list. Perhaps we could take a hint from Cotton, and include a few representations of ants, bluebottles and moths in a corner of the fly-box? The *ant*, certainly, is worth carrying, because when fish are taking the naturals in hot weather they may become so preoccupied as to accept only a close copy. And the Daddy is a great fish-catcher.

The word *terrestrial* clearly develops from L. *terra*, 'earth', and in our sense dates from Shakespeare's *Merry Wives*, 1598: 'Giue me thy hand, terestiall...'. In the (non-human) sense of 'terrestrial animals, orders or families' the first attestation dates to 1842 ('*Terrestrials*... the name of a section of the class *Aves*...').

thermocline   The *thermocline* is that sub-surface zone of transition in a stratified lake between the higher, warmer water of the *epilimnion* and the colder, deeper water of the *hypolimnion*. The word is first attested in 1898 (*Nat. Science*: 'As regards the production of the Thermocline, Prof. Birge believes that... it is due to the concurrence of gentle winds and hot weather').

Lakes tend to become stratified during the summer unless there is sufficient wind and wave action to mix the water. And in conditions of stratification, trout will most often be found in the epilmnion, feeding on *daphnia* and other zooplankton. During the day, when the zooplankton lie deep, trout might be found feeding in the thermocline, but not below it (since the hypolimnion is effectively barren of food); at dusk and at night, when the zooplankton migrate towards the surface, fish will follow the food out of the thermocline and into the warm, surface waters of the lake. These points are admirably detailed in Greenhalgh, 37-43.

thorax   A term from L. *thōrāx*, first attested in 1400 ('Thorax is maad of... boonys'), meaning in our sense the segmented 'chest' on a natural fly, especially on a *nymph* or *pupa*. The thorax contains the wings of the adult fly (or the *sub-imago* in the case of *duns*); when the nymph or pupa hatches, it typically does so by splitting the nymphal or pupal *shuck* from the thorax.

The thorax is perhaps most prominent on the nymphs of *upwinged flies* (the *olives* and related species), and several anglers and entomologists have suggested that since this is a prominent feature of the natural insects, it should also be a key feature of the corresponding artificial. Most redoubtable of these anglers were perhaps Frank Sawyer and Oliver Kite (see *nymph fishing*), who dressed their artificial olive-suggesting nymphs with fine wire, forming a hump of wire as the foundation of the thorax, over which pheasant tail or other *herls* were doubled and redoubled to complete the thorax outline.

But the thorax is also a prominent feature on the bodies of upwinged duns, containing as it does the wings of the *imago*, and this feature has received rather less attention from fly-dressers (again with the exception of Kite, whose famous Imperial has a body 'made of about four undyed heron primary herls, doubled and redoubled to form the thorax, in the usual Netheravon manner' – *A Fisherman's Diary*, 113). Recently, however, a style of dressing has been developed by Neil Patterson (see *Funneldun*) which incorporates the thorax as a standard, and key, feature of the dressing. See also *abdomen; shoulders*.

throat hackle A *hackle[1]* on an artificial fly dressed on the underside of the hook and at the head of the fly only is said to be a *false hackle* or *throat hackle*.

tinsel A material used to form bodies and ribbing on artificial salmon, sea trout and trout flies. Flat tinsel is used to form bodies; fine flat or oval tinsel is used for ribbing (also to form the *tag* on many salmon patterns).

Our sense of the word is defined as 'very thin plates or sheets, spangles, strips . . . or some gold- or silver-coloured alloy, used chiefly for ornament; now esp. for cheap and showy ornamentation, gaudy stage costumes, anglers' flies, and the like'. The first angling attestation dates from 1867 (F. Francis, *Angling*: 'Silver tinsel and twist').

Tinsel, then, seems at first glance to have been used as a fly-dressing material at some time during the mid-19th century, possibly because of the influence Irish fly-dressers were then having on the dressing of salmon flies, and the availability of relatively exotic materials. And there is little doubt that it was during the 19th century when tinsel first came to be used systematically on anglers' flies. Yet John McDonald (*Quill Gordon*, 94) notes that Richard Franck (*Northern Memoirs*, 1694) advised salmon fishermen to use flies incorporating 'glittering tinsel and multiple wings', so it is possible that tinsel was used sporadically in earlier centuries. See also *topping*.

tip As noted under *tag*, some fly dressers refer to the floss, *tinsel* etc. wound round the hook shank at the tail of a salmon fly as a *tip* (unfortunately current usage is complicated here: others also refer to floss etc. wound round the shank at the tail of a trout fly

as a 'tag'). Trench, for example (p.136) refers to a fully-dressed
Irish salmon fly of the mid-19th century as incorporating 'tip,
tag, tail, butt...' (etc.). But the most usual term is *tag*.

   Tip, in its sense 'slender extremity or top of a thing... apex,
very end' derives from MLG. or Du., and is first attested in
English in 1440 ('Typpe, or lappe... of the ere').

tippet[1] The *tail* of several patterns of trout fly is formed by strands
of golden pheasant *tippet* (a yellow-gold barred black feather from
the neck of the bird), and this is how the word is defined in e.g.
Courtney Williams's 'Glossary of terms'. In its sense 'part of an
artificial fly', the first attestation dates from 1867 (and Francis –
again – who was the authority consulted by the OED's first compilers). The etymology of the word is uncertain, perhaps deriving
ultimately from OE *tæpped*, 'carpet, hanging', or possibly being
a diminutive of *tip*.

tippet[2] The piece of *nylon* nearest to the fly on a single-fly *leader*
is sometimes referred to as the *leader tippet*, or simply the *tippet*
(but perhaps today more commonly referred to as the *point*). In
this sense ('length of twisted hair or gut forming part of a fishing
line') the word is first attested in 1825 (Jamieson: '*Tippet*: one
length of twisted hair...').

topping Artificial salmon and sea trout flies, especially those of
a traditional construction, are sometimes dressed with a small
golden pheasant *topping* for the tail of the fly, and a larger topping
dressed over the wing, the tips of both toppings intersecting neatly
behind the wing of the fly. (The toppings come from the golden
pheasant's crest.) In Kingsmill Moore's words (he was here writing of his own excellent invention, the Kingsmill): 'My black fly
stood surrounded by a halo of pale golden light, a halo which was
to prove deserved' (p.82).

   Although I cannot be entirely sure, this style of dressing seems
to have derived from Ireland during the 19th century. During
this period, Irish fly-dressers 'lived near seaport markets where
they found gold and silver tinsels, colored silks, bright feathers,
and other delights of man's eye' (McDonald, 94), and certainly
by 1848, F. Tolfrey (in *Jones's Guide to Norway*) gives dressings
for what Trench (*Hist. Angling*, 136) calls 'the new Irish creations,
complete with tip, tag, tail, butt, body, ribbing, body-hackle,
shoulder-hackle, under-wing, upper wing, topping, cheek, and
head'. Also, the fact that the salmon flies shown in Bainbridge's
Fly Fisher's Guide (1816) do not include toppings (although they
do include multi-feathered wings), suggests that the topping
comes in with Irish brilliance during the mid-19th century. This
is further attested by a quote from Thad Norris (*The American*

Angler's Book, 1864), who wrote that 'The gaudy Irish flies tied for the Shannon would frighten the salmon in this side of the Atlantic...' (cited by McDonald, 94).

_ *Topping* derives from *top* + *-ing*. The earliest sense of *top* was 'a tuft, crest or brush of hair' (e.g. 1205 Layamon's *Brut*: 'Bi þone toppe he hine nome Al swa he hine walde of-slean'). *Topping* itself is first attested *c.*1390 (*Gawain and the Green Knight*: 'Ðe tayl & his [a horse's] toppyng twynnen of a sute, and bounden boþe wyth a bande of bryʒt grene' – this is a description of the terrifying Green Knight's terrifying horse, whose tail and crest were matched and bound in a green band). See also *butt²; tube fly*.

trail   The older sense of the term *trail* (also the practice of *trailing*) is detailed by H.T. Sheringham in *Elements of Angling* (1908):

> There is what may by courtesy be termed spinning, the practice of trailing (it is often erroneously called "trolling") for big lake trout in Ireland and Scotland. The angler simply sits in the stern of a boat and lets his spinning bait trail thirty yards or more behind while somebody else rows...(cited in Falkus, *Sea Trout Fishing*, 391).

This lugubrious 'art' would seem to have no part, then, in the present work, since it does not involve fly-fishing. But the term *trailing* is also used of the fairly common practice of allowing the line and flies to trail behind the boat as it is being rowed upwind between *drifts*, a way of allowing the flies to be at least in the water during a period of otherwise useless fishing time. Occasional trout (and salmon) are taken by this method (when anglers may also speak of a fish being taken 'on the trail'), but on some waters, especially the commercially-run rainbow trout fisheries, it is banned, perhaps because, as a method, it is open to abuse (e.g. the use of lead-cored lines and large *treble hooks* might possibly *foul-hook* fish). But elsewhere it is used as a quite legal 'minor tactic', especially on salmon and sea trout lochs. Sidney Spencer, for example, wrote as follows:

> I did take off the sea trout cast and replace it with one of 8-pound nylon carrying two sixes – one a Dunkeld and the other a Sweep: as we left the shore I put out about fifteen or twenty yards of line and allowed it to trail astern. In a rough wave salmon will often take a trailed fly when they won't look at one cast to them and worked...(*Game Fishing Tactics*, 64).

Trailing the fly behind a drifting boat (rather than a boat being rowed) is also mentioned by Greenhalgh, who writes that trailing a *lure* on a quick-sinking line is 'the fly fishing equivalent of trailing a spinner behind a boat' (p.149).

In the sense 'fish by trailing a bait from a moving boat', *trail*

is first attested in 1857 ('Another cluster of fishing boats...
apparently trailing for fish' – but this is perhaps sea fishing), and
again, in our specific sense, in 1864 (Thoreau, *Maine W.*: 'My
companion trailed for trout as we paddled along'). And see also
troll.

travelling fly   The *Travelling Fly* has to be mentioned in the same
shamefaced whisper as that other great taker of salmon, the *Garden
Fly*. The only reference to this superb euphemism I know comes
in Kingsmill Moore, who refers to his early days fishing the Erne
in August, 'where I was taught to fish a single-hook prawn on a
fly rod. This method was forbidden, but was winked at when the
best of the season was over. The ghillie would ask you if you
would like to try the "travelling fly", and out of his pocket would
come a shrimp ready mounted...' (p.67).

The adjective *travelling* does seem to have had a specific angling
sense, meaning 'a tackle which permits the bait to travel or move
down the swim' (1867, F. Francis *Angling*: 'This kind of fishing,
which is called "traveller" fishing (the float being the traveller)...'), so it seems very possible that the term travelling fly (i.e.
a 'fly' – a prawn – allowed to travel down the swim or pool)
develops from this usage. See also *lie²*.

treble   Also *treble hook*, this is a form of *hook* used in salmon and
sea trout fishing, where it is dressed with, typically, a floss wool
or *tinsel* body with a hair *wing* and fished singly on the *point* of
the *leader*. (Sea trout fishermen seem to favour 'outpoint trebles'
in this context.) The advantage of the treble hook is that it gives
a very secure hold in the mouth of a fish; the hook is also relatively
heavier than a single iron, and so fishes a little deeper in the water
when fished e.g. on a floating line. A typical example of the word's
usage is the following, where Arthur Oglesby is writing of spring
salmon fishing:

> For the best chance of sport, the early-April temperature
> should be about 46 deg. F. for the water, and about 52 deg.
> F. for the air... In these conditions, I would opt for a full
> floating line, but with a fly which is sufficiently heavy to get
> down a bit below the surface – probably a size 4 treble would
> do ('The search for a springer' in *T&S*, January 1990, 23).

Treble hooks also form the business end of *tube flies*, and are
affixed to some *dapping* flies as dangling appendages (see *flying
treble*).

It is difficult to reconstruct when the treble hook was first used
in fly-fishing. It seems to have been used in spinning for pike
(and possibly for salmon) during the 19th century, but it may
have been in sporadic use earlier: an illustration in the 1760 edition

of *The Compleat Angler*, for instance, shows two treble hooks, although these seem, judging by the illustration, to have been hooks used in dead-baiting (Trench, 66). But of its systematic use in fly-fishing I have been able to find no trace until the 20th century. Jock Scott, for example, writing in 1963, stated that

> In my young days, sunk flies [for salmon] were tied on enormous hooks, either single or double. Now these hooks required a good deal of force to bury them over the barbs, and a fair proportion of hooked fish were thereby lost. Nowadays the flies are often mounted on small treble hooks, and the percentage of losses has dropped considerably (in *The Complete Fly-Fisher*, ed. C.F. Walker, 26).

This at least suggests that the dressed treble was unknown in salmon fly fishing until relatively recently. Its use certainly gained ground after the publication of Richard Waddington's books on salmon (the first, *Salmon Fishing: A New Philosophy*, being published in 1947), since Waddington is a firm believer in the merits of trebles, and indeed designed a range of patterns to be fished on them.

trichoptera   This is the Latin term for the Order of the various *sedge* flies. The word develops from Gk *trichopter* ('a member of the group *Trichoptera*, of neuropterous insects, characterized by specially hairy wings; a caddis-fly...'), and is first attested in 1826 (Kirby's *Entomology*: 'The existence...of the collar in the trichoptera'), also in 1835 (Kirby again: 'The *Trichoptera*...have four hairy membranous wings').

As noted in the entry under sedge, these flies are immediately recognisable by their four mottled-brown wings, which lie on their backs like a roof when the fly is at rest, and by their long *antennae* (see also Clarke, *Pursuit of Stillwater Trout*, 69). The flies are common on both still and running water during the summer and autumn, and may provoke spectacular *evening rises*. For further information on the habits and angling history of these flies see *caddis; pupa*.

troll   As noted under *trail*, there is some confusion between *trail* (or *trailing*) and *troll* (or *trolling*). The older sense of the word *trail* denotes the practice of trailing a spinning bait behind a moving boat; the newer sense refers to the practice of trailing flies thus. But trolling has an older history: the word ultimately derives from an Old French verb *troller*, 'to quest, to go in search of game', and the first attestation of the word dates from 1651 (Barker, *Art of Angling*: 'The manner of his trouling was with a hasell rod'). Indeed trolling, as a practice, has a long history. It will be recalled, for example, that in 1682 Thomas Nobbes brought out a book with the not immediately fetching title of *The Compleat Troller* (the second attestation of the word in English dates from this work: 'In some places, they troll without a rod . . .'). Nobbes fished entirely for pike, and he fished for them using dead bait (mounted for some unknown reason backwards on a double hook), which he retrieved *sink-and-draw* (see Trench, 58-9).

The fact that he worked a dead-bait in this way helps to define the subsequent scope of the term *trolling*. John Bickerdyke, for example, in *The Book of the All Round Angler* (1888) wrote of trolling that it 'is the use of a dead-bait which does not spin, and is worked with a sink-and-draw motion in the water' (cited in Falkus, *Sea Trout Fishing*, 389). This form of trolling he distinguishes from *trailing*, which involves trailing a spinning bait at some fixed distance behind the boat.

The confusion between the two terms has been given more impetus of late, since some stillwater fly-fishermen on the big English Midland lakes have developed a modified form of trailing – which they call either 'trailing' or 'trolling' – using a *lead-cored line* and a large fly (sometimes a *tandem-hooked lure*, or even a big *tube fly*; and see *Northampton style*) trailed at depth behind the boat. While this is clearly a good method of searching the water, and while it does seem to account for big fish (particularly, large brown trout) I have little direct experience of it; nor am I entirely certain that this technique should be included here.

trout   For information on the species of trout found in the British Isles, and of the history of fishing for them, see *brown trout*, *rainbow trout*, *sea trout*, and entries cross-referenced under those heads. I will add nothing here beyond an etymological note.

The trout first occurs in English literature during the 11th century, when Ælfric's *Colloquy* (a set of dialogues penned to help schoolboys learn to use language) was Englished. One of these dialogues concerns a fisherman. (Others, incidentally, treat of the fowler and the huntsman: is it a literary coincidence that the 15th-century *Treatise*, and of course Walton, should begin with imaginary dialogues concerning the respective merits of hunting, fowling, and fishing?) Ælfric's fisherman, however, was evidently a netsman, and perhaps a spear-man as well, since a whale-hunt is mentioned. Most importantly, though, his questioner asked the fisherman 'What sort of fishes do you catch?' and the fisherman replied 'Ælas, ond hacodas, and scēotan' – Eels, and pikes, and trouts. The word *scēote*, used in the plural by Ælfric (the *-an* Old English plural ending is still with us in words such as 'oxen, children, brethren'), derives from the verb *scēotan*, to shoot, dart, or rush. The OED, interestingly enough, cites *shoat* as a term for 'a fish resembling the trout, but smaller, found in Devon and Cornwall', and suggests that the term survives in dialect usage until the late 19th century (although what this trout-resembling sprat actually is, or was, I have little idea). But whatever the subsequent history of the word, it is a suitably apt term: it is rather comforting to think that our ancestors saw the trout as a darter and a shooter of currents.

Then comes the Conquest, and the word *trout* enters the language from Norman French (although it is recorded, once, in late Old English as *truht*, where the <h> is pronounced like the <ch> in *loch*; this eventually gives rise to a variant pronunciation in *truff*); the Norman borrowing decisively ousts the older term *scēote*. Our word *trout* therefore ultimately derives from Latin *tructus*. It first appears in a fishing context, of course, in the *Treatise*, where the trout was described as 'a ryght deyntous fyssh and also a ryght feruente byter'. It is not impossible that the etymological change, the change from *scēote* to *truht*, betokens a wider change in the way the fish was thought about – and fished for. If I am right in suggesting that fly-fishing (and possibly all rod-and-line fishing) comes to England from the Continent as a result of the Norman Conquest (and see *fly*; *rod*), then it is hardly surprising that the native term should ultimately be ousted by the Continental one: the trout was not, as in Old English, merely a darter and a source of food, but a source of food ('deyntous fyssh) *and* a sporting fish ('a ryght feruente byter'). But unfortunately, this kind of history is difficult to prove because of the lack of records from the relevant centuries.

tube fly   Also *tube*; a kind of *lure* used in salmon (and some sea trout) fishing, consisting of a plastic (or copper) tube through which the end of the *leader* is threaded, the tip of the line being then fastened to a *treble* hook of a size to match the size (and weight) of the tube. The tube itself is invariably dressed with some form of hair *wing*; such a dressing is mobile and attractive in the water, and the treble has good hooking properties. These flies are preferred today by salmon anglers fishing the *sunk line* in early spring (where a two-inch copper tube, perhaps a Willie Gunn, is a favoured fly), but may also be fished in smaller sizes during the lower waters of summer, e.g. as in the following: 'Last year, on a Sutherland river, I was exceptionally lucky...in warm weather with warm water (over 60 deg. F.) using very small transparent plastic tubes ([quarter inch] or smaller) with virtually no dressing' (T.J. Manners, 'Thoughts on salmon flies', *T&S*, January 1990, 28).

Tube flies seem to have been developed during the middle of this century. As Jock Scott wrote in 1963, 'more and more fishermen are trying out the tube form of fly and its variations . . .' (*The Complete Fly-Fisher*, ed. C.F. Walker, 26). See also *treble*.

turle knot   The Turle is used to join trout flies to the *leader*, especially *dry flies* and flies tied the smaller sizes of *hook*. In its 'two-circle' form, it is also used to join salmon flies to the *point*. In this last guise it is a particularly useful knot because, since it tightens behind the eye of the fly, and since the *low water irons* have upturned eyes, the knot helps the fly to swim on an even keel.

My impression is that this knot was developed after the coming of *nylon monofilament*. It is not described in any of the old, standard works on e.g. salmon fishing (Chaytor in particular). I believe Turle was the name of the knot's inventor, although I may be wrong. See also *knots*.

Ulcerative Dermal Necrosis or **UDN**   A disease which attacks all salmonids, but most particularly the salmon itself.

Although this disease has been known about for some time, outbreaks seem to have begun around 1965, when UDN first made itself manifest in Ireland, but quickly spread to all parts of the British Isles. At the time of writing, there are sporadic instances of the disease over the country, but UDN does not seem to be as prevalent and widespread as it was during the late 1960s. (The OED dates the first attestation of this abbreviation, significantly, to 1968 and the *Irish Veterinary Jrnl*: 'This paper describes the symptoms . . . and bacteriology of UDN'.)

Theories have differed as to the precise nature of UDN, but it is now generally accepted that the disease is due to a 'virus infection with secondary bacterial symptoms' (*T&S*, February 1968). The disease begins with 'grey, necrotic patches of red, bleeding ulcers' (*T&S*, January 1969) which are characteristically found on or around the head of the fish, these ulcers are quickly attacked by fungus, and fish mortality is subsequently high. (The eggs of diseased fish, however, are evidently not affected, and if the fish can reach the *redds* in time, *spawning* may be completed.) The fungal infection of fish carrying UDN must not be confused with the disease furunculosis, which attacks all species of fish (salmon *kelts* are susceptible to this too); UDN is salmonid-specific (grayling, for example, were badly affected in some areas during the late 1960s).

There is unfortunately no complete answer to the source and cause of the present outbreak. One theory at the time was that the disease was caused by atomic waste, but that was proved untenable. More likely is that UDN is some sort of unisolable virus – like the common cold in man – which may appear and disappear in an irregular way. As with the common cold, no cure has so far been found.

It is possible, though, that UDN will disappear again once nature is allowed to take a hand. Time must pass. There was evidently an outbreak of UDN (or something very like it) in the 1870s (Tweed was badly affected 1879-93), and that abated gradually over about ten years. The present outbreak is taking longer, but it is to be hoped that the disease is eventually worsted. Rivers full of fresh, clean water would undoubtedly help.

upwinged flies   This is the simple, all-embracing term for that
great Order of flies, the *Ephemeroptera*, contrasting with e.g. the
'flat-winged flies' (*stone-flies*) and flies 'with roof-shaped wings'
(the *sedges*). As Goddard notes, the flies gain their name from the
fact that when a *hatch*[1] occurs, 'they look like a fleet of miniature
yachts sailing down the river' (*Trout Fly Recognition*, 16). See also
dun; olive; mayfly[1] etc.

Vendace A species of *whitefish*, *Coregonus albula*, closely related to the *pollan*. They are found in the English Lake District, as well as (at least reputedly) in one or two Border stillwaters: Bassenthwaite is said to hold a stock of the fish, and this is borne out by e.g. the *Angler's Guide to the Lake District* (2nd edn, 1987): 'One of the rare species of . . . fish is also present . . . This is the vendace, a small silvery fish which generally inhabits the deeper water around seventy foot. It is not encountered very often in this lake . . .' (p.10). In the other Lake District water once reputed to hold stocks of the fish, Derwentwater, the species appears to be extinct. This also appears to be the case on those Border waters around Lochmaben near Dumfries (and see below).

As with the other whitefishes, the vendace is said to live on plankton and other small food-forms at depth. It apparently spawns in mid December to early January.

The word derives from OF *vendese*, *vendoise*, and is first attested in 1684 (*Scotia Illustrata*: 'Piscis in Lacu Mabano, Vandesius'). Loch Maben was always known for this species, as also in the following: 'It [the gwyniad] is the same with the Ferra of the lake of Geneva, the Scheeley of Hulse Water, the Pollen of Lough Neagh, and the Vangis and Juvangis [sic] of Loch Mabon' (1769 Pennant, *Brit. Zool.*). See also *powan; schelly* etc.

ventral fins These are the pair of fins found on the underside of the fish (i.e. on its belly), sometimes also called the *pelvic fins* (see e.g. Maclean, *Trout and Grayling*, 19). Their purpose seems to be to help the fish 'plane' up or down, to help it turn in the water, and to help it brake suddenly (see here Sosin & Clark, 30-1).

voe fishing A form of *sea trout* fishing, practised, usually with fish-suggesting flies or other *lures*, around the *voes* of the Shetland Isles and elsewhere:

Fishing the voes, or kelp tangles, is a well established method in many parts of Scotland and Ireland. When rivers are too low for sea trout to run, these fish browse along the kelp beds feeding on crustaceans and other fare. Anglers who specialise in voe fishing are most active in June, July and early August. The angler selects a spot on the coast adjacent to a river which has runs of sea trout . . . It is a good plan to fish down with the last of the ebb and up with the young flood. The flies are cast and drawn until one finds the speed and manner that interests the fish most... ('Fly Fishing for Sea Fish' in *Sea Angling*, ed. Wrangles, 94).

Although the first attestation of the word *voe* (which derives from ON *vág-r*, Norw. *vaag*) dates from 1688 (Wallace, *Descr. Orkney*: '*Voe*, a Creek or Bay, or firth, or inlet'), the earliest reference to this form of fishing that I have been able to find dates from 1899, and the first edition of Grey's *Fly Fishing*. There, he wrote of the 'most interesting' form of sea trout fishing to be found in the Shetlands, the fishing 'in the voes in salt water'. In this intriguing chapter, Grey recorded that on one voe he had a dire morning followed by a strangely productive afternoon, and 'a delightful reaction from despair to good spirits' after taking a basket of sea trout weighing 16lbs. But he also cautioned that he 'had much to learn about that voe and the sea trout there. They moved.with the tide, and we had to understand their habits and follow their movements' (p.176). This seems to be true of much voe fishing: local knowledge, and an understanding of wave, wind, tide, and the fickle moods of the fish, seem to be essential for success.

Another reference in the literature comes from Farson's classic *Going Fishing* (1st edn, 1942), where he wrote of 'one voe where we tried vainly for sea trout, using chamois imitation sandeels. It was in the burn tumbling down into this coloured estuary that, after catching several normal sea trout...I lost two monsters; one, well over eight pounds, which I held on a 3X cast for two hours and forty minutes...' But the joy of Farson's description of voe fishing really lies in passages such as the following:

The softly waving seaweed forms a brown lace around the rocks of the voe. It waves to you, rising and sinking softly with the long Atlantic swells. The seas foam up white, and run back hastily with little whispering regurgitations, to lie still, so that the white tracery of tiny bubbles fades away, and you look sheer down through blue-green depths...Cliffs rise above, towering overhead to break off in turreted battlements against the rounded clouds. Black ravens sail out of them, hanging in the vast emptiness. The rocks are red, mauve, scarlet. Walls, leaning towers, two-hundred-foot spear-points of red granite (p.69).

A third, more contemporary reference not exactly to 'voe fishing', but to saltwater fishing off the West coast of Ireland, may be found in Falkus, *Sea Trout Fishing*, revised 2nd edn, chapter XIV.

Wading   It is curious that *wading* does not seem to be depicted in angling prints until the 19th century. Does this mean that wading was not practised until then? Not at all. As Hills noted, in Cotton's time the fisherman 'waded, but only sparingly' (*History*, 78). The first reference to wading known to me comes in Venables, *The Experienced Angler* (1662), where he wrote that 'in great rivers you must wade, as I have known some, who thereby got the sciatica, and I would not wish you to purchase pleasure at so dear a rate' (facsimile, 58). (There is little new in fishing. In 1968, Reg Righyni wrote that 'as a matter of policy, I try to avoid any wading at all in winter. If I am fortunate enough to live to a ripe old age, I hope I shall be able to spend it on the riverside and not in an armchair crippled by rheumatism', *Grayling*, 44).

So Venables noted the practice, but was not exactly an enthusiast. By the 19th century, however, wading had become more common, especially for salmon fishermen:

> [The 17th-century fisherman] did not possess the hardihood of Scrope [*Days and Nights of Salmon Fishing*, 1843], who tells you never to go into water deeper than the fifth button of your waistcoat, and even this is inadvisable for tender constitutions in frosty weather. He advises those who are delicate and wade in February when it freezes very hard, to pull down their stockings and examine their legs. Should they be black or even purple it might perhaps be as well to get on dry land, but if they are only rubicund you need not worry . . . (Hills, *History*, 78).

But Scrope, on his own testimony, had an elective affinity with water, as he affirmed in the following passage – which also suggests that by the mid-19th century, rubber wading trousers had been invented by 'Macintosh':

> I declare, then, that I, Harry Otter, am by nature a person of considerable aquatic propensities, having been born under the sign of Aquarius, or Pisces, – it matters not which. My delight in water, however, has its limits, and extends only to external applications: the placid amusement of wading in a salmon river is very much to my taste – quite captivating. Showers, and even storms, if not of too long a continuance, are exceedingly refreshing to my person; but I must in candour admit that the

254

decisive action of a water-spout may not possibly be so gratify-
ing – *ne quid nimis*. Macintosh's invention I consider as wholly
uncalled for, accounting it, as I do, an unpardonable intrustion
to place a solution of Indian-rubber between the human body
and a refreshing element. It is like taking a shower-bath under
shelter of an umbrella (from Gingrich, 118).

By the end of the century, however, deep wading for salmon
had become a standard practice, and so had body waders,
although these were cumbersome to wear; and one-piece thigh
waders had also been developed:

The lightest and most comfortable form of waders for water
meadows, or shallow water free from large stones or rocks, is
that with long waterproof stockings coming well up on the
thigh, and with indiarubber soled boots, the whole in one
piece. These waders are not the most lasting, nor do they soon
dry inside, but the convenience of being able to slip them on
and off easily is very great. A heavier kind with more leather
and nailed soles lasts longer. In salmon fishing, and in many
trout rivers, wading trousers nearly up to the arm-pits, separate
brogues and outside socks are needed. If one has to walk much
from pool to pool they are a terrible discomfort. I hate the
putting on of my wading trousers, the wearing of them, the
walking in them, and the sight of them altogether, but I prefer
them infinitely to fishing from a boat. They hamper one in
every possible way, but they do not destroy one's independence
(Grey, *Fly Fishing*, 1st edn, 232-3).

The techniques of wading have changed little since then, although
waders have, naturally, improved in quality. One last thing to
note is that where one does wade, one should not be put off from
wading deep. Fish are surprisingly little alarmed by it (providing
it is carefully and quietly done), and it allows one much better
coverage of the water.

Wading derives ultimately from OE *wadan*, 'to go, advance';
by the 13th century a sense specific to water ('to walk through
water or any liquid . . .') had developed, as attested by the following: 'Oc on swimmeð bi-forn, and alle ðe oðre folezen, weðer so
he swimmed er he wadeð' (1220 *Bestiary*).

The term *waders* is first attested in 1841 (J.T.J. Hewlett, *Peter
Priggins*: 'Mud-boots, waders, and snow-boots').

wading-staff An implement employed by salmon (and some sea
trout) fishermen wearing body *waders* in order to steady themselves in strong currents. A makeshift *wading-staff* can be made
by weighting a long *landing net* handle at the bottom end, carrying
the net itself on a lanyard, whereby the net may be swung round

from the back to test the stream-bed as the angler moves between casts. But for large, deep rivers such as the Spey or the lower Lune, it is better to carry a proper wading-staff: as Taverner & Scott put it, a 'strong wading-staff completes the list of the salmon-fisherman's equipment' (*Salmon Fishing*, p.60).

walking   Salmon, sea trout and other fish may be *walked* during the *play*; walking the fish is a very effective method of bringing a hooked fish back towards the angler once it has run downstream:

> Walking a fish up is a simple trick by means of which it can be persuaded to move upstream... The rod-point is lowered, the line held and the angler walks gently upstream dragging the fish after him; but the line should be held delicately, so that it can be released if the fish should start to run. The whole manoeuvre should be carried out boldly and it is essential that the tension of the line be even (Taverner & Scott, *Salmon Fishing*, 228).

Falkus (*Sea Trout Fishing*, 236ff.) also describes how walking a hooked fish (a sea trout) 'is advisable... as soon as possible whenever you are in a position to do so. It takes the heart out of him, reduces his resistance and shortens the fight...' But, Falkus truly adds, '[y]ou are not indulging in a trial of strength but the art of gentle persuasion...': 'I must make it absolutely clear that when "walking" a fish you do *not* tow him up the pool. Nor do you try to pull him along... [T]here is no question of trying to force him...'.

Taverner and Scott's description of walking ('dragging the fish...') does perhaps imply too much force. When the fish has been hooked, or after its first run has stopped, one 'feels' for the fish, and with a quiet, even pressure on the line walks backwards. Sensitivity – '*hands*' – is what counts. But it is a most useful part of playing a fish.

A modification of the same tactic can be used when a large brown or rainbow trout is hooked on stillwater from a boat. One needs a co-operative *gillie* or boat-partner to row steadily upwind, or into deeper water, while the hooked fish is quietly 'towed' behind the boat. This is particularly useful (I believe) with very big trout, who (sometimes) seem to take a while at the beginning of the play to realise that they are in fact hooked, that the pressure of the iron in their jaw means danger. Then is the time to walk – to 'row'? – the fish away from the shallows and their potential snags.

water knot   Fly-fishing's oldest knot; see *knots*.

water-louse   The *water-louse* is properly a species of *Asellus*, also sometimes called the *hog-louse*. It is common on lakes and slowly flowing rivers, and an important food-form where it occurs, often eaten by trout and grayling. As C.F. Walker noted, 'The fresh-water louse (*Asellus*) . . . is . . . found in still or very sluggish water, often in prodigious numbers. [Like the *shrimp*], [b]oth these crustaceans live on the bottom or in weed-beds, and their young resemble the adults . . .' (*Lake Flies and their Imitation*, 73).

But it seems to have taken time for anglers to realise that the hog-louse is important, despite C.F. Walker's comments (and despite the fact that this insect is mentioned – and a plate of it given – in Harris). More recently, though, Church & Gathercole (p.57) devote a couple of pages to 'Shrimps and Hoglice', and record catching some big trout from deep water at Rutland which had been feeding heavily on these crustaceans.

There seem to be few current artificial patterns, although C.F. Walker did give a dressing (*Lake Flies*, 161). Since the natural is not unlike a wood-louse, one useful fly is a heavily leaded, large Hare's Ear (tied with dark hair from the outside of the ear), but more specific representations would be quite possible to construct.

water meadow   Part of the original system of irrigation through which chalk streams flow. The water meadows were bisected by a series of *carriers* and ditches, through which the water flow was controlled by *hatches*[2]. The hatches were opened in winter, and the meadows flooded; then the hatches were closed in the spring, and the meadows allowed to dry. A good description of this vanishing landscape can be found in Sawyer's *Keeper of the Stream*, 17ff; and of course the landscape of the water meadows forms a large part of much fishing writing about the chalk streams.

weed   Something about weed in rivers can be found under *ranunculus*, but of course a healthy river contains many more species of weed than this. Macan & Worthington, for example, write that the Itchen not only holds water crowfoot, but also the water parsnip (*Sium erectum*), the marestail (*Hippuris vulgaris*), and the bur-reed (*Sparganium simplex*), among others (*Life in Lakes and Rivers*, 89). Not all these plants are totally welcome, however, and one worrying feature is the spread of Canadian pondweed (*Elodea canadensis*) on both river and stillwater. The spread of this pest has been hastened by the fact that chemicals used in farming leach out of the land and find their way into lakes and rivers (see also *eutrophication*):

> One of the aspects of these chemical fertilisers that may not be widely known is their affinity to adhere to soil particles. When water containing these chemicals becomes turbid, the normally soluble chemicals bind with mud and silt particles

to become insoluble, and when the turbidity declines, these
bonded particles fall to the bottom of the loch/lake...They
are now available to plants which can only absorb nutrition
through their roots, plants such as canadian pondweed. This
is the foul fiend that is doing its level best to throttle such
diverse waters as Bewl Water and Loch Harray. Soluble or
insoluble, these chemicals are not so slowly destroying our
fishing heritage (Stan Headley, 'Trout in the '90s', *T&S*,
January 1990, 7).

weed-cutting   In rich waters, both rivers and lakes, weed has to
be cut when it is so thick that it is impeding the water flow and/or
making fishing impossible. The old-fashioned way of cutting weed
was to use a long underwater saw (formed by jointed saw-blades)
operated by two men, one on each end of the saw. This is back-
breaking work, but quiet and very specific. Today several alternative weed-cutting machines have been developed. See also
ranunculus.

weight forward   A type of *fly line* developed during the mid-20th
century. The weight is concentrated in the first thirty feet of the
line, and the rest of the line, sometimes called the 'shooting line',
is uniform in diameter. This profile makes for longer casting, and
the line is favoured by e.g. bank fishermen on lakes and reservoirs.
It is also a useful line for throwing into a wind; and a good line
for a beginner to practice casting with (since there is always the
same length of line aerialised on the back-cast, distance being
achieved by *shooting the line* on the forward throw). See also *shooting head*.

wet fly   A *wet fly* is a fly designed and presented so that it fishes
below the surface, thus also *fishing the wet fly* and/or *wet fly fishing*.
Wet fly fishing is therefore distinct from *dry fly* fishing, where the
fly is designed and presented so that it fishes on, or in, the surface;
in addition, in dry fly fishing on rivers, the fly is usually cast
upstream, whereas in wet fly fishing on running water, the fly or
flies may be cast either upstream or downstream (see below).

In practice, wet fly fishing may shade into *nymph fishing*, but
this last term usually applies, on running water at least, to a single
fly fished upstream, whereas in upstream wet fly fishing, one or,
typically, more flies are fished. There is a further distinction
between upstream wet fly fishing and nymph fishing in that in
the last, the fly is a copy of a natural nymph; in the first, the fly
or flies may copy either natural nymphs, or drowned *duns* and
other insects.

Broadly speaking, anglers speak of fishing the wet fly for brown
trout on rivers, for sea trout, and for trout and sea trout on lake

and loch, where the wet fly, especially fished from a boat, is a widespread technique (see *boat fishing*; *dibble* etc.). *Salmon* fishermen, too, of course, present a sunken 'fly' (perhaps better described as a *lure*) to the fish, but – perhaps because of that very distinction between *fly* and lure – do not speak of 'wet fly fishing for salmon' but rather, of '*sunk line fishing*' (fishing deep with a sinking *fly line*) and of '*greased-line fishing*' (fishing a sunk fly nearer the surface on a floating line).

Mention of upstream and downstream wet fly fishing points to one of the most enduring topics in all fly fishing: how should the wet fly be presented? There are many good arguments for upstream presentation; but also good arguments for fishing the fly or flies downstream in some fishing situations.

Historically, it seems that the fly was first presented downstream. This is at least implicit in the *Treatise* (although no specific instructions were given there), but it is certain that the flies were intended to be fished sunk (although not deeply sunk), and likely that they were fished downstream. Hills, for example, wrote of 'the method of fly fishing which prevailed [in the 15th century] and long after. Casting downstream with the wind behind you and using a hair line...' (*History*, 24). And again, Hills noted that at the time of the *Treatise*, 'the fly must have been cast, but how we know not. It can only have been cast down wind or in a calm, for the rod and line used could not have cast upwind... it is not a very extravagant guess to assume that the usual practice was to fish down stream and to draw the fly, keeping it near the top of the water' (*History*, 34). But it is at least possible that, with a howling upstream wind, the 15th-century fly fisher could have thrown his fly upstream over a rising fish.

By Cotton's time, there had been improvements in line-making, and the fairly steeply *tapered* lines of the 17th century could have been cast either up or downstream, although the wind still largely dictated matters. Downstream wet fly was still, perhaps, the usual method, but upstream fishing was also possible, as here: 'The best Instruction I can give you, is, that, seeing the wind curles the water, and blows the right way, you would now angle up the still deep to day...' (Cotton, 302). But it was Cotton's contemporary, Venables, who first wrote of systematic upstream fishing, contrasting it with the downstream wet fly using arguments that one could still hear today. The following is surely one of the most significant passages in the history of the wet fly:

And here I meet with two different opinions and practises, some will always cast their fly and bait up the water, and so they say nothing occurs to the fish's sight but the line; others fish down the river, and so suppose, the rod and line being long, the quantity of water takes away, or at least lessens the fish's sight; but others affirm, that rod and line, and perhaps yourself, are seen also. In this difference of opinions I shall only say, in small brooks you may angle upwards, or else in great rivers you must wade... besides, casting up the river you cannot keep your line out of the water, which has been noted for a fault... and they that use this way confess, that if in casting your fly, the line fall into the water before it, the fly were better uncast, because it frightens the fish... My opinion is, therefore, that you angle down the river... (facsimile, 58).

The debate between upstream and downstream wet fly had been fairly joined. (The fly, of course, was still fished sunk. The floating fly is not fished purposely for another two centuries.)

This brings us to the history of the wet fly between Venables and Stewart, whose *The Practical Angler* (1857) is the next major landmark. This history has been so well summarised by Hills that I can do no more here than to paraphrase his findings. Hills took eighteen writers on fly-fishing between c.1650 and 1857, six from each century, and recorded which of them fished upstream, which downstream, and which both. It is a fascinating history. Franck (writing in 1694) fished downstream, as did Barker (1651). Cotton (1657) usually fished downstream, but also fished upstream if the wind blew upstream; he is therefore neutral. Chetham (1681) generally fished down, but fished upstream in clear water with the natural fly; with the artificial, however, he invariably fished down, so must be classed as a downstream man. The same is true of John Smith (*The True Art of Angling*, 1696). Hills's comment at this point is that by the end of the 17th century, four writers fish downstream, and two are neutral, 'inclining rather to down than to up, but showing that an upstream school existed' (*History*, 105).

Then to the 18th century. Bowlker (1747) fished up ('when you see a Fish rise... the best way is to throw a yard above him... and let your fly move gently towards him, by which means you will show it to him more naturally' – a striking quote). Best (1787), Howlett (*Angler's Sure Guide*, 1706) and Brookes (*Art of Angling*, 1740) all fished downstream. Shirley (*Angler's Museum*, 1784) followed Bowlker in fishing upstream. Scotcher (*Fly-Fisher's Legacy*, c.1800) was neutral. The totals for the 18th century are therefore three writers in favour of down, one neutral, and two in favour of up.

In the 19th century, Davy (*Salmonia*, 1828) fished up. Penn (*Maxims*, 1833) fished both up and down, but is generally in

favour of up. Stoddart (1835) fished down (but must also have
fished up, since he mentioned the floating fly). Ronalds (1836)
fished across and down. Younger (1840) fished up and across.
Fitzgibbon (*Handbook of Angling*, 1847) is on the whole to be
counted as being in favour of upstream fishing. Therefore the
19th century has four writers in favour of upstream fishing, and
two in favour of downstream. By the time Stewart was writing,
then, the balance had tipped in favour of the upstream wet fly
(and see Hills, *History*, 104-07).

Stewart's greatness lies in his ability to put arguments shrewdly.
I summarise his arguments for upstream fishing here.

(a) the trout lies with his head upstream, and is constantly
looking upstream for his food. Therefore the angler fishing
downstream is visible, whereas the angler fishing upstream, i.e.
from behind the trout, is not (Stewart: 'The first and greatest
advantage is, that the angler is unseen by the trout').

(b) the wet fly cast across the current, and allowed to swing
round downstream, presents the fly unnaturally; the fish does not
expect his food to drag across the current (Stewart: 'by [upstream
fishing] the angler can much better adapt the motions of his flies
to those of the natural insect').

(c) the trout hooked on a downstream fly is liable to scare other
fish in the vicinity during the play (Stewart: 'fishing up . . . does
not disturb the water so much . . .').

(d) many fish simply pluck at the downstream wet fly, whereas
the upstream man stands a better chance of hooking his fish securely as the strike pulls the fly into the fish's mouth
(Stewart:'[another] advantage of fishing up . . . is the much greater
probability of hooking a trout when it rises').

These, certainly, are powerful arguments. Yet they are not
entirely conclusive. Many anglers on the rain-fed rivers during
the later 19th century still fished downstream, and even on those
rivers which were to become the hallowed ground of the dry fly,
downstream fishing was practised. In *A Summer on the Test*, Hills
noted that both Hawker and Durnford, for example, fished down
and across (although upstream fishing had been practiced in
Hampshire from at least the late 17th century). What, then, are
the arguments for downstream fishing? (It should be noted that
these arguments are rarely put, perhaps because, as Hills wrote
(*History*, 109), they 'differ from theory'.)

(a) in theory it is true that an angler fishing upstream is less
visible to the fish, but the downstream fisher can lessen the problem by throwing a long line, by making use of bankside cover (a
point insisted upon as early as the *Treatise*), and/or by deep

wading. Moreover, the relatively broken water surface of rain-fed rivers can also help to conceal the angler.

(b) it is true that the downstream wet fly can, if fished thoughtlessly, *drag²* unnaturally. But again, water does not flow at an even pace, and a natural insect is not washed downstream at a steady rate, but faster, or slower, as the current and its features (rocks, weed-beds) dictate. In other words, the natural insect moves inconstantly. Other things being equal, the current has much the same effect on a sunk fly presented on fine nylon. Moreover, the travel of the fly can be slowed by *mending* the line (a practice not available to Stewart).

(c) in theory, upstream fishing would appear to disturb the water less. But a fish hooked on a fly fished downstream may of course be *walked* upstream (a common tactic when fishing pool-tails for sea trout at night). And when brown trout are feeding hard, the water is seldom disturbed for long.

(d) in theory, upstream fishing should allow one to hook more fish. And it is true that one does get fruitless plucks and knocks on the downstream wet fly. But these are often caused by the flies fishing too quickly. If the fly is fished at the correct pace relative to the strength of the current (and if the size of the fly is correct, relative to the strength of the current), then fish rise to, and turn down with, the fly with confidence, giving a firm indication on the line and allowing the angler to tighten into the rise. I would also add that it is essential to leave the fish time to turn away and down with the fly: many fish are missed on the downstream wet fly because the rod is held too low, and a taking fish thus feels immediate resistance from the rod and line. It is (usually) far better to fish with the rod point up, leaving a bow of line between rod-tip and water.

(e) a last argument for downstream fishing. One always knows where the flies are, and one is always in touch with them. Therefore one (almost) always knows when a fish has risen. This can sometimes be a problem in fishing the wet fly upstream in fast water.

So much for the history and theory behind both methods. Both are used today, for brown trout, grayling, and sea trout, although for the latter, downstream fishing is perhaps the more usual method, perhaps because the rivers where the fish are found are relatively large, relatively swift-flowing, and may, after a fining summer flood, be tinged with peat-stain. (Night fishing for sea trout is perforce carried out downstream.) My own practice, along with that of many other anglers, is to fish the wet fly upstream on brooks, becks and small rivers, upstream, or across and downstream on the middle reaches of rain-fed waters, and downstream when the water is high in spring and autumn, or when a gale of downstream wind makes upstream fishing impossible. It seems a sensible sort of compromise; Venables, I think, would have agreed.

It remains to discuss the relationship between the two great methods of wet fly fishing, and the various different designs of wet fly. That there is such a relationship no one will be tempted to deny who has spent some little time examining the different representations, say, a Large Dark Olive (dry patterns, such as the Rough Olive or *Greenwell's Glory* with their stiff hackles and/or upright wing, are naturally exempt from this discussion). Take, first, the Waterhen Bloa, one of the North Country flies tied with a sparse body of mole lightly dubbed on primrose silk, and an equally sparse slate-grey hackle from the outside of a waterhen's wing. This could serve as a representation of a hatching *nymph*, or as a copy of a drowned dun. In its first role, it could be fished on the *point* of a cast, and fished either up or downstream. Fished upstream, the soft hackle will have kick and life in the current, and the fly could be fished on the top *dropper* as a copy of a *dun*. Fished downstream on the point, the fly will be fishing perhaps a foot under the surface, the mobile hackle will similarly be tumbled by the current, and that is a good representation of a swimming nymph.

Next take a darkish wet Greenwell's, tied with a sloping wing and a sparse ginger hackle. As Kingsmill Moore put it, this is a kind of 'compromise' fly (*A Man May Fish*, 46). It is clearly a copy of a drowned dun, although perhaps, in a quick current, it might be mistaken for a hatching nymph. But the sloping wing, set to the hook at an angle of 45 degrees or less, gives the game away. It is intended to be fished downstream, or rather, across and downstream, near the surface (but not so near the surface that it drags and causes a wake, which would be disastrous).

Next, take a Clyde-style dressing, with a short body of dubbed mole or water-rat and an upright starling wing. Again, the upright wing indicates that this fly is meant to be fished upstream. If fished downstream, it would certainly cause a fish-scaring, unnatural wake. Therefore you would put it on the top dropper, and cast it upstream.

Finally, take a Blue Quill. This is perhaps a little light for the Large Dark Olive, but it will serve. It is tied with a *quill* body (quill is hollow and floats well) and a sharp, blue or blue dun hackle, usually a cock's (Courtney Williams, 107-08). It is in fact similar to a dry fly, and would float if cast upstream between *false casts*. Therefore its position would be on the top dropper of a cast fished upstream; it would merely drag if fished down.

With these four different patterns, then, two are clearly designed to be fished up, or up and across, one is designed to be fished downstream, and one, the Waterhen Bloa, could be fished either up (on the top dropper) or down (on the point). It is strange to find that this balance between patterns, favouring the upstream fly, echoes the balance between upstream and downstream fishing touched on earlier. But it is, perhaps, hardly surprising.

On fishing the wet fly for sea trout, see *sea trout*; *fly*. On fishing the wet fly on lakes and lochs see *bumble*, *fry*, *drift* etc. and for stillwater nymphs and wet flies see *buzzer*, *midge*, *pupa*, *sedge* and the entries cross-referenced there. In general see *salmon*, also *nymph fishing*, *creeper*, *stone-fly*. On wet fly leaders and leader-construction see *cast[1]*, *leader*.

whisks The *tails* of an artificial fly (particularly of those flies representing natural insects) are typically constructed of strands of *hackle* fibre, and are sometimes called *whisks*.

whitefish The various species of the family *Coregonus*, which typically live in deep and/or isolated lakes, having survived there since the last Ice Age. The classification of the various species is a complicated matter: some, for example, write of the whitefish family as being divided into three groups, those of the *lavaret* (including the *gwyniad*, the *powan* and the *schelly*), the *vendace* (including the vendace(s) of the Lake District and the Borders, along with the *pollans* of Ireland), and the *houting* (a very rare migratory species).

The whitefishes are of relatively little importance to fly-fishermen owing to their localised distribution and presumed feeding habits (they are only rarely caught on the surface with flies); further information about these various fish, and about the origin of their names, can be found under the relevant key-word entries.

white trout The *sea trout*, *Salmo trutta trutta*, is almost universally known in Ireland as the *white trout*. As Fallon puts it, 'in this land of white trout he is whiter than white and is known by no other name, whether sewin or peal or even sea trout' (p.85). See also *boat fishing; drift* etc.

whitling This is yet another term for the *sea trout*, especially the sea trout *herling* (= sea trout grilse). The word is sometimes confusingly rendered as *whiting*, although the form in *-ling* is accurate and appropriate, deriving from 'white+ling', where *-ling* is a diminutive suffix (compare e.g. *foundling* etc.). The OED dates the first attestation of the word to 1597, but the given definition is '[a] fish of the salmon family, not certainly identified; app. the young of the bull-trout, *Salmo eriox*'. Nowadays, at least, the word is used to refer to (the silvery-white colour of) small sea trout when fresh off the tide, and is used in Scotland, particularly, I think, in the far north-west. The first time I came across this word was in a postcard from a schoolfriend many years ago, who, enjoying a house party up at Tongue, wrote that he had taken one or two half-pound whitling. I thought he had been sea fishing.

willow-fly   The *willow fly*, *Leuctra geniculata*, is one of the group of *stone-flies*. Goddard (*Trout Fly Recognition*, 126) writes that it is 'very abundant and . . . widespread over the whole of the country except East Anglia and Ireland'. It hatches in late summer and autumn, especially on rain-fed rivers, where these hatches may coincide with those of late-hatching *needle-flies* (both insects are, moreover, superficially similar in appearance).

wind   Stillwater trout fishermen (especially those *boat fishing*), and those searching for sea trout in the lakes and lochs of the far north and west, pray for wind. A flat calm on the loch is usually held to be a difficult fishing condition, perhaps because after it has been cast, the line lands with a small pencil-streak of disturbance, and/or because the fish can see the fly or flies too clearly, and are thus aware of the deception and trap. A ruffle of wind disturbs the surface of the water, camouflaging the angler(s) to the fish's sight, and making soft presentation of the line and flies a little easier. It is also easier to present the flies on the *dibble* at some distance from the boat when there is a wind behind the casting arm. Finally, a greater variety of technique is possible when there is anything of a wind: in a calm, the fisherman is effectively bound to fish either the *dry fly* on the surface, or to fish deep with a sinking line. While both techniques will catch fish (sea trout in particular responding to a dry fly dribbled back across the calm water), when the wind blows it is possible to *drift* over likely ground, presenting the flies '*over the front*', in traditional style. A good blow on the back of one's neck also means that, where sea trout are the quarry, it is possible to put up the *dap*.

But while a sufficiency of wind is a necessary pleasure, too much wind means trouble. Black squalls can be uncomfortable and dangerous; gales mean that (if one puts out at all) the boat drifts far too fast (even when slowed by a *drogue*); and it is difficult to present the flies with any subtlety or discrimination when a Force 8 wind is blowing. And finally here, when white horses comb across the dark and storm-driven waters, it is often impossible to row home. It is necessary to beach the boat in some non-windy, secure place, and then walk in, battered and squelching.

The *Treatise* knew all about wind. In its incomparable list of 'Impediments' ('whyche cause a man to [t]ake noo fysshe') it listed the following evils:

> The tenth ['impediment'] is yf it be a tempeste. The eluenth is yf it be a grete wynde. The twellyfht yf the wynde be in the Eest and that is worste, for commonly neyther wynter nor somer ye fysshe woll not byte thenne. The weste and northe wyndes ben good but the south is beste.

(I particularly admire the fine distinction between a 'tempeste' and a 'grete wynde'.) The fact that the south and west winds (usually) bring about good fishing conditions is recorded in Walton, who institutionalised these winds in the following rhyme:

> But first for the wind, you are to take notice, that of the winds the *Southwind* is said to be best. One observes, that
>
> – When the wind is South,
>   It blows your bait into a fishes mouth.
>
> Next to that, the *West* wind is believed to be the best: and having told you that the *East* wind is the worst, I need not tell you which wind is the best in the third degree.

And yet Walton went on to observe, trenchantly, that

> as *Solomon* observes . . . *He that considers the wind shall never sow*: so he that busies his head too much about them, (if the weather be not made extream cold by an East wind) shall be a little superstitious: For as it is observed by some, That there is no good horse of a bad colour; so I have observed that if it be a cloudy day, and not extream cold, let the Wind sit in what corner it will and do its worst I heed it not . . . (108).

So perhaps what stillwater fly-fishermen should pray for is not so much what the *Treatise* called a 'whystelynge wynde' but for what the Irish call 'a soft day, thank God'.

wind-knot   The *wind-knot* should perhaps be included in some modern list of 'impediments' (see *wind*). This pest is an overhand knot which, because of poor casting technique (e.g. when throwing across, down, or especially into a wind), ties itself in the *leader*. This kind of happenstantial knot weakens the leader, which may consequently break during the *play*. (Therefore, when the *cast¹* breaks on a fish for no apparent reason, and when the *nylon* is otherwise apparently sound, a wind-knot should be suspected.)

To Cast a Trout Fly notes that wind-knots are caused 'by tipping the rod forward first [i.e. on the forward cast], then pushing it ahead, an instinctive fault when casting into the wind'. The cure is to 'bring the rod forward in one o'clock position; tip it ahead only at conclusion of the forward movement' (35). See also *cast²*.

wind-lane   A *wind-lane* is an oily-looking slick which develops on the surface of a wind-ruffled lake; these wind-lanes (there are usually many, running roughly parallel) may extend downwind for hundreds of yards. They seem to be caused by wind-action on the surface water, and, this being so, they are sometimes full of insect and other life which has been washed there; the relatively 'oily' water in these lanes also means that insects find it difficult to hatch in such channels. Consequently, trout cruise up wind-lanes, looking for easily available food. As Bob Church puts it, 'the ideal place [to fish], particularly if you're in a boat, is a "wind lane", as these calm areas amongst the ripple are usually full of food. Whether you anchor or drift slowly down one, there is no doubt that you will be covering a number of fish' (in *Trout Fishing*, ed. Mansfield, 139).

window   A fish looking up, into and through the surface, sees the external world through a circular 'hole'; outside this area of direct vision into the world, the trout sees into a *mirror* – that is, the water surface mirrors back whatever is below it (weeds, the bottom, a snail inching up a ranunculus stem...). In effect, this means that a fish seeing e.g. an angler on the bank, sees him through the *window* (and subject to the laws of refraction). But it also means that a fish seeing a *dry fly* will see it first, as it approaches from upstream, not in the window but in the mirror, where the fly's *hackle* creates, in Clarke & Goddard's words, a 'tiny starburst of light' (i.e. indentations in the surface film, see *The Trout and the Fly*, 84). Then the fly passes from the mirror into the edge of the window, and the area of direct vision: at this point, the body (and the *wings*) of the fly can be directly seen, and seen in colour. As the fly passes directly over the fish, however, in the middle of the window, its colours darken (as seen by the fish), because it is lit largely from overhead and so is seen in silhouette. (Notably, the American angler and writer, Lee Wulff, was a firm believer in the 'silhouette' theory, and designed and fished his flies accordingly; see Gingrich, 206.)

The subject of fish vision is first noted in Ronalds (*The Fly-Fisher's Entomology*, first edn, 1836), who gave a fine, and accurate, description of the topic. More recently, Clarke & Goddard give a thorough rethinking of the entire matter in *The Trout and the Fly*; and in an Appendix to the second edn of *A Man May Fish* (1979), Kingsmill Moore wrote most lucidly of the effect of waves, and of deeply stained water, on a fish's vision of the underwater fly. This appendix should really be required reading for stillwater boat fishermen.

wing   The earliest trout flies, those of the *Treatise*, were winged (usually with mallard, but also with feathers from the partridge, jay and buzzard, among others). Of course, the flies were intended to be fished sunk (see *wet fly*), but they appear to be copies of natural flies (especially *duns*). Unfortunately, since the *Treatise* gave no instructions, it is impossible to know how the wings were tied, but it is possible that they were fashioned from a single slip of feather, tied on reversed (see below) and then split with lashings of the tying silk. Only in one pattern did the *Treatise* hint at what we would call a 'split-winged' fly: this was the 'tandy [i.e. tawny] flye at saynt Wyllyams daye: the body of tandy wull, and the wynges contrary eyther ayenst other of the whitest mayle of ye wylde drake'. But it is almost impossible to be certain what this means. It is likewise difficult to know what kind of feathers were used for winging the flies of the *Treatise*: were they breast feathers, as implied by e.g. 'the blackest mayle of the wylde drake', where *mayle* meant 'breast feathers'? Or were flight feathers also used? This is at least hinted at by the fact that for eight of its twelve patterns, the *Treatise* did not specify that 'mayle' – breast feather – is to be used; but it is impossible to tell.

By the time the 17th century is reached, however, things are much more certain. Barker (*The Art of Angling*, 1651) was the first to give instructions for fly-dressing, but Venables, in particular, gives good directions for dressing wings. The commonest way, and perhaps the way of dressing inherited from the 15th century, was to tie the wings reversed, i.e. tying on the wing-slip with the tips of the feathers pointing forwards, so that the fly looks like a miniature paintbrush; then the body, and body *hackle* (if any), are formed, and the silk brought back again to the head of the fly. At this point the wing feather is divided with a pin (in Barker), and the silk carried between the two wings in a figure-of-eight binding, thus separating the fibres into two bunches. Then the wing is held or pressed upright, and some turns of silk made at the head of the fly to ensure that the wings stay upright. Barker, Venables, and Cotton (see *Angler*, 270; Cotton wrote that you should place your wing feather 'upon the back of the hook... lying revers't from the end of the shanck...') all shared this style of dressing wings. Again, it is unfortunate that we do not know for certain just how upright the finished wings were: Cotton, at least, wrote that the wings of the finished fly 'slope towards the bend of the hook' (270).

It is clear from Venables that there must have been another method of winging, one where the wing-tips were set on pointing backwards (rather than in the reversed style): 'whereas (wrote Venables) if you set the points of the wings backwards, towards the bending of the hook, the stream, if the feathers be gentle as they ought, will fold the points of the wings in the bending of the hook, as I have often found by experience' (*The Experienced Angler*, 14). This clearly suggests that some anglers made their flies like this.

There is another intriguing possibility in Venables. It is that he was the first to invent what we would now call an 'upside-down fly' (abbr. USD in e.g. Clarke & Goddard, *The Trout and the Fly*), i.e. a fly which fishes with the hook point upwards. The relevant passage is, however, obscure:

> or else [in another method of winging] I run the feathers, and those must be stripped from the quill or pen, with part of it still cleaving to the feathers, round the hook, and so make them fast, if I turn the feather round the hook; then I clip away those that are upon the back of the hook [i.e. on top of the shank?], that so, if it be possible, the point of the hook may be forced by the feathers left on the inside of the hook [i.e. below the shank?], to swim upwards...(*The Experienced Angler*, 13-14).

The passage is difficult to construe, but it is just possible that Venables was fishing something very like a USD Paradun in the middle of the 17th century.

The original, reversed-wing method survived until the middle of the 18th century (and beyond). As Hills noted (*History*, 176), this style of winging 'developed into the rolled wing, made famous by Stewart, and in general use to-day'. In rolled winging, material is taken from a single feather (say, bronze mallard), and 'rolled' into several folds (usually three folds). This rolled pad may be set on the hook in reversed style, or set on with the tips of the feathers pointing towards the bend, as in many of today's wet flies. Skues, in *Minor Tactics*, chose the rolled wing, tied reversed, for many of his wet patterns: '...a pair of wings tied in a bunch, and either left single or, preferably for our purposes, split in equal portions, and divided with the figure-of-eight application of the tying silk...' (p.26). Here it is difficult to tell whether Skues was writing of rolled wings; but his next paragraph makes this clear: '...the wings built up of a length of feather rolled into a bunch have the advantage of taking up a lot of water, and not releasing it readily; and they also assist to let the fly down more lightly on the water than so lightly dressed a fly would fall but for the wings...'. This style of wing-dressing is also known on Tweed and Clyde; several of today's fly-dressers speak of 'Clyde-style' wet flies, meaning flies with short, sparsely *dubbed* bodies and upright wings (tied rolled and reversed).

Then there are the split-winged, and double split-winged patterns which were developed for the *dry fly*. These are creations of the 19th century: Ronalds, for example, winged his Great Red Spinner with 'two pieces...from the under covert feather of a starling's wing...' (*The Fly-Fisher's Entomology*, 34), and Blacker (*The Art of Fly-Making*, 1855) gave instructions for winging flies with two slips of feather (Hills, *History*, 175). Thus the ground is prepared for Ogden (*Fly Tying*, 1879) and, supremely, Halford (*Floating Flies and How to Dress Them*, 1886). It is from Halford that the method of split-winging we know today really derives – the taking of paired feather slips from the right and left wings of a starling (for example), and the dressing of them so that they stand upright.

Lastly, as far as trout flies are concerned, there is one further method of winging that is of note. This is the 'advanced wing', where the wing is formed of a single slip of feather, is undivided, and tied so that it points forward over the eye of the hook. Courtney Williams (255-6 and Glossary) notes that this style of winging is first found on the Mole Fly (?early 20th century), where it 'balances the fly...well [and] cocks [it] better than most' (and see *cocking*). The Mole Fly has been held to represent the olives, but in France, where the fly is evidently very popular, it is also regarded as a copy of one of the *sedges*. Another fly tied with an advanced wing is the John Storey, popular in the north of England; this is a good general olive copy, but perhaps better when sedges are on the water.

We should now turn to the history of the styles of winging that have been found on the salmon fly. In brief (since relevant information will also be found under e.g. *salmon*; *topping* etc.), it seems to be the case that the first purpose-constructed salmon flies are tied with long wings: Venables, for example, writing in 1662, advised that 'the Salmon flies must be made with wings standing one behind the other, whether two or four; also he [the salmon] delights in the most gaudy and orient colours you can choose; the wings I mean chiefly, if not altogether, with long tails and wings' (facsimile, 21). Unfortunately, Venables did not state what these wings were made of. On the other hand, there were salmon fishermen who fished with what were really overgrown trout flies (such as Richard Franck, *Northern Memoirs*, 1694), with styles of winging to match.

There seems to be little development during the 18th century: two popular patterns (according to Trench, 131) were the Dragon and the Kingfisher, the first tied with a wing of peacock feather, the second with silver pheasant. Perhaps this are the linear descendants of Venables' long-winged flies. Certainly the four, sombre-looking salmon flies illustrated in Bainbridge's *Fly-Fisher's Guide* of 1816 have relatively long wings (and, on the whole, wings tied well sloping, which argues that they were tied in the usual fashion, i.e. not reversed).

Then comes the 19th century, and the phase of Irish influence on salmon fly-dressing. The wing broke out into what were truly 'orient' colours, feather-fibres sometimes being 'married' with one another in order to produce a resplendent whole, and the whole was over-dressed with a *topping*, and/or with *cheeks* of junglecock. This style of dressing seems to have lasted for the rest of the century: Francis Francis (*A Book on Angling* [1863]) gave 235 patterns of salmon fly, most being 'gaudy and orient' (and very complicated to tie, see Trench, 137).

But reaction set in with the 20th century, and Chaytor (*Letters to a Salmon Fisher's Sons*, 1919) pioneered a return to more sparse and sober dressings. This was followed, in mid-century, by experiments with hair-winged dressings, promoted, perhaps, by interest in *greased-line* fishing, and by the huge success of the Hairy Mary, a hair-wing *par excellence*. In 1963, for example, Jock Scott wrote that salmon flies

> are legion, and the fashion is changing. In late spring and in summer, the traditional feather wings are giving way to hair wings, which are more lively in the water. Wet feathers are inclined to cling to the hook and to show no signs of life in a strong stream, but hair – be it deer or stoat – does play in the current and seems to attract fish when feather wings do not. Two flies which come to mind are Hairy Mary and Stoat's [T]ail, both of which are very successful in low water' (*The Complete Fly-Fisher*, ed. Walker, 25-6).

In the same passage, the writer also drew attention to the increasing use of hair-winged *tube flies*, such as, for example, today's favourite lure for the sunk-line, the Willie Gunn tube. As Crawford Little puts it in a recent article, 'Today, if we have a strong convention in fly choice for cold-water work, it could be summed up as "any fly, so long as it is a two-inch Willie Gunn on a copper tube"' (*T&S*, January 1990, 68).

In the article just cited, Crawford Little also draws attention to two flies, the Collie Dog and the Tadpole, which have been developed within the last twenty years and which are totally radical in design, carrying wings up to nine inches long (in the case of the Collie Dog, a hank of long curly black hair from the dog's leg): perhaps these are the ultimate descendants of Venables' long-winged flies. Unfortunately, no one seems to know who invented these patterns, but, as Crawford Little notes, 'six-inch wings on two-inch tubes have firmly taken a place in accepted salmon-fly design'.

working the fly   A fly is said to be *worked* when it is cast downstream, fished sunk, and subsequently given motion by small movements of the rod tip, which cause the fly to dart minutely in the current. Some salmon fly-fishermen habitually use this technique when fishing the *sunk line*, but others work the fly only at the end of its travel, while others prefer to present the fly 'dead drift', i.e. without imparting any additional motion to the fly via the rod tip. An example is the following:

> ...he had been advised not to work the fly but to keep the point of the rod steady, while the fly was travelling round in the current, and only to give any motion to the fly, when it had reached a point directly below him and was being allowed to hang there. This was done as a final inducement to a salmon to come up to the fly...(Taverner & Scott, *Salmon Fishing*, 120).

But trout and grayling *wet fly* fishermen may also use this technique on occasion (albeit sparingly). Here is an example from Reg Righyni's *Grayling* (37):

> Len [Stott] does not follow the policy of his friend [Dr Ian Calvert-Wilson, who fishes the wet-fly upstream for grayling]. He fishes across-and-down, is a great believer in working the flies, and seldom allows them to drift naturally for long. Inching the line in with the left hand, or periodically lifting the rod tip, certainly does make the flies behave more enticingly on occasions, but the novice should not work the flies as a matter of course....

References

Anon. *c*.1420 (1496) *The Treatise of Fishing with an Angle*. The early, fragmentary text (*c*.1420) was edited by Thomas Satchell (1883); the later, full text (often misattributed to Dame Juliana Berners) was issued by Wynkyn de Worde in 1496. (The copy currently held in the Library of Trinity College, Dublin, was used in writing this lexicon.) The most recent edition of the later text of the *Treatise* is that by Professor Braekman in *Scripta I* (1980). A translation of the *Treatise* is available in McDonald, *Quill Gordon* (1972), 149-72.

Bagenal, T.B. (1970) *The Observer's Book of Freshwater Fishes* [1st edition 1941], London: Frederick Warne.

Bainbridge, W.G. (1936) *The Fly-Fisher's Guide to Aquatic Flies and their Imitations*, London: A&C Black.

Barker, Thomas (1651) *The Art of Angling*, London (cited in Hills 1973).

Barr, David (ed.) (1981) *The Haig Guide to Salmon Fishing in Scotland*, London: Queen Anne Press, Macdonald Futura Publishers.

Baverstock, L. (1970) 'River Fly Fishing', in ed. Mansfield, 7-36.

'BB' (1985) *The Fisherman's Bedside Book* [1st edition 1945], Woodbridge, Suffolk: The Boydell Press.

Beer, Jon (1989) 'Water-knot warning', *Trout and Salmon*, June issue (Letters), 30.

Bell, Terry C. (1982) 'All that glisters...', *Trout and Salmon*, December issue, 40.

Berners, Dame Juliana. *See* Anon.

Best, Thomas (1787) *A Concise Treatise on the Art of Angling*, London (cited in Hills 1973).

Blakey, Robert (n.d.; 19th century) *Angling, or How to Angle, and Where to Go*, London: George Routledge & Sons.

Caine, William (1911) 'Of graylings, large and small', excerpt (from *An Angler at Large*) reprinted in *The Grayling Society Newsletter*, Summer, 1984, 26-30.

Chaytor, A.H. (1936) *Letters to a Salmon Fisher's Sons*, 4th edition [1st edition 1910], London: John Murray.

Chetham, James (1681) *The Angler's Vade Mecum*, London (cited in Hills 1973). Excerpts from Chetham are reprinted in eds. Profumo and Swift, 116-17.

Church, Bob and Peter Gathercole (1985) *Imitations of the Trout's World*, Ramsbury, Marlborough: The Crowood Press.

Clark, John *See* Sosin, Mark.

Clarke, Brian (1975) *The Pursuit of Stillwater Trout*, London: A&C Black.

Clarke, Brian & John Goddard (1980) *The Trout and the Fly: A New Approach*, London: Ernest Benn Ltd.

Cotton, Charles *See* Walton.

Currie, William B. *See* McLaren, Moray.

Davies, W.E. (1971) *The Technique of Freshwater Fishing* [1st edition 1952], Kingswood, Surrey: Elliot Right Way Books.

Davies, W.E. (1974) *Fly Dressing and some Tackle-Making* [1st edition 1963], Kingswood, Surrey: Elliot Right Way Books.

Davy, Sir Humphrey (1828) *Salmonia, or Days of Fly-Fishing in a Series of Conversations with Some Account of the Habit of Fishes belonging to the Salmo Genus*. (As cited in eds. Profumo and Swift, 1985).

Dennys, John (1613) *The secrets of angling*. London. A substantial excerpt from this poem is reprinted in eds. Profumo and Swift, 81-3.

Dick, Lenox (1966) *The Art and Science of Fly Fishing*, Princeton, New Jersey: D. Van Nostrand Company, Inc.

Dobie, W.G.M. (1927) *Game-bag and Creel*, Edinburgh: W. Green and Son Ltd.

Evans, James (1972) *Small River Fly Fishing for Trout and Grayling*, London: A&C Black.

Fahy, Edward (1985) *Child of the Tides: A Sea Trout Handbook*, (Ireland): Glendale Press.

Falkus, Hugh (1981) *Sea Trout Fishing* [1st edition 1962], London: H.F. & G. Witherby.

Falkus, Hugh (1984) *Salmon Fishing: A Practical Guide*, London: H.F. & G. Witherby.

Fallon, Niall (1983) *Fly-fishing for Irish Trout*, Kilkenny: Roberts' Books.

Farson, Negley (1942) *Going Fishing*, London: Country Life Ltd. A classic of its kind.

Francis, Francis (1867) *A Book on Angling*, London (cited in Hills 1973). Francis was evidently the authority consulted by the original compilers of the OED.

Franck, Richard (1694) *Northern Memoirs*, London (cited in Hills 1973).

Fraser, Gordon (1987) *Mastering the Nymph*, Poole: Blandford Press.

Frost, W.E. & M.E. Brown (1970) *The Trout*, London: Collins (Fontana).

Gallichan, Walter M. (1903) *Fishing in Wales*, London: F.E. Robinson & Co.

Gathercole, Peter *See* Church, Bob.

Gingrich, Arnold (1974) *The Fishing in Print: A Guided Tour through Five Centuries of Angling Literature*, New York: Winchester Press.

'Glensman' (1990) 'Flies for a midnight killing', *Trout and Salmon*, May issue, 42-3.

Goddard, John (1976) *Trout Fly Recognition* [1st edition 1966], London: A&C Black. Indispensable.

Goddard, John (1979) *Trout Flies of Stillwater* [1st edition 1969], London: A&C Black. Also indispensable.

Grayling Society, The (1982) *The Distribution of Grayling in England, Wales and Scotland*. Compiled by David B. Liversedge. Available from The Grayling Society, a splendid body.

Greenhalgh, Malcolm (1987) *Lake, Loch and Reservoir Trout Fishing*, London: A&C Black.

Grey, Sir Edward (Viscount of Falloden) (1899) *Fly Fishing*, London: J.M. Dent & Co. Revised and enlarged edition [1930] reprinted by André Deutsch Ltd [1984] in the Modern Fishing Classics Series, edited by Antony Atha. A great book, possibly fly-fishing's best.

Haldane, A.R.B. (1944) *The Path by the Water*, London: Thomas Nelson and Sons Ltd.

Halford, Frederic M. (1886) *Floating Flies and How to Dress Them*, London (cited in Hills 1973). Gingrich (1974) devoted chapter 10 of *The Fishing in Print* to a consideration of 'Halford and Purism'; Hills (1973) gave several sections of his great work to the evolution of the dry-fly, with special reference to Halford. There are other editions.

Halford, Frederic M. (1889) *Dry-fly Fishing in Theory and Practice*, London (cited in Hills 1973). And later editions.

Hardinge, Lord, of Penshurst (1976) *An Incompleat Angler*, London: Michael Joseph.

Hardy, House of (n.d., *c.*1970-90) *To Cast a Trout Fly*, Alnwick: House of Hardy Ltd. Most useful introduction for those of us learning to cast.

Harris, J.R. (1956) *An Angler's Entomology* [1st edition 1952], The New Naturalist Series, London: Collins.

Headley, Stan (1990) 'Trout in the '90s', *Trout and Salmon*, January issue, 7.

Henzell, H.P. (1937) *The Art and Craft of Loch Fishing*, London: Allan.

Hills, John Waller (1973) *A History of Fly Fishing for Trout* [1st edition 1921], Reading: Barry Shurlock.

Hills, John Waller (1930) *A Summer on the Test* [1st edition 1924]. The 2nd [1930] edition reprinted by André Deutsch [1983] in the Modern Fishing Classics Series, edited by Antony Atha.

Holgate, James & Geoff Parkinson (1984) *An Angler's Guide to the Lake District*, Lancaster: Castabout Publications. And a later edition [1987].

Housby, Trevor (1985) *Trout Fishing*, Poole: Blandford Press.

Howlett, R(obert?) (1706) *The Angler's Sure Guide*, London (cited in Hills 1973).

Hurum, Hans Jørgen (1977) *A History of the Fish Hook*, London: A&C Black.

Ivens, Tom (1953) *Still Water Fly Fishing*, London: Verschoyle. And later editions, including e.g. the revised and enlarged 4th edition, London: André Deutsch.

Jacques, David (1974) *The Development of Modern Stillwater Fishing*, London: A&C Black.

Johnson, Stephen (1969) *Fishing with a Purpose*, London: Peter Davies.

Jukes, H.R. (1935) *Loved River*, reprinted by André Deutsch [1984] in the Modern Fishing Classics Series, edited by Antony Atha.

Kingsley, Charles (1859) *Chalk Stream Studies*. Included in *Miscellanies* (1859) and *Prose Idylls* (1873). (Cited in Hills 1973).

Kingsmill Moore, T.C. (1979) *A Man May Fish* [1st edition 1960], Gerrards Cross: Colin Smythe.

Kite, Oliver (1969) *A Fisherman's Diary*, London: André Deutsch.

Kite, Oliver (1969) 'Brown trout in chalk streams', in ed. C.F. Walker, 113-44.

Kite, Oliver (1974) 'Elements of Nymph Fishing', in ed. Mansfield 37-74.

Lapsley, Peter (1982) 'Damned limits!' *Trout and Salmon*, April issue, 51-2.

Lapsley, Peter (1988) *Trout from Stillwaters* [1st edition 1981], London: Unwin Hyman.

Lapsley, Peter (1988) *River Trout Flyfishing*, London: Unwin Hyman.

Lawrie, William H. (1943) *Practical Angling Hints and Recipes* [1st edition 1939], London and Edinburgh: Oliver & Boyd.

Little, Crawford (1988) 'Salmon on the long-wings', *Trout and Salmon*, April issue, 59-61.

Liversedge, David B. *See* Grayling Society.

Luce, A.A. (1959) *Fishing and Thinking*, London: Hodder and Stoughton.

McDonald, John (1972) *Quill Gordon* [And see Anon.], New York: Alfred A. Knopf.

McLaren, Moray & William B. Currie (1978) *The Fishing Waters of Scotland* [1st edition 1972], London: John Murray Ltd.

Maclean, Norman (1980) *Trout and Grayling: An Angler's Natural History*, London: A&C Black.

Macan, T.T. (1959) *A Guide to Freshwater Invertebrate Animals*, London: Longmans.

Macan, T.T. & E.B. Worthington (1972) *Life in Lakes and Rivers* [1st edition 1951], Fontana New Naturalist Series. London: Collins.

Manners, T.J. (1990) 'Thoughts on salmon flies', *Trout and Salmon*, January issue, 28.

Mansfield, Kenneth (ed.) (1974) *Trout Fishing* [First published as *Trout and how to Catch them*, 1970], London: Pan Books Ltd.

Markham, Gervase (1614) *The Second Booke of the English Husbandman*, London (cited in Hills 1973). This work includes Markham's *A Discourse of the Generall Art of Fishing with the Angle*, later reissued in Markham's most famous work, *The Pleasures of Princes*. An excerpt from this is reprinted in eds. Profumo and Swift, 84-5.

Marshall, Howard (1967) *Reflections on a River*. London: H.F. & G. Witherby.

Mascall, Leonard (1590) *A Booke of Fishing with Hooke and Line*. London. (Cited in Hills 1973.)

Meddings, Michael (1989) 'Cinderellas of the streams', *Trout and Salmon*, December issue, 86-9.

Muus, B.J. (1971) *Freshwater Fish of Britain and Europe*, illustrated by P. Dahlstrom. London: Collins.

Nobbes, Robert (1682) *The Compleat Troller*, London (cited in Hills 1973; see also Trench 1974).

Ogborne, Chris (1984) 'Live and let live', *Trout and Salmon*, December issue, 14-15.

Ogborne, Chris (1987) 'Loch-style today', *Trout and Salmon*, March issue, 44-5.

Ogborne, Chris (1987) 'Loch-style today', *Trout and Salmon*, June issue, 35-6.

Ogborne, Chris (1989) 'Fine, strong, but handle with care', *Trout and Salmon*, March issue, 52-3.

Oglesby, Arthur (1990) 'The search for a springer', *Trout and Salmon*, January issue,

Overfield, T. Donald (1986) *Fifty Favourite Wet Flies*, London: A&C Black.

Parkinson, Geoff *See* Holgate, James.

Parton, Steve (1987) 'Reservoir lures', in *Flies for '87*, a *Trout and Salmon* Guide to patterns, 33-4.

Pearson, Alan (1979 *Catching Big Trout*, London: Stanley Paul.

Perry, Alastair (1972) 'To Land a Salmon', *Trout and Salmon*, May issue, 50-51.

Plunket-Greene, Harry (1936) *Where the Bright Waters Meet* [1st edition 1924]. Revised and enlarged edition [1936] reprinted by André Deutsch Ltd [1983] in the Modern Fishing Classics Series, edited by Antony Atha.

Profumo, David and Graham Swift (eds.) (1985) *The Magic Wheel: An Anthology of Fishing in Literature*, London: Heinemann.

Pulman, George P.R. (1841) *Vade Mecum of Fly-fishing for Trout*, London and Axminster (cited in Hills 1973).

Radcliffe, William (1921) *Fishing from the Earliest Times*, London: John Murray.

Ransome, Arthur (1932) *Rod and Line* [1st edition 1929]. The Life and Letters Series No. 38. London: Jonathan Cape. Reprinted and issued as paperback [1980], Oxford: Oxford University Press.

Righyni, Reg V. (1968) *Grayling*. The Richard Walker Angling Library, London: Macdonald.

Righyni, R. (1973) *Advanced Salmon Fishing*, London: Macdonald and Janes (Originally published as *Salmon Taking Times*, 1965.)

Ritz, Charles (1972) *A Fly Fisher's Life* [1st edition in English 1959]. London: Max Reinhardt.

Roberts, John (1982) *The Grayling Angler*, London: H.F. & G. Witherby.

Roberts, John (1986) *The New Illustrated Dictionary of Trout Flies*, London: George Allen & Unwin.

Rollo, W. Keith (1933) *Fly Fishing* [1st edition 1931], London: H.F. & G. Witherby.

Ronalds, Alfred (1901) *The Fly-Fisher's Entomology* [1st edition 1836], London and New York: Longmans, Green & Co.

Sandison, Bruce (1987) *Trout Lochs of Scotland* [1st edition 1983], London: Unwin Hyman Ltd.

Sawyer, Frank (1958) *Nymphs and the Trout*, London: A&C Black.

Sawyer, Frank (1985) *Keeper of the Stream*, [1st edition 1952]. New paperback edition, with illustrations by Charles Jardine, published [1987], London: Unwin Hyman.

Scotcher, George (*c.*1800) *The Fly-fisher's Legacy*, Chepstow (cited in Hills 1973).

Scrope, William (1843) *Days and Nights of Salmon Fishing in the Tweed*, London (cited in Hills 1973). Gingrich (1974) gives several longish excerpts from this entertaining and instructive work.

Shedden, Colin (1990) 'Steelhead blues', *Trout and Salmon*, May issue, 44-5.

Sheringham, H.T. (1908) *Elements of Angling* (cited in Falkus 1981).

Skues, G.E.M. (1924) *Minor Tactics of the Chalk Stream* [1st edition 1910], London: A&C Black.

Skues, G.E.M. (1939) *Nymph Fishing for Chalk Stream Trout*, London: A&C Black.

Skues, G.E.M. (1949) *The Way of a Trout with a Fly* [1st edition 1921], London: A&C Black.

Sosin, Mark & John Clark (1976) *Through the Fish's Eye: An Angler's Guide to Fish Behaviour*, London: André Deutsch.

Spencer, Sidney (1934) *The Art of Lake Fishing with the Sunk Fly*, London: H.F. & G. Witherby.

Spencer, Sidney (1969) *Newly from the Sea: Fishing for Salmon and Seatrout*, London: H.F. & G. Witherby.

Spencer, Sidney (1974) *Game Fishing Tactics*, London: H.F. & G. Witherby.

Spencer, Sidney (1977) *Clear Water Trout Fishing with Worm* [1st published in 1935], London: H.F. & G. Witherby.

Stephen, Richard (1987) 'Daddy with a difference', *Trout and Salmon*, August issue, 48-9.

Stewart, R.N. (n.d.; ?1963) *Salmon and Trout*, London: Chambers.

Stewart, W.C. (1887) *The Practical Angler* [1st edition 1857], Edinburgh (cited in Hills 1973). Gingrich (1974) reprints extensive excerpts from this important work.

Stoddart, Thomas Tod (1853) *The Angler's Companion to the Rivers and Lakes of Scotland* [1st edition 1847]. (Cited in Hills 1973.)

Stuart, Hamish (*c*.1917) *The Book of the Sea Trout* (cited in Falkus 1981).

Swift, Graham *See* Profumo, David.

Taverner, Eric & Jock Scott (1972) *Salmon Fishing* [1st edition 1931], The Lonsdale Library. London: Seeley, Service & Co.

Theakston, Michael (1853) *A List of Natural Flies*, Ripon (cited in Hills 1973).

Tod, E.M. (1918) *Wet-fly Fishing Treated Methodically* [1st edition 1903], London: Sampson Low, Marston & Co. Ltd.

Trench, Charles Chenevix (1974) *A History of Angling*, London: Hart-Davis, MacGibbon Ltd.

Trout and Salmon. Issues 1968-90. Also special publications, such as *The Trout and Salmon Pocket Guide to Trout Flies*; *The Trout and Salmon Pocket Guide to Hairwing Salmon Flies*, etc. *See also* Parton, Steve.

Turner, Eric Horsfall (1966) *Angler's Cavalcade*, London: A&C Black.

Vare, Alan B. (1987) *The Hardy Book of Fisherman's Knots*, London: Camden Publishing Co. Ltd.

Varley, M.E. (1967) *British Freshwater Fishes*. Buckland Foundation, London: Fishing News (Books) Ltd.

Venables, Colonel Robert (1969) *The Experienced Angler* [1st edition 1662 (London: Richard Marriot)]. The 1969 copy is reproduced in facsimile, with an introductory biographical sketch of Venables by C.G.A. Parker, London: Antrobus Press.

Waddington, Richard (1947) *Salmon Fishing: A New Philosophy* (cited in Taverner & Scott 1972).

Walker, C.F. (1960) *Lake Flies and their Imitation*. Reprinted by André Deutsch Ltd. [1983] in the Modern Fishing Classics Series, edited by Antony Atha.

Walker, C.F. (ed.) (1984) *The Complete Fly-Fisher* [1st edition 1963], London: Barrie & Jenkins.

Walker, Richard (1980) 'Hand or reel?' *Trout and Salmon*, April issue, 73.

Walker, Richard (1982) *Dick Walker's Trout Fishing*, London: David & Charles.

Walton, Izaak and Charles Cotton. *The Compleat Angler* [1st edition 1653; 1st edition containing Cotton's work, 1676]. Many editions. The 1982 edition used here, with foreword by John Buchan, is published in Oxford World's Classics Series. Oxford: Oxford University Press.

Weaver, Mike (1989) 'A fly for tumbling streams', *Trout and Salmon*, March issue, 56-8.

Williams, A. Courtney (1986) *A Dictionary of Trout Flies* [1st edition 1949]. 1986 edition with an additional section on modern flies by T. Donald Overfield, London: A&C Black.

Williamson, Henry (1960) *The Henry Williamson Animal Saga* (includes *Salar the Salmon*, 201-375), London: Macdonald.

Willock, Colin (ed.) (1966) *The Penguin Guide to Fishing* [1st published as *The ABC of Fishing*, 1964], Harmondsworth: Penguin.

Wrangles, Alan (ed.) (1965) *Newnes Complete Guide to Sea Angling*, London: Newnes.

Yuille, John B. (1983) 'By popular demand – "gillie" again!' *Trout and Salmon*, June issue (Letters), 25.

OXFORD

MORE OXFORD PAPERBACKS

This book is just one of nearly 1000 Oxford Paperbacks currently in print. If you would like details of other Oxford Paperbacks, including titles in the World's Classics, Oxford Reference, Oxford Books, OPUS, Past Masters, Oxford Authors, and Oxford Shakespeare series, please write to:

UK and Europe: Oxford Paperbacks Publicity Manager, Arts and Reference Publicity Department, Oxford University Press, Walton Street, Oxford OX2 6DP.

Customers in UK and Europe will find Oxford Paperbacks available in all good bookshops. But in case of difficulty please send orders to the Cash-with-Order Department, Oxford University Press Distribution Services, Saxon Way West, Corby, Northants NN18 9ES. Tel: 0536 741519; Fax: 0536 746337. Please send a cheque for the total cost of the books, plus £1.75 postage and packing for orders under £20; £2.75 for orders over £20. Customers outside the UK should add 10% of the cost of the books for postage and packing.

USA: Oxford Paperbacks Marketing Manager, Oxford University Press, Inc., 200 Madison Avenue, New York, N.Y. 10016.

Canada: Trade Department, Oxford University Press, 70 Wynford Drive, Don Mills, Ontario M3C 1J9.

Australia: Trade Marketing Manager, Oxford University Press, G.P.O. Box 2784Y, Melbourne 3001, Victoria.

South Africa: Oxford University Press, P.O. Box 1141, Cape Town 8000.

OXFORD LIVES

Biography at its best—this acclaimed series offers authoritative accounts of the lives of men and women from the arts, sciences, politics, and many other walks of life.

STANLEY

Volume I: The Making of an African Explorer
Volume II: Sorceror's Apprentice

Frank McLynn

Sir Henry Morton Stanley was one of the most fascinating late-Victorian adventurers. His historic meeting with Livingstone at Ujiji in 1871 was the journalistic scoop of the century. Yet behind the public man lay the complex and deeply disturbed personality who is the subject of Frank McLynn's masterly study.

In his later years, Stanley's achievements exacted a high human cost, both for the man himself and for those who came into contact with him. His foundation of the Congo Free State on behalf of Leopold II of Belgium, and the Emin Pasha Relief Expedition were both dubious enterprises which tarnished his reputation. They also revealed the complex—and often troubling—relationship that Stanley has with Africa.

'excellent . . . entertaining, well researched and scrupulously annotated' *Spectator*

'another biography of Stanley will not only be unnecessary, but almost impossible, for years to come' *Sunday Telegraph*

Also available:

A Prince of Our Disorder: The Life of T. E. Lawrence
John Mack
Carpet Sahib: A Life of Jim Corbett   Martin Booth
Bonnie Prince Charlie: Charles Edward Stuart   Frank McLynn

OXFORD LETTERS AND MEMOIRS

Letters, memoirs, and journals offer a special insight into the private lives of public figures and vividly recreate the times in which they lived. This popular series makes available the best and most entertaining of these documents, bringing the past to life in a fresh and personal way.

RICHARD HOGGART

A Local Habitation
Life and Times: 1918–1940

With characteristic candour and compassion, Richard Hoggart evokes the Leeds of his boyhood, where as an orphan, he grew up with his grandmother, two aunts, an uncle, and a cousin in a small terraced back-to-back.

'brilliant . . . a joy as well as an education' Roy Hattersley

'a model of scrupulous autobiography' Edward Blishen, *Listener*

A Sort of Clowning
Life and Times: 1940–1950

Opening with his wartime exploits in North Africa and Italy, this sequel to *A Local Habitation* recalls his teaching career in North-East England, and charts his rise in the literary world following the publication of *The Uses of Literacy*.

'one of the classic autobiographies of our time' Anthony Howard, *Independent on Sunday*

'Hoggart [is] the ideal autobiographer' Beryl Bainbridge, *New Statesman and Society*

Also in Oxford Letters and Memoirs:

My Sister and Myself: The Diaries of J. R. Ackerley
The Letters of T. E. Lawrence
A London Family 1870–1900   Molly Hughes

THE OXFORD AUTHORS

General Editor: Frank Kermode

The Oxford Authors is a series of authoritative editions of the major English writers for the student and the general reader. Drawing on the best texts available, each volume contains a generous selection from the writings—poetry and prose, including letters—to give the essence of a writer's work and thinking. Where appropriate, texts have been tactfully modernized and all are complemented by essential Notes, an Introduction, Chronology, and suggestions for Further Reading.

'The Oxford Authors series can always be relied upon to be splendid—with good plain texts and helpful notes.'
Robert Nye, *Scotsman*

OSCAR WILDE

Edited by Isobel Murray

The drama of Oscar Wilde's life has for years overshadowed his achievement in literature. This is the first large-scale edition of his work to provide unobtrusive guidance to the wealth of knowledge and allusion upon which his writing stands.

Wilde had studied Greek and Latin and was familiar with American literature, while he was as well read in French as he was in English, following Gautier and Flaubert as well as Pater and Ruskin. Through her Notes Isobel Murray enables the modern reader for the first time to read Wilde as such admiring contemporaries as Pater, Yeats, and Symons read him, in a rich, shared culture of literary and visual arts.

This edition underlines the range of his achievement in many genres, including *The Picture of Dorian Gray, Salome, The Importance of Being Earnest, The Decay of Lying,* and *The Ballad of Reading Gaol.* The text is that of the last printed edition overseen by Wilde.

Also in the Oxford Authors:

Sir Philip Sidney
Ben Jonson
Byron
Thomas Hardy

CLASSIC ENGLISH SHORT STORIES

The four volumes of *Classic English Short Stories* have been compiled to reflect the excellence and variety of short fiction written in English during the twentieth century. Each volume covers a different period and represents the most distinguished writers of their day.

THE DRAGON'S HEAD

This collection contains stories written in the years between the turn of the century and the outbreak of the Second World War—'a restless and impatient age'. The authors include John Galsworthy, 'Saki', Naomi Mitchison, H. G. Wells, Dorothy L. Sayers, and Somerset Maugham.

THE KILLING BOTTLE

This collection brings together 12 very different authors whose short stories, written in the 1940s and 1950s, helped establish or extend their reputations as writers of stories, novels, or poetry. The 12 include Evelyn Waugh, Elizabeth Bowen, Graham Greene, V. S. Pritchett, Dylan Thomas, and Frank O'Connor.

CHARMED LIVES

This collection contains stories written in the 1950s and 1960s, many of which demonstrate the impressive and accomplished skills of Commonwealth writers who began to achieve world-wide reputations during that period, including Ruth Prawer Jhabvala, Nadine Gordimer, H. E. Bates, Bill Naughton, L. P. Hartley, and Peter Ustinov.

THE GREEN MAN REVISITED

This collection includes works written in the 1960s and 1970s by authors living all around the world, including Chinua Achebe, Kingsley Amis, Susan Hill, Olivia Manning, V. S. Naipaul, William Trevor, John Updike, and Patrick White.

THE WORLD'S CLASSICS

A 250-strong series of the finest editions of the greatest works of world literature from Homer to Hardy.

'Must now be the most wide-ranging and well-chosen list of its kind.' *London Evening Standard*

ARMADALE
Wilkie Collins

Edited with an Introduction by Catherine Peters

'it has the immense—and nowadays more and more rare—merit of never being dull'.

T. S. Eliot's appreciation of *Armadale* still stands. The third of Wilkie Collins's four great novels of the 1860s, coming after *The Woman in White* and *No Name*, and immediately before *The Moonstone* (all available in World's Classics), *Armadale* is quintessentially a novel of its decade. It deals with the emergence of the autonomous, sexually active woman from the dichotomies of Madonna and Magdalen; with the legal tangles of the unsatisfactory marriage laws; with the perception of the growing role of scientific intrusion into the privacy of the individual psyche. Above all, it explores the divided self, and the need to acknowledge the darker side of the personality: a modern theme grafted on to a traditional melodrama, and worked out with all Collins's skill in handling a complex and exciting plot.

First published in 1866, the text of this World's Classics edition is that of the one-volume 1869 edition, checked and corrected against both the first impression and the magazine serialization which preceded it.

Also available in the World's Classics:

Nicholas Nickleby   Charles Dickens
A Hazard of New Fortunes   William Dean Howells
Middlemarch   George Eliot
Melmoth the Wanderer   Charles Maturin

OXFORD BOOKS

Beginning in 1900 with the famous *Oxford Book of English Verse*, the Oxford Books series now boasts over sixty superb anthologies of poetry, prose, and songs.

'These anthologies—along with digests and reference books—are exactly what the general reader needs.'
Auberon Waugh, *Independent*

THE NEW OXFORD BOOK OF
IRISH VERSE

Edited, with Translations, by Thomas Kinsella

Verse in Irish, especially from the early and medieval periods, has long been felt to be the preserve of linguists and specialists, while Anglo-Irish poetry is usually seen as an adjunct to the English tradition. This original anthology approaches the Irish poetic tradition as a unity and presents a relationship between two major bodies of poetry that reflects a shared and painful history.

'the first coherent attempt to present the entire range of Irish poetry in both languages to an English-speaking readership'
Irish Times

'a very satisfying and moving introduction to Irish poetry'
Listener

Also in Oxford Paperbacks:

The Oxford Book of Travel Verse
edited by Kevin Crossley-Holland
The Oxford Book of Contemporary Verse
edited by D. J. Enright
The Oxford Book of Late Medieval Verse and Prose
edited by Douglas Gray

OXFORD REFERENCE

Oxford is famous for its superb range of dictionaries and reference books. The Oxford Reference series offers the most up-to-date and comprehensive paperbacks at the most competitive prices, across a broad spectrum of subjects.

THE CONCISE OXFORD COMPANION
TO ENGLISH LITERATURE

Edited by Margaret Drabble and Jenny Stringer

Based on the immensely popular fifth edition of the *Oxford Companion to English Literature* this is an indispensable, compact guide to the central matter of English literature.

There are more than 5,000 entries on the lives and works of authors, poets, playwrights, essayists, philosophers, and historians; plot summaries of novels and plays; literary movements; fictional characters; legends; theatres; periodicals; and much more.

The book's sharpened focus on the English literature of the British Isles makes it especially convenient to use, but there is still generous coverage of the literature of other countries and of other disciplines which have influenced or been influenced by English literature.

From reviews of *The Oxford Companion to English Literature Fifth Edition*:

'a book which one turns to with constant pleasure . . . a book with much style and little prejudice' Iain Gilchrist, *TLS*

'it is quite difficult to imagine, in this genre, a more useful publication' Frank Kermode, *London Review of Books*

'incarnates a living sense of tradition . . . sensitive not to fashion merely but to the spirit of the age' Christopher Ricks, *Sunday Times*

Also available in Oxford Reference:

The Concise Oxford Dictionary of Art and Artists
edited by Ian Chilvers
A Concise Oxford Dictionary of Mathematics
Christopher Clapham
The Oxford Spelling Dictionary   compiled by R. E. Allen
A Concise Dictionary of Law   edited by Elizabeth A. Martin